The Ultimate Home Diabetes Reference

American Diabetes Association Complete Guide to Diabetes, 2nd Edition

American Diabetes Association

Writer, Nancy Touchette, PhD; *Book Acquisitions,* Robert J. Anthony; *Project Manager, 1st Edition,* Christine B. Welch, Off-Press Publishing; *Editor, 2nd Edition,* Laurie Guffey; *Production Director,* Carolyn R. Segree; *Production Manager,* Peggy M. Rote; *Composition,* Harlowe Typography, Inc.; *Text and Cover Design,* Wickham & Associates; *Printer,* Port City Press.

Printed in the United States of America
1 3 5 7 9 10 8 6 4 2

The suggestions and information contained in this publication are generally consistent with the *Clinical Practice Recommendations* and other policies of the American Diabetes Association, but they do not represent the policy or position of the Association or any of its boards or committees. Reasonable steps have been taken to ensure the accuracy of the information presented. However, the American Diabetes Association cannot ensure the safety or efficacy of any product or service described in this publication. Individuals are advised to consult a physician or other appropriate health care professional before undertaking any diet or exercise program or taking any medication referred to in this publication. Professionals must use and apply their own professional judgment, experience, and training and should not rely solely on the information contained in this publication before prescribing any diet, exercise, or medication. The American Diabetes Association—its officers, directors, employees, volunteers, and members—assumes no responsibility or liability for personal or other injury, loss, or damage that may result from the suggestions or information in this publication.

♾ The paper in this publication meets the requirements of the ANSI Standard Z39.48-1992 (permanence of paper).

ADA titles may be purchased for business or promotional use or for special sales. For information, please write to Lee Romano Sequeira, Special Sales & Promotions, at the address below.

American Diabetes Association
1701 North Beauregard Street
Alexandria, Virginia 22311

Library of Congress Cataloging-in-Publication Data

American Diabetes Association complete guide to diabetes : the ultimate home diabetes reference.—2nd ed.
    p. cm.
  Includes index.
  ISBN 1-58040-038-8 (pbk. : alk. paper)
  1. Diabetes—Popular works. I. Title: Complete guide to diabetes. II. American Diabetes Association.

RC660.4 .A485 1999
616.4'62—dc21   99-049617

Contents

Foreword

One of the greatest weapons in the fight against diabetes is knowledge. Information can help people assess their risk of diabetes, motivate them to seek proper treatment and care, and inspire them to take charge of their disease for a lifetime. For almost 60 years, the American Diabetes Association has led the way in providing life-saving, life-improving information to activate people with diabetes, their families, and the health professionals who guide their care. Our mission: To prevent and cure diabetes and to improve the lives of all people affected by diabetes.

The *American Diabetes Association Complete Guide to Diabetes, 2nd Edition*, represents a landmark in our role as information provider. Within these pages, you will find expert advice, written in clear, easy-to-understand language, on every aspect of type 1, type 2, and gestational diabetes. Every word has been reviewed by experts intent on providing you with the latest and best information available on diabetes treatment and self-care. The health professionals who participated in the development of the *Complete Guide* represent a Who's Who in diabetes care and research.

Whether you have just been diagnosed with diabetes, have had diabetes for many years, or are a family member intent on learning as much as you can about this serious disease and its life-threatening complications, the *Complete Guide* can provide the information you need. We urge you to read and use the information provided to improve your diabetes control. Take your questions to your health care professionals or call 1-800-DIABETES (1-800-342-2383) for further information. But most importantly, take care of this serious disease, diabetes.

Bruce R. Zimmerman, MD
President
American Diabetes Association

Elizabeth A. Walker, DNSc, RN, CDE
President, Health Care & Education
American Diabetes Association

Acknowledgments

The American Diabetes Association is grateful to the following health care and legal experts, whose thorough reviews greatly enhanced one or both editions of this book.

Barbara J. Anderson, PhD
Joslin Diabetes Clinic
Boston, Massachusetts

Robert M. Anderson, EdD
Michigan Diabetes Research
   and Training Center
University of Michigan Medical School
Ann Arbor, Michigan

Eugene J. Barrett, MD, PhD
Department of Medicine
University of Virginia Health Sciences
   Center
Charlottesville, Virginia

Michael Berelowitz, MD
State University of New York
   at Stony Brook
Stony Brook, New York

Jean Betschart, RN, MN, CDE
Children's Hospital of Pittsburgh
Pittsburgh, Pennsylvania

Thomas Buchanan, MD
University of Southern California
   School of Medicine
Los Angeles, California

John A. Colwell, MD, PhD
Department of Medicine
Medical University of South Carolina
Charleston, South Carolina

Ann M. Coulston, MS, RD
Stanford University Medical Center
Stanford, California

Marjorie Cypress, MS, RN, CDE
Lovelace Regional Diabetes Program
Albuquerque, New Mexico

Mayer Davidson, MD
City of Hope National Medical Center
Duarte, California

Ruth Farkas-Hirsch, MS, RN, CDE
University of Washington Medical Center
Seattle, Washington

Carolyn Gaydos, MS, RD, CDE
The Johns Hopkins Hospital
Baltimore, Maryland

Michael Greene, JD
Rosenthal & Greene, PC
Portland, Oregon

Joan M. Heins, RD, MA, CDE
Center for Health Behavior Research
Washington University School of Medicine
St. Louis, Missouri

Guyton Hornsby, PhD, CDE
Department of Medicine
West Virginia University
Morgantown, West Virginia

Jerry W. Lee, MA, JD
Magistrate, Common Pleas Court
  of Wood County
Bowling Green, Ohio

Marvin E. Levin, MD
Chesterfield, Missouri

Philip Levy, MD
University of Arizona School of Medicine
Phoenix, Arizona

Mark E. Molitch, MD
Northwestern University Medical School
Chicago, Illinois

Edith Miller, MD
Department of Internal Medicine
Carolinas Medical Center
Charlotte, North Carolina

Jerry Palmer, MD
Department of Veterans Affairs Puget
  Sound Health Care System
Seattle, Washington

Richard Rubin, PhD
The Johns Hopkins University
  School of Medicine
Baltimore, Maryland

Neil Ruderman, MD, PhD
Diabetes Unit
Boston University Medical Center Hospital
Boston, Massachusetts

Barbara Schreiner, RN, MSN, CDE
Texas Children's Hospital
Houston, Texas

Leslie Schover, PhD
Department of Urology
The Cleveland Clinic Foundation
Cleveland, Ohio

Patricia Stenger, RN, CDE
Diabetes and Nutrition Center
Bangor, Maine

Neil White, MD
Washington University School of Medicine
St. Louis, Missouri

Fred W. Whitehouse, MD, FACP
Henry Ford Hospital
Detroit, Michigan

The following authors granted the American Diabetes Association permission to adapt graphs or tables that originally appeared in the following articles or chapters: Kathleen Ehmann Stanley, *Diabetes Forecast* 48:37, 1995 (box on page 3); Jay Skyler, *Therapy for Diabetes Mellitus and Related Disorders,* pages 132, 134, and 140 (graphs 1, 4, and 7 on pages 124, 126, and 129, respectively); David S. Schade, Mark R. Burge, and Patrick J. Boyle, *Diabetes Forecast* 46:34, 1993 (graphs 8 and 9 on pages 131 and 132, respectively).

Introduction:
Healthy Living Is
Good Diabetes Care

Living with diabetes is not much different than living a healthy lifestyle. Your eating and exercise plans are the same as those of anyone who wants to be healthy. Although you can't cure diabetes through healthy living, you can keep it under control.

The mission of the American Diabetes Association is to prevent and cure diabetes and to improve the lives of all people affected by diabetes. To further this mission, the Association has written this book for all people who are able to self-manage their diabetes. The *American Diabetes Association Complete Guide to Diabetes, 2nd Edition,* will encourage you to be an educated health care consumer by reading labels, asking questions, and actively participating in your own health care. You'll learn what steps to take to keep your blood sugar levels from going too far from normal levels. By controlling diabetes through healthy living, you can prevent or delay many of the complications of diabetes.

No one cares about your health as much as you do. And no one can control the choices you make better than you. But you can't do it alone. Successful diabetes management is a team effort. You and your health care providers form a support team dedicated to your good health. Learn as much as you possibly can about diabetes and how it affects you. Ask all the questions you need to have answered and become your own advocate. Your doctor, diabetes educator, or dietitian can listen to your needs, advise you on meeting your goals, and provide you with information, but it is up to you to make the decisions that affect your health and then live with your decisions.

Whether you have recently been diagnosed or have been living with diabetes for years, whether you have type 1 (immune-mediated) diabetes, type 2 (insulin-resistant) diabetes, or gestational diabetes, your concerns are basically the same: to learn to live with diabetes, to maintain a high quality of life, and to mesh the day-to-day management of diabetes into your routine. At first, the idea of trying to "master" the disease may seem overwhelming. Diabetes management can often be frustrating, even if you're an old hand at it. The trick to living with diabetes is to take it one step at a time. Don't try to master all aspects of diabetes management at once. Decide what goals are most important, and work on these first. For example, you may want to get on a regular schedule of glucose monitoring first, before you begin to fine-tune your glucose control with insulin adjustments. Or you may want to get your walking program up to five times a week before you make any more changes in your meal plan. Once your first goal becomes more comfortable, then you can work on some of your other goals.

The *American Diabetes Association Complete Guide to Diabetes, 2nd Edition,* presents information that can help you live well with diabetes. Every time you learn something more about diabetes, you increase your opportunity to live a long and healthy life. But learning about diabetes is only part of the recipe for living well with diabetes. The rest centers around self-knowledge. The best diabetes care plans are personal. Therefore, the more you know about who you are and what you want, the better you can tailor your diabetes care to fit your life.

How to Have a Healthy Life With Diabetes

- Accept the fact that you have diabetes.
- Understand that poor blood glucose control can be causing serious complications even if you feel fine.
- Create a health care team, consisting of a knowledgeable and caring doctor, dietitian, diabetes educator, and other specialists.
- Be assured that, with the help of your health care team, you can control your diabetes with healthy eating and exercise habits, self-monitoring of blood glucose, and oral diabetes medications or insulin.
- Learn all you can about diabetes: read, ask lots of questions, and attend diabetes education programs.
- Keep up-to-date on diabetes research and equipment. Obtain the supplies you need to control your diabetes.
- Know yourself. Investigate whether fatigue, mood swings, or other problems are related to your blood glucose levels.

Chapter 1:
What Is Diabetes?

When you or someone you love has diabetes, you discover that you must think about a part of life that others take for granted. Your never-changing goal becomes reaching a subtle balance between glucose and insulin. The more you learn about diabetes, the better you can be at your balancing act, and the richer your life shared with this chronic disease can be.

Types of Diabetes

Diabetes refers to a set of several different diseases. The most common types of diabetes are type 1, or immune-mediated diabetes mellitus, and type 2, or insulin-resistant diabetes mellitus. A third type of diabetes, gestational diabetes mellitus, occurs during some pregnancies.

All types of diabetes have similar symptoms, because all forms of the disease result in too much sugar, or glucose, in the blood. This is because your body is unable to remove glucose from your blood and deliver it to the cells in your body. Your cells use glucose as a source of energy in order to stay alive. But the reasons why your body cannot use glucose from the blood are different for type 1 and type 2 diabetes.

People with type 1 diabetes do not make enough insulin. Insulin is a small protein made by the pancreas that helps the body use or store glucose from food. People with type 1 diabetes can be treated with injections of insulin. In contrast, people with type 2 diabetes, like women with gestational diabetes, do make insulin, but for some reason, the cells in their bodies are resistant to insulin's action or they don't make enough insulin. In all types of diabetes, if glucose does not get into the cells and tissues that need it, it accumulates in the blood.

About half of all cases of type 1 diabetes appear in childhood or in the early teenage years. For this reason, it used to be called *juvenile-onset diabetes*. If your symptoms first appeared during the early teenage years, your doctor probably suspected diabetes right away. If you were a young child when the disease developed, it might have occurred so fast that you went into a coma, before anyone suspected diabetes. Type 2 diabetes most often develops in adulthood and used to be called *adult-onset diabetes*. Usually, it does not appear suddenly. Instead, you may have no noticeable symptoms or only mild symptoms for years

Suggested Body Weight for Adults

Height (in feet/inches), without shoes	Weight (in pounds) without clothes	
	Age 19 to 34	Age 35 and over
5'0"	97–128	108–138
5'1"	101–132	111–143
5'2"	104–137	115–148
5'3"	107–141	119–152
5'4"	111–146	122–157
5'5"	114–150	126–162
5'6"	118–155	130–167
5'7"	121–160	134–172
5'8"	125–164	138–178
5'9"	129–169	142–183
5'10"	132–174	146–188
5'11"	136–179	151–194
6'0"	140–184	155–199
6'1"	144–189	159–205
6'2"	148–195	164–210
6'3"	152–200	168–216
6'4"	156–205	173–222
6'5"	160–211	177–228
6'6"	164–216	182–234

From *The Dietary Guidelines for Americans,* U.S. Department of Agriculture, U.S. Department of Health and Human Services, 3rd edition, 1990.

before diabetes is detected, perhaps during a routine exam or blood test. *Gestational diabetes* only appears during pregnancy in women with no previous history of type 1 or type 2 diabetes and goes away after pregnancy. Pregnant women are tested for gestational diabetes.

All people with diabetes have one thing in common. They have too much sugar, or glucose, in their blood. People with very high or poorly controlled blood glucose levels share many similar symptoms:

- ■ an unusual thirst
- ■ a frequent desire to urinate
- ■ blurred vision
- ■ a feeling of being tired most of the time for no apparent reason

People with type 2 diabetes may also experience leg pain that may indicate nerve damage or poor circulation. Many people with type 1 diabetes and some people with type 2 diabetes also find that they lose weight even though they are hungrier than usual and are eating more.

Even if they have lost weight, people with type 2 diabetes still tend to be overweight. Three-fourths of all people with type 2 diabetes are or have been obese—that is, they are at least 20 percent over their desirable body weight (see the chart of suggested body weights for adults). Type 2 diabetes tends to develop in people who have extra body fat. Where you carry your excess fat may determine whether you get type 2 diabetes: Extra fat above the hips (central body obesity) is riskier than fat in the hips and thighs for developing type 2 diabetes. And leading an inactive "couch potato" lifestyle can also lead to diabetes. It also contributes to obesity.

If you have recently been diagnosed with diabetes, you are not alone. Nearly 16 million Americans—about one of every 17 people—have the disease. About 1,800 new cases of diabetes are diagnosed each day, with about 655,000 new cases each year. Ninety to ninety-five percent of all cases of diabetes in people over age 20 are type 2 diabetes. And half of all people with type 2 diabetes are unaware they even have the disease. Because of the nature of type 2 diabetes, it is possible to have mild symptoms (what you feel) or signs (what the doctor can detect) of type 2 diabetes for years before diabetes worsens. In contrast, few cases of type 1 diabetes go undetected for long. The symptoms of type 1 diabetes are severe enough that the person goes to the doctor for help.

Who Has Diabetes?

Almost 16 million Americans have diabetes. This is about 6 percent of the people in the country. In 1999, it was estimated that 500,000 to 1 million people had type 1 diabetes. It is hard to get an exact count of the number of people with diabetes because we have no nationwide diabetes registry. Slightly under half of the people with type 1 diabetes are children and teenagers age 20 and younger. Type 1 diabetes is more common in whites than in African Americans, Hispanic Americans, Asian Americans, and Native Americans.

In 1999, it was estimated that about 9.5 million people had diagnosed type 2 diabetes. Another 5 to 6 million people are undiagnosed. It is common in older people. Nearly 11 percent of Americans age 65 to 74 have type 2 diabetes. It is more common in some ethnic groups than others. In Americans age 45 to 74, over 14 percent of Mexican Americans and Puerto Rican Americans have type 2 diabetes, over 10 percent of African Americans have type 2 diabetes, and about 6 per-cent of Cuban Americans and whites have type 2 diabetes. Type 2 diabetes is even more common in Native Americans: In some groups, almost half of adults age 30 to 64 have type 2 diabetes.

About 135,000 women develop gestational diabetes each year. Of these, about 40 percent get type 2 diabetes within 15 years.

Tests for Diabetes

Although your physician may suspect that you have diabetes because of your symptoms, the only sure way to tell is with blood tests. Blood tests are used to diagnose both type 1 and type 2 diabetes, as well as gestational diabetes. Your doctor may repeat your blood tests to be sure of the diagnosis.

The blood tests are based on the fact that diabetes keeps your blood glucose, or sugar, levels above normal some or all of the time. Your blood glucose levels may be high even though you haven't eaten recently. In addition, your body cannot get rid of the extra glucose that appears in the blood after eating.

Random plasma glucose tests are the simplest way to detect diabetes. This test measures the amount of glucose in the blood at any given time and is done without fasting. If you have obvious symptoms of diabetes and the amount of glucose in your blood is 200 mg/dl or higher, your doctor will diagnose diabetes. Symptoms of diabetes include frequent urination, intense thirst, blurred vision, unexplained weight loss, and extreme tiredness.

The preferred method for diagnosing diabetes diagnosis is the **fasting plasma glucose test**. For this test, your doctor will ask you not to eat for at least 8 to 10 hours. Then, a sample of your blood is taken, and the amount of glucose present in the blood is measured. Normally after fasting, the amount of glucose is less than 110 mg/dl. But when the amount of blood glucose is greater than 126 mg/dl, the doctor will suspect diabetes. In diabetes, extra glucose remains in the blood, even after fasting, because it cannot enter the body's cells. This is due to a lack of insulin or resistance to the action of insulin. Doctors usually make a firm diagnosis of diabetes when two fasting plasma glucose tests, done on different days, are over 126 mg/dl.

If your test results are greater than 110 mg/dl but less than 126 mg/dl, you may be diagnosed with **impaired fasting glucose**. This is not diabetes, but sometimes occurs before diabetes, usually type 2 diabetes, develops. Some people with impaired glucose tolerance never get diabetes. However, some of the same problems that result from having diabetes also occur in people with impaired glucose tolerance. If you have been diagnosed with impaired glucose tolerance, your physician will want to watch carefully for diabetes. Also, you need to talk with your doctor about reducing your risk of heart disease, keeping your weight in the healthy range, and exercising regularly to lower your chances of developing diabetes.

Certain pregnant women with no history of diabetes are at high risk for developing gestational diabetes. These are women who are 25 years of age or older, are overweight, have a parent or sibling with diabetes, or are Hispanic, Native American, Asian, or African-American.

If you have any of these characteristics, your obstetrician will screen you for gestational diabetes with a **glucose challenge**. This is done between the 24th and 28th weeks of pregnancy. At this time, the hormones of pregnancy naturally begin to cause temporary insulin resistance that lasts until the baby is born. The glucose challenge helps your doctor determine whether your body is able to overcome the insulin resistance on its own. You are given a glucose drink to finish at a certain time, without regard to eating. If the glucose in your blood 1 hour later is 140 mg/dl or above, you may have gestational diabetes. Your doctor will need to give you another test, for which you may need to fast, for a firm diagnosis.

Not Sure Which Type of Diabetes You Have?

Your characteristics	Do I have type 1 diabetes?	Do I have type 2 diabetes?
Age 10 at diagnosis	Probably	Not likely
Age 20 at diagnosis	Probably	Not likely
Age 30 at diagnosis	Probably	Not likely
Age 40 at diagnosis	Maybe	Maybe
Age 50 at diagnosis	Not likely	Probably
Age 60 at diagnosis	Not likely	Probably
Age 70 at diagnosis	Not likely	Probably
Underweight at diagnosis	Probably	Not likely
Normal weight at diagnosis	Maybe	Maybe
Overweight at diagnosis	Not likely	Probably
Frequent urination, increased hunger, and thirst before diagnosis	Yes	Maybe
Large amount of ketones in urine from time to time	Yes	No
Family history of type 1 diabetes	Yes	Maybe
Family history of type 2 diabetes	Maybe	Yes
Previous gestational diabetes	No	Yes
Use insulin	Yes	Yes
Use oral diabetes medication	Only for the first few months, if at all	Yes
Use no diabetes medication	No	Yes

Diabetes: Fact or Myth?

"I used to have type 2 diabetes, but now I have type 1 diabetes. My doctor put me on insulin last year."

Lots of people, over 40 percent of adults with diabetes, use insulin. But because there are about 90 adults with type 2 diabetes to every 5 adults with type 1 diabetes, this means there are a lot of people with type 2 diabetes taking insulin. People with type 1 diabetes must use insulin to make up for their pancreas no longer making it. You don't necessarily have type 1 diabetes just because you have to take insulin. Many people with type 2 diabetes need extra insulin to overcome their body's resistance to the insulin already being made by the pancreas.

Type 1 diabetes and type 2 diabetes, while having a lot in common, are two different diseases. They have different causes. The type of diabetes you have does not change as you age or if you lose or gain weight or change treatment.

Type 1 or Type 2?

If tests reveal that you have diabetes (and you're not pregnant), your doctor must then decide whether you have type 1 or type 2 diabetes. Although the symptoms and blood test results are similar for both type 1 and type 2 diabetes, the causes are very different.

It will help your doctor to know whether there has been type 1 or type 2 diabetes in your family. Your age is not the only clue about what type of diabetes you have. It's true that most people younger than age 20 who show signs of diabetes have type 1 diabetes and that most people diagnosed with diabetes when they're over age 30 have type 2 diabetes. But there are exceptions. In some cases, families carry a genetic trait for developing type 2 diabetes as young people. And in some Native American families, obesity is so prevalent that children as young as 10 years old have type 2 diabetes.

■ If you are overweight or obese, it is more likely that you have type 2 diabetes.

■ If you suddenly developed signs of diabetes, such as frequent urination, unusual thirst and hunger, and weight loss, perhaps after an illness, and are a young adult or child, it is more likely that you have type 1 diabetes.

■ If you are not overweight and there are ketones in your urine, it is more likely that you have type 1 diabetes (see Chapter 5 on ketone testing).

■ If you are African American or Hispanic American, are older than 50, are overweight, and haven't been feeling quite "right" for a long time, it is more likely that you have type 2 diabetes.

■ If your doctor treats you with insulin injections, you could have either type 1 or type 2 diabetes.

Diabetes: Fact or Myth?

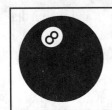

"Having a sweet tooth runs in my family. My dad got diabetes from eating too much sugar."

Eating too much of anything causes weight gain, which leads to obesity. Having a certain genetic background predisposes you to diabetes. Being overweight can be the trigger that causes type 2 diabetes to show itself. Lots of people with type 2 diabetes have the one-two punch of diabetes in the family and poor eating and exercise habits. Whether the excess pounds are from eating candy or bagels or meat loaf makes little difference.

Eating too much sugar doesn't cause diabetes. But eating too much sugar isn't healthy for anyone. It can cause tooth decay, and most important, leads to excess pounds. Sweets contain lots of simple carbohydrate, which may fill you up without giving you much nutritional benefit, and sometimes fat. Having a candy bar before lunch makes it easier to pass up the vegetable soup.

Who Gets Diabetes?

The risk factors associated with type 1 or type 2 diabetes are different. For both type 1 and type 2 diabetes, having a family history of diabetes puts you at a higher risk for developing the disease than for a person with no family history of diabetes. However, many people with type 1 diabetes have no known family history of the disease. Type 1 diabetes is more common among whites than among members of other racial groups. In contrast, members of Native American, African American, and Hispanic ethnic groups are at higher risk for developing type 2 diabetes. Perhaps the genetic make-up of nonwhites predisposes them to the obesity and diabetes that tend to result from a 20th-century sedentary American lifestyle.

Do You Have MODY?

Other types of diabetes also exist that do not fit the type 1 or type 2 profile. For example, Maturity-Onset Diabetes of the Young (MODY) usually affects young adults, but can also affect teens and children. It can be misdiagnosed as type 1 in younger patients. Adults with MODY develop diabetes at a younger age than most type 2 patients and do not tend to be overweight or sedentary. In the past, people with MODY were often told they had a form of type 2 diabetes. Doctors now know that MODY is caused by a genetic mutation that leads to impaired insulin secretion. Insulin resistance, which is often found in type 2 diabetes, does not usually occur in MODY. If you have MODY, you do not have type 2 diabetes. Some people with MODY have been told they have "type 1.5" diabetes.

If you have MODY, or suspect you may have MODY, talk to your doctor about developing a specialized diabetes management plan. You may want to consult with an endocrinologist or see a diabetes specialist. You may be able to control your blood glucose levels through diet and exercise alone, at least for a while. However, therapies that work for people with type 2 diabetes do not always work for people with MODY. You may have more success with insulin therapy or oral agents that stimulate insulin secretion. Talk to your doctor to determine the best course of treatment for you.

A major difference in the characteristics of individuals with type 1 and type 2 diabetes is the age of onset. Typically, type 1 diabetes develops in individuals under the age of 40. Half of all people diagnosed with type 1 diabetes are under the age of 20. In contrast, most of the people diagnosed with type 2 diabetes are over the age of 30, although type 2 diabetes is on the rise in teenagers. The risk for type 2 increases with age. Half of all new cases of type 2 diabetes are in people age 55 and older.

Type 2 diabetes is more common in overweight and obese individuals, whereas body weight does not seem to be a risk factor for type 1 diabetes. Type 2 diabetes is often found in women with a history of giving birth to babies weighing more than 9 pounds and in women who were previously diagnosed with gestational diabetes. In both men and women, high blood pressure and very high concentrations of fats in the blood are more common in people with type 2 diabetes.

You can't get diabetes—either type 1 or type 2—from stress, exposure to someone who already has diabetes, or from something you ate. And although diabetes may reveal itself after an illness or a stressful experience, these may have only speeded up the appearance of the disease.

Causes of Type 1 Diabetes

In people with type 1 diabetes, the immune system mistakenly destroys the insulin-producing beta cells in the pancreas, treating them as if they were a foreign invader. This is called an *autoimmune response*. Autoimmune responses also occur in other diseases such as multiple sclerosis, lupus, and thyroid diseases like hypothyroidism (Hashimoto's disease) and hyperthyroidism (Graves' disease). Researchers do not know exactly why this happens. But for diabetes, researchers have found many factors that appear to be linked to type 1 diabetes. These include genetics, autoantibodies, viruses, cow's milk, and oxygen free radicals.

Genetics

Scientists have long suspected that heredity plays a role in diabetes, especially in type 1 diabetes. This is because type 1 diabetes seems to run in families—if your mother or father had diabetes, for example, you are more likely to develop the disease than someone without a family history. Also, type 1 diabetes seems to be more common in certain racial groups. Whites, for example, are more likely to develop the disease than are people from other racial backgrounds. Type 1 diabetes occurs in less than 1 in 100,000 people in Shanghai, China, but occurs in greater than 35 in 100,000 people in Finland.

Everyone is born with a set of instructions that tells the cells in your body how to grow, live, and function. These instructions lie in the particular chemical sequence of units known as bases that make up the DNA in every cell in your body. Each cell in your body contains 46 chromosomes, which are made up of DNA and protein. Each DNA strand is like a long string that contains millions of bases. Along the strand lie the genes, unique segments of DNA that tell your cells what kind of protein to make.

But just as books sometimes contain typographical errors, so too does the sequence of DNA. If there is a mistake, or mutation, in the DNA within a gene, then a faulty protein may be made that can't do its job. Scientists are trying to determine how mistakes in specific genes cause diabetes. If mutated genes occur in germ cells—the eggs and sperm—then the DNA mutations can be passed on from generation to generation.

Researchers have identified several different genes that might make a person more likely to develop type 1 diabetes. However, they have not found one single gene that makes all people who inherit it develop the disease. Instead, it seems that there are several genes known as "diabetes susceptibility" genes.

One particular set of genes that may predispose a person to diabetes is responsible for the human leukocyte antigens, or HLAs. These genes code for certain proteins called *antigens,* which identify a person's own cells as "self." They tell the immune cells not to destroy the cells that are part of a person's body. Scientists believe that some HLA antigens incorrectly identify the beta cells as non-self. Then the immune cells, which normally destroy foreign invading cells, destroy these cells. This is called *autoimmunity*—an immune attack on a person's own cells. In type 1 diabetes, the insulin-producing cells of the pancreas are destroyed in an autoimmune attack, and the body can no longer make insulin. This destructive process occurs over many months.

Each person has many kinds of HLA genes, and thus there are many types of HLAs. Each person inherits one of each kind of HLA gene from each parent. One type of HLA gene, known as HLA-DR, is most strongly linked to type 1 diabetes. There are many variations of HLA-DR, but 95 percent of people with type 1 diabetes have the DR3 form, the DR4 form, or both. This makes researchers suspect that having the DR3 and DR4 variants may make a person more likely to get type 1 diabetes. However, this is not the whole answer, because 45 percent of people without type 1 diabetes have the DR3 or DR4 variants. Also, variants of another HLA gene, known as HLA-DQ, may also play a role in type 1 diabetes.

Just because a person inherits a susceptible HLA variant doesn't mean that person will develop diabetes. Most people with DR3 or DR4 variants remain healthy. But if there is a family history of type 1 diabetes, then screening may help predict the risk of developing the disease. For example, brothers and sisters of a person with diabetes who have two of the same HLA-DR variants have a 15 percent chance of getting type 1 diabetes. But if they share only one variant, the risk is only 5 percent. If no variants are the same, the risk of developing type 1 diabetes is 1 percent or less.

The more we study how people get type 1 diabetes, the more we understand that the answers are not simple. No one event or characteristic seems to bring on diabetes. Researchers have identified several other gene clusters on different chromosomes in addition to these HLA variants that may also play a role in type 1 diabetes.

Autoantibodies

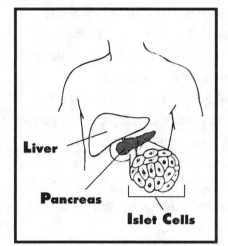

The immune system protects you from disease by killing germs and other foreign invaders. It does this largely through the action of white blood cells, or lymphocytes. T lymphocytes, or T cells, can attack foreign cells directly. B lymphocytes, or B cells, produce special proteins called *antibodies* that recognize the shapes of molecules on the surface of specific invaders.

B cells sometimes manufacture antibodies that recognize a person's own cells. These self-recognizing antibodies are called *autoantibodies*. Autoantibodies are found in many people with autoimmune disorders, but three autoantibodies are especially common in people with type 1 diabetes. These antibodies recognize:

■ islet cells (beta cells are just one type of islet cell in the pancreas)

■ insulin

■ glutamic acid decarboxylase, a protein made by the beta cells in the pancreas. This protein is also called GAD, or the 64K protein.

These three types of autoantibodies all seem to act as markers. Researchers believe that these antibodies contribute to the demise of the beta cells of the pancreas by identifying which cells are to be attacked. It is really the T cells that ultimately destroy the insulin-producing cells of the pancreas. Of people newly diagnosed with type 1 diabetes, 70 to 80 percent have antibodies to islet cells, 30 to 50 percent have antibodies to insulin, and 80 to 95 percent have antibodies to GAD.

The antibodies may be present several years before diabetes is diagnosed. The islet cell antibodies disappear later on. Because these antibodies are so common in people with type 1 diabetes and because they so often appear before the symptoms of diabetes appear, researchers are finding that they are useful in screening people for type 1 diabetes who are at high risk for the disease. Although the risk for developing diabetes may only be 1 to 10 percent for people with a parent or sibling with the disease, a much higher percentage of people who also have antibodies to islet cells develop type 1 diabetes within 5 years. And for many, having combinations of these antibodies and certain HLA genes results in an even higher risk.

By testing relatives of people with type 1 diabetes for autoantibodies, doctors and researchers can often predict who is likely to develop the disease. This could be especially useful as new therapies emerge, because they can be started before damage to the pancreas is too extensive. For example, by identifying people who are likely to develop type 1 diabetes at an early stage, researchers may be able to treat with insulin or drugs that suppress the immune system and thus prevent the T cells from destroying the beta cells in the pancreas.

Some people with a high risk of getting type 1 diabetes have participated in studies to see whether immunosuppressants such as azathioprine or cyclosporine delay or prevent the onset of the disease. Researchers are also testing to see whether long-acting insulin, oral insulin, or nicotinamide can delay or prevent diabetes. These studies suggest that azathioprine or cyclosporine can reduce the dose of insulin needed in people who have already developed type 1 diabetes, if the drug is started at the time the disease is diagnosed.

Other therapies may also be tested as researchers learn more about how autoantibodies contribute to diabetes. For example, if autoimmunity to GAD turns out to be a primary trigger of type 1 diabetes, it might be possible to develop a vaccine that would protect people from developing the disease.

Viruses

Perhaps surprisingly, many scientists also suspect that viruses may cause type 1 diabetes. This is because people who develop type 1 diabetes have often recently had a viral infection, and "epidemics" of type 1 diabetes often occur after viral epidemics. Viruses, like those that cause mumps and German measles and the Coxsackie family of viruses, which is related to the virus that causes polio, may play some role in causing type 1 diabetes.

A small region of the GAD molecule is almost identical to a region of a protein found in the virus known as Coxsackie B4. The two similar protein regions probably have similar shapes and may be recognized by the same T cells. Thus, to a T cell hunting for foreign invaders, the GAD protein, which is part of the body, might look the same as the Coxsackie virus protein, which is part of an invading cell. After a viral infection by the Coxsackie virus, the T cell, bent on destroying the invading virus, might actually destroy the body's own beta cells that bear the GAD protein. This would destroy the cells that produce insulin and result in type 1 diabetes.

Other theories may also explain how a viral infection might lead to diabetes. Some researchers believe that when a virus infects a body, it might somehow change the structure of the antigens on the surface of the islet cells. If this occurs, then the altered antigen might appear to be foreign to the immune system, and a person's own insulin-producing islet cells might be destroyed.

Gian Franco Bottazzo, a well-known diabetes researcher, has another theory. He believes that diabetes is a relatively new disease caused by a slow-acting virus. Although such a virus has not been found, Bottazzo holds that the virus causes the immune system to attack proteins in the pancreas. A drastic increase in the number of cases of type 1 diabetes occurred on the island of Sardinia, Italy, in the 1960s and in Finland in the 1970s, and he believes that such a slow-acting virus could be the culprit.

Cow's Milk

It seems unlikely, but different kinds of food may play a role in the development of type 1 diabetes. For example, one group of researchers found a connection between being fed cow's milk early in life (before three or four months old) and type 1 diabetes. They showed that children newly diagnosed with type 1 diabetes have higher amounts of antibodies that recognize a specific protein in cow's milk. These autoantibodies appear to bind to a protein that sometimes appears on the surface of the insulin-producing beta cells in the pancreas after an illness. The researchers speculate that, after an illness, the transient protein may appear on the surface of beta cells. The immune response to the milk protein might be to then recognize the beta cell surface proteins and attack the beta cells, leading to a destruction of the insulin-producing cells of the pancreas, and thus, to type 1 diabetes.

However, other researchers have looked for but not found an increased risk of type 1 diabetes if cow's milk is given early in life and if breastfeeding is done for a short period. Cow's milk is only one kind of food that may play a role in the development of type 1 diabetes. Studies in diabetes-prone rats show that withholding wheat and soy helps delay or prevent diabetes.

Oxygen Free Radicals

No, these are not part of some terrorist organization, but they may as well be. Oxygen free radicals, formed as a by-product of many chemical reactions in the body, wreak havoc wherever they go. Normally, the body has ways of quenching free radicals. But smoke, air pollution, diet, and even genetics can contribute to the formation of excessive amounts of free radicals, which the body cannot always handle. Uncontrolled, the reactive molecules can destroy the body's own cells as well as bacteria. Oxygen free radicals contribute significantly to the aging process and to the development of several other diseases. Researchers have implicated free radicals in the development of amyotrophic lateral sclerosis (ALS), or Lou Gehrig's disease, a degenerative neuromuscular disease.

Some researchers believe that oxygen free radicals may also contribute to type 1 diabetes. Islet cells have very low levels of the enzymes that break down free radicals. Thus, agents that increase free radical production could result in destruction of pancreatic cells. If this is true, then researchers may be able to develop drugs that block the formation of free radicals in the islet cells.

Chemicals and Drugs

Several chemicals have been shown to trigger diabetes. Pyriminil (Vacor), a poison used to kill rats, can trigger type 1 diabetes. Two prescription drugs, pentamidine, used to treat pneumonia, and L-asparaginase, an anticancer drug, can also cause type 1 diabetes. Other chemicals have been shown to make animals diabetic, but scientists don't know for sure whether they have the same effect in humans.

It is unlikely that either genetics or environmental factors alone cause diabetes. But it does appear that a person could start with a genetic susceptibility—the inheritance of a particular set of genes. If this person is then exposed to some environmental "triggering" factor, such as a virus or a chemical, then diabetes may develop. Although no one is destined to develop diabetes with certainty, a person's heredity increases the odds.

Causes of Type 2 Diabetes

The reasons that type 2 diabetes occurs are different from those that trigger type 1 diabetes. Unlike people with type 1 diabetes, who become unable to produce insulin, people with type 2 diabetes produce insulin. But, either the body does not respond to insulin's action—it's resistant—or there is just not enough insulin to go around—there's too much body for the amount of insulin that's made. Either problem leads to the same outcome: insulin can't deliver glucose to the cells that need it, and there's too much glucose in the blood.

Virtually all cells in the body contain special proteins called *receptors* that bind to insulin. They work like a lock and key. In order for glucose to enter the cell, insulin (the key) must first fit into the insulin receptor (the lock). But for some reason, in some people with type 2 diabetes, there is a faulty lock, or insulin receptor. The key doesn't open the lock, and glucose is shut out of the cell. And in some people with type 2 diabetes, there are not enough locks, or insulin receptors, on the cells to allow enough glucose to enter. But for most people with diabetes, it's not so much that the key doesn't fit the lock, but that insulin doesn't work properly. In rare cases, the insulin is mutated, or built incorrectly, and does not fit the insulin receptor.

In addition to problems with insulin and the insulin receptor, in many people with type 2 diabetes, the beta cells in the pancreas do not produce enough insulin. Without enough insulin to meet the body's needs, glucose levels rise and diabetes results. Scientists do not know why the pancreas does not function well in these people. Some believe that the system that controls glucose levels in the blood and tells the pancreas to make more insulin does not function properly. Others think that the pancreas, after many years of working overtime, overproducing insulin to overcome insulin resistance, simply begins to "burn out."

Although researchers do not fully understand why type 2 diabetes develops, they have uncovered many factors that may contribute to the disease.

Genetics

Genetics also appear to play a role in how type 2 diabetes develops. Like type 1 diabetes, type 2 diabetes also appears to run in families, and it is most likely due to the inheritance of certain genes. The link to genetics seems even stronger in type 2 diabetes than in type 1 diabetes. If a person with type 1 diabetes has an identical twin, there is a 25 to 50 percent chance that the twin will develop diabetes. But if a person with type 2 diabetes has an identical twin, there is a 60 to 75 percent chance that the person will develop diabetes.

More evidence for the role of genes in type 2 diabetes comes from studying minorities. Compared with whites, African Americans, Asian Americans, Hispanic Americans (except Cuban Americans), and Native Americans all get type 2 diabetes more often. Native Americans have the highest rate of type 2 diabetes in the world. Hispanic groups, such as Mexican Americans, that share genes with Native American groups (where there has been cultural mixing) have a higher rate of type 2 diabetes than Hispanic groups, such as Cuban Americans, where less intercultural contact has occurred.

Researchers have not yet isolated a single "type 2 diabetes" gene, but they are finding errors in several that may contribute to type 2 diabetes. For example, researchers have identified a protein called *PC-1* that shuts down the insulin receptor, which creates insulin resistance. This protein is prevalent in most people with type 2 diabetes, compared with people without diabetes. For some reason, too much of the inhibitor protein is made in some people, and the insulin receptor cannot do its job properly, which can lead to insulin resistance.

Researchers believe that the genes that lead to obesity may also play a role in diabetes. In mice, scientists have identified a gene they called the *obese gene*. The obese gene appears to regulate body weight by making proteins that affect the center in the brain that tells you whether you're full or hungry. When the obese gene is mutated, the mice become obese and develop type 2 diabetes.

Age, Obesity, and Lifestyle

The most important environmental trigger of type 2 diabetes appears to be obesity. Obesity is defined as weighing more than 20 percent of your desirable body weight. Genetics may play a role in obesity and, thus, in triggering type 2 diabetes.

In some way, having too much body fat promotes resistance to insulin. This is why, for so many years, type 2 diabetes has been treated with diet and exercise. Losing weight and increasing the amount of muscle while decreasing the amount of fat helps the body use insulin better. There is also a link between type 2 diabetes and where your body is too fat. People with central body obesity, which means carrying excess fat above the hips, have a higher risk of developing type 2 diabetes than those with excess fat on the hips and thighs.

Central body obesity, as well as overall obesity, is more common in African Americans than in whites. This may be one reason why type 2 diabetes is also more common in African Americans than in whites.

Age also appears to play a role. Half of all new cases of type 2 diabetes occur in people over age 55. Because people tend to gain weight as they age, many researchers think that the reason more older people develop diabetes is because more older people are overweight.

Leading an inactive, sedentary lifestyle and consuming a high-calorie diet can also lead to type 2 diabetes, presumably by contributing to obesity. Obesity, as well as type 2 diabetes, are common in Asian Americans and Hispanic Americans who have "westernized" their eating and activity habits.

Causes of Gestational Diabetes

Like the other types of diabetes, the exact cause of gestational diabetes is unknown. However, experts do have some clues.

Hormones

During pregnancy, the placenta, which is the organ that nourishes the growing baby, produces large amounts of various hormones. Hormones are important for the baby's growth. However, these hormones may also block insulin's action in the mother's body, causing insulin resistance. All pregnant women have some degree of insulin resistance.

Gestational diabetes usually appears around the 24th week of pregnancy. This is when the placenta begins producing large quantities of the hormones that cause insulin resistance. For this reason, the period between the 24th and 28th weeks of pregnancy is a good time to screen for gestational diabetes.

Genetics

Because insulin resistance, rather than underproduction of insulin, seems to cause gestational diabetes, it is more like type 2 diabetes than type 1 diabetes. And having gestational diabetes increases your chances of someday developing type 2 diabetes (but not of developing type 1 diabetes). Researchers suspect that the genes responsible for type 2 diabetes and for gestational diabetes may be similar.

Some women show signs of high blood glucose even before the 28th week of pregnancy. Doctors believe that these women probably had diabetes that was unrecognized before the pregnancy began. The weight gain and hormonal changes of pregnancy stressed the body and revealed the diabetes. This can happen with either type 1 or type 2 diabetes. Doctors would carefully watch what happens after the pregnancy in order to diagnose type 1 or type 2 diabetes.

Obesity

Gestational diabetes is more common in groups that have more obesity. For instance, it is found more often in areas with a large number of Hispanic Americans, in whom obesity is more common. Obesity can trigger gestational diabetes as well as type 2 diabetes.

Historical Perspective

For thousands of years, doctors have recognized diabetes as a disease, but did not understand its cause. An early Egyptian medical text written around 1550 B.C., called the *Ebers Papyrus,* describes a condition of "passing too much urine." The Greek physician Aretaeus, who lived in the second century A.D. gave diabetes its name, for a Greek word meaning "siphon" or "pass through." Aretaeus observed that his patients' bodies appeared to "melt down" into urine.

People observed early on that the urine from people with diabetes was very sweet. In fact, one way to diagnose diabetes was to pour urine near an anthill. If the ants were attracted to the urine, it meant that the urine contained sugar. By the eighteenth century, physicians added the Latin term *mellitus* to diabetes, which describes its sugary taste.

In 1776, scientists discovered that the sugar glucose was in the blood of both people with diabetes and people who didn't have diabetes. That led them to suspect that people with diabetes pass sugar from the blood to the urine. But they didn't know how.

Then in 1889—more than 100 years after glucose was found in blood—two German physiologists, Oskar Minkowski and Joseph von Mering, found quite by accident that the pancreas was involved in diabetes. While studying how fat is metabolized in the body, they decided to remove the pancreas from a laboratory dog. Much to their astonishment, the dog urinated again and again. Proving that science rewards a prepared mind, the scientists had the foresight to test the dog's urine for glucose. Sure enough, the dog had developed diabetes when its pancreas was removed.

This led the scientists to suspect that some substance in the pancreas somehow prevented diabetes. As scientists embarked on a 30-year quest to find that magic substance, people with diabetes were subjected to a host of so-called cures, including bloodletting, opium, and special diets. Unfortunately, none of these measures helped the disease. Although some diets did seem to help some older people with diabetes, they did nothing for severely affected young patients. These patients typically died within several years of developing the disease.

In 1921, Dr. Frederick Banting, a young surgeon just out of medical school, had a breakthrough. He had the idea to isolate the groups of cells called the *islets of Langerhans* in the pancreas. Working in the laboratory of a senior faculty member at the University of Toronto, Professor J.J.R. Macleod, an authority on carbohydrate metabolism, Banting began his experiments. Macleod teamed Banting with a young medical student named Charles Best.

Using experimental dogs, Banting's approach was to tie off the pancreatic duct—which connects the pancreas to the intestine. This would destroy most of the tissue of the pancreas, which would no longer be able to secrete its digestive enzymes into the intestine. Banting guessed that the islets of Langerhans secrete something directly into the blood and that these cells would survive. At long last, Banting and Best succeeded in treating a dog with diabetes using extract from the islet cells.

Within 6 months after their success with the diabetic dog, the two scientists injected their extract into Leonard Thompson, a 14-year-old boy who was dying from diabetes, but the boy remained ill. A biochemist working in Macleod's laboratory, J.B. Collip, purified the extract, and the experiment was repeated 12 days later. This time the scientists succeeded, and Thompson, emaciated from diabetes, began to gain weight and lived for 15 years with regular insulin injections, until he died from pneumonia. In 1923, Banting and Macleod were awarded the Nobel Prize in Medicine for their discovery. Feeling that their collaborators had been slighted, Banting shared his prize money with Best, and Macleod shared with Collip. The team had made an important discovery leading to a diabetes treatment that is still in use today.

Chapter 2: Diabetes Management

How you manage your diabetes depends on your personal goals and needs. Here are some treatment options you might want to consider.

Nan has two small children and is 32. After a flu-like illness, her thirst, weight loss, and almost constant need to urinate brought her to the doctor, who started her on insulin therapy and a meal plan. She's wondering what will happen if she loses control when her children need her.

Jesse is a grandfather of four who is 64. Although he tried to keep his weight down and do some walking, his doctor's prediction of diabetes came true. His mother lost both legs below the knee, and eventually her life, because of diabetes.

William is a junior high school student who likes books and dirt bikes. His cousin Sarah, a grown-up, has diabetes. William must take insulin and is worried about all the needles and what his friends will think.

Alvin, 49, knows that he needs to cut back on fried foods to lower his blood fat levels and help his weight problem. He's thinking of going to a health club.

Anita has gestational diabetes. She is worried for her baby's safe arrival and about her chances of having diabetes permanently.

Marie is an avid shopper and walker at 68 who wants to do more to increase her chances of living longer. She got diabetes at age 40 and has spent time learning how to make insulin adjustments based on her blood glucose records.

In diabetes, the message that "no two people are exactly alike" comes across loud and clear. This is because diabetes involves hormone action and metabolism, which vary from one body to the next, plus human behavior, which also varies from one person to the next. Mix the biological processes with the personal preferences, and you end up with an almost endless variety of responses to diabetes. Therefore, everyone with diabetes deserves an individualized diabetes care plan.

Despite their differences, Nan, Jesse, William, Alvin, Anita, and Marie all have something in common. They have chosen to accept their diabetes and meet the basic challenges it poses. To have as normal a lifestyle as possible, they must:

■ prevent short-term problems such as blood sugar levels that are too low (hypoglycemia) or too high (hyperglycemia)

■ prevent or delay some of the long-term problems diabetes can bring, such as damage to the nerves, kidneys, eyes, or heart and blood vessels.

Meeting these goals by taking care of themselves on an everyday basis can mean things like:

■ avoiding extremely high blood sugar levels

■ avoiding severe low blood sugar or unconsciousness

■ keeping up normal growth, if you're young

■ maintaining a healthy body weight and physical fitness

■ enjoying normal sexual function

■ living a healthy lifestyle, with regular school or job attendance and fun social activities.

Are these goals worth pursuing for you? If so, you're ready to deal with your diabetes with a positive approach, one that leads to short- and long-term benefits for you and your family.

Designing Your Diabetes Plan

As you and your health-care team design your diabetes care, you'll need to set some "big picture" goals. Any kind of diabetes treatment should be able to help you meet the basic diabetes management goals listed above. The methods you use to meet these treatment goals always include some form of meal and exercise planning and may also include a medication plan (see table).

You have the best chance of meeting or exceeding your goals if your treatment plan is tailored to your own style and needs. Bring as much of yourself into your diabetes care plan as you can. This can be as simple as finding healthy recipes for your favorite foods at holidays or as complicated as finding out a way to meet the demands of your unpredictable work

Common Diabetes Treatments

Type of therapy	Goals of therapy
■ Meal plans	■ Control weight ■ Control blood glucose levels ■ Control blood lipid levels ■ Reduce chances that you'll need additional medications
■ Exercise plans	■ Maintain muscle tone and physical fitness ■ Lower blood glucose levels ■ Lower blood lipid levels ■ Increase sensitivity to medications ■ Aid meal planning in controlling weight
■ Oral diabetes medications	■ Reduce blood glucose levels by improving insulin release, reducing available glucose, and/or decreasing insulin resistance
■ Insulin injections	■ Make up for the body's inability to produce insulin ■ Reduce blood glucose levels by improving insulin action and overcoming insulin resistance

schedule. Even though most diabetes care plans include diet, physical activity, and insulin or oral medications if needed, your plan needs to be just for you. What might work for a sedentary person with type 2 diabetes is not suitable for an active person with type 1 diabetes. Speak up if you feel you can't live with the plan being offered to you. If you can't stick to it, it's not going to help you. Two people may be diagnosed with the same type of diabetes, but each person needs a diabetes management plan designed specifically for them.

When you sit down with members of your health-care team to tailor a treatment plan to your needs, be sure to consider the following:

- your age and your physical abilities
- what type of diabetes you have
- how long you've had diabetes
- whether you have signs of any diabetes complications. For instance, do you need to lower your blood pressure or blood fats or watch your kidneys' health?
- how often and what happens when you have very low blood glucose levels
- what kind of lifestyle you lead. For instance, are you a stay-at-home type? Do you like to travel? Are you in charge of others?
- your favorites kinds of exercise, if any, and when you like to work out
- your occupation. For instance, what would happen if you had very low blood glucose on the job?
- how much support you have from family, loved ones, and friends. For instance, how much time do you spend alone? Are you able to get around by yourself? Does your family want to help you?

Your potential diabetes management tools are many. Included in your bag of tricks are insulin, oral diabetes medications, healthy eating habits, regular exercise habits, and a can-do, take-charge attitude about your diabetes. Another big player in your diabetes management is self-monitoring of blood glucose (SMBG). This is a tool that lets you make an immediate reading of your blood glucose level using a drop of blood, usually from your fingertip. When you apply the blood to a glucose test strip, you can match the color change to a chart to find your glucose level or insert the test strip into a glucose meter that will tell you the glucose level. When you know what your blood glucose level is at a given moment, you can make informed diabetes management decisions. Maybe you decide to take a brisk walk when you find your blood glucose level is a little high after lunch. Or perhaps you just don't feel right, and after a test, you know that it's because your blood glucose is at 60 mg/dl, so you decide to eat a small box of raisins. To satisfy your curiosity, you can take as many readings each day as your budget and your fingertips can handle. You can find more information about SMBG in Chapter 5.

Type 1 Diabetes Management

Because your body no longer makes insulin, insulin injections play a big role in your diabetes care plan. How much insulin you need to take depends on what your body's level of blood glucose is, or what you predict the level will be after a meal. Naturally, food also plays an important role in your diabetes management plan, because it contributes glucose to your blood. Usually, physical activity can lower your blood glucose level, decreasing your need for insulin. So, you'll need to account for exercise and physical activity in your diabetes management plan.

Insulin Therapy

Most people with type 1 diabetes take insulin by injecting it with a standard needle and syringe. The goal is to mimic normal insulin release as closely as possible. Normally, a low level of insulin is available in the blood at most times. This is a background, or basal, level of insulin. After meals, insulin release goes up, just enough to clear the glucose in the meal from the blood. To imitate this sequence, you can develop a regular schedule of insulin injections using faster-acting forms of insulin or combinations of both slower-acting and fast-acting forms of insulin (see Chapter 4 for a lot more about insulin and insulin plans).

Some people use insulin pumps to dispense fast-acting insulin at a steady background, or basal, rate and to provide extra insulin to cover meals. Although most insulin pumps in use today are carried around on a belt, researchers are working to develop a pump that is placed inside the body. Ideally, scientists would like to make a pump that senses the amount of glucose in the blood and delivers the right amount of insulin, as needed. So far, the most difficult part has been creating a glucose sensor. No matter what method is used, the goal is still the same—to deliver insulin to cells so they can take in glucose.

Your type of insulin therapy should relate directly to your health and your lifestyle choices. Your chosen therapy may be as simple as keeping your blood glucose levels from shooting too high after meals or falling too low between meals. Or your therapy may be more challenging: trying to keep after-meal blood glucose levels as close as possible to those of someone without diabetes.

A common type of insulin therapy is taking your insulin in one or two shots a day. This means using long-acting insulins, or a combination of long- and short-acting insulins. Most diabetes doctors would tell you that type 1 diabetes cannot be successfully controlled with one or two shots a day. Under this plan, there are many hours at different times of the day that your blood glucose level is high.

An insulin plan that includes three to four, or even more, injections of insulin per day leads to fewer times when blood glucose levels are high. People who take shots this many times each day usually use a long-acting insulin to control background blood glucose levels and fast-acting insulin to cover meals. They inject fast-acting insulin before meals to lower the blood glucose rise that occurs as food is digested.

The food you eat and the exercise you get go hand-in-hand with your insulin therapy. To know how much insulin you'll need at each shot, it helps to know what your blood glucose level is now (you know this by blood glucose testing), what you're planning to eat (so you'll be able to estimate how much your blood glucose will increase), and what glucose-lowering physical activities you'll be doing. Of course, healthy eating and regular exercise are a part of anyone's healthy living plan. But for you, knowing how these two daily features move your blood glucose level up and down is essential.

There is more information about insulin therapy and different insulin plans in Chapter 4, and more about healthy eating is in Chapter 8. Read about exercise for people with type 1 diabetes in Chapter 9.

Pancreas Transplantation

So far, the only way to treat type 1 diabetes is to give the body another source of insulin. Usually, this is done through injections of insulin. However, new experimental approaches also show some promise.

Patients with type 1 diabetes have experienced miraculous results from pancreas transplants. Typically, part or all of a new pancreas is placed in a patient in the pelvic area. The old pancreas is left alone; it still makes digestive enzymes even though it doesn't make insulin. Living relatives can donate a portion of their own pancreas, or the organ can be obtained from someone who has died but made provisions to donate organs. People with successful pancreas transplants may no longer need to take insulin and may have normal glucose levels in the blood. In addition, many of the side effects that often accompany diabetes are also prevented, or at least slowed. Most people with nerve damage who receive a pancreas transplant do not get worse and sometimes show improvement.

The downside to pancreas transplantation is that the body treats the new pancreas as foreign. The immune system attacks the transplanted pancreas. People with pancreas transplants must take powerful immunosuppressant drugs to prevent rejection of the new pancreas. Drugs that suppress the immune system can lower resistance to other diseases such as cancer and bacterial and viral infections. Doctors do not usually recommend pancreas transplantation for a patient with type 1 diabetes unless the patient is also receiving a new kidney. The pancreas transplant adds little further risk and offers huge benefits. However, these patients usually have much damage from the complications from diabetes. This, plus the major stress of the surgery, may be why 15 percent of all patients who receive a new pancreas die within 5 years.

Islet Transplantation

Researchers are experimenting with the idea of transplanting only the islet cells of the pancreas. These are the cells in the pancreas that secrete insulin. The islets also sense glucose levels in the blood and dispense the right amount of insulin to the blood.

Scientists believe that transplanting islet cells is less dangerous than transplanting the whole pancreas. They have developed ways to prepare islet cells from the pancreas. However, they still do not know for sure how many islet cells are needed and where they should be placed in the body. Also, immune rejection of islet cells is an even bigger problem than in pancreas transplants. Some scientists surround the cells in a protective membrane before transplanting them. Other scientists are trying to change the cells before transplanting them to trick the immune system into thinking they are part of the body. Sometimes the islet cells are exposed to cold temperatures or ultraviolet light, so that the cells of the immune system cannot recognize the foreign antigens on the surface of the transplanted cells. Another method is to transplant the islet cells directly into the thymus, a gland in the neck, where some immune system cells grow and learn to tell the difference between self and nonself. If exposed to transplanted cells as they mature, immune system cells might think the transplants are part of the body.

The biggest problem with both pancreas and islet cell transplantation is the shortage of organ donors. Only 7,000 to 9,000 bodies are donated for organ transplants each year in the United States—too few to supply pancreas cells for everyone with type 1 diabetes.

Type 2 Diabetes Management

You can manage type 2 diabetes by many methods. Not everyone with type 2 diabetes needs pills or insulin. Most people who are newly diagnosed are put on a new eating and exercise plan. For many, eating healthy portion sizes of low-fat foods and getting a regular workout is all they need to keep blood glucose levels near normal. Others need to add to this plan the extra glucose-lowering power of oral medications or insulin.

There is a range of different reasons why people develop type 2 diabetes.

■ Your muscle and fat cells often are resistant to the action of insulin. In this case, a regular exercise program and weight loss, often in addition to medication, can help.

■ Your insulin-releasing pancreas cells may not release enough insulin to meet your needs. In this case, insulin or oral diabetes medications are helpful.

■ Your liver may release too much glucose. In this case, metformin can be helpful.

Sometimes it's possible to figure out which of these problems is causing type 2 diabetes. This helps your doctor match the treatment to the cause. And often, type 2 diabetes seems to be caused by a combination of these problems.

Whether you should take oral medication, insulin, or any medication at all and what sort of insulin or medication plan you should follow really depends on how your body is dealing with the glucose it makes. Doctors may tailor the treatment approach by your usual fasting blood glucose levels. Ideally, you will want to keep your glucose levels as close to normal as you are able. This means fasting blood glucose levels under 110 mg/dl and after-meal blood glucose levels under 140 mg/dl.

Treatment Approaches by Fasting Blood Glucose Levels

Fasting blood glucose level (mg/dl)	Treatment, in addition to regular medical visits
Under 110	Healthy eating and exercise habits
110 to under 126	Meal planning and regular exercise
126 to 200	Meal planning and regular exercise
	Oral diabetes medications or insulin
Over 200	Meal planning and regular exercise
	Around-the-clock insulin coverage and/or oral diabetes medications

Food and Physical Activity

The accepted, tried and true treatment for type 2 diabetes is a balance of diet and exercise. Even if medications are prescribed, healthy eating and exercise habits continue to be key in caring for your type 2 diabetes. Most people with type 2 diabetes are advised to lose weight and improve their physical fitness. This can help to lower the body's resistance to insulin. The severity of type 2 diabetes can be greatly reduced by maintaining a healthy body weight. Even a modest weight loss can have benefits.

By building a healthy lifestyle around a low-fat, well-rounded diet and regular exercise, it is possible to control body weight and insulin resistance. Exercise helps by taking some glucose from the blood and using it for energy during a workout, an effect that lasts even beyond the workout. Healthy eating, especially controlling the amount of food eaten, helps glucose levels stay lower. As your level of physical fitness improves with regular exercise, so does your body's sensitivity to insulin.

Insulin Therapy

For people with a milder form of type 2 diabetes, insulin is almost never prescribed. If you have fasting blood glucose levels less than 126 mg/dl, you have type 2 diabetes that can usually be controlled through diet and exercise. But not all people with type 2 diabetes can control blood glucose levels by diet and exercise alone. Often, people start out treating diabetes with exercise and diet, then add an oral medication. Eventually blood glucose–lowering insulin injections are also needed. A few people need insulin temporarily after diagnosis to control very high glucose levels and then find that, because of good results with diet and exercise, they can stop taking insulin, at least for a while.

Your doctor may suggest that you start insulin therapy when diet, exercise, and oral medications together haven't been able to keep blood glucose levels low. This doesn't necessarily mean your health is getting worse, only that you need more help dealing with your body's resistance to insulin.

Somewhere around 30 to 40 percent of people with type 2 diabetes use insulin. You are more likely to use insulin the longer you've had diabetes. A typical plan is two insulin doses per day. In this plan, each dose contains some fast-acting insulin and some longer-acting insulin, either mixed together in one syringe or injected with two syringes. The fast-acting insulin lowers the blood glucose level after the next meal, and the longer-acting insulin lowers the glucose levels between meals.

If your fasting blood glucose level is between 126 and 200 mg/dl, your doctor may prescribe insulin therapy. If so, it will probably be given at background, or basal, levels. Because your pancreas releases enough insulin to cover your meals (provided they are of a healthy portion size), you only need help controlling hyperglycemia between meals. One or two injections of intermediate- or longer-acting insulin might work well for you. One approach is to inject long-acting insulin at supper or bedtime to control fasting blood glucose level. During the day, you would control blood glucose levels with meal planning and exercise and perhaps oral diabetes medications.

Diabetes: Myth or Fact?

"Dad has a touch of diabetes. Nothing to get worried about."

Despite what you might read in the newspaper or be told by friends or relatives, there really is no such thing as a "touch" of diabetes. What people may be talking about is type 2 diabetes that responds well to healthy eating and regular exercise and hasn't shown any signs of damaging body parts. Or they may be describing gestational diabetes or impaired glucose tolerance.

The reality is that diabetes is a serious, life-long disease. Describing someone as having a touch of diabetes is like saying a woman is "a little bit pregnant"—it just isn't true because both are "yes or no" conditions.

Once diagnosed, diabetes doesn't go away, although there may be times in your life when it's easier to control. If this happens, you may be tempted to think your diabetes is cured, but don't forget that there will also be frustrating periods when nothing you do seems to help keep blood glucose levels low. Body changes can make glucose control more difficult—aging, fat gain, an injury that makes it harder to get regular exercise, or a gradual or total shutdown of insulin production. When these things happen, you'll need to adjust your diabetes therapy to match your body's new needs.

If you are able to control your blood glucose level by overcoming your urges to overeat and avoid exercising, you have "easily" controlled diabetes.

If you have a fasting blood glucose level greater than 200 mg/dl, you may require around-the-clock insulin coverage. Your doctor will recommend against a plan of one or two injections with longer-acting insulins, because you need more help lowering glucose levels after you eat. Your doctor may suggest one or two doses of intermediate-acting insulin to cover your basal insulin needs, but may add injections of short-acting insulin before meals to help lower glucose levels after meals. You and your health care team need to arrive at a schedule of insulin types and injection times and doses by trial and error, much like a person with type 1 diabetes would. People with severe type 2 diabetes have a deficiency of insulin that is often difficult to distinguish from type 1 diabetes. If you have type 2 diabetes, however, you are not likely to develop ketosis.

In people with type 2 diabetes, the body becomes more resistant to insulin as glucose levels remain out of control. That means that you may be treated with insulin when your diabetes was first diagnosed to gain control of your blood glucose levels. For many people, as the changes in blood glucose level become less erratic, there is less insulin resistance. After gaining better control, you may find that oral diabetes agents, or even a diet and exercise program alone, may be enough to keep your blood glucose levels in balance—without added insulin.

Look for more information on insulin and insulin plans in Chapter 4.

Oral Diabetes Medications

Before prescribing any oral drug, your doctor will probably first suggest a meal plan and a program of regular exercise. However, you may need a little more help lowering blood glucose levels. Many people with type 2 diabetes can achieve blood glucose control through diet, exercise, and the use of oral medications.

You should continue to follow your eating and exercise plans even if you start taking an oral diabetes medication.

Most diabetes oral agents are sulfonylurea drugs. The effects of sulfonylurea drugs on blood glucose levels were discovered by accident in the 1940s (they were used as antibacterial drugs during World War II). Sulfonylureas lower blood glucose levels by encouraging the pancreas to produce and release more insulin. Scientists have many leads on how these drugs accomplish this.

Seven different sulfonylureas are prescribed in this country: tolbutamide (brand name Orinase), tolazamide (Tolinase), acetohexamide (Dymelor), glyburide (DiaBeta, Glynase, or Micronase), glipizide (Glucotrol), chloropropamide (Diabinese), and glimepiride (Amaryl). Glimepiride is the newest sulfonylurea to be approved.

Until 1994, sulfonylureas were the only oral medication for type 2 diabetes available to Americans. In December 1994, metformin (brand name Glucophage) was approved for use by the Food and Drug Administration. It belongs to a different class of drugs called the *biguanides.* Biguanides help people

How Metformin Helps

- Metformin can help some people lose weight by causing loss of appetite. That's good because many people with type 2 diabetes are overweight and may gain weight with sulfonylurea or insulin therapy. Losing weight can help patients gain blood glucose control.
- Metformin does not cause hypoglycemia. This is a side effect of sulfonylurea drugs (and insulin).
- Metformin causes the level of fats in the blood to drop. This can help many people with type 2 diabetes who have high cholesterol.

with type 2 diabetes differently than sulfonylureas. Biguanides lower blood glucose mainly by putting a brake on the liver's release of stored glucose. They also hinder the absorption of glucose from food being digested in the small intestine. Biguanides may also lower insulin resistance in the muscles. Because metformin acts to decrease glucose release rather than increase insulin activity, there is little risk of very low blood glucose levels (hypoglycemia). Metformin has the added advantages of helping lower high blood fat levels and promoting weight loss.

Metformin can be used along with a sulfonylurea or insulin. Because they work in different ways, metformin and sulfonylureas are often prescribed together. They can be very effective for patients who are poorly controlled just on sulfonylureas and a meal plan. Metformin is particularly useful for people who are allergic to sulfa drugs.

A new class of drugs used to treat type 2 diabetes is the thiazolidinediones. Troglitazone (brand name Rezulin) helps people with type 2 diabetes who have high blood glucose levels despite using insulin. This pill lowers insulin resistance, but how it does this is still being studied. Troglitazone may enable you to reduce your insulin dose. Extra benefits are lower triglyceride levels and increased high-density lipoprotein cholesterol levels. Two other drugs in this class, pioglitazone (Actos) and rosiglitazone (Avandia), were approved by the FDA in 1999.

In 1996, doctors started prescribing acarbose (Precose) for some people with type 2 diabetes. Acarbose and miglitol (Glyset) are members of the alphaglucosidase inhibitor class of drugs. These drugs help keep after-meal blood glucose levels from going as high as they could by temporarily blocking the action of a group of enzymes that helps you digest starches. This improves long-term glucose control as shown by lowered glycated hemoglobin levels. A lot of people who take these drugs complain of intestinal gas and diarrhea, but these side effects often diminish with continued use or dose adjustments, and the improvement it can offer in glucose control may make them useful drugs for you.

A final class of drugs is the meglitinides. Repaglinide (Prandin) stimulates insulin release by the pancreas in response to a meal. If you have problems with your blood

Oral Diabetes Medications at a Glance

Generic name	Brand name	Usually taken	Action usually lasts
Tolbutamide	Orinase	2 or 3 times/day	6 to 12 hours
Chlorpropamide	Diabinese	Once a day	Up to 60 hours
Tolazamide	Tolinase	1 or 2 times/day	12 to 24 hours
Acetohexamide	Dymelor	1 or 2 times/day	12 to 24 hours
Glipizide	Glucotrol Glucotrol XL	1 or 2 times/day Varies	12 to 24 hours Up to 24 hours
Glyburide	DiaBeta, Micronase, Glynase PresTab	1 or 2 times/day Varies	16 to 24 hours 12 to 24 hours
Glimepiride	Amaryl	Once a day	Up to 24 hours
Metformin	Glucophage	2 or 3 times/day	4 to 8 hours
Troglitazone	Rezulin	Once a day, with meal	Up to 24 hours
Acarbose	Precose	3 times/day, with meals	4 hours
Miglitol	Glyset	3 times/day, with meals	4 hours
Repaglinide	Prandin	3 times/day, with meals	4 hours

glucose rising immediately after a meal, repaglinide may be a good choice for you.

Sulfonylureas, metformin, and the other drugs come in tablet form. Make sure you know how often and how much you should take, before you leave the doctor's office. Also, ask your doctor about possible side effects, and any signs of side effects that you should be on the lookout for.

Choosing an Oral Diabetes Medication. All oral diabetes medications must be prescribed by a doctor. Your doctor will take into account your lifestyle, physical condition, and personal needs before prescribing any particular drug or combination of drugs.

■ Generally, you should not use an oral agent if you have type 1 diabetes (acarbose or miglitol may prove helpful to people with type 1 diabetes). They are usually only prescribed for people with type 2 diabetes.

■ Not everyone with type 2 diabetes will be helped by oral diabetes medications. Oral medications are more likely to lower blood glucose levels in people who have had high blood glucose levels for less than 10 years, who are normal weight or obese, who are willing to follow a healthy meal plan, and who have some insulin secretion by their pancreas. The drugs work poorly in people who are very thin.

■ You should not take a sulfonylurea if your pancreas no longer secretes insulin; if you are pregnant or planning a pregnancy; or have significant heart, liver, or kidney disease.

■ During severe infections or major surgery, your doctor may recommend that oral diabetes medications be replaced or supplemented with insulin injections, at least temporarily.

■ You should probably avoid sulfonylurea drugs if you are allergic to sulfa drugs. Ask your doctor if there is another drug that might work for you. Metformin may be of some help to you. However, you should not take metformin if you have kidney, heart, or liver disease.

■ If you are taking troglitazone (Rezulin), pioglitazone (Actos), or rosiglitazone (Avandia), your liver function will be monitored through blood tests, because of the possibility of liver damage in rare instances.

■ Oral diabetes medications vary in price. This may affect your choice of drugs.

There can be big differences in timing and duration of action of different oral diabetes medications. For example, tolbutamide has a minimal risk of hypoglycemia and may be safest for an elderly person living alone. But other medications, such as chlorpropamide and glyburide, can have longer lasting glucose-lowering effects. Also, different people can also respond differently to the same dose of any oral agent. To evaluate these issues, or if you feel that your oral diabetes medication is not doing what it should, talk to your health care team.

Cautions for Use. All sulfonylurea drugs increase the risk of hypoglycemia, especially if you skip meals or drink too much alcohol. Be sure to talk to your doctor about the symptoms to watch for and any precautions you need to take while on your oral medication. Teach your family and friends the warning signs of hypoglycemia. Together, make a plan of action for dealing with unexpected lows.

Oral agents can have other side effects. For example, they can interact with alcohol to make you feel flushed, nauseated, or have a rapid heartbeat. This is especially true with chlorpropamide. In rare cases, chlorpropamide can cause your body to retain water, causing headache, sleepiness, nausea, and sometimes convulsions. Skin rashes can occur with sulfonylurea use. If you notice any changes in your behavior or your body after starting a course of oral diabetes medications, be sure to tell your doctor.

Drug Interactions. You and your doctor should talk about medicines other than your diabetes medications, either prescription or over the counter, that you are currently taking or might be thinking of taking. Are there any medicines you take when you are coming down with a cold? In bed with the flu? Get a sudden headache? If you take aspirin or thyroid or high blood pressure medicine, medicine to lower blood cholesterol, or cold or allergy remedies, tell your doctor. Sometimes, drugs that are safe by themselves can interact with each other to cause sickness or conditions that can be difficult to diagnose. Some drugs can lower or raise blood glucose levels. This must be accounted for so that your blood glucose levels don't go too low or stay too high. What looks likes hypoglycemia may really be caused by a drug interaction and can be mistreated. Many drugs interfere with the way the body uses and eliminates oral diabetes medications. These drugs can indirectly cause hyper- or hypoglycemia.

Looking Ahead. After taking an oral diabetes medication for a while, you may find that you can consistently achieve normal fasting blood glucose levels. If you have normal readings for several weeks or months, it's possible that you can control your blood sugar levels by meal planning and regular exercise alone. Ask your health care team whether they can suggest that you start a trial of diabetes control with no pills—just meal planning and regular exercise. If you do this, make sure to keep monitoring your blood glucose and stay in close contact with your health care team.

There is a possibility that oral medications won't help you at all. Or they may help, but only for a while. In people who have initial success with a sulfonylurea, about 5 to 10 percent stop responding within a year. Eventually, at least another 50 percent will stop responding. If oral treatment fails to help you achieve your target blood glucose levels, your doctor may want to add insulin to your diabetes care plan, with or without continuing your oral diabetes medication. You may resist your doctor's suggestion to start the insulin-and-needles routine, but the reward will be improved blood glucose levels. The risk of hypoglycemia may increase with this treatment plan, until you and your doctor find the right doses. Make sure to pay special attention to instructions and medication techniques and schedules. Write all instructions down until you feel comfortable with the new treatment. Know the symptoms of hypoglycemia, and make sure you know how to treat it in advance.

Gestational Diabetes Management

Pregnancy demands more insulin than normal because of the increased production of hormones that lead to insulin resistance. People with gestational diabetes and people with type 2 diabetes all have insulin resistance. The pancreas is unable to produce enough insulin to overcome the insulin resistance. Because of this similarity, both diseases are treated by meal planning and regular exercise. But, should diet and exercise not keep blood glucose levels low, insulin is the next course of action. Oral diabetes medications can cause birth defects and are not prescribed during pregnancy.

Blood glucose goals are tighter for pregnant women than for most people with type 2 diabetes. This is because of the harmful effects that too much glucose in the mother's blood can have on the growing baby, as well as the pregnant woman. For women who have type 1 or type 2 diabetes before becoming pregnant, keeping blood glucose levels low even before pregnancy decreases the risk of birth defects in the baby. (Chapter 11 has more information about pregnancy and women with preexisting type 1 or type 2 diabetes.) But in gestational diabetes, which is usually not diagnosed until more than halfway in the pregnancy, the problem is not the possibility of birth defects. By the halfway mark in the pregnancy, the baby's organs are already formed. The last half of the pregnancy is when the baby grows larger. Too much glucose in the mother's blood during the last half of pregnancy can lead to a baby that is too large to be delivered safely. This condition is called *macrosomia*. Because of macrosomia, women with gestational diabetes have a higher risk of delivery by cesarean section. Also, you may need to deliver the baby early if he or she grows too large too fast. An early delivery puts the baby at a higher risk for respiratory distress because the lungs are about the last organ to mature.

Women with gestational diabetes are also at higher risk for toxemia, a condition in pregnancy in which blood pressure is too high. Swelling of legs and arms commonly goes along with toxemia. Toxemia can be dangerous for the mother and baby and can mean bed rest for the mother until delivery.

A doctor will start treating your gestational diabetes based on the results of your 3-hour glucose tolerance test. If your fasting blood glucose level (taken at the start of the test) was normal (under 105 mg/dl) but your glucose tolerance test results were

Sample Blood Glucose Goals in Gestational Diabetes

 Note that these goals are considered normal for a person without diabetes and are general goals for women with diabetes during pregnancy. Your goals need to be individualized.

- Fasting blood glucose . . . . .90 mg/dl or less
- Before-meal blood glucose . . . . .105 mg/dl or less
- One hour after a meal . . . . .130 mg/dl or less
- Two hours after a meal . . . . .120 mg/dl or less

in the diabetic range, your doctor may recommend nutrition therapy, perhaps with a prescription for exercise, if you are able. If your fasting blood glucose was over 105 mg/dl, you will probably start insulin therapy, too. Because of the emphasis on keeping blood glucose levels low, you will need to test your blood frequently, perhaps four or more times a day.

Nutrition Therapy

For many women, making healthy food and portion choices is enough to keep blood glucose levels within the ranges your doctor recommends. Using mild exercise to lower blood glucose levels may also be included in your diabetes management. Even women with special needs during pregnancy can almost always swim or walk to keep active. Your goals during pregnancy may also focus on limiting the amount of your weight gain. This is especially important because many more overweight or obese women develop gestational diabetes than those with a normal weight. For instance, in women who were obese before pregnancy, recommended weight gain may be limited to 15 pounds.

Healthy food choices play a key role in managing gestational diabetes. You may need to refresh your knowledge of nutrition basics, so it's important that you meet with a registered dietitian. You may need to set a daily calorie goal based on the amount of weight you should gain during the pregnancy.

Insulin Therapy

Because normal blood glucose levels are so important during pregnancy, if you are having any problems reaching your target ranges, your doctor may recommend insulin therapy. Your insulin resistance is at its highest during the third trimester of pregnancy. Therefore, your doctor may start you on a large total dose of insulin each day, for example 20 to 30 units. This might be a mixture of short- and intermediate-acting insulins. This can be given once, usually before breakfast, if fasting blood glucose levels are low. Or the dose can be divided into several injections

Diabetes: Myth or Fact?

"Because I have gestational diabetes, my child or I will get diabetes."

The risk of your child someday developing diabetes is low. This risk seems to go up with the birth size of the baby. Studies have shown that the larger your baby is at birth, the greater the chance that he or she will develop obesity. Signs of obesity can be seen as early as 7 or 8 years of age. If your child develops obesity during youth or adolescence, there's also a chance that he or she will develop glucose intolerance, and possibly diabetes, as an adult. Your best bet to keep your child's risk of diabetes as low as possible is to keep your blood glucose levels as close to normal while you have gestational diabetes.

However, your risk of getting diabetes permanently is high. Although your blood glucose levels may return to normal after delivery, you need to be checked for diabetes every year. The risk of developing type 2 diabetes 5 to 15 years after gestational diabetes is between 40 and 60 percent, compared with about a 15 percent risk in the general population. Being obese increases the risk of getting type 2 diabetes after having gestational diabetes to a 3 out of 4 chance. What an incentive for keeping a healthy body weight (see Chapter 1) and getting plenty of exercise!

a day, similar to tightly controlled type 1 diabetes, if you need help reducing fasting glucose levels.

Because insulin resistance is so high late in pregnancy, very low blood glucose levels, leading to hypoglycemia, are rare. However, if you seem prone to hypoglycemia, remember that the safest times to exercise are after meals, when you are less likely to develop hypoglycemia.

Don't be alarmed if your total insulin dosage increases as your pregnancy continues. This does not mean your diabetes is getting worse, only that your insulin resistance is increasing, which is normal. You may need to make changes in your insulin dosage as often as every 10 to 14 days.

Look for more information on insulin and insulin plans in Chapter 4.

Chapter 3: Good Health Care and Your Health Care Team

Good diabetes care is a team effort that involves you, your family and friends, your physician, and other health professionals to meet your different needs. Be assertive—take charge of your own health. Gathering a diabetes care team can mean a little extra effort, but the payoff is worth it.

Living with type 1 or type 2 diabetes can seem overwhelming. Whether you have just been diagnosed or have had diabetes for a while, many questions are likely to arise. Do I have to take insulin? How often should I test my blood sugar? Can I exercise? What should I eat? How should I take care of my eyes? My feet?

Diabetes affects many aspects of health and daily living. Fortunately, you can manage by gathering a team of health care professionals to help you adjust to your new lifestyle and fine-tune your routines now and then. Your health care team is key in helping you manage diabetes. But remember that you are the team captain—you call the shots. So choose team members whom you trust and who think as you do about diabetes care. Working together, you can learn to live well with diabetes.

Getting Started

You may not be used to "shopping" for health care. But if you have a chance to choose your health care team members, take advantage of it and look for health professionals who follow these three Rs:

- **Recognize** you as an individual and are willing to devise a plan that you can live with. Don't settle for a meal plan containing foods you don't like or an exercise prescription you can't follow. You and your health care team should agree on steps you can and are willing to do.

- **Respond** to your questions and concerns. You and your family members should be able to ask questions openly and trust that the health professional will take the time to listen and answer you patiently, completely, and honestly.

- **Recommend** the best possible strategies for the care and management of diabetes. All professionals should be aware of and follow standards of care recommended by the American Diabetes Association.

PROFESSIONAL	DEGREE	LOOK FOR	CONSULT FOR
Physician	MD or DO	Specialization in diabetes, such as board certification in endocrinology	Medical management of diabetes, including oral agents or insulin, and the detection of complications
Nurse educator	RN, BSN, MSN	Certified Diabetes Educator (CDE)	Counseling you on diabetes self-care, including following a diet, taking your medicines, doing blood tests, or managing sick days or stress
Dietitian	RD	CDE is desirable	Helping you to develop or alter your diabetes meal plan, lose weight, or follow dietary restrictions (such as cutting dietary sodium or fat)
Eye doctor	MD specializing in ophthalmology, or an optometrist	Familiarity with diabetic eye disease	Detecting and treating diabetic eye disease such as retinopathy; ophthalmologists treat eye disease with laser therapy or eye surgery
Podiatrist	DPM	Experience treating diabetic foot problems	Treating foot problems, including calluses, sores, or ulcers; helping you prevent future foot injury.
Mental health professional	MD (Psychiatry); MS, MED or PhD (Psychology); MSW (Social Worker); LPC (Counselor)	Experience treating diabetes	Helping you cope with depression, anxiety, or other mental health problems
Exercise specialist	Various: BS, MS, or PhD, or RN	CDE is desirable	Helping you develop and stick with an exercise plan and working with your doctor to help you exercise safely
Pharmacist	RPH or PharmD	Experience counseling people with diabetes	Providing information and counseling about diabetes drugs and self-care products (such as meters)

Whatever your preferences, keep in mind that assembling the perfect team and developing a plan may take some time. Your plan will need fine-tuning along the way. Try to choose team members willing to help you adapt to changes along the way.

The Team Captain: You

In finding your health care team, you will choose professionals with expertise in different aspects of diabetes care. A dietitian may advise you of the foods to fit into your meal plan. An exercise physiologist may help you find an exercise plan that fits your interests and schedule.

In the end, though, you are the one who follows the diet and exercises and takes the necessary medication. Your health care team can offer you advice, but it's up to you to make the decisions that will safeguard your health. After all, you are the team captain and no one knows you better. You will be the first one to detect any problems. Trust your instincts and listen to your body.

Even if you have done everything your team members advise, something may not feel quite right. Maybe your diet

Reasons to Contact Your Diabetes Care Team

■ You're having frequent or severe low blood sugar

■ Your blood sugars are consistently higher than your targets

■ You've noticed a change in your vision

■ You're confused about how to take a medicine

■ You're having unexplained high or low blood sugar reading

■ You're having trouble following your meal or exercise plan

■ You develop feelings of numbness or tingling in your hands or feet

■ Your skin is dry or you have a sore

■ You feel depressed or anxious about having diabetes

or insulin dose needs an adjustment. Your health care team members can't help you make the necessary adjustments if they don't know there is a problem. So stay in contact. Your team members are counting on you to tell them what you know about your body and how it responds to diabetes.

As team captain, your job is to choose the other members of your team. Think of your primary care physician as your co-captain. You may also want to pick a diabetes educator, a dietitian or nutritional counselor, and other health care specialists that may be called upon as needed. This could include an eye doctor, a podiatrist, a counselor (psychologist, social worker, or psychiatrist), and an exercise physiologist.

Sometimes, diabetes professionals will already practice together in a center that specializes in diabetes care. Or your primary care physician may routinely work with some of these professionals. If not, you may have to assemble your own group. If your doctor doesn't have a diabetes educator or dietitian on staff, ask him or her to recommend one as well as other professionals you may want to have on your team.

It's a plus if the members of your team are comfortable communicating with each other. That is often the case if they are highly recommended by your doctor. But you should also pick team members that you feel comfortable with. Don't be afraid to shop around a little and find the team members that best suit your needs.

In assembling your team, don't forget your fans—family and friends that will lend support, help, and understanding on a daily basis. They need to be prepared to deal with your day-to-day routines—what time you test your blood glucose, for example. And you may also need their help should any emergency arise.

Also, don't forget community resources. Many hospitals and community health groups offer classes and support groups for people with diabetes. Here you can receive valuable information and answers to your questions about dealing with the disease. Class instructors and support group members may also be able to provide referrals to other health care professionals that specialize in diabetes care.

Choosing a Physician

As you start to choose your health professionals, it may help to listen to the experience of other people with diabetes. Consider the stories of James and Helen, decades apart in age, but sharing an initial sense of confusion and a little fear about finding good care for diabetes.

James had just started college 500 miles away from home when he was diagnosed with type 1 diabetes. Mastering glucose control by blood glucose monitoring, insulin shots, and a carefully controlled diet was confusing and a little scary, especially because he was also trying to get used to college life. Being so far from home, he knew he would have to find a new doctor near campus. He would have to see a doctor at least every 3 months, and perhaps more often while he was trying to get his diabetes under control. He wasn't sure he could get home that often and wanted someone nearby in case of an emergency. Besides, his familiar family doctor was not an expert in diabetes and suggested that he find a local physician with expertise in managing the disease.

Helen was just starting to plan for her early retirement. Over the past ten years she had put on a little extra weight. Between taking care of the kids and working long days at her high-level government job, she had little time for exercise and was always eating on the run. Her health care maintenance had fallen by the wayside also. Although she visited her gynecologist every year or so, she hadn't seen a general practitioner or had a complete physical in nearly a decade. She was looking forward to doing some traveling, taking up some new hobbies, and starting an exercise program, when she learned that she had type 2 diabetes.

Both James and Helen needed to find new physicians who had experience in coordinating the care for people with diabetes. Although James and Helen had different types of diabetes, they both had similar concerns and needs in finding the ideal doctor. Helen wrote down a list of the important qualities she was seeking and was able to express what she was looking for in a doctor.

"I wanted someone who would really listen to me and answer my questions in English, not doctor-ese. So many times, doctors have treated me as though I were a child whose only duty was to obey. Well, I'm the one who has diabetes, and I'm the one who's got to take care of it. I guess I just want a doctor who won't talk down to me, who would treat me as another professional."

James is also concerned about communication:

"It's hard to talk to doctors sometimes. I mean, a lot of times, I nod my head as if I understand something when I really don't. But there's a lot of stuff I'm worried about. Like, someone told me that a lot of men with diabetes become impotent. I want to know if that's true and whether there is anything you can do to prevent it."

Both Helen and James realized that they would need the services of other health care professionals. For Helen, this meant wanting to consult an exercise physiologist to start a fitness program:

"I've been meaning to start exercising—for about the last 20 years. But there have always been so many reasons not to—the kids, my job, it being too hot or too cold outside. To be honest, I'm also a little embarrassed about having people see me exercising at my weight. I'd like to see someone who could help me get over my excuses and help me ease into activity gradually."

For James, the biggest issue was seeing a dietitian for advice on fitting diabetes care into college life and cafeteria food:

"I've always been laid back about schedules. I never eat breakfast, and if I don't like what the cafeteria is serving, I'll just have pizza or something later on. Now that I'm taking insulin shots, I know I can't do that anymore. But I'm hoping that a dietitian can help me be a little flexible about when and what I eat."

Like James and Helen, you may have personal concerns about diabetes. Before you choose a doctor, you may want to schedule an appointment to talk with several candidates. Some health care professionals may charge an "interview fee," so be sure to ask about this ahead of time.

Come to your interview with questions you would like answered. If necessary, write them down in advance and don't be afraid to look at them during your interview. Write down answers to your questions during the interview, if need be. Here are some common questions and concerns you might discuss with the doctor:

- Where did you do medical school? Are you board certified in endocrinology or internal medicine? Do you hold professional memberships in associations such as the American Diabetes Association, The Endocrine Society, or the American College of Physicians?

- What percentage of your patients have diabetes? Are they mostly patients with type 1 or type 2? How many patients like me do you see each month?

- What insurance do you accept? Are you a provider in my PPO plan? If I require a referral to a specialist, do you have colleagues who also participate?

- How often will regular visits be scheduled? What tests are conducted routinely?

- Who covers for you on your days off?

- What procedures should be followed in the event of an emergency? What conditions indicate an emergency? How do I know whether I should call you?

■ Are you associated with other health care professionals so that I can benefit from a team approach?

■ Are you likely/willing to try new approaches/therapies to diabetes management, or do you prefer to wait until new methods have stood the test of time?

After the interview, take time to reflect on it. How did it feel? Were you comfortable with the doctor? Did the doctor seem concerned about you as an individual? Was the doctor willing to work with you to achieve your health goals? Did you feel free to express your feelings? Did you feel that the doctor was listening to you? Were you given sufficient time to get all your questions answered or did you feel rushed? Did the doctor seem directive or nondirective—is he or she likely to tell you what to do or let you make your own decisions in your management plan?

In addition to your interview, you may also want to get a sense of the doctor from his or her staff and other patients.

Is the doctor's office convenient enough for you to get to regular appointments? Maybe the closest endocrinologist is 50 miles away and you would like someone closer. In that case, you might want to find an internist or general practitioner with expertise in treating patients with diabetes.

Are the doctor's current patients satisfied? Is it easy enough to get an appointment? Does the doctor meet his or her appointments? Ask other people who see this doctor. You can also contact your local ADA chapter for recommendations, or receive referrals from a physician you know and trust. Also your local hospital or community health organization may provide referrals. Professional medical societies may also provide recommendations.

Is the office neat and clean? Is the staff polite? Are you accommodated at your scheduled appointment time or are you kept waiting? Are educational materials on display?

The Rest of the Team

I t's unlikely that you will learn all you need to know about managing diabetes in a one-hour appointment with your doctor. Because diabetes is such a complicated disease that affects many different organ systems in your body, you will benefit from the addition of other health care professionals to your management team. Your best resource for recruiting other team members is probably your doctor. It is important not only that your doctor communicates with other members of your team, but also that they are able to communicate with each other about any changes that may arise in your diabetes management plan. To ensure this, make sure that they each have the phone numbers, fax numbers, and e-mail addresses of other members of the team.

Your Diabetes Educator

R on took his insulin faithfully every day—a shot before breakfast and another in the evening. He had apparently mastered near-perfect glucose control. However, he began to notice hard lumps surrounding the injection site on his abdomen. His primary care physician recommended that he meet with a nurse educator or diabetes nurse practitioner to work on improving site rotation.

Paul had been trying to quit smoking for several years. He sometimes went for weeks or even months without having a cigarette, but always started up again. Recently, he had been diagnosed with type 2 diabetes. He wondered how his smoking might affect his diabetes and wanted advice on how to quit. His physician put him touch with a diabetes educator.

If you have questions like Ron's and Paul's about managing your diabetes, a diabetes educator can help. She or he can address any of the concerns or questions you may have about

Finding a Recognized Diabetes Education Program

In addition to meeting one-on-one with a diabetes educator, you may also want to participate in a diabetes education program. Your local American Diabetes Association chapter can refer you to a program that has been recognized as meeting National Standards. This means that it can provide you with quality diabetes education. Education programs that meet the National Standards cover all of the following topics:

■ General information about diabetes and its causes

■ Adjusting psychologically to caring for diabetes

■ Using family and friends for support and teaching them about diabetes

■ Understanding your eating plan and the importance of matching your insulin dose to the amount and nature of your meal portions

■ Exercising wisely to manage blood glucose and avoid hyperglycemia

■ Taking medications such as insulin effectively

■ Balancing nutrition, exercise, and insulin

■ Testing your blood glucose accurately and recording it properly

■ Dealing with hypoglycemia and hyperglycemia—their symptoms, causes, and treatments

■ Managing sick days

■ Preventing and treating long-term complications

■ Maintaining good hygiene, including skin, foot, and dental care

■ Weighing the benefits and responsibilities of care, avoiding complications, and understanding the effects of smoking and alcohol on diabetes

■ Using the health care system and your health care team to help you manage your diabetes. Locating community resources to help you with all aspects of diabetes. If you participate in such a program, have the program's staff write to inform your physician of what you did in the program.

diabetes. Diabetes educators, for example, may give you background information about the biology of diabetes, teach you how to take insulin or check blood glucose levels, explain how to handle sick days and pregnancy, or discuss the effects of lifestyle habits on blood glucose control.

A diabetes educator is usually a registered nurse (RN) with special interest and training in caring for people with diabetes. An educator may also be a dietitian, pharmacist, or a physician. The initials CDE (for certified diabetes educator) indicate that the professional has passed a national exam in diabetes education and is up-to-date about diabetes care. CDEs often work in the offices of doctors who treat many patients with diabetes. The American Association of Diabetes Educators can also provide local referrals (see Resources).

Your Dietitian

*A**lthough Marie had lived with diabetes for three years and had good glucose control in the past, she recently noticed that her blood glucose levels had been getting higher. She wondered whether changing her diet might bring her glucose levels to closer to normal.*

At his last physical exam, Charles gritted his teeth as the nurse pumped the blood pressure cuff tight. He was surprised when he heard the two numbers that indicated his blood pressure was too high. His doctor advised him to exercise, lose weight, and eat a low-sodium diet to help reduce his blood pressure. His physician suggested a visit with his dietitian for advice on how to cut down on fat and sodium without sacrificing the foods he loved or upsetting his glucose balance.

Even if you aren't having problems with diabetes care, it is a good idea to see a dietitian once or twice each year. A registered dietitian (RD) is a member of your health care team who has training and expertise in food and nutrition. For both type 1 and type 2 diabetes, whether or not you take insulin or other medication, a balanced meal plan is critical to living well with diabetes. A dietitian can help you develop a meal plan that you can live with and will help you understand the importance of nutrition in managing diabetes. You may want help in adapting your diet to special goals, such as losing weight, reducing dietary fat or sodium, or complementing a regular exercise program. Your dietitian can help ensure that your diet achieves these goals and that it accommodates your likes and dislikes, work schedule, and lifestyle.

How to Afford a Dietitian

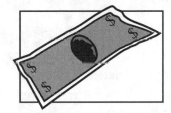

The best way to afford your visit to the dietitian is obvious: get your health insurer to pay. Unfortunately, that's not always easy. Here are some tips that can increase your chances of getting your claim paid:

■ Call your insurer first. You may be lucky and have an insurer who will pay without a fuss. If so, ask what paperwork you will need to submit.

■ Submit a claim after each visit to the dietitian. Include a written referral from your doctor; it should not prescribe "nutrition counseling" or "nutrition education" but fancy sounding language such as "medical nutritional therapy for diabetes management."

■ If you are turned down, resubmit your claim. This time, document how your visit to the RD can save the insurer money. For example, you can cite the Diabetes Control and Complications Trial, which proved that complications can be prevented or delayed with good control.

■ If you are turned down, ask for your claim to be reviewed. Many insurers will tell you no at first, only to eventually cover some or all of the claim. In writing, ask for your disputed claim to be reviewed. Follow up with phone calls. Write down the names and titles of the people you call and the dates when you spoke. It pays to be persistent, so continue to write letters and make phone calls until either you or your insurer decide to pay for treatment.

Does your meal plan need a change or adjustment? If you can answer yes to any of the following questions, then your meal plan may need a tune-up:

■ Has it been more than a year since your dietitian or physician reviewed your meal plan?

■ Is your blood glucose level or body weight more difficult to control than usual?

■ Are you bored with your meals?

■ Have you started an exercise program or changed your insulin regimen since your last nutrition check-up?

■ Have you decided to aim for blood glucose levels that are closer to normal?

■ Have you been diagnosed with high blood pressure, high cholesterol levels, or kidney disease?

■ Have you recently become pregnant?

■ Are you entering menopause?

To find a dietitian, ask your primary care physician for a referral or contact your local hospital, American Diabetes Association chapter, or The American Dietetic Association. In choosing a dietitian, look for the initials RD (registered dietitian). This indicates that the dietitian has passed a national credentialing exam. Many states also require a license, and you may see the initials LD (licensed dietitian) after a dietitian's name. Some dietitians are also CDEs.

During your first visit, your dietitian will assess your dietary needs, a process that generally takes an hour and a half. Follow-up visits usually take 30 minutes. Follow-up visits allow for sharing further helpful information, progress checks, and adjustments to your meal plan. Even though your diabetes management may seem to be on target, don't neglect periodic follow-up visits with your dietitian.

Dietitians can advise you on many useful strategies:

■ how to use the *Exchange Lists for Meal Planning,* published by the American Diabetes Association and The American Dietetic Association

■ how to count dietary carbohydrate and fat and make adjustments in your insulin dose

■ how to read food labels

■ how to handle eating out in restaurants, and

■ how to make healthy food choices when grocery shopping.

Dietitians may also provide you with a wealth of nutritional resources, such as cookbooks and reading materials, so you can learn how to prepare easy, nutritious, and satisfying meals. Your dietitian may also provide advice on how to integrate your meal plan with that of the rest of your household. In fact, the healthy eating plan that's good for you is good for everyone in your family. You'll learn that, with practice, you can maintain good glucose control even when eating in ethnic restaurants, at a party, or after Thanksgiving dinner.

Your Exercise Physiologist

Whenever she exercised, Terry's heart pounded, she broke into a cold sweat, her body grew shaky, and she became exasperated—the classic signs of a hypoglycemic reaction. She was exercising to make herself feel better, not worse. Terry's doctor referred her to an exercise physiologist who helped her coordinate exercise with balanced glucose levels and a snack schedule.

Howard, while not completely sedentary, had been traveling a lot lately and over the past year had let his fitness program fall by the wayside. When he learned he had type 2 diabetes he was determined to control it through diet and exercise. A former rock climber, he wondered if he dared take up the sport again.

You know you ought to exercise, but where do you begin? If you haven't been very active in the past you might want advice on how to get started. If you have a favorite sport or activity you might want to learn how best to integrate it into your diabetes management plan. A person with knowledge of the science of exercise and training in safe conditioning techniques is in the best position to help you design a fitness program you can live with. To find a qualified exercise physiologist, ask your primary care physician or other members of your health care team. In choosing an exercise physiologist, look for someone who holds a master's or doctoral level degree in exercise physiology or a licensed health care professional who has received graduate training in exercise physiology. You may want someone certified by the American College of Sports Medicine, to ensure that your exercise physiologist has the skills necessary to design a safe, effective fitness program to suit your needs.

Exercise physiologists can help you design a tailor-made fitness program, set realistic goals, and offer tips for staying motivated to stick with your exercise routine. Whatever your exercise goals—to improve cardiovascular fitness, lower blood glucose levels, lose weight, or develop muscular strength and flexibility—your exercise physiologist can help you achieve those goals. Even if you have arthritis, are overweight, experience any complications of diabetes, or have been sedentary and want to become more active, an exercise physiologist can develop an exercise program to accommodate your specific needs. But before embarking on any new exercise program, make sure to clear it with your physician. Also make sure that your physician and exercise physiologist are in contact.

Your Mental Health Counselor

Shelly, a middle-aged woman with type 2 diabetes, prides herself for her success in keeping her diabetes under control. But whenever she finds that her blood glucose level is higher than she likes to see, she feels like a failure. She mopes around and thinks, "I can't do anything right."

Everything seemed to be going well for Michael. He had made the final cut on the high school soccer team and seemed to have a good shot at starting forward. He had just started dating a girl in his biology class, and he was keeping up his grades. But then he started feeling ill and was diagnosed with type 1 diabetes. What would his team members think? Would he have to give up soccer? Would his new girlfriend think he was some kind of freak?

In addition to creating physical and metabolic problems, diabetes can also wreak havoc on a person's thoughts and feelings, often making people with the disease feel as if they have somehow failed. Both Shelly and Michael could probably benefit from seeing a therapist, such as a social worker, family therapist, psychologist, or psychiatrist. Such mental health professionals can help people deal with some of the personal and emotional aspects that are inevitably associated with diabetes.

A **social worker** should hold a master's degree in social work (MSW), as well as training in individual, group, and family therapy. Social workers can help you cope with many concerns related to diabetes, including problems within the family, coping with workplace situations, and locating resources to help with medical or financial needs.

A **marriage and family therapist** should hold a master's or doctoral degree in a mental health field and additional training in individual, family, and marriage therapy. These therapists can help you with personal problems in family and marital relationships and problems on the job.

A **clinical psychologist** usually has a master's or doctoral degree in psychology and is trained in individual, group, and family psychology. You may visit a clinical psychologist to help you through a particularly stressful period over the course of several weeks or months, or on a longer term basis to work through more deep-seated problems.

Tip: Getting a child or teen to buy into and stick with a diabetes management program can be a huge challenge. Make sure your child's health care team includes a mental health professional. This team member will work with your child and you to identify the behavioral, emotional, and social issues confronting your child and offer solutions to problems, such as modifying goals.

A **psychiatrist** is a medical doctor with training in the relationship between physical well-being and mental health. Psychiatrists with expertise in treating people with diabetes can help you understand how the physical problem of diabetes can also affect your mental health. Psychiatrists prescribe medications or hospitalization for emotional problems, if needed.

If you feel that you need some extra help coping with the emotional burden of diabetes, don't be afraid to communicate your feelings to your primary care physician, who can recommend an appropriate health care professional.

Your Eye Doctor

Rose first detected problems with her eyes one afternoon while playing a round of golf. As she was about to tee off, she had difficulty finding the flag on the green, even though it was only a par 3 hole. Instead, she saw strange blotches moving around her field of vision. A quick call to her primary care physician assured her that she needed to see an eye specialist.

For anyone with either type 1 or type 2 diabetes, eye care is an important priority. By maintaining close control of blood glucose levels, you can prevent some of the long-term effects of diabetes and preserve your eyesight. An eye doctor monitors changes in your eyes, especially those changes associated with diabetes. He or she then determines what those changes mean and how they should be treated. For example, changes in the tiny blood vessels that supply your retina—the part of the eye that detects light and thus visual images—could be an early sign of diabetic retinopathy. Left untreated, diabetic retinopathy can lead to blindness.

Although your primary care provider will look at your eyes during the course of your yearly physical examination, you also need to have them more thoroughly examined by a trained eye specialist. If you are between the ages of 12 and 30 and have had diabetes for at least 5 years, or if you are over 30 when you are diagnosed with diabetes, you should have a comprehensive eye and visual exam conducted by an eye doctor every year. Also, if you notice any changes in your vision or you are pregnant or planning a pregnancy, you should also be examined.

Ophthalmologists are physicians qualified to treat eye problems both medically and surgically. Retina specialists are ophthalmologists with further training in the diagnosis and treatment of diseases of the retina. Optometrists are trained to examine the eye for certain problems, such as how well your eyes

Taking Care of Your Eyes

 Have a thorough eye exam at the time of diabetes diagnosis if you are over 30 and yearly thereafter. If you are between 12 and 30 and have had diabetes for at least 5 years, also have a comprehensive yearly exam.

■ After the initial exam, see an eye doctor familiar with retinopathy and other diabetes complications of the eyes once a year.

■ Call your doctor if you notice changes in your vision, but don't panic. Highs and lows in your blood glucose level may cause temporary blurring in your vision.

■ Keep your blood glucose levels under control. You will help prevent damage to the small blood vessels that run through your retina.

■ Have regular blood pressure checks, and work to keep your blood pressure in the healthy range.

■ Discuss your exercise program with your eye doctor. Some activities can raise the pressure inside your eyes and lead to bleeding in the retina.

■ If you have retinopathy, avoid taking birth control pills because they may affect the clotting of your blood or increase your blood pressure.

■ Get early treatment for eye problems! Early intervention, such as laser treatment for retinopathy, cuts the risk of blindness by 90 percent.

can focus. While they can prescribe corrective lenses, they do not perform laser surgery to correct retinopathy. If you require surgery, ask your primary care physician or regular optometrist for referrals in selecting an ophthalmologist to serve on your health care team.

Schedule an appointment with an ophthalmologist if you, your primary care physician, or your optometrist notice any of the following signs:

■ unexplained visual problems, such as spots, "floaters," or cobwebs in your field of vision, blurring or distortion, blind spots, or eye pain or persistent redness

■ trouble reading books or traffic signs or difficulty distinguishing familiar objects

■ increased pressure within the eye, which could be a warning sign of glaucoma. Some primary care physicians and most optometrists routinely test for this.

■ any retinal abnormalities. Most internists, family practitioners, and optometrists will test for this but should refer problems with the retina to an ophthalmologist.

■ leaking of blood vessels that supply the retina, which leads to retinopathy, is the main cause of blindness in people with diabetes.

In choosing an eye doctor, try to find one that has experience treating patients with diabetic retinopathy and is familiar with laser therapy and vitrectomy. Also ask your eye care specialist the following:

■ What percentage of your patients have diabetes?

■ Do you perform eye surgery? This is usually limited to ophthalmologists.

■ Are you a retina specialist? This is important because eye disease in people with diabetes affects the retina, that part of the eye that detects visual images.

■ Will you send regular reports and keep in touch with my regular physician?

Your Podiatrist

After an early morning jog, Janet noticed a sore on the ball of her foot as she was removing her sock. Her physician recommended that she see a podiatrist, who confirmed that Janet had a foot ulcer. Fortunately, Janet caught it early enough to be treated.

Foot care is especially important for people with diabetes, because they are prone to poor blood circulation and nerve disease in the extremities. In addition, people with diabetes are also likely to develop infections that often appear in the feet. Even small sores can turn into serious problems quickly. Any foot sore or callus should be checked by your regular physician or podiatrist. Don't try to treat any foot problems yourself.

Podiatrists graduate from a college of podiatry with a Doctor of Podiatric Medicine (DPM) degree. They also complete residencies in podiatry and can perform surgery and prescribe medication for your feet. Podiatrists treat corns, calluses, and foot sores to prevent more serious problems from developing. They can also show you how to correctly trim your toenails and how to buy shoes that fit properly. To find a podiatrist, ask your primary care physician for a referral, or check with local hospitals or your local American Diabetes Association affiliate or chapter. During your initial visit, ask what percentage of patients have diabetes.

Your Pharmacist

Evelyn ached all over. Last night, she barely slept because of her stuffy nose and headache. She decided she needed a liquid nighttime cold medicine so she wouldn't have to spend another night like that. At the drugstore, there were so many choices, Evelyn decided to ask the pharmacist help her choose which medicine would work best for her. Her blood

Taking Care of Your Feet

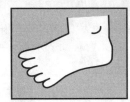 Keep your feet clean and dry. Wash them every day with a mild soap. Dry them off carefully, especially between the toes. If the skin on your feet is too dry, apply a lotion thinly everywhere but between the toes.

■ Start each day with fresh, clean socks or stockings.

■ Inspect your feet and between your toes daily. You should look for swollen areas, red areas, and cuts or breaks in the skin and feel for very cold areas (this could mean poor blood circulation) and very warm areas (this could mean infection).

■ Never go barefoot. Although this is a good rule for everyone, it is really important for people who have lost sensation in their feet.

■ Make a habit of cutting your toenails straight across. This helps you avoid ingrown toenails.

■ Wear only comfortable, well-fitting shoes. Don't expect to break in new shoes—they should feel comfortable right away. Shoes made of leather help your feet get the air circulation they need to stay healthy.

■ If you have a loss of sensation in your feet or have neuropathy, you may not be able to trust how a shoe feels to decide whether the fit is good for you. Find a shoewear specialist who is trained to fit people with diabetes (see Resources).

■ Never try amateur surgery on your feet. Have your doctor or podiatrist treat calluses, corns, plantar warts, and the like.

■ Get early treatment for foot problems! Call your doctor or podiatrist if you have
    ■ an open sore (ulcer) on your foot
    ■ any infection in a cut or blister
    ■ a red, tender toe—possibly an ingrown toenail
    ■ any change in feeling, such as pain, tingling, numbness, or burning
    ■ any puncture wound, such as if you step on a nail or thorn.

glucose levels were already running high because of her cold, and she didn't want to get any more out of control.

A pharmacist has a wealth of good information on medicines: what's in them and how they interact with each other. Pharmacists are highly trained professionals who must know about the chemistry of products they dispense and what impact, both good and bad, medications have on the body. Therefore, they can also give advice on how a particular medicine might affect your glucose control.

It is important to find a pharmacy you like dealing with and stick with it. This way, the pharmacist can keep an accurate and up-to-date profile of your medical history, allergies, and medications. Pharmacists do more for you than fill your prescriptions. They alert you to the potential common or severe side effects of any drug you are going to take. And, if they know you and your health status, with each new prescription, they will review your medication profile to see if any of the medications you currently take might possibly interact with your new prescription. For example, if your pharmacist knows you take a certain kind of sulfonylurea as a diabetes medication, he or she may recommend a cold medicine with little or no alcohol to avoid any possible interaction between the two medications. So, in addition to asking your doctor, you can also ask your pharmacist to recommend over-the-counter medicines for colds or other minor illnesses.

Your Dentist

Ryan didn't worry too much about dental care. He brushed his teeth two or three times a day and rinsed with one of those antiplaque rinses. He knew dental hygiene was important for someone with diabetes, and he tried to floss whenever he could. But it was one of those things that kept slipping his mind. Then one day he noticed *that his gums were starting to bleed when he brushed them. Maybe a trip to the dentist was in order.*

Bacteria, especially those that thrive in the mouth, love sweets. And when you have high glucose levels, your saliva makes your mouth an inviting home for the bacteria that cause gum infections. Having diabetes further complicates matters because it's harder for your body to fight off infections once they start. To prevent gum disease, see your dentist or dental hygienist every six months for a thorough teeth cleaning. Make sure your dentist

Taking Care of Your Mouth

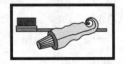 Poorly controlled diabetes can cause severe gum disease and abcesses in young and old. So keep monitoring your blood glucose level.

■ Have your teeth cleaned and checked by the dentist at least every 6 months.

■ Brush at least twice a day to fight plaque. Use a soft nylon brush with rounded ends on the bristles. Tilt the bristles at about a 45-degree angle against the gum line and brush gently in a scrubbing motion. Brush front and back and also brush the chewing surfaces.

■ Brush the rough upper surface of your tongue.

■ Use dental floss once a day to remove bacteria from between your teeth. Special floss holders and various types of floss are available to make flossing easier.

■ Call your dentist if you find:

■ your gums bleed when you brush or eat

■ your gums are red, swollen, or tender

■ your gums have pulled away from your teeth

■ pus appears between your teeth and gums when the gums are touched

■ any change in the way dentures or partial plates fit

■ any change in the way your teeth fit together when you bite

■ persistent bad breath or a bad taste in your mouth.

knows that you have diabetes and ask him or her to observe your brushing and flossing techniques to make sure you're doing everything correctly. In addition to scheduling regular visits, call your dentist if you notice any signs of gum disease.

Your Dermatologist

When he was a teenager, Robert never thought that dry skin would be a problem. But ever since he had been diagnosed with type 1 diabetes last year, his skin was always dry and itchy. Even his feet cracked and peeled, and nothing seemed to help. His doctor referred him to a dermatologist to find a solution to this common problem.

When blood glucose levels are poorly controlled, the body produces extra urine to rid itself of excess blood glucose. This results in dehydration, which causes dry skin. Having diabetes also increases your risk of developing skin infections, especially if your diabetes is not well-controlled. For instance, staphylococcal skin infections can cause itchy spots on buttocks, knees, and elbows. Your best weapon against dry skin is to closely monitor blood glucose levels and keep your glucose within your target ranges through diet, exercise, and medication.

Should a skin infection or other skin problem develop, see a dermatologist right away, when treatment is most effective. Dermatologists are medical doctors with special training in skin disorders. Your physician or local American Diabetes Association affiliate or chapter can provide a referral for a dermatologist, if needed.

Taking Care of Your Skin

■ Keep your skin clean. If you have dry skin, use a superfatted soap such as Dove, Basis, Keri, or Oilatum.

■ Dry off well after washing. Be sure to prevent moisture in the folds of the skin, such as the groin area, between the toes, under the breasts, and in armpits where fungal infections are more likely. Try using talcum powder.

■ Avoid very hot baths and showers if you have loss of sensation because you can easily burn yourself without knowing it.

■ Prevent dry skin. When you scratch dry, itchy skin, you can break the skin and open the door to bacteria. After you dry off from a shower, you may need an oil-in-water skin cream such as Lubriderm or Alpha-Keri. On cold and windy days, you may need to moisturize often to prevent chapping.

■ Wear all-cotton underwear, which allows air to circulate better than other types. Don't use feminine hygiene sprays.

■ Drink lots of water, unless your doctor advises otherwise.

■ Treat cuts quickly. For minor cuts, clean the area with soap, water, and hydrogen peroxide. Lightly dress with a Telfa pad wrapped with a knot of gauze or secured with paper tape. Do not use antiseptics such as Mercurochrome, alcohol, or iodine because they irritate the skin. Only use antibiotic creams and ointments for a few days without consulting your doctor.

■ Call your doctor if you find:

   ■ redness, swelling, pus, or pain that might indicate a bacterial infection

   ■ jock itch, athlete's foot, ringworm, vaginal itching, or other signs of a fungal infection

   ■ blisters or bumps anywhere, especially on the backs of your fingers, hands, toes, arms, legs, or buttocks—these are signs of poor glucose control

   ■ rashes, bumps, or pits near insulin injection sites.

Getting the Most Out of Your Health Care Team

You've chosen your health care team. Now what? Your physician may already use a team approach to diabetes and may already be in contact with other team members. If they are not already in touch, make sure all team members know about everyone on your team. Ask your health care team to consult with each other whenever appropriate. Be sure that they have each other's phone numbers and addresses. If you are making any lifestyle adjustments—quitting smoking, starting a weight loss diet, or taking up jogging, for example—make sure you notify all team members.

Remember, your health care team is there to help you manage your diabetes. They can serve as a wealth of information to provide you with all the resources you need to make the decisions that affect your health. But you are the one who ultimately makes the decisions and puts your health care plan into action.

The Importance of Communication

To work together as a team you must be able to communicate with your fellow health care team members. It's not always easy to communicate, especially when you're feeling nervous, worried, or under pressure. Sometimes people can feel intimidated by doctors and health care professionals. However, just remember that they are there to help you. But to best help you, they need to know what is on your mind. Only you can tell them how you are feeling and what special concerns you might have. Here are a few tips for establishing a smooth line of communication between you and your health care professional:

■ Share the conversation. Your doctor or health care professional should talk about 60 percent of the time and you
should talk about 40 percent of the time. It's important to
speak up and express your concerns, but it's also important
to listen to what the health care professional has to say.

■ If the vocabulary becomes too technical or the concepts too
complex and you don't understand, speak up. Ask for an
explanation of anything you don't understand. Write down
any information or instructions. And don't worry about feeling "stupid" or worry that this is something you should
already know. It is important that you thoroughly understand
everything that your health care professional is telling you.

■ Don't be afraid to bring up sexual or personal topics. Your
team members are professionals and are prepared to help you
deal with even the most sensitive topics.

■ Don't be afraid to discuss money. Health care professionals
realize that financial worries can contribute to patient anxiety, and most will be willing to discuss payment options.

■ Consider bringing a spouse or support person to sit in on the
visit.

■ If you don't feel comfortable with any member of your
health care team or feel that you are not communicating
effectively, consider interviewing other professionals until
you find someone you feel at ease with.

What to Expect

The first step in proceeding with your diabetes care plan
will probably be to meet with your primary care physician. Whether you have type 1 or type 2 diabetes and
have just been diagnosed or have lived with the disease for
years, your doctor should provide you with certain basic care.
This should include a complete physical exam once each year.
A complete medical history should be conducted during the

first visit. You should be tested for glycated hemoglobin every three months, and you should discuss contingencies and changes in management on an as-needed basis.

Visiting Your Physician

Yearly physical examinations are important for everyone as a preventive health measure, but are especially important for people with diabetes. If you have diabetes, you have a greater risk for developing diabetic complications, including damage to the eyes, kidneys, nervous system, heart, and circulatory system. You are also more susceptible to developing infections. That's why a thorough examination is in order to make sure your whole body is functioning properly.

If you are seeing your primary care physician or other health care professional for the first time, you will most likely be asked to provide a medical history. The forms and questionnaires may vary, but all will want the same basic information. Although many questions may refer to matters that you consider private, it is important to answer honestly and trust that your health care team will maintain confidentiality.

Because, information related to your medical history will often be hard to recall—when was your last immunization, or how old were you when you contracted mumps?—ask that a questionnaire be mailed to you in advance. That way, you can answer all the questions more accurately and at a leisurely pace. The more complete and correct the picture you provide, the better your health care will be.

Most histories include questions about the health of your close relatives. Think about the general health and specific diseases that have occurred in your family, especially your mother, father, grandparents, sisters, and brothers. You will also be asked to provide a general inventory of your past and present health problems, such as back pain, appendicitis,

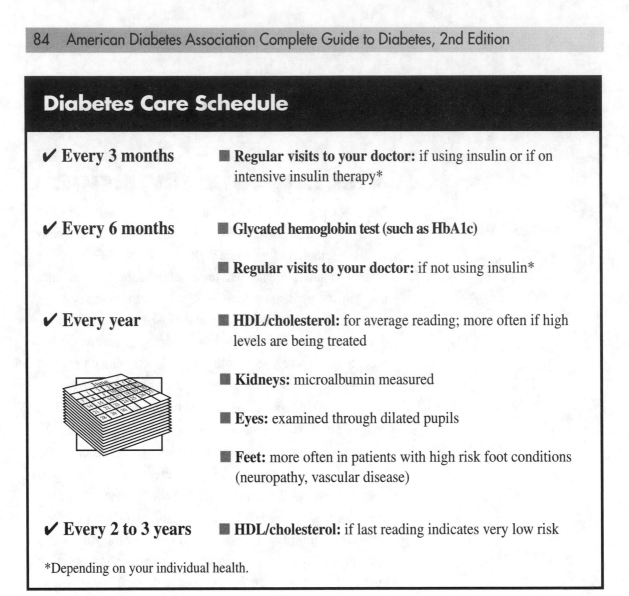

Diabetes Care Schedule

✔ **Every 3 months**   ▪ **Regular visits to your doctor:** if using insulin or if on intensive insulin therapy*

✔ **Every 6 months**   ▪ **Glycated hemoglobin test (such as HbA1c)**

▪ **Regular visits to your doctor:** if not using insulin*

✔ **Every year**   ▪ **HDL/cholesterol:** for average reading; more often if high levels are being treated

▪ **Kidneys:** microalbumin measured

▪ **Eyes:** examined through dilated pupils

▪ **Feet:** more often in patients with high risk foot conditions (neuropathy, vascular disease)

✔ **Every 2 to 3 years**   ▪ **HDL/cholesterol:** if last reading indicates very low risk

*Depending on your individual health.

headaches, and depression. Do not deny or try to hide any illnesses, such as psychiatric disorders or AIDS.

Dig out a record of your immunizations. You may even need to call past health care providers for dates and names of procedures. Here are a few health-related questions you might be asked:

▪ What medications are you currently taking?

▪ Do you smoke? Have you ever smoked? If so, how much and for how long?

■ Do you have any allergies?

■ Have you ever been pregnant? What was the outcome?

■ When were your last chest X-ray, eye exam, and dental exam?

■ Have you ever been treated by a psychiatrist?

■ Have you recently lost or gained weight? What was your maximum weight? What did you weigh at the diagnosis of diabetes?

■ Have you ever been rejected for health insurance or employment for a medical reason?

■ Do you use any street drugs?

Some of these questions may be difficult to answer. You may not remember or you may not want to be reminded. Make an attempt to overcome your fears of being judged harshly by what you put on the form. A concerned health care professional will use this information to provide you with the best possible care—not to criticize you. What is important is achieving good health.

Getting Physical

After taking a medical history, your primary care physician will give you a complete physical exam. In fact, your physician should give you a complete physical once each year. A physical examination begins with a discussion between you and your doctor. This will include a review of your blood glucose measurements and discussion of your insulin therapy and other medications, diet, and exercise programs. You should bring your doctor up-to-date on any changes you have made in lifestyle or habits. Maybe you just quit smoking or started an exercise program. If you feel a need to consult one of the other professionals on your team, now is the time to ask about it. If you feel that there are any parts of your treatment plan that are not working, tell your doctor. Also, keep your doctor informed of what treatment options are successful.

A good physical will also include a close examination of all the parts of your body, from head to toe. Your doctor is trained to detect small problems and prevent them from becoming bigger problems and will examine all of the following, and perhaps more:

- **Total body weight.** Talk to your doctor about the body weight that you think is best for you and whether you have any difficulty maintaining that weight.

- **Blood pressure and pulse.** Ask you doctor what your current readings are and whether these fall within the normal range. If not, ask what levels are best for you to achieve and how to go about it.

- **Eyes.** Your primary care physician will check your eyes for problems and ask about any changes in your vision. Make sure to keep him or her abreast of any changes that have occurred even if you are also seeing an eye-care specialist.

- **Heart and lungs.** The doctor will most likely listen to your heart and lungs through a stethoscope. Sometimes an electrocardiogram or stress electrocardiogram may be performed to detect symptom-free heart disease. Such tests measure the electrical activity and pumping of your heart muscle and can detect many subtle abnormalities.

- **Feet.** Removing your shoes and socks each time you visit—not just during your yearly physicals—will remind your doctor to check your feet. Your doctor should check your feet for pulses, reflexes, calluses, infections, and sores. She or he will also look for any loss of feeling or prickly feeling that could indicate neuropathy.

- **Skin.** Your skin, your largest organ, will be examined by sight with special attention to insulin injection sites.

- **Nervous system.** Your doctor will check your reflexes and your sensitivity to the sharpness of a pin or the light touch of cotton or a brush. If you are experiencing any persistent problems, such as dizziness on standing, pain, burning

Tip: Children whose diabetes is not well-controlled sometimes are slow to grow and mature. So, the doctor should measure height at every visit, not just the first one. The doctor should also check the progress of sexual maturation.

sensation, numbness in your legs or arms, constipation, diarrhea, difficulty urinating, or difficulty with erection or sexual satisfaction, make sure to mention them.

■ **Mouth and neck.** Your doctor will exam your gums, teeth, mouth, and throat. She or he will feel for swelling in the glands in your neck and ask you about your brushing and flossing habits. Your doctor will also assess the function of your thyroid gland during your initial physical examination.

■ **Blood.** A sample of blood will be withdrawn to test for glucose levels and glycated hemoglobin. A fasting lipid profile, which measures cholesterol and triglycerides, will be performed to determine the levels of these fats in your blood. Your doctor will also assess kidney function by measuring urea nitrogen and serum creatinine concentrations in the blood.

■ **Urine.** Kidney function is also assessed by testing urine for ketones, glucose, and protein. People with diabetes are more likely to have urinary tract infections because of the high concentrations of glucose in urine and the loss of the sensation of knowing when the bladder is empty or full because of neuropathy. If you have any symptoms of infection, a urinary culture may also be performed.

■ **Vaccinations.** People with diabetes are more likely to develop complications from the flu or pneumonia. Ask your doctor about vaccines to prevent these conditions.

■ **Other tests.** Some tests may be performed by other members of your health care team. For women, this should include a Pap smear, mammogram, and gynecological and rectal exam. Contraceptive use and pregnancy planning should also be discussed. Men should receive prostate and rectal exams. Both men and women should have their stool samples tested for blood to detect colon cancer.

Tip: If you have type 1 diabetes, you have a five times greater risk of also someday developing thyroid disease, which is another type of autoimmune disease. Make sure your doctor evaluates you for thyroid disease.

■ **Specific problems.** Your doctor may ask you to explain any unusual concerns you may have, such as a sore shoulder or abdominal pain. If you are experiencing any sexual or personal problems, don't be afraid to bring them up.

Beyond the yearly physical, your doctor should also check your glycated hemoglobin, using the HbA1c test for example, every six months. Measuring your glycated hemoglobin tells your doctor how well you are achieving good blood glucose control. You need this test whether you use insulin or not. The reading tells your average blood glucose reading from the last six months and can predict the likelihood of future eye, kidney, and nerve disease. Ask for the results of your glycated hemoglobin test. You are aiming for an HbA1c level of less than or equal to 7 percent. According to research, this is a reading that will help you prevent future complications.

Your doctor should check the results of the glycated hemoglobin test against your own self-monitoring records. Be sure to discuss your blood glucose readings (always bring your log book) with your doctor at every visit. If your daily blood glucose tests are in range but your glycated hemoglobin is too high, you and your doctor should discuss ways to better control and monitor your blood sugar levels. You should have some idea why your tests might show good blood glucose readings when your overall blood glucose measure is too high.

Talk to your doctor about what to do on sick days. Even a mild cold can throw off blood glucose levels, usually by making them higher than normal. Ask what symptoms to be on the lookout for and when you should call the doctor. What precautions should you take when you feel under the weather?

Other changes in your health may result in return trips to the doctor more often than every three months. If you're just starting insulin or are changing your dose and your glucose is not in control, you may need to see your doctor as often as every day for a while, until your blood glucose is in control.

Or if you are trying to control high blood pressure, you may need to monitor your blood pressure often, in the doctor's office or elsewhere, and keep records of the readings.

Glycated Hemoglobin Testing

WHAT IS THE GLYCATED HEMOGLOBIN TEST?

Blood is collected from a vein during a visit to your doctor. In the lab, a technician measures the concentration of hemoglobin molecules, which are found in red blood cells, that have glucose attached to them. This tells you what your average blood glucose level was over the past three to four months.

HOW DO I INTERPRET THE RESULTS?

The measure is given as a percentage. A 9% level means that 9% of your hemoglobin molecules are glycated. People without diabetes have about a 5% reading.

WHAT IS GLYCATED HEMOGLOBIN?

Hemoglobin links up (or glycates) with the glucose in your blood. The more glucose available in your blood, the more hemoglobin will become glycated. Once glycated, the hemoglobin stays glycated until the red blood cell's life is over. This averages about 120 days.

WHY IS THIS TEST USED?

Long-term, or overall, glucose control is just as important as control throughout each day. This test gives you a "long" view of your blood glucose control because as old red blood cells are dying, new ones are taking their place. If your blood glucose was high last week, then more of your hemoglobin was glycated than usual. Your blood glucose might be back under control this week, but your red blood cells will still be carrying the memory of last week's high blood glucose level.

HOW LONG IS THE MEMORY OF THIS TEST?

Your glycated hemoglobin reading is not a simple average of all the blood glucose level ups-and-downs over the past three to four months. It is a weighted average. You never have a complete turnover of red blood cells all at once. Some are dying as others are just coming on board. There are always more young cells than old cells. About half are newer cells, ones formed within the last month. So your glucose levels in the last month count for about half of your glycated hemoglobin measure, and cells from the previous two to three months make up the other half of the measure.

IF MY BLOOD GLUCOSE CONTROL IMPROVES, HOW LONG DOES IT TAKE TO SEE RESULTS?

It takes about three to four months to see all the results of an improvement (or worsening) in blood glucose control. This is why there's really no need to have the test more often than every three months. However, if you are newly diagnosed and may have been far out of control for a while, your doctor may want to take measures every two weeks until you improve. Very big changes in blood glucose control can be seen within two weeks. Or, for someone who is pregnant and seeking very tight glucose control, glycated hemoglobin may be measured every month or two to make sure that the treatment plan is getting results.

HOW DO MY BLOOD GLUCOSE TESTING RESULTS RELATE TO MY GLYCATED HEMOGLOBIN RESULTS?

Measuring glycated hemoglobin gives you the big picture. Self-monitoring of blood glucose gives you a snapshot of the moment. Let's say you have type 2 diabetes, and you test your blood glucose once a day, before breakfast. The level is usually around 120 mg/dl. But your last glycated hemoglobin test was just over 10%, which corresponds to an average daily blood glucose of around 250 mg/dl. This would mean that your after-meal blood glucose levels must be getting pretty high, so some changes in food choices, portion sizes, or medication dosage are in order.

WHAT SHOULD MY GLYCATED HEMOGLOBIN MEASURE BE?

There is no straightforward answer to this question. The number you're aiming for depends on what kind of test your doctor's lab uses. A 9% in one test could be the target result, but in another test, 9% is too high. Also, glycated hemoglobin goals need to be individualized to the kind of control you're aiming for. However, research has shown that keeping HbA1c 7% or under helps you avoid diabetes complications of the kidneys, eyes, and nerves.

Glycated Hemoglobin Measurements

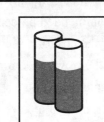

Glycated hemoglobin by the HbA1c measurement method (%)	Average blood glucose level (mg/dl)
4	60
5	90
6	120
7	150
8	180
9	210
10	240
11	270
12	300
13	330

Tip: What to ask:
- What is the diagnosis and how was it determined?
- What treatments are available and which are most effective? most risky? most commonly used?
- What treatment do you suggest and why?
- What is the success rate for this treatment?
- Is the treatment reversible?
- What are the potential side effects and complications of the treatment and how likely are they?
- Is the problem or treatment likely to affect my diabetes control?
- Will the treatment require hospitalization? For how long? Will I need follow-up care?
- Are there any hidden costs associated with this treatment, such as repeated blood tests, physical therapy, or postoperative nursing care?
- Is this an experimental treatment? Will I be participating in research? Will I be part of a placebo/control group or will I receive treatment? If this is the case, you may need to evaluate the potential risks and make sure they do not outweigh the benefits. If this is a research protocol, are more conventional treatments available should this one fail?

Second Opinions

*H*ermes experienced seven serious episodes involving blackouts, fainting, dizziness, and even cardiac arrest over the course of two years. His doctor blamed it on "some latent viral infection" that crops up from time to time. When he asked his doctor for a second opinion, he was told he didn't need one. Finally, after much persistence, his doctor referred him to a diabetes specialty clinic, where his problem was eventually diagnosed and treated. No matter how much you trust your doctor and other health care professionals, there may be times when you would like a second opinion. This could occur when your doctor recommends surgery, long-term medication, or other treatments that will drastically affect your lifestyle. You may also want a second opinion if you have a problem for which your doctor says there is no known therapy or calls the problem incurable.

Check with your insurance company to determine whether medical costs for a recommended procedure are covered. Also ask whether they cover the cost of a second opinion and whether they pay only their own recommended consultants. Some insurance companies insist on a second opinion before they will fully cover certain treatments.

When searching for a physician to provide a second opinion, first ask your physician or other doctor you trust. Look for a doctor who is board certified in the field in which you are seeking information, such as cardiology, surgery, or endocrinology. Be sure to tell the physician about your diabetes. If the problem is diabetes related, or you suspect that it is, call your local American Diabetes Association chapter for the names of specialists in your area (see Resources). For non-diabetes–related problems, try calling the appropriate department of a major medical center or teaching hospital and ask for the names of specialists in the field.

Chapter 4:
The Ins and
Outs of Insulin

Get to know insulin. All people with type 1 diabetes need to use it. Many people with type 2 diabetes or gestational diabetes also use insulin for good blood glucose control.

Since its discovery in the 1920s, scientists have learned a great deal about insulin. They know a lot about how it normally works in people without diabetes. And they also know that when insulin is absent or doesn't do its job, people develop diabetes.

Insulin is a hormone. Hormones are chemical signals made by the body that tell various parts of the body how to do their jobs. Some hormones control how the cells in the body grow. Some control how the body uses food and energy to live. And other hormones help muscles to contract, blood to clot, or the heart to beat.

One of insulin's most important jobs is to help cells use glucose. Insulin acts like a key to unlock the door that lets glucose into the cell. Cells in the body use glucose as a source of energy that they need to live. Without energy, the cells in the body cannot survive. Insulin also helps the body to store extra fuel as fat.

In people with type 1 diabetes, the body does not make enough insulin. This is because most of the cells of the pancreas that make insulin have been destroyed by the immune system. Eventually, all of the cells that make insulin are destroyed and no insulin is produced. That is why type 1 diabetes is also called *immune-mediated diabetes*. People with type 1 diabetes are treated with injections of insulin to keep healthy.

In people with type 2 diabetes, insulin is produced, but the cells do not respond to insulin as they should. Glucose has a hard time getting out of the blood and into cells. For some people with type 2 diabetes, diet, exercise, and oral diabetes medication together can control glucose levels in the blood without insulin injections. But for many people with type 2 diabetes, diet, exercise, and oral diabetes medication are not enough to control blood glucose. These people with type 2 diabetes need to take insulin.

Insulin Type

Insulin is a small protein called a *polypeptide.* It is made up of a chain of small units, known as amino acids. In the early days, only pork and beef insulins were available. These insulins were made from grinding up the pancreases from pigs and cows and purifying the insulin protein. They acted rapidly to lower blood glucose levels. They also were used up rapidly by the body and had to be injected before each meal and at bedtime. The purity and strength of early insulin preparations were not always reliable.

For many years, purified preparations of animal insulins were widely used. However, human insulin is now used much more often. There is a ready supply of human insulin. It is not harvested from actual pancreases but is made with the help of genetic engineering. The human insulin gene, which tells cells what sequence of amino acids is needed to make the insulin protein, is put into bacteria that multiply rapidly. The bacteria are "tricked" into making human insulin.

If you were diagnosed with insulin-requiring diabetes in the past decade, you were probably put on human insulin. If you have been living with diabetes for a long time, you may still be using animal insulin. Your doctor may not suggest switching to human insulin if your diabetes is well-controlled using animal insulin. The big advantages to human insulin are that it is easy to make and it is unlikely to cause an allergic reaction. Some people are allergic to animal insulin, because the body sees it as a foreign substance.

Action Times

People may respond to preparations of insulin and insulin mixtures differently, so it is important to find the type of insulin that works best for you. Each type of insulin has a different action time, a term that describes the length of time they take to begin acting and how long their effect lasts. The action times of insulin are due to the following three features:

■ **Onset:** The length of time it takes for insulin to reach the blood and begin lowering blood glucose levels.

■ **Peak time:** The time during which insulin is at its maximal strength in lowering blood glucose levels.

■ **Duration:** The length of time in which insulin continues to lower blood glucose.

The first type of insulin that was made available is known as regular insulin. Regular insulin is short acting and must be injected several times throughout the day. Regular insulin begins working rapidly and is used up quickly by the body. As shown in the table on insulin action times, regular insulin begins to act within an hour. A newer form of rapid-acting insulin, lysine-proline (or lispro) insulin, goes to work within minutes. An

Insulin Action

Insulin type	Onset (hours)	Peak (hours)	Usual effective duration (hours)	Usual maximum duration (hours)
Rapid acting				
Human lispro	Within 15 minutes	1 to 1.5	4 to 5	4 to 5
Short acting				
Human regular	0.5 to 1.0	2 to 3	4 to 6	5 to 7
Intermediate acting				
Human NPH	2 to 4	4 to 10	10 to 16	14 to 18
Human Lente	3 to 4	4 to 12	12 to 18	16 to 20
Long acting				
Human Ultralente	6 to 10	14 to 24	18 to 20	20 to 36

intermediate-acting insulin, NPH (neutral protamine Hagedorn), contains a molecule known as a protamine that slows down how fast the body absorbs insulin. Because the insulin reaches the blood more slowly, the onset, peak, and duration times are longer. By using a slower-acting insulin, you can get by with fewer injections each day. For example, a mixture of NPH and regular insulin injected at breakfast can last until dinnertime. By taking this, you may be able to avoid an injection at lunchtime.

People who are allergic to the protamine in NPH can consider using lente, another intermediate-acting insulin. An even longer acting insulin, ultralente, provides a continuous level of insulin with almost no peak effect. In some people, human ultralente insulin may really act more like an intermediate insulin. Whenever your doctor advises you to change insulin, you may have to adjust to the speed of action of the new type of insulin in your body.

All insulins used for injections have added ingredients. These prevent bacteria and molds from growing and help keep insulin from spoiling. Intermediate- and long-acting insulins also contain ingredients that prolong their action times. If you think you may be experiencing an allergic reaction to your insulin preparation, talk to your doctor.

Premixed Insulin

Your doctor might advise you to take a mixture of regular and NPH insulin in one injection. You can mix them yourself (see Appendix for instructions). Or, you can buy the insulin already mixed. Mixtures of regular and NPH insulins come in various combinations that make it more convenient and easier to handle. For example, you can buy a 50/50 mixture of NPH and regular insulin, or you can buy a mixture that contains 30 percent regular insulin and 70 percent NPH. You can also mix the rapid-acting insulin, lispro. Premixed insulins are useful for people with busy schedules who are looking for time-saving measures. They can also be helpful for people with eyesight or

Tip: The signs of a local allergic reaction to insulin are:
- Dents under the skin at injection sites
- Redness at injection sites, either persistent or temporary
- Groups of small bumps, similar to hives
- Swelling at injection sites.

Which Short-Acting Insulin Is Best For You?

 What would you do with an insulin that goes to work lowering your blood glucose level within 15 minutes after injection? You'd probably get even better blood glucose control than you do with regular insulin.

A faster-acting insulin, called the *lysine-proline analog,* has been available for several years. It can be used by people with type 1 or type 2 diabetes, and it pleases many of those using it. The faster action of lispro insulin means people can do a better job of timing their insulin versus their food.

The lispro insulin is in a form that the body can absorb right away, without having to break it down. With regular insulin, the body needs to reduce the insulin protein chain to a smaller size before it can be absorbed and go to work. It can take over 30 minutes from the time regular insulin is injected until it starts working on cells. With lispro, this time is cut in half. So, there's less room for error with the lispro insulin. It goes to work almost as fast as naturally produced insulin does.

This faster-acting insulin may give you a lot more flexibility without sacrificing good blood glucose control. For instance, if you want an extra helping at a meal, you can take care of the carbohydrates with a booster shot right away. You may even be able to wait until you know how much carbohydrate you've eaten to inject this insulin. Also, because lispro doesn't remain in the body as long as regular insulin does, you may experience fewer episodes of hypoglycemia. Ask your doctor whether you could benefit from using this faster-acting insulin.

Insulin type	Onset	Peak	Duration
Natural	Immediate, when needed	30 to 60 minutes	2 to 3 hours
Human lispro	Within 15 minutes after injection	1 to 1½ hours	4 to 5 hours
Human regular	30 to 60 minutes	2 to 3 hours	5 to 7 hours

dexterity problems that make drawing different amounts of insulin from two different bottles difficult.

Even though you can buy mixtures of regular and NPH insulin or can mix them yourself, make sure to talk to members of your health care team before you make any changes in the insulin you take. Never mix types of insulin without the okay of your doctor. Mixing regular insulin with lente or ultra-lente insulin can be more complicated. These longer-acting insulins can interfere with fast-acting insulins and lead to unpredictable results. Fast-acting insulins are not always readily absorbed by the body when mixed with slower insulins. If your injection schedule calls for taking both regular and lente insulin at the same time, try to inject them immediately after mixing. If you have any questions or notice that you don't get the response you expect from the regular insulin, talk to your doctor. He or she may want to increase the amount of regular insulin in the mixture or switch to lispro insulin.

Before you leave your doctor's office, be sure you understand:

■ what type of insulin you will be taking and the name of the insulin

■ symptoms of high and low blood glucose that could indicate a problem with your insulin regimen

■ where you should inject it

■ whether you need to prepare any mixtures

■ how often to give yourself injections

■ the best hours of the day to take your insulin

■ how to store your insulin

Don't be afraid to take notes or ask questions about anything that's not clear. Even if you have taken insulin before, you might want to review your insulin schedule on a return visit, especially if you are experiencing any difficulties. You might also want to go over any changes in your schedule that your doctor has recommended. Make sure you understand

Tip: Crossing time zones can confuse your insulin schedule. You may need to make a new plan for timing your insulin injections. You may also need to adjust your total daily insulin dose. When traveling east, you get a shorter day and need less insulin. When traveling west, you get more hours in a day and need more insulin. Keep your watch on your home time until the first morning after you arrive in a new time zone. Check your blood glucose level more often than normal. For more on insulin and travelling, see page 103.

how to time injections with mealtime. Go step-by-step through a typical day. Also, talk about how to adjust for an unusual day. What happens if you oversleep, get sick, travel across time zones, or plan to be unusually active?

Insulin Strength

When insulin was first manufactured, different batches often had different strengths. This made it difficult to know how much insulin was needed to lower blood glucose to the right level. Later, the strength of insulin became standardized, but it was available in several different strengths. This often made it confusing, trying to figure out how much insulin to take.

Today, if you buy insulin in this country, you don't have to worry about the strength. Nearly all insulin preparations sold in the United States today are of the same strength: U-100. This means that they have 100 units of insulin in every cubic centimeter (cc), of fluid. U-40, a more diluted insulin, has been discontinued. U-500, a highly concentrated preparation, is available only by special order for people who have developed insulin resistance and need to take extremely high doses of insulin. Hospitals sometimes use U-500 insulin for emergencies.

Diabetes: Myth or Fact?

"Once I open a bottle of insulin, I need to keep it in the fridge."

To get the most life out of your insulin supply, keep open bottles "comfortable," not too hot or too cold. If you'll use up a bottle of insulin within a month, keep it at room temperature. If it takes longer than a month to use up, it's best to keep it refrigerated, but warm up the syringe before you inject. Injecting cold insulin can make the injection uncomfortable. Keep unopened bottles in the refrigerator.

Freezing can cause the insulin ingredients to "unmix." Because insulin is a protein, it will unfold (denature) at hot temperatures, such as those reached inside a locked car in the summer.

Insulin syringes also come in different sizes that match the strength of insulin. If you travel outside of the United States, bring along sufficient insulin and matching U-100 syringes. You could end up taking the wrong dose if you don't match insulin strength with the right syringe. If you are planning a long visit outside the country and can't bring along all the supplies you need, remember that you will need a U-40 syringe to use the U-40 insulin found in Latin America and Europe. Your doctor can help you adjust your dosage.

Buying and Storing Insulin

Don't assume that most pharmacies will charge the same price for insulin. The same insulin at one pharmacy or outlet may be several dollars cheaper than that found somewhere else, so it pays to shop around. You might receive a discount for buying certain quantities at your pharmacy or by ordering through the mail. Be sure to ask your pharmacists whether they offer discounts for large orders. Your insurance company or managed care provider may have an agreement with "preferred pharmacies" to offer insulin at reduced rates. Check with your insurance company or managed care provider to see whether they offer this service. By using these services you may be able to keep your costs down. But if you decide to buy insulin in bulk, check the expiration date. You don't want to buy a big supply of insulin if most of it will expire before you have a chance to use it.

In choosing a pharmacy, convenience may be just as important as cost. You may want a pharmacy that is close by or one that delivers your insulin to you. This can be convenient, especially if you are very busy, ill, or housebound. Also, think about the pharmacist. Is the pharmacist easy to talk to? Does he or she seem willing to answer your questions?

Storing Insulin

Unopened (unused) bottles	→	Stored in the refrigerator	→	Discard after date given on bottle
Opened bottles	→	Stored in the refrigerator	→	Discard after 3 months
Opened bottles	→	Kept at room temperature	→	Discard after 1 month

Once you find a pharmacy that you like, try to develop a relationship with the pharmacist. Don't just ask for NPH insulin. Ask questions. Check to make sure you have the desired brand name, strength, and kind. You may want to bring along an empty bottle to make sure you get exactly the same thing each time. Before you pay, double check to see that you have what you want. If something doesn't look quite right, or if you are uncertain, be sure to ask your pharmacist.

If you use one or more bottles of insulin each month, you don't have to worry about storing the bottle you are using in the refrigerator in between injections. Store only unopened bottles of insulin in the refrigerator. The expiration date on a bottle of insulin applies to bottles that have not been opened and have been stored in the refrigerator. If you keep an open vial of insulin at room temperature for more than a month, the insulin may become contaminated or lose its strength. Throw away bottles that have been used for a month and kept at room temperature. If you go through bottles slowly, write the date you first open a bottle on the label. For certain insulin preparations, such as Novo-Nordisk's Novolin 70/30 Penfill and Prefilled, manufacturers recommend against using it for more than seven days after opening it. The label, or your doctor, should explain why special storage might be needed.

One good reason to store the insulin you're using at room temperature is that injecting cold insulin can make the injection feel more uncomfortable. If your insulin is cold, draw it up into the syringe, then warm it up by gently rolling it back and forth in your hands.

If you are traveling and keep your insulin stored in a cooler, make sure the insulin doesn't freeze or come in contact with ice. Storing insulin at temperatures colder than 36°F can cause it to clump. Also, try to avoid getting insulin too hot or leaving it in direct sunlight for too long. Insulin spoils if it gets hotter than 86°F. The general rule of thumb is, if the temperature is comfortable for you, your insulin will be okay, too.

Never use insulin if it looks abnormal. Regular and lispro insulins are clear. If you use regular or lispro insulin, always check for any floating particles, cloudiness, or change in color. This could be a sign that your insulin is contaminated or has lost its strength.

Other types of insulin come as suspensions. This means that the material is not completely dissolved, and you might

On the Go With Insulin

 ■ Wear a medical ID bracelet or necklace that says you have diabetes.
■ Don't get separated from your supplies. Use a tote bag to carry with you your insulin, syringes and/or insulin pump and infusion sets, lancets, glucose meter, blood and ketone test strips, glucagon kit, glucose gel or tablets, and snacks.
■ Take twice as much insulin and blood testing equipment as you think you'll need. Getting extra diabetes supplies when you're away from home can be difficult.
■ Keep insulin out of direct sunlight and protect it from very hot or very cold temperatures. If flying, keep your insulin supply with you instead of packing it in bags that might get too hot or too cold (such as in an airplane baggage compartment).

be able to see solid material floating in liquid. However, it should look uniformly cloudy. If you are using NPH or lente, check that your insulin is free of any large clumps of material. You should not use any insulin if you see large chunks of material floating around. These changes could mean that crystals or aggregates are forming and the insulin is spoiled or denatured. This can be caused by too much shaking of the insulin bottle or storing insulin at temperatures that are either too hot or too cold.

If you have been instructed to dilute your insulin, use only the diluent recommended by the manufacturer. Properly diluted insulin is good for four to six weeks stored in the refrigerator.

If you find anything wrong with your insulin right after you buy it, return it immediately. If the condition develops later, try to figure out whether you have handled or stored the insulin the wrong way. If not, talk to your pharmacist about a refund or exchange.

Using Insulin

Most people with diabetes use a needle and syringe to get insulin into their bodies. Once you learn how, this should be a quick and relatively painless task. If you have problems with your vision or using your hands, some of the injection aids now available may solve the problem.

Using a syringe is just one way to get insulin into your body. Advanced delivery systems such an insulin pump may work better for some people. Jet injectors use high pressure to pass insulin through the skin. Whatever you choose, the basic purpose is the same: to deliver insulin into the fat that lies just under your skin.

Other ways to deliver insulin may become more widely available in the future. One exciting prospect is an insulin infusion device that is implanted into the body. With this, you might be able to go 2 months without having to worry about refilling it. And scientists hope that, one day, they will be able to make a device that measures your blood glucose level and delivers the proper amount of insulin, automatically.

Injecting Insulin

Injecting insulin today is a lot less painful than it used to be. You can choose between disposable syringes with lubricated microfine needles and insulin infusers. There are many helpful devices that make injecting with a syringe possible for almost anyone.

Syringes. Today's smaller gauge needles are slimmer, have sharper points, and are specially coated to slide into the skin smoothly. If you are already using these needles and your injections are still uncomfortable, talk to your doctor or diabetes educator. You may need to go over your injection technique to make sure you are doing everything properly. Trying to relax before injections can help. Tense muscles can make the injection hurt.

Keeping your injection site clean will reduce the risk of developing an infection. But you don't have to use alcohol to clean your skin before injecting the needle. Soap and water works fine. If you use alcohol before injections, make sure the alcohol dries before you inject, or it could cause stinging. See the Appendix for more tips on injections and reusing your syringe and needle.

Buying syringes. The syringe consists of a needle, barrel, and plunger. Syringes come in different sizes. It is important to match the size of your syringe to the strength of your insulin. Almost all insulin in this country is U-100, so you will need U-100 syringes.

It is also important to match the size of the syringe to the dose you'll take with it. You want a syringe that will hold your entire dose of insulin. For example, if you need to take 45 units of insulin, you would want to use a 50-unit syringe to hold all your insulin. A 30-unit syringe (the next smallest size) is handy for giving yourself injections of 30 units or less. Likewise, if you need to inject very small doses of insulin, 1/2 unit for example, use syringes that have 1/2 unit marks (such as a Terumo 1/4 cc syringe) to keep doses accurate.

Also, check to see whether you can read the markings on your syringe. U-100 syringes are available that can hold different amounts of insulin. A 100-unit syringe holds 100 units of insulin in a volume of 1 cc (or 1 ml). Each line marks 2 units of insulin. A 50-unit syringe holds 50 units of insulin in 0.5 cc of liquid, and each line marks one unit. A 30-unit syringe holds 30 units of insulin in 0.3 cc, and each line marks one unit. You will need to measure out each dose in units. So, if you can't see the lines marked on the syringe, you will have problems getting an accurate dose. Perhaps using a syringe with a different color plunger would make it easier to tell when the syringe is filled to the right level. Your pharmacist or another member of your health care team should know what supplies are available to help you. Another good source of information is the *American Diabetes Asssociation Resource Guide* published yearly by *Diabetes Forecast,* the member's magazine of the American Diabetes Association. The *Resource Guide* is also available in single copies from the American Diabetes Association (see Resources).

If you are planning to travel or will be away from home, take along a doctor's prescription for syringes. You might also ask him or her to write a letter stating that you have diabetes and indicating what type of insulin you use. Some states require a prescription to purchase supplies. If you have problems getting supplies while traveling, try a hospital emergency room.

Reusing syringes. There is no right or wrong answer to the question of whether you should use your insulin syringes over again. It's really up to you. Reusing syringes can save money. And it creates less medical waste to litter the environment. Before plastic syringes were available, people routinely boiled and reused glass syringes. There is no evidence that you are more likely to become infected if you reuse a syringe—as long as you maintain it properly. If you choose to reuse syringes, the American Diabetes Association offers guidelines for maintaining them properly (see Appendix).

Most manufacturers of disposable syringes recommend that they be used only once. This is because syringes cannot be guaranteed to be sterile if they are reused. If you have poor personal hygiene, are ill, have open wounds on your hands, or have a low resistance to infection for any reason, you should not reuse syringes.

The most important advice about syringe reuse is this: never let anyone use a syringe you've already used, and don't use anyone else's syringe—ever.

Syringe disposal. How you get rid of your syringe can affect everyone who might come in contact with your trash. This includes the members of your family, neighbors, your trash collector, and people using beaches and other public areas. So it's important that you do it safely. Never toss a used syringe directly into a trash can. Syringes and lancets and any other material that touches human blood is considered medical waste and must be handled carefully. Before deciding what you will do, you might want to check with your local health department. Some towns and counties have special laws or rules for getting rid of medical waste.

The best way to keep anyone from reusing your old syringe is to dispose of it appropriately. Don't use scissors to cut off the needle. This could send the needle flying and could hurt someone or become lost. It's best to buy a device that clips, catches, and contains the needle. These devices, called *safe-clips,* are available at most pharmacies. You might want to pull out the plunger and push the needle into it. Now you can easily and safely bend the needle until it breaks off and put the plunger with the embedded needle back into the syringe.

Tip: Each fall, the American Diabetes Association publishes the *Resource Guide,* a supplement to *Diabetes Forecast.* You can also buy the guide separately. The *Resource Guide* lists the latest offerings of diabetes tools from manufacturers.

If you don't destroy syringes, recap them if you can do it without sticking yourself with the needle. Place the entire syringe into an opaque (not clear) heavy-duty plastic or metal container with a screw cap or other tight-fitting cover. Make sure that the syringes will not come out of the container once they have been sent to the dump. Don't use a breakable container or one that will allow a needle to poke through and stick someone. When traveling, if possible, bring your unused syringes home. Pack them in a heavy duty container, such as a hard plastic pencil box.

Injection Devices. Talk to your doctor or your diabetes educator if you are having problems with any aspects of insulin injection. There are alternatives to injecting by syringe, such as the insulin pump or jet injector. And there are products available that make giving an injection easier. Ask your doctor for samples of some of the insulin-injection aids before you buy anything. This way you can see if any new product is right for you before you invest your money.

Insertion aids. An automatic injector shoots a needle into your skin painlessly. You hardly know what hit you. Some automatically release the insulin when the needle hits your skin. With others you have to press the plunger on the syringe. An automatic injector can be useful if you have arthritis or other problems that make it difficult to hold a syringe steadily. If you cringe at the thought of injecting yourself or don't like the sight of needles, an automatic injector may be for you.

Infusers. This aid reduces the number of times you have to stick a needle in your skin. With a special catheter needle, you insert an infusion tube into your abdomen or other convenient site. This can remain at the injection site for two or three days. You can inject insulin into a special tube that reseals itself after each needle entry. The risk of local infection is higher with this device, so you may have to pay more attention to sterile technique than with the usual syringe and needle method. Infusers are usually sold in boxes of four or ten. Ask your doctor if you can try one before committing to a whole box.

Jet injectors. If you want to be free of needles altogether, then consider a jet injector. The insulin is shot out so fast that it acts like a liquid needle, passing insulin directly through the skin. If you fear needles, or want to take several injections each day, a jet injector may be a wise choice.

The downside is that jet injectors are expensive. Check with your insurer about whether they will cover the cost of this device. Although you will save on the cost of needles and syringes, there may be a hefty initial cost. Ask to test a jet injector before buying. Bruising can be a problem, especially in thin people, children, and the elderly, all of whom have less fat under the skin.

About every two weeks, the jet injector must taken apart and boiled and sterilized. Germicidal cleaners can be used if they do not irritate your skin. This can make cleaning easier, because you don't have to take apart and reassemble the injector. Nevertheless, this can be time-consuming. Ask your doctor, diabetes educator, and others you know who have used them what they think of jet injectors.

Pen injectors. An insulin pen looks just like an ink pen. Instead of a writing tip, it has a disposable needle, and instead of an ink cartridge, there is an insulin cartridge. These pens are popular because they are convenient and accurate in dose. You don't have to worry about filling syringes or carrying them with you when you are away from home. Each pen cartridge contains 150 units of insulin that can be delivered in the amounts you need. Cartridges of lispro insulin, regular insulin, premixed 70/30 insulin, or NPH insulin are available. You decide the number of units you want, set the injector for that dose, stick the needle in your skin, and inject the insulin. This makes them useful for multiple dose schedules. Pen injectors are conveniently portable because you don't have to carry around a bottle of insulin.

Aids for the visually impaired. Several products are available that make it easier for people who are visually impaired. These include:

■ Dose gauges to help you measure your insulin accurately—even mixed doses. Some click with every 1 to 2 units of insulin you measure, and others have Braille or raised numbers.

■ Needle guides and vial stabilizers help you insert the needle into the insulin vial correctly. Some of these will also let you set a desired dosage level.

■ Syringe magnifiers can enlarge the measure marks on a syringe barrel. One model combines a magnifier with the needle guide and vial stabilizer. Another clips around the syringe and magnifies the scale.

Some of these aids only fit certain brands of syringes. Make sure that any aids you purchase will fit the equipment you already have. Some of these aids can be used along with some of the devices discussed above. In addition to injection aids, you can also buy blood glucose meters for the visually impaired (see Chapter 6).

Injection Site Rotation

It's really up to you to decide where you want to inject your insulin, as long as you inject into an area that contains fat. You may find it easier to use the abdomen than the thigh. Maybe not. The important thing is that you have choices. Wherever you choose to inject, you will want to inject at different sites within that body area so that you don't develop problems in and under the skin. You may find that it works best to rotate injection sites within one general area such as the abdomen rather than rotate randomly to sites in different areas of the body. However, some people achieve consistent results by doing all morning injections at one site, such as the buttocks, and all evening injections at a second site, such as the abdomen. You will probably get the most predictable results if you are consistent. That's because insulin is absorbed at different rates in different body areas. That could cause your body to respond to each insulin injection differently and lead to large fluctuations in blood glucose levels. By injecting in the same general area you can have better control of your insulin schedule. Once you have used each injection site within a body area, you can start over in the same body area. There are many opinions on the best way to rotate injection sites. Talk to your diabetes educator about the best method for you.

Typical Injection Sites. Insulin works best when injected into a layer of fat under the skin, above the muscle tissue. Several areas of the body have enough fat tissue under the skin for insulin injection. The abdomen, except for a two-inch circle around the navel, is used most commonly. Insulin injected in this area is absorbed most quickly and at the most consistent speed (from one injection to another). Another suitable area is the top and outer thighs. This is best used when you are in a sitting position. The backs of the upper arms, the hips, and the buttocks also work well. Some people, especially those with a large body size, have other options. For example, the lower back can also be a good injection site, as long as there is enough fat under the skin. Wherever you choose to inject, keep these basics in mind:

■ Divide the body area into injection sites about the size of a quarter. Try to make each new injection at least a finger-width away from your last shot. You may need to devise a way to remember where that last site was.

■ When injecting into the arm, use the outer back area of the upper arm, where there is fatty tissue. Avoid the deltoid muscle, the large triangular muscle that covers the shoulder joint. Don't inject into muscle tissue anywhere in the body.

■ Inject anywhere there is fat on the abdomen except for the 2-inch space around the navel. This has tough tissue that causes erratic insulin absorption.

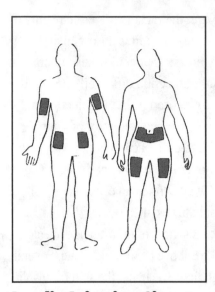

Insulin Injection Sites

■ Avoid injecting too close to moles or scar tissue anywhere in the body.

■ When injecting in the thighs, shoot for the top and outside areas. If you inject the inner thighs, rubbing between the legs may make the injection site sore. Also avoid the bony area above the knees where there isn't much fat.

Differences in Insulin Absorption. Insulin is absorbed most quickly (and at the most consistent speed) when it is injected into the abdomen, more slowly when injected into the arms, and slower still when injected into the thighs and buttocks. Many doctors recommend the abdomen because it absorbs insulin at the most consistent rate. If you have been injecting insulin into your abdomen for several weeks, you probably know how long it will take for the insulin to go into effect. This predictability has probably helped you achieve good glucose control.

If you were to suddenly switch to injecting insulin into your thigh, you might experience a different response. You might find that it takes longer for your insulin to take effect. Then it would be more difficult to meet your target blood glucose levels without adjusting what time you eat.

However, there are cases in which you might want to take advantage of this. Suppose you are still having swings in blood glucose levels or your rotation pattern doesn't give you the results you expect. Some doctors recommend a different approach to site rotation. This approach uses the different rates of absorption to even out swings in glucose levels. Here's how it works.

Suppose you need a fast response from your insulin in the morning because you like to eat a big breakfast. But you want a slower response from your nighttime insulin because you like to go to bed early and want your nighttime insulin to last through the night. In the morning you might want to inject your insulin into your abdomen where it will be absorbed quickly. At bedtime, you may want to choose your thigh as an injection site, where it would have a slower response. Based on this knowledge of your needs, your doctor or diabetes educator might suggest a rotation plan in which you would inject the abdomen every morning and the thigh every evening. You would continue to follow a site rotation plan within each area.

Other factors, such as body temperature, diet, exercise, and level of stress, affect your body's response to insulin. In general, anything that increases the blood flow to an area increases insulin absorption. Your response to insulin could even be the opposite of what you might expect, based on where you inject. For example, playing soccer for two hours may cause your insulin to be absorbed more quickly than usual so that your blood glucose level isn't where you expect it to be. So what can you do? Routinely test your blood glucose. It is the only way to make sure you are having the response you had planned. Then you'll know if your site rotation plan is working for you.

Exercise and Injection Sites. Strenuous exercise of muscles near an injection site can make the insulin act more rapidly than normal. This is because there is an increased flow of blood to exercising muscles. That doesn't necessarily mean that you should stop injecting insulin in the areas of your body you use during exercise. But if you notice that your insulin is peaking faster than you would expect when you exercise, you might want to think about the absorption rate. In general, it's a good idea to avoid strenuous exercise during the peak action times of your insulin. Insulin plus exercise can lead to very low blood sugar (hypoglycemia).

When you exercise, you have to decide whether to eat more or take less insulin. That's because exercise and insulin both decrease the amount of glucose in the blood. And you don't want your blood glucose levels to get too low. With experience, you'll learn how to balance all of these things. Frequent blood glucose monitoring will help you figure out these ups and downs in blood glucose.

Skin Problems and Injection Sites. Two main skin problems can occur at insulin injection sites: lipoatrophy and hypertrophy. With lipoatrophy, fatty tissue under the skin disappears and causes dents in the skin at the injection site. Hypertrophy is the overgrowth of cells, usually fat cells, that makes the skin look lumpy. It can look similar to scar tissue. By rotating the injection site, you can avoid some of these problems. There is also the possibility that some of the problems are caused by the type of insulin you are using.

Lipoatrophy is probably caused by an immune reaction, although its exact cause is not known. Your body is responding to insulin as an injected "foreign" substance. This problem is not common with human insulin. Make sure you are using highly purified insulin, preferably human or pork. Young women are more likely to develop atrophy. If you are bothered by these dents in your skin, or find them unsightly, ask your doctor about changing to human insulin, if you haven't already. Human insulin can be injected into the margins of the dented area as a way to build up fat and get rid of the depressions. This is not a quick fix and may take several months for improvement. A good plan for site rotation can help prevent this problem.

Hypertrophy is not an immune reaction, so you don't have to change your insulin if you are having this problem. But you do need to change injection sites to avoid this. When the same sites are used over and over again, fat deposits can accumulate in the area. This is also called *lipohypertrophy.* You may be reluctant to change because injections seem less painful in these areas. This can be true because the hypertrophy can numb the area. On the other hand, injections can sometimes be more painful in these areas. You should rotate injection sites because the abnormal cell growth can limit the absorption of your insulin. Do not inject into the lumps. Insulin action can be restricted by not being able to move through the tissue. Inject away from the lumps. A member of your health care team should check your injection sites periodically.

Insulin Pumps

Insulin pumps have come a long way in recent years. These nifty devices are miniature, computerized pumps, about the size of a call-beeper, that you can wear on your belt or in your pocket. A pump sends a steady, measured amount of insulin through a piece of flexible plastic tubing to a small needle that is inserted just under the skin and taped in place. This way of delivering insulin is called continuous subcutaneous insulin infusion, or CSII. At your command, the pump can also send a surge, or bolus, of insulin into your body. You will do this just before eating to adjust for the rise in blood glucose that will come as your food digests.

If you use insulin frequently, you have probably thought about getting an insulin pump from time to time. But maybe it seemed too costly or inconvenient. Maybe you didn't like the idea of being hooked to a machine or changing your diabetes care routine so abruptly. Now is the time for a second look. Pumps today weigh less than four ounces, so they are easy to wear. You can remove the pump for an hour or two for special occasions and still maintain glucose control. At $3,000 to $5,000, the cost of a pump is high. But with a doctor's prescription, and persistence on your part, some insurance companies will pay for all or part of it.

Paying for the Pump. Insulin pumps are expensive. They can cost up to $5,000. Monthly maintenance can run about $300, including insulin, infusion sets, and blood testing supplies. If your insurance company knows the value of insulin pumps and will cover them, you're all set. But some insurance companies won't pay the start-up or maintenance costs of the pump. What to do?

■ Keep asking! Eventually, because of the results of the Diabetes Control and Complications Trial, more insurers will cover the cost of the pump. Keep in mind that it took many years, much research, and lots of people asking to convince insurance companies to pay for other therapeutic measures, such as prescription footwear, that have long-term health benefits.

■ Your doctor should be your most convincing advocate. He or she may have to write several letters and make several calls to your insurance company with details of your need for the good glucose control that's possible on the pump.

■ Ask your diabetes educator to also write to your insurance company.

■ Work on writing effective, informative letters. All letters should stress how better control means fewer and less severe diabetes complications in the long run—which is also less expensive for the insurance company in the long run.

How Pumps Work. The pump is a little marvel of technology:

■ It beeps if clogged.

■ It lets you know when the batteries run low.

■ It has dosage limits to stop an accidental overdose.

■ You can program it to change the amount of insulin pumped to match your metabolism.

However, insulin pumps are not foolproof. Although they will alert you when a clog stops the flow of insulin, they will not identify a slow flow. Even if you are using an insulin pump, you will still need to monitor your blood glucose frequently.

Pumps use phosphate-buffered regular or lispro insulin because the buffered insulin is less likely to clog the pump. The insulin is pumped from a filled syringe inside the pump through thin plastic tubing to a needle or catheter inserted under the skin. Depending on the size of a syringe and your insulin needs, the pump can hold a 1- or 2-day supply of insulin. The tubing comes in different lengths, but it is long enough to allow plenty of slack for normal body movement. The insulin pump sends a continuous flow of insulin that trickles through the tube into the injection site at a slow, steady (basal) rate, day and night. The basal rate for pumps can be adjusted from 0.1 to 10 units per hour, depending on your metabolism. Before you eat, you push a button to deliver an extra portion of insulin, called a *bolus*. You can program, or adjust, the size of the bolus, depending on how much carbohydrate you will be eating in your meal. Delivering a bolus of insulin is just like injecting your premeal shot of insulin when you are on a multiple injection routine—without the shot! Usually, you won't have to take an extra bolus when you eat between meals, unless the snack is large.

Your doctor will help you calculate your basal and bolus insulin doses. The total basal dose over a day is some percentage of the total daily insulin dose that you've been injecting, perhaps 40 to 50 percent. The other 50 to 60 percent of your daily insulin dose is divided into the before-meal bolus doses, most of it at breakfast and dinner, and the remainder at lunch and bedtime. You will need to know how these doses were chosen, so you can learn to adjust them for fine-tuning.

A big advantage to using a pump is that you will have flexible insulin coverage for meals and snacks. You will have to spend a lot of time at the beginning to find the best basal rates, to find out when you need to adjust the basal rate, and to figure out how big a bolus you will need for each meal. You'll probably want to learn how to estimate the number of grams of carbohydrate in your meals so you can take the needed number of insulin units. This will help you even out your after-meal blood glucose levels. You'll avoid having big changes in blood glucose level throughout the day. Eventually, this will lead to a more flexible eating schedule. Pumps still cannot automatically sense your body's need for insulin. It doesn't adjust by itself. You still need to take blood glucose readings throughout the day.

Where will you attach the needle for the insulin pump? Many people choose the abdomen for insulin delivery. This area is convenient to use and gives a reliable, uniform absorption of insulin. How you insert the insulin needle will be different for different brands of infusion sets. With the Sof-set infusion set, you use a needle to insert a catheter and then remove the needle, leaving the soft catheter under your skin. With other sets, you insert a short needle. Pumps are easy to remove temporarily because, after clamping the tubing, you can leave the infusion set (the needle and tubing or the soft Teflon catheter) in place. You reattach only the pump. Some infusion sets even have a quick-release feature.

You don't have to worry that it will hurt when you exercise or if someone bumps into your pump or infusion area. The needle or catheter should be painless and comfortable at all times. If you see any redness or swelling at the infusion site, remove the needle or catheter right away and find a new infusion site. Persistent problems (lasting longer than 24 hours) should be discussed with your health care team.

Every 1 to 3 days, you'll need to replace the infusion set and move to a new insertion site. This is a part of good insulin pump technique. It helps you avoid infection at the insertion site or a clog in the infusion set. Place the new insertion site at least one inch away from the last insertion site on the abdomen. Just like with syringes, you need to avoid inserting the needle in scar tissue or moles and use a site rotation schedule.

Using the same insertion site too often or for too long can cause the same skin problems that develop when you don't rotate your syringe injection sites. Scarring can occur. Check your injection site every day to make sure no insulin is leaking out.

The pump should be worn at all times. If you take the pump off, you'll need to resume a schedule of insulin injections. However, it is possible for you to take off the pump temporarily, but not for more than 1 to 2 hours. Your blood glucose levels will get high again quickly because you don't have any longer-acting insulin. You may want to unhook during lovemaking or other physical activities that can lower blood glucose level. How long you can keep the pump off without an injection depends on how active you are when the pump is off. A dancer might be able to keep it off during an entire performance because exercise lowers blood glucose levels naturally. Through experience and testing, you will figure out how long you can keep the pump off before you need to put it back on or take an insulin injection.

Like all things worthwhile, using a pump successfully takes practice. You will most likely have problems here and there. Perhaps the most common problem is mysterious high blood glucose levels. This occurs quickly when clogged or kinked tubing stops the flow of insulin and pressure builds up in the

Unexplained High Blood Glucose Levels on the Insulin Pump

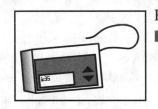

Have you considered?

■ The insulin: Is it buffered? Is it expired? Has it been exposed to extremes in temperature? Does it look clumped or filled with particles? Is the vial nearly empty? Have you used it for more than 1 month?

■ The insertion site: Have you placed the needle in or near a scar or mole? Near your beltline or other area where there's friction from clothing? Does the site hurt? Is it red or swollen?

■ The infusion set: Did the needle come out? Is insulin leaking around the infusion site? Is there blood or air in the infusion line? Is there a kink in the line? Did the line come loose from the pump? Has the infusion set been in place for more than two days? Think about changing the infusion line.

■ The insulin pump: Is the basal rate set correctly? Has the battery run down? Was the cartridge of insulin placed correctly? Is it empty? Was the pump primed with insulin when a fresh cartridge was put in? Is the pump just not working correctly?

infusion line. Your pump will sound an alarm if this happens. This is not the only reason for high blood glucose levels. For instance, an infection or inflammation at the insertion site can develop and delay the absorption of insulin. See the box on page 119 for other things to consider when you have unexplained hyperglycemia on the pump.

Should You Use a Pump? Maybe you're already having trouble sticking to your current testing and injection routine. Then a more intense schedule, such as multiple daily injections or an insulin pump, may not be for you. However, the possible benefits may motivate you to a new level of commitment.

A major advantage of a pump is that you don't have to stop what you're doing to fill a syringe. Your insulin is delivered at the push of a button. You can do this anywhere and any time.

Pumps are also precise. You can set them to pump out as little as one tenth of a unit (0.1 unit) of insulin per hour. This may help you get a level of blood glucose control that you never imagined.

People who have an urgent or special need to gain tight control or flexibility may be best suited to using a pump. Maybe you're planning a pregnancy and want the tightest control possible. Maybe you have to work odd hours at your job and it's hard enough to balance work, family, and meals during the week without having to adjust to a new injection schedule every weekend. Maybe you have had unwanted swings in blood glucose injecting intermediate- or long-acting glucose and you'd like to keep your blood glucose in check. People who want an insulin plan that adapts to day-to-day changes in their lifestyle might like an insulin pump.

Choosing a Pump. There are two insulin pumps on the market today—the MiniMed 507C and the H-TronVplus models. Your doctor or diabetes educator may prefer one brand over the other. Ask them for their thoughts on each model. Your best bet may be to talk to other people who use pumps. Find out what they like and what they don't like about each model. Here are a few things you might want to know:

- Is it waterproof? The H-Tron is waterproof. The MiniMed is splashproof and has a waterproof pouch. Both models must be removed if you want to dive into a pool, but you can shower or swim with either. However, for convenience you might want to remove them anyhow.

- Can you adjust the basal rate for different times of day? Your pump can alter the rate up to 24 (H-TronVplus) or as many as 48 (MiniMed 507C) times a day. For example, your basal rate is likely to be greater from 3 a.m. to 7 a.m. than during the rest of the day.

- Both pump manufacturers offer a 24-hour toll-free number. You will want to talk to service people about problems when you suspect the pump isn't working correctly.

- What kind of warranty does the manufacturer offer?

- How often do you have to change the batteries? How easy are the batteries to find, and how expensive are they? Batteries usually last two to four months.

Insulin Plans

How often should you inject insulin? There is no answer that is right for all people at all times. Different plans suit different people, depending on how easily controlled blood glucose swings are and how well the person with diabetes understands what foods and physical activity, and even stress, do to their blood glucose levels.

With **type 1 diabetes**, the pancreas no longer secretes insulin. The goal of insulin therapy is to mimic a normal pancreas as closely as possible. This requires multiple daily injections of insulin or the use of an insulin pump and frequent blood glucose monitoring.

Type 2 diabetes can have different causes. In some people, not enough insulin is produced in relation to how much is needed by the body. In addition to meal planning and exercise, people with this problem may need to take insulin. In others, the cells in the body resist the action of the insulin that is produced. In addition to diet and exercise, people with this problem may need oral diabetes medications. In still others, both of these problems may occur. Therapies for type 2 diabetes may have to take into account both lack of insulin and resistance to insulin. Because their bodies make and release natural insulin, people with type 2 diabetes may be able to control blood glucose by changing their eating and exercise habits. Others will need oral diabetes medication and still others will need insulin in addition to diet and exercise.

When Will Insulin Take Effect?

Type of insulin	When taken	When it's active	Blood test that shows its effect
Rapid or short acting	With or before a meal	Between that meal and the next meal	After that meal and before next meal
Intermediate acting	Before breakfast	Between lunch and dinner	Before dinner
Intermediate acting	Before dinner or bedtime	Overnight	Before breakfast
Long acting	Before breakfast or before dinner or half dose at each time	Overnight, because short-acting insulin hides its effect during the day	Before breakfast

Some women with **gestational diabetes** can control the high blood glucose levels caused by insulin resistance without insulin therapy. Others need the help of an injection of intermediate- and short-acting insulin, usually given at night.

Insulin plans can use one or two types of insulin. This means using lispro (rapid acting) or regular (short acting) insulin, and, for some people, also using a longer-acting insulin. When deciding what insulin plan to recommend, your doctor will consider how to match your personal needs, both medical and practical, to a combination of insulin type, dose, and schedule. To understand this plan, it helps to know when the different injections of insulin are likely to have an effect on your blood glucose levels (see the table).

Most insulin plans, especially those for people with type 1 diabetes, try to mimic the effects a normal pancreas could produce (see Graph 1, page 124). A pancreas puts out a steady stream of insulin (a basal or baseline dose) day and night. It also secretes an extra dose of insulin (a bolus) in response to meals. This is the way insulin plans using the insulin pump are usually set up. If insulin injections are preferred, doctors may prescribe a longer acting insulin to mimic the basal insulin secretion. To substitute for the bolus of insulin, a dose of rapid-acting (lispro) or short-acting (regular) insulin is usually given before each meal. What combination of short- and long-acting insulins you use is up to you and your doctor. Together, work out a plan that will suit your lifestyle and diet. If you think your plan is not working out for you, talk to your doctor.

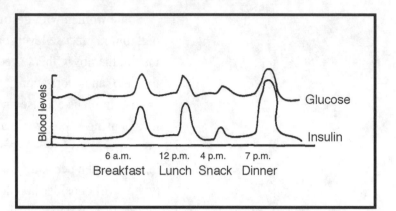

Graph 1: Typical changes in glucose and insulin levels over 24 hours in someone without diabetes.

One Shot a Day

It sounds too good to be true—and it probably is. A single shot of intermediate-acting insulin will stay in your blood stream for only 18 hours. This will leave you without any available insulin for about 6 hours. Let's say you give yourself an injection at 7 a.m. What problems could arise? Graph 2 shows how much insulin will be available, based on average absorption rates and action times of intermediate-acting insulin. If you look at graph 2, you'll notice the following:

■ Even though you inject at 7 a.m., it takes a while for the insulin to kick in. You won't have any insulin coverage for 2 to 4 hours. That may take care of lunch, but what about breakfast?

■ You are most likely to become hypoglycemic when the insulin peaks 7 to 10 hours later. So you will have to match your eating schedule to your insulin schedule.

■ You will have no insulin coverage for much of the night, because the insulin fades out after 18 hours—and it's only 1 a.m.

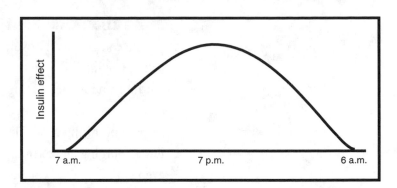

Graph 2: One shot of intermediate-acting insulin.

For most people with diabetes, one shot a day is not adequate. Your glucose level will be out of control for many hours each day, which will put you at higher risk for complications. Long-lasting insulin may be able to cover your low-level background glucose levels, but you need more insulin to lower glucose levels after meals.

You should have your major meals during the peak action time of insulin. Can you always eat at the same time? Does your schedule allow it? Are your family and friends available to eat dinner when your insulin is peaking? Although this insulin plan is very easy, it is not very flexible. It locks you into a more rigid lifestyle than you probably want to have. And it leaves big holes in your insulin coverage.

There are always exceptions, and a schedule such as this might work for some people. For example, in some people with type 2 diabetes, natural insulin just needs a boost. Some take insulin only at night to control fasting blood glucose levels. In some people with type 1 diabetes, the pancreas still secretes some insulin in the honeymoon phase, if you have just been diagnosed with diabetes. But unless you fall into one of these categories and your doctor recommends it, this schedule is not advised.

More Than One Shot

You can get better coverage by splitting your intermediate-acting insulin dose into two shots. These can be given in the morning and in the evening. Usually, the morning shot will contain more insulin than the evening shot. Graph 3 shows the amount of insulin available if you split your intermediate dose into a morning and evening shot. However, you'll notice that even with this plan, you may have a period in the early morning, between 3 and 10 a.m., when your insulin may be low.

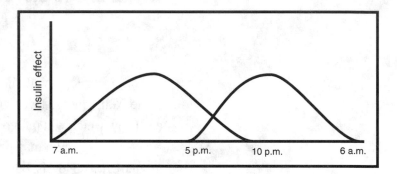

Graph 3: Intermediate-acting insulin split into two shots.

Or, you might take two injections of long-acting insulins. Graph 4 shows how long-acting insulin given at breakfast and supper provides round-the-clock coverage of basal amounts of insulin.

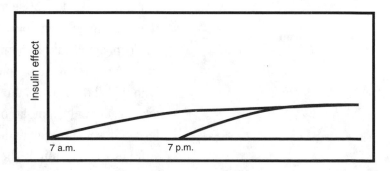

Graph 4: Long-acting insulin split into two shots.

One way to improve your coverage is to also mix rapid- or short- and intermediate-acting insulins in each dose. Usually this approach of splitting and mixing insulins combines lispro or regular and NPH insulins. Doses are taken about 30 minutes before breakfast and dinner, as shown in Graph 5. In this plan, regular insulin goes to work within 30 minutes. As regular insulin decreases, the intermediate insulin starts to work. Just when the intermediate insulin starts to wear off before dinner time, another mixed dose is given. Again the regular insulin kicks in early, and the intermediate insulin picks up the slack to carry you through the night.

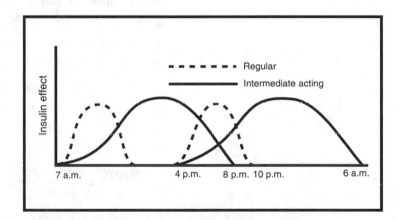

Graph 5: Split and mixed regular and intermediate insulin in two shots.

It may take a little experimenting to figure out how to best mix short- and intermediate-acting insulins. You may want to start out using a 2 to 1 ratio of intermediate-acting insulin to regular insulin (2 parts intermediate, 1 part regular). You may have to change the ratio until you are getting the results that best suit you. You may find it convenient to buy a premixed formula, such as a 70/30 mixture of NPH/regular. Or you may prefer to split and mix the doses yourself. This lets you change the amount of regular or NPH independently of each other. You may find this helpful when trying to account for activity level and food intake.

Don't forget that lente and ultralente insulin must be injected right after mixing them with regular insulin. Otherwise, the action of regular insulin will be lessened. If you find that regular insulin is not acting as rapidly as you would expect, you may have to increase the amount of regular you take or switch to the more rapid-acting lispro. To get around this, some people take regular in separate shots from lente or ultralente, but at the same time of day. Of course, you'll have to give yourself more shots each day if you follow this approach.

If you are using a two-shot plan using split and mixed doses of intermediate-acting and lispro or regular insulin, you will need to keep close tabs on your body's response. This means that you should monitor your blood glucose levels before each meal. You may need to monitor at other times as well. A two-shot program gives you better control than a single-shot plan but still keeps you closely tied to a regular meal schedule and a regular pattern of activity. This is because you cannot make short-term adjustments in longer-acting insulins. Only lispro or regular insulin can be adjusted immediately to respond to a blood glucose test or change in schedule.

If you find that you have high blood glucose levels in the morning, you may want to move your evening insulin shot from dinner time to bedtime. This will make insulin available a little later during the course of the night to keep your glucose levels in check. Make sure that your glucose levels are in balance during the evening hours, if you try this adjustment.

You may find that you have low blood glucose in the early morning (around 2 or 3 a.m.) with the two-shot plan. If this is the case, think about a three-shot plan. With this, you would give yourself a mixture of short and intermediate-acting insulin at breakfast, a short-acting insulin at dinner, and an intermediate-acting insulin at bedtime. The insulin levels throughout the day are shown in Graph 6.

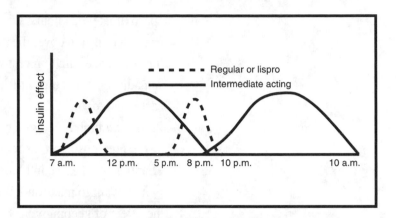

Graph 6: Three shots: split and mixed morning dose, regular dinner dose, and intermediate evening dose.

The more often you inject insulin, the more opportunities you have to fine-tune your control. One example of such a flexible insulin plan also uses three shots a day. This plan can provide glucose control when you take a rapid- or short-acting insulin injection before lunch and a mixture of rapid- or short- and long-acting insulins before breakfast and supper (Graph 7). The long-acting insulin provides a basal dose of insulin over

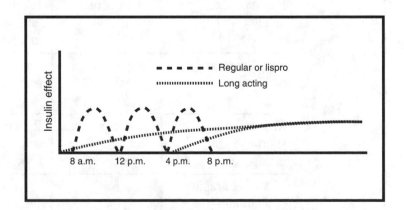

Graph 7: Three shots: split and mixed morning dose, regular dose, split and mixed evening dose.

approximately 24 hours, with no peak. The injections of lispro or regular insulin cover the three meals. To make this plan work for you, make sure to monitor your blood frequently. Then you can adjust the amounts of lispro or regular insulin given before each meal to

■ lower a high blood glucose level not sufficiently lowered by the previous lispro or regular injection

■ anticipate the rise in blood glucose caused by the next meal.

You want to make sure that the adjustments you make have the effect of keeping your blood glucose levels within your target range.

Examples of Insulin Plans

	Before breakfast	Before lunch	Before dinner	Before bedtime
	Mixture of rapid or short and intermediate acting		Mixture of rapid or short and intermediate acting	
	Mixture of rapid or short and intermediate acting		Rapid or short acting	Intermediate acting
	Rapid or short acting	Rapid or short acting	Intermediate or long acting plus rapid or short acting	
	Rapid or short acting	Rapid or short acting	Rapid or short acting	Rapid or short and intermediate acting
	Mixture of rapid or short and long* acting	Rapid or short acting	Rapid or short acting	
	Mixture of rapid or short and intermediate acting			

*The long-acting insulin dose can also be taken at bedtime or before dinner or split in half, with half taken before breakfast and half before dinner.

Timing Your Insulin Injections

Knowing when to give your injection, or take your premeal bolus by pump, can be confusing. Regular insulin is taken before meals or very big snacks to counteract the increase in blood glucose that will occur as food is absorbed. Ideal timing is pictured in Graph 8. Insulin starts to work lowering blood

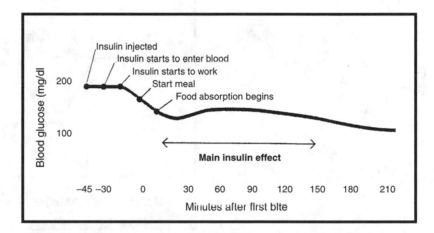

Graph 8: Ideal timing of regular insulin in relation to meals.

When to Inject Insulin Before Meals

If blood sugar level 45 minutes before meal is:	Inject regular insulin:
below 50 mg/dl	When completing meal
50 to 70 mg/dl	At mealtime
71 to 120 mg/dl	15 minutes before meal
121 to 180 mg/dl	30 minutes before meal
over 180 mg/dl	45 minutes before meal

glucose as food increases blood glucose levels. If regular insulin is taken too close to the start of a meal, the food will cause blood glucose levels to go too high before the insulin has had a chance to be absorbed for use. An example of inadequate timing of regular insulin injection, which results in hyperglycemia, is shown in Graph 9.

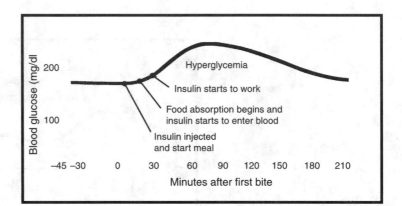

Graph 9: Inadequate timing of regular insulin in relation to a meal.

How much in advance of your meal you need to take insulin depends on insulin type and your blood glucose level before the meal. Try testing about 45 minutes before you plan to start eating. If your blood sugar level is high (see chart), you need to inject insulin quickly to help counteract your already high blood glucose level before food sends it even higher. If your blood sugar level is low, you need to wait to inject closer to the time you'll start eating. Remember, regular insulin takes about 30 minutes to go to work taking glucose from the blood into cells. Lispro takes about half that time.

Intensive Insulin Therapy

Sometimes, despite your best efforts, you may feel that you are not quite in control of your diabetes. Perhaps a change is in order. One option is intensive insulin therapy. A ten-year study called the Diabetes Control and Complications Trial showed that patients with type 1 diabetes who maintained blood glucose within narrow or near-normal ranges (known as tight blood glucose control) reduced their chances of developing most complications associated with diabetes. But is it for you? Ask yourself the following:

- Am I unhappy with my control of blood glucose?
- Do my blood glucose tests frequently show unexpected levels, high or low?
- Do I have any signs of the complications of diabetes?
- Do I lack the amount of energy I need to participate in all my activities—both day and night?
- Do I want more flexibility in my lifestyle for timing meals, exercise, and other activities?

If you answer yes to any of these questions, you may want to investigate the idea of intensive insulin therapy. See Chapter 7 for more information.

Chapter 5: Achieving Glucose Control

Each day, you try again to solve the diabetes challenge: How to keep blood glucose near normal with so many things pushing it up or down.

Why Control Glucose?

Why should you have to pay special attention to your glucose levels? If you take insulin or oral diabetes medications regularly and watch your diet, shouldn't that take care of everything? Probably not. For people with diabetes, blood glucose levels change throughout the day. This is especially true for people with type 1 diabetes, but people with type 2 can also experience big swings in glucose:

▲ Food pushes the blood glucose level up.

▼ Insulin or an oral diabetes medication brings it down.

▲ Stress drives it up.

▼ Exercise can bring it back down.

▲ Illness makes it rise.

Diet, activity, stress, and overall general health all affect blood glucose levels. Everyone with diabetes responds somewhat differently to each of these. It would be wonderful if there was a magic formula to tell you how to arrive at the right blood glucose level. Instead, you'll need to discover how each of these factors affects your blood glucose level. As you do this, you are likely to feel frustrated at times. Knowing how much to eat, how much to exercise, and how much insulin or medication to take are not always easy to figure out. Look to your health care team for support. They can work with you to create a plan to best achieve blood glucose control. More than likely, your plan will include self-monitoring of blood glucose (SMBG).

Testing = Control

SMBG allows you to make decisions about your diabetes management. You wouldn't want to guess which road to take on a car trip—why guess how much insulin to take or how much to eat? Your blood glucose test should act as your road map, telling you which turns to take.

Here's something else to keep in mind: If your blood glucose levels swing too high or too low during the course of the day, you could develop some serious problems. Some of these problems can be risky in the short term and result in a life-threatening crisis. For example, if your blood glucose levels drop too low and you are not treated, you could become unconscious. Other problems can develop that may not cause an immediate emergency but could lead to severe complications over time. People with a history of chronic high blood glucose levels can develop debilitating eye disease, kidney disease, circulation problems, or nerve disease.

The best way to lead a normal and healthy lifestyle is to take charge of your diabetes. You do this by controlling glucose levels with food, exercise, and medication. And the single most important thing you can do for yourself is keep track of the amount of glucose in your blood on a regular basis. Instead of saying "I feel great" or "I feel lousy," take measurements and keep records. These records tell you how well your diabetes plan is working. Monitoring is the only way to know how your body responds to food, insulin, activity, and stress. Without knowing this, you can't make improvements in your diabetes care plan. Trial and error—and a little patience—will help you achieve better control.

What Affects Glucose in the Blood?

Food

Your body breaks down the carbohydrate in the food you eat to glucose. Glucose travels through your blood to nourish every part of your body. When you eat, the amount of glucose in your blood goes up. How much your blood glucose rises after a meal depends on many things. Different foods have different amounts of carbohydrate and will produce different amounts of glucose. How much of a food you eat at one time changes how much glucose is produced. Carbohydrates come in several forms that take various amounts of time to break down. Sugars break down faster than starches. Also, foods that contain fat or protein plus carbohydrate can slow down the digestion rate. High-protein foods can raise blood glucose levels but do this more slowly than foods containing mostly carbohydrate.

One take-charge tool is to learn on a day-to-day basis how the food you eat affects your blood glucose levels. You may be surprised at how your glucose levels respond to different foods. Measure your blood glucose one to two hours after you eat particular foods. Do you find that your blood glucose rises faster with carrots than sweet potatoes? Or faster with mashed potatoes than with ice cream? What about a serving of meat versus a slice of bread? By figuring out how your body responds, you can make adjustments in your plan, so that your blood glucose will not rise too high, too quickly.

A key to managing your diabetes is to plan your meals carefully. But you needn't feel like you're the only person who has to pay attention to what you eat. When you develop an eating plan for diabetes, you're doing the same thing that millions of Americans without diabetes are already doing—

eating a healthy, balanced diet. And today, more Americans are finding that eating a healthy diet makes them feel better everyday and over the long haul.

You will want to match what you eat with the amount of insulin or oral diabetes medication in your blood. It may take you a while to learn how your body responds to the insulin you take and to the food you eat. A registered dietitian can help you balance your diet and insulin intake. If you are taking other medications to help control blood glucose, your dietitian can also help you balance your food intake and response to medication. Make sure that you develop a meal plan that fits your tastes. If there are particular foods you want to include, ask your dietitian for a plan that will include them. That way, you will be more likely to stick with your eating plan.

Insulin

As your body digests the food you eat, glucose builds up in the blood. In people without diabetes or in many people with type 2 diabetes, glucose signals the body to release insulin. Insulin then lets glucose into the cells that need it. Without insulin, cells in the body can't get the energy they need to live and grow. In people with type 1 diabetes, the body no longer makes insulin. Glucose can't get to the cells that need it. In people with type 2 diabetes, the body makes insulin, but the insulin has problems in getting enough glucose into the cells that need it.

The body carefully balances the amount of glucose and insulin in the blood. It works almost like a thermostat. When there is too much glucose in the blood, insulin is released. Insulin reduces the amount of glucose in the blood. Then, when glucose levels drop, insulin is no longer secreted. The body balances the amount of insulin and glucose to keep glucose at a fairly even level throughout the day. It keeps a little bit of insulin ready to go to work at a moment's notice. For meals, it does a good job of releasing the right amount of extra insulin in time to clear glucose from the blood before glucose levels climb too high.

The goal for people with diabetes is to try to strike a balance between insulin and glucose, much like the body does naturally. Too much insulin, and glucose levels may fall too fast or too low. Too little insulin, and glucose builds up in the blood. For people with type 1 diabetes, this goal can be reached by using insulin carefully. By testing blood glucose levels before and after meals, you can become experienced at knowing how much a given dose of insulin will reduce your blood glucose level.

If you use insulin, timing your injections and meals is important. You should eat meals and snacks when insulin has had time to act. If you eat too soon after an injection, your glucose can climb too high. If you wait too long after an injection, your blood glucose can fall too low. This is also a consideration if you are taking any type of sulfonylurea, an oral diabetes medication that lowers glucose by increasing insulin release. Also, where you inject insulin can affect timing. Many people have found that they get the most reliable timing in insulin action when they use the abdomen as the injection site.

For an idea of how to time insulin injections according to the level of blood glucose before eating, see Chapter 4. You should inject regular insulin 30 to 45 minutes before you eat, so the insulin is ready when glucose enters the blood. Lispro can be injected at or just before meal time.

You also need to match the amount of insulin you take to the amount of food you eat. If you inject the usual dose of insulin and then eat more dinner than you had planned, you may end up with high glucose. On the other hand, if you don't eat as much as you thought you would, your blood glucose level will drop too low.

Even if you eat the same amount and exercise the same amount every day, you won't always be able to control how your body takes in and uses the insulin you inject. The amount of insulin your body absorbs can change as much as 25 percent from day to day. This is especially true for NPH insulin. So don't be disturbed by differences. The way to adjust for these changes is to test your blood glucose and increase or decrease your next insulin dose.

For more information on food, see Chapter 8.

Exercise

If you are used to exercising and you have just been diagnosed with diabetes, you might be wondering whether you will be able to continue your workouts. (Of course you will!) If you are not yet in the swing of things, it's time to think about beginning an exercise program. Everyone needs to be physically active—it's good for your overall health. It can help prevent heart disease and cancer. Regardless of your type of diabetes, exercise can have many positive benefits.

Not only does exercise make you feel and look good, it improves blood flow and muscle tone. It can even beat stress. Aerobic exercise gives your heart and lungs an especially good workout. It makes your heart pump harder and gets the blood flowing through even your smallest blood vessels. This helps prevent the circulation and foot problems that people with diabetes can get. Walking may be the best all-around exercise. It's something that almost everyone can do.

When you exercise, your muscles work harder and use up their glucose stores for fuel. When the glucose stored in muscle runs low, glucose from the blood is used. Exercise can help use up some of the glucose that builds up in the blood. And exercise has another bonus for people with diabetes. It seems to make muscles and other tissues more sensitive to insulin, so less insulin is needed to move glucose out of the blood and into muscle cells. If you exercise regularly, you may be able to eat a little more or inject a little less insulin. Some people with type 2 diabetes find that they no longer have to take insulin or other diabetes medication once they start a regular exercise program. However, you should never start an exercise program or make changes in your diet, insulin, or medication without first talking it over with your health care team.

Exercise is truly one very important part of the diabetes care plan for people with type 2 diabetes. You can count on regular exercise to help with your weight control and to increase your body's sensitivity to insulin and other medications. Exercise may be more important than eating healthy meals. For people with type 1 diabetes, exercise does not really help control diabetes. It has definite benefits, such as lessening your risk of cardiovascular disease and cancer, helping with weight control, and allowing you to use less insulin on the days you work out. But instead of using exercise to control your diabetes, it is something you must account for in terms of food and insulin. That is, on days you have a one-hour aerobics class after dinner, you may be able to eat an extra helping of the main dish at dinner or inject less insulin.

Because of diabetes, when you exercise, you need to take special precautions. You should make sure that your blood glucose levels don't drop too far too fast. This can happen in the hours after exercise, more commonly in people with type 1 diabetes. This is when your muscles take glucose from the blood to restore their glucose reserves. So even if your glucose level seems normal right after exercising, don't assume it will stay that way during the hours following your workout. It's a good idea to check blood glucose levels several hours after exercising.

On the other hand, if your blood glucose levels are too high (over 250 mg/dl) while you exercise, activity may cause your blood glucose level to go up rather than down. Hard exercise with too little insulin can make the liver release stored glucose.

For more on exercise, see Chapter 9.

Stress

Everyone seems stressed out these days. And living with diabetes adds even more stress to your life. People with diabetes sometimes try to do more than everyone else, just to prove that diabetes doesn't make them any different. But you, too, need to allow yourself enough time to relax and recover from the stresses of everyday life.

Stress can produce hormones that can shoot your blood glucose levels up and out of your desired range. This can contribute to ketoacidosis, which can lead to diabetic coma—a life-threatening situation. Stress can also be a hidden contributor to unexpected swings in blood glucose levels. The effect of an angry driver who cuts you off on the interstate can't be as easily measured as grams of carbohydrate, units of insulin, or calories burned during exercise. When you can't figure out why your blood glucose level is so high despite "doing everything right," think about the stresses in your life. Also, think about how you respond to stress. Do you eat when you are under stress? This can bring up blood glucose levels. Do stressful situations make you more active than usual? This response can decrease blood glucose levels.

Illness

When you're sick, your body is also stressed. To deal with this stress, your body releases hormones that help you fight disease. But these hormones also counteract the effect of insulin in lowering blood glucose and cause a rise in blood glucose levels. Sickness can cause your diabetes to go out of control. Extremely high blood glucose levels caused by illness

Sick Day Action Plan

 Before your next illness, decide on an action plan with your health care team. It should include the following:

- When to call the doctor.
- How often to test for blood glucose.
- Whether you should perform urine ketone testing. Ketones are produced when fats instead of glucose are used for energy. Most commonly, this is a sign that not enough insulin is available to help your body break down glucose. (Less commonly, when carbohydrates are very restricted, such as when very tight control is the object, ketones can appear in the blood. This is called *starvation ketosis*.) When blood glucose levels are high during illness, ketones can appear if extra insulin is not given.
- Medication changes that might be needed. You need to know how much extra insulin to take to bring down unusually high blood glucose levels. If you take oral diabetes medications, you need to know whether you should continue taking them or increase or decrease the dose.
- Whether you need to have antinausea suppositories or over-the-counter cold or flu or cough medications on hand, which ones are good choices, and when to take them.
- What foods and fluids to take during your illness.

can also lead to diabetic ketoacidosis in people with type 1 diabetes and to hyperosmolar hyperglycemic nonketotic syndrome (HHNS) in people with type 2 diabetes. (See the section on emergencies, below.)

Blood glucose monitoring is especially important during any bout of sickness. Even if you have type 2 diabetes and only monitor once a day, you may want to keep a closer check during times of illness. Be sure to talk to your health care team before you get ill about what you should do in the event of illness. You and your health care team can work together to come up with a plan to help you handle common illnesses such as colds or the flu.

Other than eating chicken soup and drinking lots of liquids, here are a few things you should do when you are feeling under the weather:

■ Always take your normal dose of insulin—even if you can't eat. Your doctor may even prescribe more insulin to take care of the excess glucose your body releases when you are sick. You and your doctor should agree on what blood glucose levels call for a change in your insulin dose.

■ If you take oral diabetes medications, take your medication. Sometimes on sick days you may temporarily need to take insulin. Talk to your doctor about this during a normal checkup, before you get sick, so you can work out a plan in advance.

■ Monitor your blood glucose and ketone levels about every three to four hours. If the levels are too high or you are pregnant, you may need to monitor more often.

■ Substitute sick-day foods for normal foods if nausea and vomiting are making it difficult to eat. Talk to your dietitian about which sick-day foods will cover your basic eating plan. Prepare a sick-day plan before you even become sick. Try to keep some comforting foods like rice, soup, or frozen fruit bars on hand, especially during the cold and flu season.

■ Drink plenty of caffeine-free liquids. If you are losing fluids by vomiting, fever, or diarrhea, you may need nondiet soft drinks or sports drinks with sugar or carbohydrate. This can help prevent the hypoglycemia caused by not eating or taking extra insulin. If vomiting or diarrhea are severe, try sipping 3 to 6 ounces an hour to keep blood glucose stable.

■ Keep on hand a fever thermometer and a small supply of common sick-day medications that are safe to take. These should be approved in advance by your doctor.

Some of the cold medicines sold over-the-counter to treat colds and flu should not be taken by people with diabetes.

Many cough and cold remedies labeled "decongestant" contain ingredients (such as pseudoephedrine) that raise blood glucose levels and blood pressure. Do not take any over-the-counter medication without first talking to your doctor.

In addition to some of the medicines in cough and cold remedies, some contain sugar and alcohol. Make sure you read the label and find out exactly what "active ingredients" as well as "inactive ingredients" any medication contains. A small amount of sugar is probably fine, as long as you are aware you are taking it. If you will be taking frequent or high doses of a particular medicine, try to find a sugar-free version. Alcohol is a common ingredient in nighttime cold medications such as Nyquil. Be sure you eat something before you take any medication that contains alcohol. Otherwise, your blood glucose level may fall too low.

Pain medications are also usually safe in small doses. You don't have to worry about taking an occasional aspirin for headache or fever. Also, many doctors prescribe a daily coated "baby" aspirin to protect against cardiovascular disease. This is safe for people with diabetes. Ibuprofen is not safe for anyone with kidney disease. People with diabetes should not take ibuprofen unless a doctor advises it. This drug could cause acute renal failure in people with kidney problems.

When to Call the Doctor. You should call your doctor if:
- You have been sick for one or two days without improvement
- You have had vomiting or diarrhea for more than 6 hours
- Self-testing shows moderate to large amounts of ketones in your urine
- You are taking insulin and your blood glucose levels continue to be over 240 mg/dl after taking two or three supplemental doses of regular insulin as prearranged with your doctor
- You are taking insulin and your blood glucose level is under 60 mg/dl (hypoglycemia)

■ You have type 2 diabetes, you are taking oral diabetes medication, and your premeal blood glucose levels are 240 mg/dl or higher for more than 24 hours

■ You have signs of extreme hyperglycemia (very dry mouth or fruity odor to the breath), dehydration, or loss of mental competence (confusion, disorientation)

■ You are sleepier than normal

■ You have stomach or chest pain or any difficulty breathing

■ You have any doubts or questions about what you need to do for your illness.

When you call, your doctor will want you to have some information ready. Keeping records during your illness will make it easier for your doctor to determine how sick you are. This will also help you and your doctor keep track of your progress in getting well. Your doctor will want to know:

■ Your blood glucose level and your urine ketone results, starting when you first realized you were ill

■ What insulin doses and diabetes pills you have taken and when you took them

■ Other medications you have taken

■ How long you have been sick

■ Your temperature

■ How well you can take foods and fluids

■ If you have lost weight while sick

■ Any other symptoms you may have

■ Your pharmacist's phone number.

Self-Monitoring Your Blood Glucose

You can keep your long-range diabetes management goals, such as staying healthy, on track by making and aiming for shorter-term goals. Shorter-term goals in diabetes management usually focus on measurements of your blood glucose level that you take yourself, which is called self-monitoring of blood glucose, or SMBG.

Who Needs It?

If you have type 1 diabetes, you need to test. If you have type 2 diabetes and take insulin or oral diabetes medications, you need to test. If you have gestational diabetes and take

Diabetes: Myth or Fact?

"I can tell my blood glucose level without testing."

Some people with diabetes claim they have a sixth sense: knowing their blood glucose level. It would be a wonderful sense to have, but it's just not reliable. Testing by SMBG is the only way to go.

However, you can learn more about sensing the clues your body or behavior gives about your blood glucose level by attending a class or series of classes on hypoglycemia prevention and recognition. This education can be very valuable to anyone with diabetes, but especially for people who have stopped recognizing symptoms of severe low blood glucose (hypoglycemia unawareness). Just as jet pilots can be trained to recognize and react to signs of oxygen deprivation, you can become better aware of your cues of possible hypoglycemia:

■ autonomic: heart rate, trembling, sweating

■ mental: slow thinking and lack of concentration and coordination

■ mood: irritation or aggression

■ food: skipping meals

■ insulin: taking it earlier

■ exercise: working out harder or longer.

Cues for hyperglycemia are much harder to detect. Look for increased thirst and urination and blurry vision.

Training leads you right back to your glucose meter. Many people who have gone through a blood glucose awareness program learned just how poor they were at predicting their blood glucose levels. Now, they test more often than ever.

insulin, you need to test. Insulin and oral diabetes medications are powerful drugs that lower blood glucose. You can tell how well they are doing their job by keeping tabs on your blood glucose. It's an important skill, well worth developing, to learn how much of these medications you need to take to counter the after-meal blood glucose rise. SMBG will also let you see how exercise affects the amount of medication your body needs. Also, when you use these medications, you put yourself at risk for low blood glucose levels. SMBG will tell you if your blood glucose is low, so you don't have to guess. It can also guide you in deciding how much treatment you need.

If you have type 2 diabetes or gestational diabetes and manage it with an eating and exercise plan, you don't need to worry about low blood glucose levels. However, SMBG has great benefits for you. It gives you feedback on how well your diabetes care is working. Positive feedback may be a wonderful source of encouragement for you. You can see the effects of your exercise program or food choices on your blood glucose levels. For pregnant women, it guides the treatment adjustments that will help keep you and your baby healthy.

How Much Testing?

You and your health care team need to decide how often you will measure your blood glucose. This depends on your reasons for self-monitoring blood glucose. Blood glucose levels in type 1 diabetes tend to fluctuate quite a bit throughout the day. If you use the results of each test to adjust your next insulin injection or your food intake, then you need to check your blood glucose level each time you plan an injection or a meal. This would mean three to four tests a day.

On the other hand, maybe you've opted for a more relaxed schedule. If you are just trying to prevent hyperglycemia and ketosis, you may only be taking one or two insulin shots each day. If this is the case, you may decide to monitor just two times each day.

If you aim for blood glucose levels close to normal, it's essential to test at least four, and sometimes five, times a day. You would test before each meal and before bedtime every day and in the middle of the night (around 3 a.m.) about once a week. Studies have shown a relationship between the number of tests a day and the level of glucose control. When monitoring drops to less than four tests a day, glucose control worsens.

Blood glucose levels in people with type 2 diabetes are more stable over the course of a day and do not need to be monitored as often. If you take oral diabetes medications, you don't need as many tests as someone taking insulin. You can't use the results to fine-tune your next dose. You will test frequently while your health care team is trying to find the best dose of medication for you or when there's a change in your care plan (such as a new exercise routine). Finding the best dose of oral medication can be as tricky as finding the right amount and timing for insulin injections. While you are making adjustments, you could be surprised by unexpected bouts of hypoglycemia. During this period, test your blood glucose once or twice a day (before breakfast and either before dinner or before going to sleep at night). Occasionally, you may want to test two hours after breakfast and dinner to see how well the medication or your meal plan is working. Your monitoring records will help you and your health care team decide what changes, if any, are needed. But once your blood glucose levels are closer to normal, testing one or two times a day may be fine for you.

If you manage your type 2 diabetes without medications, once your blood glucose levels are under control, you might test once or twice a day, or three or four times a week. You should also test when you're curious about what your blood glucose level might be, such as after a special dinner or an extra-strenuous workout.

How often you test depends on how often you're willing to prick your finger, what your schedule permits, and what supplies you can afford. More frequent testing means you have to spend more money on supplies.

Sometimes you might not be feeling quite right and you don't know why. Monitoring your blood glucose may tell you what the problem is. Maybe you're feeling sweaty and a little shaky after a 3-mile run. Maybe you're just tired from the workout, or maybe you're having a low blood glucose reaction. Without monitoring, you may tend to eat because you think your blood glucose level is too low, when it is really too high. Only by monitoring your blood glucose can you tell what your body really needs.

Over time, you will gain confidence in your ability to manage your diabetes. You may think it's okay to test less often. Beware! It's tempting to think you can tell what your glucose level is by the way you feel. But research shows that most people cannot guess their glucose level reliably. Guessing is dangerous, especially if your blood glucose levels tends to swing with little warning.

When to Test?

Once again, this depends on your particular reasons for testing. You have many choices. Test whenever you like. However, if you are on the lookout for patterns, there are standard times to test:

- before breakfast, lunch, and dinner (or an especially big snack)
- before you go to bed
- one to two hours after breakfast, lunch, and dinner (or an especially big snack)
- at 2 or 3 a.m.

When to Do Extra Tests

- When you're ill
- If you suspect low blood glucose
- Before you drive (if you take insulin or sulfonylureas)
- When you're physically active
- If you start taking a nondiabetes medication that affects blood glucose levels or your ability to recognize low blood glucose warning signs: talk to your pharmacist and doctor about these possibilities
- If you have frequent insulin reactions overnight or wake up with very high blood glucose levels
- When you are changing your insulin injection plan, your eating plan, or your exercise plan
- When you have lost or gained weight
- When you are pregnant or thinking about becoming pregnant
- When you have trouble recognizing the warning signs of hypoglycemia
- When your levels have been dangerously high or low (outside your acceptable range)
- When you are on intensive insulin therapy.

If you have type 2 diabetes or gestational diabetes managed without medications, you can learn a lot by testing your blood glucose levels regularly. It helps you keep track of your diabetes control. You can do this by measuring your fasting (pre-breakfast) blood glucose levels every day. If you want to know how high your blood glucose rises after eating your Aunt Mary's Famous Fudge Cake, do a test one or two hours after you eat it. If you have type 2 diabetes and need positive reinforcement for weight loss, do a test in the morning before you eat and compare it to tests you did in the first month after you were diagnosed.

Blood Glucose Goals

Time of test	Person without diabetes	Person with diabetes
Before meals	Less than 110 mg/dl	80 to 120 mg/dl
Before bedtime	Less than 120 mg/dl	100 to 140 mg/dl

Tip: Blood glucose goals for children are looser. For example, the target range may be 100 or 200 mg/dl. Most children under the age of 6 or 7 are not yet able to be aware of and respond to oncoming low blood glucose, and it's very important to limit episodes of low blood glucose. Tailor goals to the age and abilities of the child and be flexible with goals as the child grows.

Your Blood Glucose Goals

Choosing blood glucose goals can be easy. You can simply follow guidelines supported by the American Diabetes Association (see table). However, these goals may not be easy for you to reach. Or they may not be appropriate for you because of a health problem. Your goals may be consistently higher. Why not see what your blood glucose levels are before and after meals and before bed and compare them to the goals in the table. Perhaps you can make small changes, a few at a time, to slowly lower your blood glucose levels. Changes may include:

■ how much food you eat
■ the kinds of food you eat
■ how much exercise you get
■ how much insulin or medication you take.

Whether you have type 1 or type 2 diabetes or gestational diabetes, the goals of achieving control of blood glucose levels are similar: to keep blood glucose as close as possible to that of a person without diabetes. For many people with diabetes, getting normal blood glucose levels (like a person without diabetes) just isn't realistic or even desirable. For instance, if you are elderly and live alone, you may be more concerned with preventing severe low blood glucose than avoiding long-term complications. You and your health care team should decide together what goals are best for you. The goals need to be based on you: your needs, lifestyle, and health. You will be able to reach realistic goals. You will not be able to reach unrealistic ones, and setting, but not reaching, them will only hurt your self-confidence.

Write down an acceptable blood glucose range for you at this time. The range could be something like 70 to 200 mg/dl. This means that any reading under 70 mg/dl is too low. Anything over 200 mg/dl is too high. This range includes lower blood glucose levels for before meals and somewhat higher glucose levels one or two hours after meals. As you gain greater glucose control, you will see the high end of the range come down.

Dealing With Your SMBG Results

After diligently monitoring your blood glucose levels, don't forget to keep track of your results. Although a reading that is too high or too low can alert you to a dangerous situation, it's the patterns in blood glucose readings throughout the day or from day to day that give you clues about your diabetes control. The only way to see the patterns in blood glucose levels is to record your results.

Ask your doctor or diabetes educator for a record book with an easy-to-use format. You can also make your own. Some blood glucose meters store 10 or 20 or up to 250 test results. This saves you from having to write the results down each time, but you will still have to see if there are any patterns in your blood glucose readings by charting out the results. Make sure to show the members of your health care team the results of your monitoring.

When you are new to SMBG, your concern is doing the test correctly. But even if you are getting consistent results, you may want to have your diabetes educator watch you do a test, to make sure you're doing everything properly. Blood testing skills can slip over time. There's information on blood testing accuracy in Chapter 6.

Sometimes you will be faced with an unexpectedly high or low reading. Try to figure out what could have caused this. You might already know why the reading could be higher than normal. Maybe it's that extra helping of mashed potatoes you ate at dinner or that slice of pie you usually avoid. If that's the case, don't berate yourself. Forgive yourself and be glad you know why it's so high. If you have a series of high or low results that you can't explain, contact your health care team as soon as possible.

As you get the hang of monitoring, you will come to know what to expect your readings to be at certain times of the day. If your readings are consistently higher or lower than recommended, or if you get a reading that is unexpectedly high or low, this could indicate a problem. Discuss with your health care team in advance what you should do if your readings are way off scale. If you detect patterns in your glucose levels that indicate a need to adjust your regimen, let them know. For example, you may find that your blood glucose levels tend to be high when you test in the morning. This could be because your body is "rebounding" from a very low blood glucose level while you sleep. Try testing your blood around 3 a.m. If you discover hypoglycemia, treat it as you normally would.

Monitoring can be frustrating. Despite all your best efforts, you may sometimes come up with readings that are too high for no apparent reason. But if you find that you're avoiding testing, ask yourself why. Are you trying to avoid facing some of the problems in managing diabetes that are bound to occur at some time or other? If so, ask for some support from your health care team. They are convinced of the importance of SMBG to your health. They can help you track down the culprit. You may need to change your eating habits or your medication plan. But don't give up on testing.

Emergencies

Dealing with high and low blood glucose levels is a fact of life with diabetes. People with type 1 diabetes are more susceptible to swings in blood glucose levels than are people with type 2 diabetes. But all people with diabetes should be aware of possible emergencies that can occur. It is important that you learn to recognize the warning signs and to have a plan for dealing with them. Discuss with your health care team what you should be on the lookout for and what you should do if you suspect an emergency situation may be developing. Also talk to your family, friends, and coworkers about what to do in an emergency. If you are in danger, you may not always be able to handle the situation yourself. Being prepared is your best bet, and frequent monitoring of blood glucose will prevent most emergencies.

Your potential emergencies are caused by glucose levels that are either too high or too low. The most common condition is hypoglycemia, or low blood sugar. This is a problem for those

Brittle Diabetes?

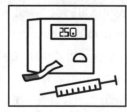
You used to hear the term brittle diabetes often—before blood glucose monitoring became possible for everyone. It refers to wide, unpredictable swings in blood glucose. Now, it's rarer for people with diabetes to be clueless, and frustrated, about why they can't control blood glucose levels.

Why do blood glucose levels swing so wide? The changes can be created by several factors, working alone or together. Food is not absorbed in the same amount of time every time you eat. Insulin is absorbed at different rates from under the skin. The stresses and strains of everyday living create the release of different amounts of stress hormones at different times.

Brittle Diabetes? (continued)

Has SMBG made brittle diabetes extinct? For most people, yes. A regular program of testing yields plenty of clues about why your blood glucose levels go up and down. But some people's bodies have exaggerated responses to food, medication, and stress. They may inject the same dose of the same insulin at the same time of day and eat about the same thing every day, but their blood glucose levels are high one day and low the next. Extremely uncontrollable swings in blood glucose level are primarily a problem for people who inject insulin.

Figuring out why this happens takes some doing. Some places to start looking for answers are:

■ **Timing of insulin injections:** Are you giving your regular insulin a full 30 to 45 minutes to get ready to work before you eat? See the chart in Chapter 4 on timing insulin injections according to premeal blood glucose levels.

■ **Insulin dose:** Are you sure you are measuring your dose accurately? Also, too much insulin at one time can take varying amounts of time to work. Would using an insulin pump help? It delivers the same size dose spread out over time.

■ **Injection sites:** Are you on a regular rotation schedule? Insulin is absorbed at the most consistent rate from the abdomen.

■ **Injection depth:** Do you inject your insulin at the same depth each time?

■ **Blood flow:** Do you inject into areas where muscles are at work? Is your home hot and your office cold? Do you smoke? Working muscles and warm temperatures speed up absorption. Cool temperatures and tobacco slow down absorption.

■ **Hypoglycemia:** Do you have frequent bouts of very low blood glucose? Your body's natural defenses to this (glucose release from the liver) can be spoiling your insulin's work.

■ **Neuropathy:** Do you have nerve damage that affects your absorption of food? Nerve damage can slow digestion or can produce unexpected bouts of diarrhea.

■ **Dehydration:** Do you have sustained periods of high blood glucose that drain your body of fluids? The less water in your body, the harder it is for your insulin to flow into tissues.

Causes of Hypoglycemia

- Too much insulin
- Too little carbohydrate
- Too little food
- Too much exercise
- A delayed meal
- Alcohol on an empty stomach

taking insulin or oral diabetes medications (sulfonylureas). Dangerously high levels of blood glucose can lead to diabetic ketoacidosis (DKA) in people with type 1 diabetes. People with type 2 diabetes can develop hyperglycemic hyperosmolar non-ketotic syndrome (HHNS) if glucose levels climb too high. DKA is rare in people with type 2 diabetes; HHNS is rare in people with type 1 diabetes. Both DKA and HHNS can lead to coma, shock, respiratory distress, and death, if not treated promptly.

Hypoglycemia

Hypoglycemia is not unusual for people with diabetes who take glucose-lowering medications, such as insulin (then it's called an "insulin reaction") or a sulfonylurea drug. It occurs when blood glucose levels get too low. At the beginning of a hypoglycemic reaction, you might feel dizzy, sweaty, shaky, or faint. If untreated, you could lose consciousness or have seizures.

On average, people with type 1 diabetes have one or two episodes of hypoglycemia each week. It is much less common in people with type 2 diabetes. Hypoglycemia is usually caused by insulin doing its job too well. In people without diabetes, the body stops releasing insulin before glucose levels fall too low. But in people with diabetes, especially those injecting insulin, there is no shutdown in insulin release.

Another interesting, if frustrating, fact about diabetes is this: The body's use of insulin is inconsistent. Even if you always give yourself the same dose of insulin or oral diabetes medication, you could end up with more than enough insulin to handle the glucose in your blood. This can happen even when you are doing everything, including eating, the same as usual.

How much insulin your body needs can change. This depends on many things:

- how much food you eat
- what kind of food you eat
- how much exercise you get
- when you exercise versus when you take your medication
- where you're injecting insulin
- the state of your health
- how much stress you're under.

It's impossible to control all of these things perfectly each day, no matter how hard you try. And insulin will do its job of clearing glucose from the blood even if it means that blood glucose levels fall too low. Hypoglycemia usually occurs just before meals, during or after strenuous exercise, or when insulin is peaking. Sometimes you may even get hypoglycemia during the night when you are sleeping.

Looking for Hypoglycemia

The symptoms (what you feel) and signs (what someone else can see) of hypoglycemia are divided into two groups:

- Caused by effect of low blood glucose on autonomic nervous system: shakiness, nervousness, sweating, irritability, impatience, chills and clamminess, rapid heartbeat, anxiety, light-headedness, and hunger
- Caused by effect of low blood glucose on the brain: sleepiness, anger, stubbornness, sadness, lack of coordination, blurred vision, nausea, tingling or numbness in the lips or tongue, nightmares, crying out during sleep, headaches, strange behavior, delirium, confusion, personality change, and unconsciousness

Low Blood Glucose Symptoms. It's important that you learn your own signs of hypoglycemia. Different people may experience different feelings during hypoglycemia, so it is important to know what signals your body gives during a low glucose reaction. The only sure way to know whether you have hypoglycemia is to test your blood glucose. Your signal to test may include shakiness, nervousness, sweating, chills and clamminess, rapid heartbeat, trouble concentrating, headache, dizziness, light-headedness, moodiness, clumsiness, tingling in your face or lips, extreme hunger, or irritability. These symptoms can happen at any time. You could even wake up in the middle of the night with a nightmare because of hypoglycemia.

Each person's reaction to low blood glucose can cause a different set of symptoms. It's unlikely that you will have them all. Some of the symptoms, such as nervousness, shakiness, hunger, and light-headedness, are considered early warning signs. They are called *autonomic symptoms* because low blood sugar affects the autonomic nervous system of the body to create these symptoms. The autonomic nerves control many of the things the body does automatically, without your having to think about them: opening blood vessels, making your heart beat, and controlling your breathing. Sometimes, you might not notice the autonomic symptoms at all. You might be anxious about a test or new job. Or your heart may be beating faster because you just got a speeding ticket.

Some of the symptoms of hypoglycemia appear due to the effect of prolonged low blood glucose on the brain. These include anger, sadness, lack of coordination, and blurred vision. It may be hard to know if you are sad because of hypoglycemia or because you had a fight with a friend. When in doubt, don't wait for the symptoms to go away. Test your blood, because that's the only way you can tell for sure.

Tip: How do you know whether you have had a hypoglycemic reaction during the night? Certain symptoms may tell you. Do you find your pajamas and sheets damp in the morning? Have you had restless sleep and nightmares? When you wake up, do you have a headache or still feel tired? You may have to test your blood around 2 or 3 a.m. a few times and try to match your results with your food, exercise, and medication doses from the previous day and evening. This will help you pinpoint what is really going on.

Some people have a hard time detecting oncoming hypoglycemia. If you have had episodes of low blood glucose often, especially if you have had diabetes for many years, you could lose the ability to feel the early warning signs of hypoglycemia. People who tend to miss the early symptoms are said to have *hypoglycemia unawareness.* If you have hypoglycemia unawareness, you can have a severe hypoglycemic episode unexpectedly. People who practice tight control of blood glucose levels increase their chances of having low blood glucose reactions. Having many episodes can cause you to stop sensing the warning signs of hypoglycemia. This can

Hypoglycemia Unawareness

Some people lose the ability to know when their blood glucose level has fallen to a dangerous level. They are missing the early warning signs of hypoglycemia. For many people, the first symptom of low blood glucose is impaired thinking.

Hypoglycemia unawareness seems to occur more often in people who tightly control their blood glucose. It is common in pregnant women. There is some evidence that frequent bouts of low blood glucose can bring on hypoglycemia awareness. Avoiding even mild hypoglycemia can help restore awareness of symptoms. Sometimes this means increasing blood glucose goals to higher numbers, such as increasing between meal goals to 140 mg/dl instead of 120.

If you or your health care team suspect that you have hypoglycemia unawareness, you need to establish some safety nets:

■ Increase the number of times you test your blood glucose every day

■ Always test before driving

■ Discuss your hypoglycemic episodes with your health care team so you can look for patterns to use as warning cues

■ Expect to educate more of the people you're with everyday about hypoglycemia and how to help you.

lead to even more episodes of very low blood glucose. For these reasons, blood glucose testing has added importance for people in intensive diabetes management programs and for people who have hypoglycemia unawareness.

Hypoglycemic symptoms can serve as important clues to whether you are having a low glucose reaction. But they are not always the full story. Sometimes the symptoms could be due to something else. Unless you test your blood glucose level, you could overtreat or overreact, causing glucose levels to soar.

Maybe you have read that hypoglycemia occurs when your blood glucose levels fall below 50 mg/dl. But many people may have blood glucose readings below this level and feel no symptoms. Others may start to have symptoms of hypoglycemia when their blood glucose levels are higher than 50 mg/dl. All this can be very confusing. To start, ask your doctor what glucose levels to look out for when you suspect hypoglycemia. Make note of the symptoms you are experiencing. You will soon learn what level is too low for you.

Treatment. If you think you are having a hypoglycemic reaction, you need to first test your blood glucose level. Talk to your health care team about the blood glucose level at which you should begin treatment. Although it's always best to test before treating, this may not always be possible. What if you don't have your glucose testing equipment with you? Should you wait until you get home? No! Treat your symptoms immediately. Never wait until you get home, especially if you have to drive.

When you are having severe hypoglycemia, you need to eat or drink a sugar that can be rapidly absorbed from your digestive tract and into your blood. But that doesn't mean you should go overboard on sweet foods, especially if you are on a weight-reducing diet. Make sure to use some restraint so your blood glucose levels don't go soaring in the other direction.

Tip: One way to gauge how much glucose to take during a hypoglycemic reaction is to do a little test. When your blood glucose is about 100 mg/dl or less, take your favorite fast-acting sugar. Wait 15 minutes, then retest. Did your blood glucose rise 25, 30, or 50 mg/dl, or more? This will give you an idea of how to treat your hypoglycemia. You'll be less likely to overtreat low blood glucose if you can predict how much your treatment will increase blood glucose. Ask your health care team what blood glucose levels to aim for following treatment of hypoglycemia.

There are many choices of fast-acting sugars. Don't use chocolate or candy bars to treat low blood sugar. The fat in those foods slows down absorption.

You're best prepared for low blood glucose if you carry around a measured amount of "pocket sugar." This should be about 10 to 15 grams of glucose (about 1 Fruit or 1 Starch Exchange). The easiest and most convenient fast-acting sugar is found in glucose tablets or gel, available at pharmacies. Two to five glucose tablets or one package of glucose gel (check the labels to be sure of the dose) will bring quick relief.

After taking your quick-fix treatment for hypoglycemia, retest your blood after 15 minutes. If you still have low blood glucose, you may need to take another dose of 10 to 15 grams of carbohydrate. If your next meal or snack is more than 30 minutes away, have a follow-up snack after you have treated your hypoglycemia. Call your doctor before your next dose of medication.

Severe Hypoglycemia. If symptoms of hypoglycemia go unnoticed, or ignored, you could develop severe hypoglycemia. When your blood glucose level is very low for too long, your

Fast-Acting Sugars for Hypoglycemia

Each of these has 10 to 15 grams of carbohydrate for treating hypoglycemia:

- Two to five glucose tablets
- Two tablespoons of raisins
- Half a can of a regular soda
- Four ounces of orange juice
- 5 to 7 Lifesavers
- 6 jellybeans
- 10 gumdrops
- 2 large lumps or teaspoons of sugar
- 2 teaspoons of honey or corn syrup
- A tube (0.68 ounces) of Cake Mate decorator gel
- 6 to 8 ounces of skim or 1% milk

brain does not get enough glucose and you can lose consciousness. This is a real emergency. The best way to deal with severe hypoglycemia is to take precautions so that it doesn't happen in the first place. Be alert to your symptoms and treat yourself right away. Don't wait to see if it gets worse or put off treatment until a more convenient time. Also, your family, friends, coworkers, and whoever you spend time with need some training. Either you or a member of your health care team should instruct them on the signs of severe hypoglycemia, and what to do should it develop. If you are elderly and taking oral diabetes medications (sulfonylureas) or insulin, you are at especially high risk for developing severe hypoglycemia.

During a hypoglycemic reaction you can become so confused and irritable that you refuse help. Those around you may have to be persistent to get you the help you need. They can save you from a coma and a trip to the hospital by insisting that you take some form of glucose quickly. Your life will be easier and safer if those with whom you spend the most time can spot a low glucose reaction and know what to do about it.

If you become unconscious, someone else must take over. You will not be able to eat or drink anything. But your blood glucose levels need to go up immediately. The safest remedy is to get a glucagon injection. Your helper should call for emergency help at once if he or she does not know how to inject glucagon. Glucagon is a hormone made by the pancreas that causes the liver to release glucose. It also inhibits insulin release. Glucagon will not work on someone who has no glucose stored in the liver. This can happen in cases of starvation or chronic hypoglycemia or in people who are alcoholics.

If you are prone to hypoglycemia, you'll need to train someone you trust how to inject glucagon. Talk to your doctor about whether you should buy a glucagon kit, which is available by prescription. If so, ask your family or close friends to

Tip: If you live alone, you may be concerned about having a severe hypoglycemic reaction while you are sleeping. Your best bet is to monitor your blood glucose levels before you go to sleep and occasionally during the night. If your blood glucose level is dropping, eat a small protein-filled snack before going to sleep.

learn with you how to use glucagon so they know what to do. The kit has a special glucagon syringe that is filled with a diluting solution. Kits usually last a year before the glucagon and diluting solution expire (check the date on the box). However, if you premix the glucagon in diluting solution, the mixture only lasts about 48 hours and should be kept refrigerated.

After you have been treated with glucagon, you may vomit, so your head needs to be elevated above your stomach. You should respond to glucagon within 5 to 20 minutes. When you are awake enough to chew and swallow, you should have some clear fluid, such as 7-Up, to settle your stomach and then eat a substantial snack, such as a roll with peanut butter or half of a cheese sandwich. If you do not respond to the first shot, your helper should repeat your injection and get emergency help right away.

If you have such a low blood glucose level that you have to take glucagon, be sure to let your health care team know. Also tell them if you are having frequent bouts of even mild hypoglycemia. By working together, you might find a pattern in your insulin, diet, or activity routine that may be causing the hypoglycemia. With clues, you and your health care team can do some problem solving and decide on some changes to prevent these bouts of hypoglycemia.

You need to wear medical identification jewelry or carry a medical information card. This gives others the information they need to help you during a bout of hypoglycemia. If you use insulin or an oral diabetes medication (sulfonylurea), be prepared to treat low blood glucose at all times.

Pregnancy. Pregnant women are especially motivated to keep tight control over blood glucose levels. In addition, many pregnant women become desensitized to low blood glucose levels, and some experience hypoglycemia unawareness. Thus, they are more likely to have mild and moderate bouts of hypoglycemia. That's why it is so important to develop and keep up a blood glucose testing routine and to test when hypoglycemia is most likely, in between meals and in the middle of the night. You need to treat any blood glucose level under 60 mg/dl.

If you are pregnant and become unconscious, special precautions are necessary. The baby may be harmed more by high blood glucose and ketone levels and by drastic changes in blood glucose than by the hypoglycemia itself. Therefore, your doctor may suggest that you receive only half of the normal dose of glucagon at the beginning of a severe episode of hypoglycemia. After 10 minutes, if you do not regain consciousness or blood glucose levels do not rise, you need another shot. Make sure that those with whom you spend time know that you are pregnant and know what to do if you develop severe hypoglycemia.

Exercise. Exercise lowers blood glucose levels, so you have to be extra careful to avoid hypoglycemia during exercise. Try not to overdo it by working out really hard especially when you are alone. Instead, exercise at a pool or gym where others are around. If you can't get to a gym, jog or cycle with a friend. If you'll be burning a lot of calories, make sure to have a healthy snack beforehand. For more information about matching food needs to exercise, see Chapter 8.

If you do feel as though you are becoming hypoglycemic while you are exercising, stop at once! Don't say, "I'll just do one more lap," or "Just five minutes more won't hurt." Test your blood glucose level right away and eat a fast-acting sugar snack if you need it. If you want to continue your workout, eat a snack and take a 15-minute break before starting back. If you don't do this, your blood glucose level will drop again, quickly. Studies show that hypoglycemia is even more likely to occur 4 to 10 hours after your exercise, than during the activity or shortly after. Monitor your blood levels after exercising to find out how your body reacts.

Sexual Activity. If you are prone to hypoglycemia when you exercise or at night, you may also have a low blood glucose reaction following sexual activity. This can be especially true if you are intimate at night. This is when your blood glucose levels typically dip, so you may need to adjust your insulin or have a snack before or after sexual activity. Be especially careful if you are combining sexual activity with alcohol.

Heart Disease. Hypoglycemia can cause your heart to beat faster than normal. If you have heart disease, talk to your doctor about how hypoglycemia might affect your particular condition. Your doctor may recommend that you keep your blood glucose levels a little higher than normal to reduce the risk of developing hypoglycemia.

Alcohol. Alcohol lowers blood glucose levels. Normally, when your blood glucose levels begin to drop too low, your liver will convert stored starch to glucose. This helps protect you from a severe reaction temporarily and gives you time to recognize and treat hypoglycemia. But alcohol interferes with this process. If you drink alcohol, you may lapse into a severe state of hypoglycemia with little warning. There's more information about alcohol and your meal plan in Chapter 8.

Dawn Phenomenon. Your body has a normal mechanism that wakes you up and gives you energy to start the day. Your body responds to the wake-up call of the growth hormones. These hormones depress the activity of insulin, allowing blood glucose to rise between around 4 and 8 a.m. This is called the dawn phenomenon. The dawn phenomenon can be one reason for blood glucose readings and ketone levels that are quite high when you wake up.

If high morning blood glucose levels seem to occur mysteriously, discuss the problem with your health care team and talk about the best way to treat it. You may need to eat less food at breakfast or the night before or increase your pre-breakfast insulin dose. Let your health care team know what choices you would prefer.

Hyperglycemia

Having chronically high levels of glucose in your blood or achieving poor glucose control can lead to many of the complications of diabetes over time. But blood glucose levels can also become dangerously high in the short term and cause a life-threatening situation that could result in coma or death. It is important to know what the warning signs are and how to treat it. But it's best to prevent the situation from ever occurring.

Type 1 Diabetes. Having too little insulin in your body leads to too much glucose. A rare and serious, but totally preventable, emergency can arise if you ignore high blood glucose. Diabetic ketoacidosis (DKA) occurs when you don't get enough insulin, which is mostly a problem for people with type 1 diabetes.

It can start innocently enough: you skip a dose of insulin, or you don't notice that the insulin in the bottle you've been using has gone bad, or you've got a clog in your insulin pump tubing. But an undetected high blood glucose level, combined with not testing your urine for ketones, can buy you coma, shock, pneumonia, difficulty breathing, and even death. Small children can also develop swelling of the brain (cerebral edema). DKA can occur in people with type 1 diabetes who have not yet been diagnosed, but once insulin therapy has begun, you can always avoid it, if you do the tests.

People tend to get DKA for one of two reasons. Psychological or social pressures may cause people to stop taking their insulin. Teenagers may not be emotionally prepared to take on the burden and responsibility of self testing and injections. Or they may feel embarrassed by having a condition that sets them apart. Some teens may even stop taking their insulin as a way of rebelling or dealing with the frustration of having diabetes. Emotionally or mentally disturbed adults may drop their therapy.

DKA can also develop during periods of stress or illness. When the body has to deal with a bacterial infection, a sickness such as the flu, or a stressful situation, hormones cause the liver to release stored glucose. These hormones also block the effects of insulin.

Anytime your body doesn't have enough insulin, muscles can't take in the glucose that they need. They feel starved, so your body breaks down fat for energy. Ketones are the by-products of this breakdown. If ketones form faster than your body can get rid of them in the urine, they build up in the blood. Ketones poison the blood with acidic products. At the same time, glucose spills into your urine, your kidneys produce more urine, and you get dehydrated. When you have dehydration and ketones in the blood, you've got DKA.

Sometimes when you are sick and can't eat, you may think, "I shouldn't take insulin today." But this is the worst thing you can do. Even though you aren't feeding your body, it still needs insulin to cover its 24-hour insulin needs, plus you are producing extra glucose. So, in addition to your usual dose of insulin, you may need extra insulin.

Sick days call for more frequent blood glucose monitoring and urine testing for ketones. Do both at least every four hours until you're feeling better. Any time you feel queasy or are vomiting, even if your blood glucose doesn't test high, you need to check your urine for ketones. A buildup of ketones can cause nausea.

If your urine shows trace or small amounts of ketones, that's not so bad. Even people without diabetes have measurable ketones in their urine when they are sick. If your urine has moderate or large amounts of ketones, call your health care team immediately. You probably need to take extra regular insulin right away and need the advice of your health care team. If urinary ketones do not promptly go down, or if you are vomiting and it cannot be controlled, you need emergency help at once. Make sure that those who spend time with you know what to look for and what to do if DKA should occur.

Signs of DKA. DKA gives plenty of warning before it happens. If you regularly test your blood glucose several times during the day, you won't miss the most important warning sign: high blood glucose (over 250 mg/dl). Call a member of your health care team if you have an unusually high blood glucose level and any of the following:

- lack of appetite
- pains in your stomach
- vomiting or feeling sick to your stomach
- blurry vision
- fever warm, dry, or flushed skin
- difficulty breathing
- feelings of weakness
- sleepiness
- a fruity odor on your breath
- classic signs of hyperglycemia: intense thirst, a dry mouth, and the need to urinate frequently.

Fast Action for Ketones

If you do have high ketones, along with high blood glucose levels, you will have to lower them immediately. This can be done by:
- Taking additional insulin: Consult with your health care team to know how much additional regular insulin you may need.
- Drinking plenty of water: This helps to prevent dehydration.
- Avoiding exercise: Exercise just causes more fat-burning because there isn't any insulin. If you continue to exercise, you could counteract the effects of taking extra insulin.

Type 2 Diabetes. Compared with people with type 1 diabetes, people with type 2 diabetes do not have dramatic swings in blood glucose levels. But they can sustain high blood glucose levels over prolonged periods without even knowing it. This can wear on the body and cause diabetic complications. By monitoring your blood glucose levels regularly you can guard against chronic hyperglycemia.

Acute hyperglycemia can occur in people with type 2 diabetes and is life-threatening. Hyperglycemia in people with type 2 diabetes does not usually produce ketones. But blood glucose levels can soar to over 600 mg/dl and even as high as 1,000 mg/dl. This sometimes happens before diabetes is diagnosed. Extreme hyperglycemia can induce a coma.

Hyperglycemic hyperosmolar nonketotic syndrome (HHNS) occurs almost exclusively in people with type 2 diabetes. It can happen to people who manage their diabetes with diet and exercise only, those who use oral diabetes medications, and those who use insulin. Most cases occur in people who don't use insulin. One-third of all cases of HHNS are caused by undiagnosed diabetes. In many instances, people have just let their diabetes go out of control for too long. HHNS can be caused by stress, alcohol, untreated infection, diuretics, or even a stroke. Sometimes even something simple, like not being able to get a glass of water when you want one, can contribute. This occurs more often in people who have restricted mobility, such as the elderly, or in people who cannot take proper care of themselves. Also, many elderly people lose their sense of thirst and may not drink enough fluids.

The process that leads to HHNS is this: blood glucose levels go higher and higher, urine output goes up, and dehydration sets in. This process may go on for days or weeks. Extreme dehydration eventually leads to confusion and lack of ability to even get a drink or make it to the toilet. With that much glucose in the blood, plus the fluid loss, blood gets thicker. Eventually, the severe dehydration leads to seizures, coma, and death.

Signs of HHNS. Because vomiting is not usually a sign of HHNS, people often become much sicker than those with DKA before they are diagnosed. If you experience any of the following signs, your blood glucose level should be checked at once and a doctor should be called. Be sure those around you know what to do, because you may not be able to react.

■ dry, parched mouth

■ extreme thirst, although this may gradually disappear

■ sleepiness or confusion

■ warm, dry skin with no sweating

■ high blood glucose: if it's over 350 mg/dl, call your health care team; if it's over 500 mg/dl, have someone take you to the hospital immediately.

If you are testing your blood glucose levels even once a day, you'll be alerted to high blood glucose levels well before the process that leads to HHNS gets going. Because illness can make blood glucose levels rise, you'll want to test three to four times a day when you're sick. It's also very important to drink plenty of caffeine- and alcohol-free fluids. You may need to take insulin, even if you don't ordinarily use it.

Besides illness, certain situations can increase your risk for HHNS.

■ **Medications.** Ask your doctor, pharmacist, or other member of your health care team about glucocorticoids (steroids), diuretics, phenytoin (Dilantin), cimetidine (Tagamet), and beta blockers, especially Inderal. If you take any of these medications, you need to test your blood glucose regularly.

■ **Treatments.** HHNS can occur in people having peritoneal dialysis or intravenous feedings because of the large amounts of glucose used. If you're on either of these treatments, you need to test your blood glucose regularly.

■ **Nursing homes.** About one-third of the cases of HHNS occur in people living in nursing homes. This can happen when residents have to wait for staff to offer them something to drink, and they may get dehydrated. Insist on regular blood glucose monitoring.

Chapter 6:
Diabetes Tools

The average person with diabetes spends $2,500 each year at the pharmacy. You'll need medications, test strips, a blood glucose meter . . . so, it pays to make informed choices.

Mastering the lifestyle skills—food, exercise, and stress management—is key to managing your diabetes care plan. But that's only half the battle. Taking charge of your diabetes also means mastering the science and technology that underlies the disease.

This means understanding the medical basis of diabetes and becoming familiar with the tools of the trade. All of the various supplies that can help you keep your diabetes in control form a sort of high-tech toolbox. This toolbox consists of everything from the simple finger-stick lancet and visually read test strips to the latest computerized blood glucose management systems.

As with any tool, each piece of equipment must be carefully chosen to suit your individual needs. Once chosen, you must learn to use and properly maintain the equipment in your diabetes toolbox. It may seem a bit overwhelming at first, but your health care team is there to help you with these challenges. Talk to them. Ask them what they would recommend and what their other patients like or dislike about various tools and systems.

The best catalog for a diabetes toolbox is the *American Diabetes Association Resource Guide,* published every year by *Diabetes Forecast* magazine (see Resources). This guide lists and describes all available diabetes care tools on the market. The next best references are the regular advertisements and the Shopper's Guide section in *Diabetes Forecast.*

You can find information about insulin and insulin pumps in Chapter 4.

Blood Glucose Meters

In your efforts to control blood glucose levels, your blood glucose meter is essential. Only by keeping close tabs on your blood glucose levels and recognizing when they are abnormal can you take steps to remedy the situation.

There are many different brands of blood glucose meters on the market today that detect how much glucose is floating around in the blood. Most meters rely on one of two different methods to detect glucose in the blood. Some meters use a chemical that changes color when it comes in contact with glucose. With these meters, a drop of blood is placed on one end of a plastic test strip, which changes color, depending on the amount of glucose in the blood. The strip is then inserted in the meter, which measures the color intensity and produces a computer-translated electronic readout of how much glucose (mg/dl) is in your blood.

Other meters measure an electric current in the blood that depends on the amount of glucose present. With these meters, blood is also placed on a small area of a test strip. A special enzyme transfers electrons from glucose to a chemical in the strip, and the meter measures this flow of electrons as current. The amount of current depends on how much glucose is in the blood. This weak current flows through the strip and is measured in the meter. The meter produces an electronic reading of blood glucose levels (mg/dl) in the blood.

There is a new glucose meter on the market that allows you to take blood from any part of your body, not just your fingertips. Check the *American Diabetes Association Resource Guide* for more information. And the Food and Drug Administration is currently reviewing two new types of glucose meters. One is a glucose sensor that is placed under your skin and takes a glucose reading every five minutes. Another is a watch that you calibrate once in the morning, then wear on your wrist all day. A sensor interprets samples of your perspiration and gives you glucose readings when you need them. Both of these meters promise more comfort and ease of use to people with diabetes, so watch for them.

Meters that use a color assay and those that measure a current are about the same in precision (how close readings of the same sample are to each other) and accuracy (how close the reading is to the actual amount). All meters perform the same basic job of measuring the amount of glucose in blood. But all meters are not created equal, even among meters of the same type. Some models may fit your needs better, depending on your particular lifestyle. To choose the right meter, you may want to consider several aspects.

Insurance Coverage

Before you invest in any meter, check with your diabetes center, insurance plan, or company health program. They may pay for only specific meters or have a cost allowance. Also, find out if you are covered for the test strips and the quantity allowed.

Your Budget

You may be surprised when you go to buy replacement strips for your meter. The meter that seemed like a bargain at the time of purchase may turn into a major expense when it comes time to pay for strips, especially if you don't get reimbursed for them by your health care insurance. In the long run, the strips will cost you more money than the meter itself. Most meters will only use one kind of strip. Make sure you check the cost of the strips your meter uses before you buy it. Several independent manufacturers now make generic strips that work in meters that are based on a color change. They are still working on generic strips that can be used in brand-name electronic meters. But make sure your meter can use the generic strips before you buy them. Some manufacturers will not support you if you run into trouble using anything other than the recommended strips. Check the *American Diabetes Association Resource Guide* and ads for lists of companies that sell generic strips.

Your Dexterity

Some blood glucose meters are about the size of a credit card. Some even come as small as a pen. Others are more like a calculator. You may find the smaller models difficult to manipulate. If you have trouble with small hand and finger movements, you may want to consider a larger meter. However, these might be heavier and more difficult to carry around. Also, consider what strips you need to use for your meter. Some come packaged in a vial, while others are individually wrapped in foil. The foil wrappings can be difficult to remove, so you may want to avoid brands that require this type of strip.

Your Schedule

If your life is a constant battle with the clock, stay away from devices that require too much time. Some meters can measure blood glucose just 12 seconds after a drop of blood lands on the strip. These ultra-fast devices can be especially useful in work and social situations where a few minutes here and there really do make a difference.

Your Vision

Whether you have severe visual impairment or just have a hard time focusing on small print, you may want to bear this aspect in mind when choosing a meter. Several companies offer products for visually disabled users. Meters are available with built-in voice modules or separate plug-in voice synthesizers. Otherwise, look for a meter with a large digital display if you are having difficulty seeing.

If you have any degree of color blindness, test-drive a few different models. Make sure that you have no trouble reading the digital display. Some meters have black and gray displays while others feature red or green numbers that may be difficult to distinguish.

If you have even some vision loss, perhaps a close companion or family member can help. Make sure that they are trained in the use of your meter and the other components of your diabetes toolbox.

Support System

If you are using a meter for the first time, consider one that offers a video that teaches you how to do the test. A picture or visual image can make a seemingly complicated procedure look crystal clear. Also make sure that the company has a 24-hour toll-free number to call, should you have questions about the meter. Sometimes a quick phone call may clear up a simple problem. Also check that your health care team is familiar with the model you purchase and that supplies are available in your geographic area.

User-Friendliness

Make sure your meter or monitoring system is easy to handle. Several features can make meters easier to use. Models that don't require wiping strips can eliminate messy problems with disposing of a blood sample. Some models require a bigger sized drop of blood. Ask how much blood is required for each model you might be considering. With some models too little blood may give a faulty reading and you may need to repeat the test. This can be inconvenient at best but could be more of a problem for those with poor circulation in their hands or who must test in cold environments.

Accuracy

Testing strips can vary from batch to batch. There may be differences in the amount of chemical on the strips in each batch. So, when you open a new batch of strips, you must standardize or calibrate your meter to make up for these small differences. If you don't calibrate, all your results with the new strips may read as higher or lower than they really are. Some machines calibrate all by themselves—you don't have to do anything when you open a new batch of strips. With some glucose meters the procedure can be a little tedious. Some models have a two-step procedure that uses a special strip. If you lose the instruction manual that comes with your meter, don't panic. Instructions for calibration are included in every new package of strips.

Calibrating your meter for every new batch of strips is one way to ensure that your meter is measuring your glucose level accurately. But there is one more thing you must do to make sure you are getting the right readings. Even the best glucose meters can drift from time to time and give higher or lower readings than they should. To get around this you need to test your machine every month using a standard solution known as a "control" solution that contains a known amount of glucose. If you measure the amount of glucose in this standard solution in your meter and your meter shows a reading that is either too high or too low, your machine could be giving you a faulty reading. But first check to see if your problems are being caused by old or damaged test strips. Then call the manufacturer of your meter. There may be something wrong with your meter. You can usually order a vial of standard glucose solution by calling your machine's manufacturer. All have toll-free numbers.

Getting good accuracy also depends on your blood testing technique. There are easy ways to test how well you are using your meter. Take your meter with you when you visit your doctor or diabetes educator and have him or her watch your technique. Or, have your doctor or diabetes educator measure your blood glucose level with his or her meter and compare those results to yours. Or, measure your blood glucose level with your own meter when your blood is drawn for laboratory glucose tests. Record your results. The two readings are best compared

Diabetes: Fact or Myth?

"I've been testing my blood glucose level for years. With all my practice, I get accurate results every time."

Researchers found that practice, at least in the area of blood glucose testing, does not make perfect. Fresh from training by a diabetes educator, people start off getting accurate results. But, as time goes by, they begin to get sloppy. Accuracy actually decreases over time.

You can avoid this source of error in your blood testing results by having your technique checked at every visit with your doctor or diabetes educator. Here are some potential problem areas for you and your health care team to watch:

■ **Your blood.** Are you getting enough blood on the test strip? With many older meters, it's important to cover the pad on the strip completely. To increase blood flow, wash your hands in warm water, hang your hand down, and massage your hand from your palm out to the fingertip before pricking. You may find it less painful to prick the side of your finger, rather than the fleshy pad. Allow the blood to fall onto the test strip pad without actually touching your finger to the pad. The oils from your skin could cause your meter to give you an inaccurate reading. For some strips, once the drop is on the pad, try not to smear it, and don't add more blood. If your meter requires that you wipe excess blood from the test strip pad, make sure you use only the material (for instance, a cotton ball or sterile pad) the meter manufacturer recommends. The fibers from the wiping material could reduce meter accuracy.

■ **Test strips.** Are your strips fresh? Be aware of the expiration date. Look for color changes on the strip pad, which can indicate chemical spoilage. Avoid exposing the strips to light. Are you taking the time to calibrate your meter to each new batch of test strips? There are variations from one batch to another, even when they are made by the same manufacturer.

■ **Your meter.** Check your meter regularly with the control solution specified by the meter's manufacturer. Look in the instructions that came with the meter if you've forgotten how to do this. If your meter can be cleaned, do it periodically. You'll find a build-up of blood, dust, and lint.

when you are fasting. If you have just eaten, the comparison may not be accurate, because shortly after a meal, fingertip (capillary) blood glucose can be higher than that drawn from a vein.

When your lab-tested blood results are available, compare the numbers by the two methods. If you are using a meter that tests "whole blood," your results should be within 15 percent of the lab's results. (Some meters test "serum blood," the same as a lab, so your values should be fairly close.) For instance, if the lab results were 150 mg/dl, your technique and meter are accurate if your results were within the 127 to 173 mg/dl range. If your result was off by more than 15 percent, go over your technique with your diabetes educator or doctor. If they can't find any reason why your technique shouldn't be getting you accurate results, it's time to suspect that something may be wrong with your meter. Call the manufacturer, and ask about getting a replacement meter.

Meter Size

If you're on the move and don't relish the idea of lugging around a lot of excess baggage, consider investing in a pen- or card-sized meter. They slip easily into a shirt pocket or small purse. But be careful—they could get lost in a deep dark handbag or backpack. The larger sized meters stick out in either situation. If you do opt for the smaller version, make sure it's easy enough to handle.

Meter Memory

If you carry your meter around with you during the day, you may want one that stores more than one result in its memory. At night you can jot down the day's readings in your logbook. Some meters can store up to 250 meter readings that you can copy into your record book and take along on your trip to your physician or diabetes educator. On the other hand, if you take all of your readings at home with your logbook close at hand, meter memory may be less important. Either way, you will want the members of your health care team to go over the results of your log when you visit.

Data Management Systems

Diabetes management is much more than blood glucose readings. And data management systems can do much more than store blood glucose readings. These sophisticated meters can store many test results and information on time, date, insulin doses, exercise, and food intake. Some will allow you to store the number of grams of carbohydrate eaten. Some even have built-in alarm clocks. The most advanced systems can load all of this data into your or your health care team's computer. Surprisingly, data management systems don't cost too much more than regular meters. Most run $75 to $100 and often come with big rebates. These systems can give you a detailed picture of your overall diabetes management plan. (But, they won't eliminate your need to graph out your results, day by day, so you can see the trends in your blood glucose levels.) Before you buy a system, check to see if your health care team recommends one too. If so, make sure your system is compatible with theirs. Also call the manufacturer's toll-free number and ask them exactly what you will be getting. They should be willing to answer any questions you may have.

If you are a computer buff, you can also buy computer programs that take data management systems one step further. You can enter the data by hand or through an electronic download from your system. The program can then provide a trend analysis, averages, graphs, printouts, and more. This can make it easier for you and your health care team to pinpoint any problem areas that might arise. Check ads in the *American Diabetes Association Resource Guide* for these products.

Don't buy a high-end blood glucose data management system unless you can afford the extra $30 to $50, compared to lower-end models. Many people find that they can get along with a good logbook. This is especially true if you have type 2 diabetes and require less frequent monitoring. However, if you have type 1 diabetes and are managing your diabetes through intensive treatment, you might decide it is worth the extra cost.

Language

Some meter systems can display in English, Spanish, and even up to seven other languages.

Battery and Machine Replacement

Yes, glucose meters need batteries, too. But each model handles batteries differently. For some models you can buy the battery and insert it into the meter yourself. Some of these batteries can be fairly expensive and difficult to find. Other meters use standard equipment batteries—the same kind you might use in your flashlight or remote control. And some meters have no replaceable batteries. Before you buy any meter, find out what type of replacement battery it uses, whether the batteries are easy to find, and how expensive they are. With daily use, batteries generally have to be replaced every 1,000 readings. Most manufacturers will tell you how long the meter's batteries will last. Some companies will replace batteries for you, and others simply replace the whole meter. Companies that replace the whole meter usually have a toll-free number available. You can order the new meter by express delivery. The company supplies an envelope to ship back the old meter. Usually, you miss testing for no more than 2 days. During this period, you can test by using visually read blood glucose strips.

Blood Contamination

Contamination can be a serious concern if you have a blood-borne illness such as hepatitis or HIV infection. If this is the case, you will want to keep the handling of blood samples to a minimum. Consider late-model meters with no-wipe strips that absorb the whole blood sample. Also, don't share meters in which blood can contaminate the meter itself.

Convenience

If you commute to work, or split your time between two locations, you might want to buy two meters (make sure they use the same brand of test strip). You can keep one at home and the other at work. Lugging your meter back and forth every day can be a bit of a nuisance. Not only will you avoid the inconvenience, you will also avoid the hazard of forgetting to bring the meter back home or to work with you. If you use two meters, finding ones with memory will be less of an issue. You will need two logbooks to record the results from tests of both meters.

If the meter of your dreams turns out to be a real lemon, take heart. Many companies will provide you with a rebate for the return of any model meter. This rebate is good toward the purchase of their meter. Look for ads in *Diabetes Forecast* for companies that offers such trade-in deals. But before you trade in your current model make sure other conditions aren't causing your problems. Low iron, anemia, very low blood pressure, edema in fingers, and certain medications can also cause problems in getting accurate blood glucose readings.

Test Strips

The test strips that go in blood glucose meters are described in the section on blood glucose meters. You'll need to know about other kinds of test strips, too.

Visually Read Glucose Strips

There may be times when you can't use your blood glucose meter. Maybe it needs new batteries. Maybe you forgot it at work. Although these circumstances can usually be avoided in the United States, it might not be so unusual in developing countries where modern supplies often are in short demand. If you are traveling, you might find that you will have to fall back on visually read blood or urine strips. Visually read strips can also come in handy if your meter malfunctions, or you suspect it is malfunctioning for some reason. With visually read strips, you match the color of your test strip to a color chart on the side of the vial to estimate your blood glucose level.

Color patches for visually read strips usually progress in increments of 20 to 30 mg/dl. Readings can be educated guesswork. Some people with years of experience can read visually read strips as accurately as a meter. Visually read strips cost about the same as color-developed meter strips.

Glucose also shows up in your urine, and there are visually read strips that can tell you if glucose levels in your urine are too high, but they cannot measure levels that are too low. However, testing urine glucose is a poor way to determine your blood glucose level. For one thing, glucose doesn't show up in the urine until blood glucose levels are already quite high. And, urine glucose tests tell you how much glucose you had in your blood a few hours ago. This information is not useful for deciding insulin dosage, handling emergencies, or even evaluating your overall treatment program. Your health care team will discourage you from basing your diabetes management on urine glucose tests only.

If you have nothing else available use urine glucose strips to test your urine glucose. This will give you a ballpark estimate, but remember that these readings may not reflect your current blood glucose level. Also, urine glucose measurements can be altered by vitamin C, aspirin, fluid intake, dehydration, and failure to completely empty your bladder on your last trip to the bathroom.

If you have any degree of color blindness, check with your health care team to see what brand of strip might work best for you.

Visually Read Strips for Urine Ketones

If you don't have enough insulin available, your body will burn fat instead of glucose. This can happen when you don't inject enough insulin or when your body counteracts insulin's efforts with counterregulatory hormones, as during illness. Some of the products of fat burning are ketones. Ketones are a toxin to your body. It's important to detect them before they grow to large levels. This is why testing for urine ketones is important for people with diabetes, especially people with type 1 diabetes who do not make any insulin. People with type 2 diabetes usually produce some insulin and so are less likely to develop ketoacidosis. However, everyone with diabetes needs to know how and when to use ketone test strips.

To test urine for ketones, you use a visually read strip made to detect ketones in the urine. Ketone strips vary in how much time is needed between applying urine and reading the result—as little as 15 seconds or as long as 2 minutes—so it's important to know what timing is required for the strips you are using. Some ketone strips also measure glucose and have two test pads on each strip. Know which pad measures ketones and which color chart on the strip vial to compare it with.

Always Test for Ketones

- When your blood glucose readings are over 240 mg/dl
- When you are ill, especially when you have high fever, bouts of vomiting, or diarrhea
- During pregnancy, daily before breakfast (fasting)
- During acute stress, whether it is physical (such as surgery) or psychological (such as a new job)
- When you are chronically tired
- When you have fruity breath, vomiting, breathing difficulties, or are having a hard time concentrating.

The individually foil-wrapped ketone strips are the most expensive up front, but they last longer. Because you are unlikely to need to test ketones very often, they save you money in the long run, compared to ketone strips that come unwrapped in a vial. These will all spoil at the same time, probably about 6 months after you open the vial. However, each foil-wrapped strip has its "own" expiration date.

There are several reasons why you might have ketones in your urine. They can show up because of:

- too little food (this is called starvation ketosis and is usually seen when meals are very restricted in calories)
- hypoglycemia or low blood glucose (when no glucose is available, your body breaks down fat into glucose)
- hyperglycemia or high blood glucose (high blood glucose levels are a sign that insulin is not available to let glucose into cells. Your body breaks down fat because it can't use the glucose in the blood)
- illness
- lack of insulin
- effect of anti-insulin hormones

Unlike glucose levels, ketone levels aren't given in exact units like mg or dl. Instead, the side of the vial reads from

Fast Action for Ketones

If you do have high ketones, along with high blood glucose levels, you will have to lower them immediately. This can be done by:

- Taking additional insulin: Consult with your health care team to know how much additional regular insulin you may need.
- Drinking plenty of water: This helps to prevent dehydration.
- Avoiding exercise: Exercise just causes more fat-burning because there isn't any insulin. If you continue to exercise, you could counteract the effects of taking extra insulin.

zero and trace to small, moderate, and large. Some brands just score with + signs. If you read anything with more than zero or an occasional trace, ask your health care team what levels are dangerous for you. If you are getting levels higher than that, you may need to take prompt action. Always call your health care provider if you have ketones. Ask your health care team in advance what you should do.

Talk to your health care team members about what readings to look out for, and what to do should you have high ketones. Do this on one of your regular visits, before an emergency situation develops. There is more information on hyperglycemia and ketosis in Chapter 5.

If you are colorblind, check with your team members to see what brand of strip will be best for you.

Lancets

Many blood glucose meters come with a finger-sticking device and a few lancets. A few have the lancet built into the meter. If this device works for you, fine. But be aware that there are several kinds of devices and lancets. And not all lancets fit all finger-sticking devices. Make sure that you can get replacement lancets to fit your device. Check the prices for the replacement lancets in any instrument you are considering purchasing. Also know that different lancets will produce different sizes of blood drops. Make sure the device you are considering will help you get a drop of blood that is large enough to cover the test pad on the strips your meter uses. Finger-sticking devices often have two different caps or an adjustable tip that control how deep the lancets poke your finger. Use the shallowest poke possible to draw blood. It hurts less, and causes less scarring of your fingers. Lancets are sterile the first time only. Don't share lancets or lancing devices.

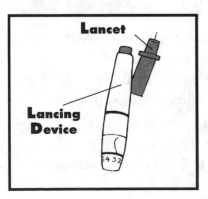

Making Mail Order Work for You

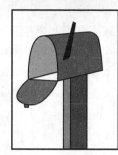

Purchasing your diabetes supplies, like insulin and test strips, through a mail-order supplier can be one way to save money when buying bulk. Here are some tips to help you use mail-order services wisely:

- If you live in a warm climate or order during the summer, ask how perishable items will be shipped. Insulin is sensitive to heat. Strips can spoil in excessive heat. Overnight shipping is best for these items.

- Find out prices by shopping around. Most mail-order firms have toll-free telephone numbers.

- When you start a new drug, whether it is insulin or an oral diabetes medication, buy it from a pharmacy. Your doctor may need to adjust the dosage—or take you off the drug altogether.

- Don't buy large quantities of a drug until your doctor has found the safe, effective dose for you. All medications require a doctor's prescription, but your doctor may want to make changes in your dose especially if the medication is new to you.

- Buy drugs you need now from the pharmacy. Use mail-order firms to buy drugs you use regularly to maintain your diabetes.

- If you depend on Medicare to help you pay for supplies, note that prices shown in advertisements or quoted over the phone may differ from the amount that Medicare will reimburse for that item. You may need to pay the difference.

- Order your supplies far enough in advance so your current supply won't run out before the new supplies arrive.

- Ask your doctor about generic drugs. Savings offered by mail-order firms come routinely from substituting generics for brand-name drugs.

- Inspect your prescription drugs carefully when they arrive. If they look different, call your supplier to double-check. Get the name of the generic's manufacturer for your records.

- Always follow your doctor's orders when taking prescription drugs. If the instructions that arrive with your medications differ from those your doctor gave you, call your doctor and ask which instructions to follow.

- Always keep copies of any orders you send through the mail. If you call in your order, be sure to write down when you placed the order and what you ordered.

- Inspect insulin vials carefully for signs of damage or crystallization on the inside of the vial. Call the doctor or mail-order firm immediately to report spoiled insulin.

- Check the expiration date on each item that arrives. If you'll need the item in 6 months, make sure it doesn't expire in 2 months. Send back all items with expiration dates that are "just around the corner."

Some people use lancets without the automatic lancing device to sample their blood. This takes some practice. If you can do it, you can save some money, and you won't have to lug the lancing device around with you. But many people find that the automatic lancing device is handy. It produces a uniform-sized stick and it enables you to poke fingers on either hand with the same ease. If you have trouble with your dexterity, look for an automatic lancing device that resets easily with a simple push-pull movement. The newest lancet uses a tiny laser beam to create a small hole for blood sampling.

Setting the Record Straight

One of the most important tools in your diabetes toolbox is also the most overlooked. The low-tech logbook may not look like much, but it will tell you and your health care team how well you are managing your diabetes and will alert you and them to any red flags that could signal a serious problem. Everyone gets a free logbook when buying a new meter. Many pharmacies don't carry logbooks because the meter manufacturers provide them to health care professionals instead. Ask your health care team if they can give you a logbook. You can also probably find logbooks through most mail order houses. Or call the toll-free number for your meter manufacturer to request more. You could also consider photocopying blank pages and compiling them in a loose-leaf notebook, or creating your own custom logbook.

You may want a lot of room to write in your logbook. Consider buying a spiral bound notebook or using a loose-leaf notebook, where you can add pages as needed, to jot down extra notes. You may find it useful to have extra space to record different symptoms and situations that could be relevant to your health. Your logbook is an important tool for

Sample Logbook Page for Blood Sugar Records

Month _____   Year _____

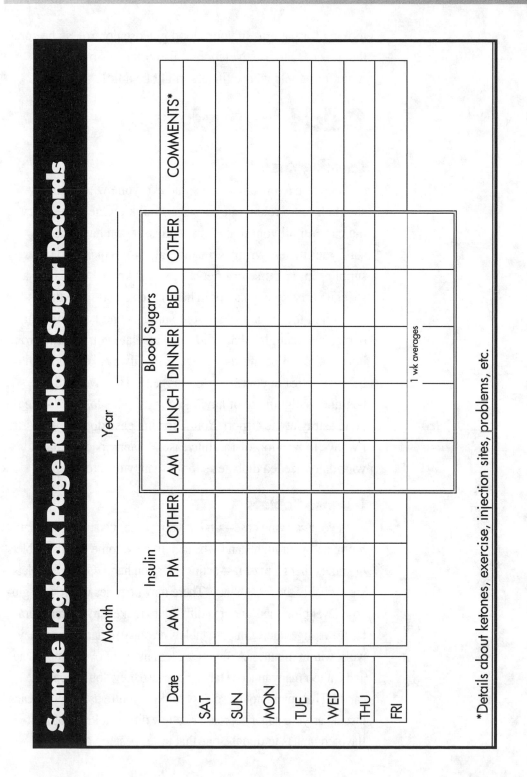

Date	Insulin				Blood Sugars					COMMENTS*
	AM	PM	OTHER		AM	LUNCH	DINNER	BED	OTHER	
SAT										
SUN										
MON										
TUE										
WED										
THU										
FRI										

1 wk averages

*Details about ketones, exercise, injection sites, problems, etc.

looking for patterns in your blood glucose control, so be sure that it is easy to use. Notebooks also offer lots of room to write for people whose fingers might be a little stiff.

Odds 'n Ends

Carrying Case

There are a few other items that everyone with diabetes should have to round out his or her tool kit. One is the carrying case for all your diabetes supplies. If you have tried to stuff your meter, syringes, insulin, alcohol wipes, and other supplies into a purse or briefcase, you'll know how handy a special carrying bag can be. These cases can do two things for you. First, they organize all your supplies and keep them in one convenient place. Second, they insulate your insulin from hot or cold temperatures. For traveling always keep your diabetes supplies in your carry-on luggage. This avoids the beginner's nightmare of having your supplies lost in a suitcase gone astray at the airport. Your carrying case doesn't necessarily have to be a top-of-the-line case. A fanny pack that holds your daily needed diabetes supplies can work, too.

Glucose Tablets

In your carrying case—and in your purse, your car, your bathroom, and your nightstand—be sure to have some glucose tablets or some other form of fast-acting sugar on hand. Glucose tablets are probably the most handy. There may be times when your glucose level plummets and it is difficult to make it to the refrigerator for orange juice. Glucose tablets are easy to handle and they work within minutes. And you are less likely to overcompensate and eat too many glucose tablets because they don't seem like candy. That might not be so easy to do if you're using jelly beans instead as your sugar source. Try a few different kinds of fruit-flavored tablets to find the one that tastes best to you.

Personal Identification

Don't forget to put some form of personal identification in your tool kit. This should identify you and your medical condition in case you become unconscious or injured. The Medic Alert Foundation keeps updated medical information available on computer, 24 hours a day (see Resources). Other information cards, pendants, bracelets, and tags have all the necessary information printed right on them. Kid-sized, kid-colored, and designer IDs are available.

Shopping Around

Shopping for your diabetes tools may take a little practice. For example, if you are in the market for a new meter, you may have to first check your insurance or Medicare coverage. Otherwise, you may find what you think is the perfect meter for you, only to find that your insurance won't cover the cost. Many insurance companies follow Medicare guidelines for deciding what to reimburse. Currently, Medicare beneficiaries are covered for monthly glucose-testing supplies and one meter per year. Your insurance may cover the meter and the strips or just one of these.

Meters are usually deeply discounted by the manufacturer. The real investment in a glucose meter is in the strips you must buy on an ongoing basis. To get the latest information on the model you are interested in and any accessories it may require (such as strips and batteries), call the manufacturer's toll-free number and talk to someone in customer service.

If your insurance offers meters and strips through a mail-order program, you needn't worry about bargain hunting. However, you will need to get a physician's prescription to be reimbursed for the meter and strips. You may also need to show a physician's prescription for insulin and syringes to get reimbursed.

If your insurance doesn't cover the costs of supplies, check out the *American Diabetes Association Resource Guide.* You'll probably find a bargain, especially if you are shopping for strips. Most ads and mail-order houses offer better prices than you'll find at the local pharmacy. Pharmacies generally offer much smaller selections of equipment. However, if you have a good relationship with your pharmacist, you may ask him or her to order the machine you want. Although pharmacies can be more expensive, establishing a good working relationship with your pharmacist can save you a lot of running around in the long run. Pharmacists can often give you information on the ins and outs of many different products and models.

When dealing with mail-order houses, you have to pay extra attention to timing. Be sure to order your strips, insulin, and other equipment at least two weeks in advance of when you think you'll need them. Otherwise, you may find yourself high and dry without medication or test supplies. This is especially true if your meter requires special strips. Also, if you are insured, starting up with a mail-order house may take additional time up front while the paper work is processed. The company must confirm your insurance coverage before filling your first order.

Another shopping option is to visit a diabetes specialty store. To find one near you, call your local American Diabetes Association chapter (see Resources) or check in the phone book under Medical Supplies or Diabetes. If you are lucky enough to have one nearby, you may be able to get many nonprescription items and diabetes information and support in one easy stop. Some pharmacies specialize in diabetes supplies and carry a large number of meters and other supplies. You may also find a selection of healthy foods, books, and information on local diabetes events and organizations. Many diabetes shops have a knowledgeable staff who can help you compare models, answer your questions, and provide training on complicated tools.

Most grocery store and chain pharmacies carry diabetes supplies. If your neighborhood store doesn't carry your brand of strips or meter, ask the pharmacist if a sister store does. Often stores in neighborhoods with many elderly people will carry more brands of supplies. Local pharmacists will know the products that they sell and will be able to spend time training you to use your purchase. This is a real, convenient advantage.

Stretching Your Diabetes Dollars

Living with diabetes can eat a major hole in your pocketbook. Here are a few money-saving tips to consider:

■ Test blood glucose on a regular basis. Skipping tests may at first seem to save money. But in the long run it could cost you more if your diabetes is often out of control and you end up with complications.

■ Think about using syringes more than once. There is no evidence that reusing syringes increases your chances for infection, if you follow proper precautions. Ask your health care team if it's safe for you and how to care for your syringes.

■ Ask your health care team about using generic blood glucose testing strips and whether your meter accuracy will be affected.

■ Seek out rebates and trade-in discounts on meters.

■ Take care of your equipment. Keep it clean and dry and keep it accessible.

Chapter 7:
Intensive Diabetes Management

If you are motivated and physically and financially able, you can capture the benefits of near-normal blood glucose control.

When Katherine was diagnosed with diabetes, she was heartbroken. She had witnessed the devastation of the disease through her mother, who had lived with diabetes for thirty years. She stood by as her mother first lost her eyesight, then suffered a leg amputation, and finally succumbed to kidney failure. Katherine did not want to face the same ordeal. She felt she had no choice until she heard about the results of the Diabetes Control and Complications Trial. . . .

It always seemed obvious that keeping blood glucose levels as normal as possible would prevent diabetic complications. That's what researchers thought, but couldn't prove for sure. What if something else related to diabetes caused the complications? What if controlling blood glucose had no effect on complications? In fact, some studies had suggested that controlling blood glucose would have no effect on, or might even worsen, complications.

Then, in 1993, researchers confirmed what many diabetes health professionals and people with diabetes had long suspected. The Diabetes Control and Complications Trial (DCCT) showed that by keeping blood glucose levels under tight control, you can delay or even prevent many of the complications of diabetes. One group of people participating in the DCCT had drastic reductions in the occurrence of diabetic eye, kidney, and nerve diseases. This study confirmed that it was the excess sugar in the blood of people with diabetes that, after many years, caused them to develop problems with their eyes, nerves, blood vessels, and kidneys. The DCCT only looked at people with type 1 diabetes, but the results of another study conducted more recently called the United Kingdom Prospective Diabetes Study (UKPDS) show that tight blood glucose control can also help people with type 2 diabetes. (For more on the results of the UKPDS, see page 213.)

Maintaining tight control over blood glucose levels is almost like taking on a second career. It requires added commitment and effort, and is more costly in the short term than standard diabetes management programs. Each person needs to decide for him- or herself if the benefits of tight blood glucose control outweigh the possible disadvantages.

Standard Diabetes Control Versus Tight Control

In 1983, the National Institute of Diabetes and Digestive and Kidney Diseases began the DCCT. The goal was to see whether keeping blood glucose levels as close to normal as possible would reduce the complications of diabetes. The ten-year DCCT compared how different levels of glucose control in people with type 1 diabetes affected some of the problems related to the disease: retinopathy, neuropathy, nephropathy, and cardiovascular disease. The idea was not to compare two types of diabetes management. Instead, the study measured what would happen to people with standard glucose control versus exceptionally tight blood glucose control.

The 1,441 people who volunteered for the study were divided into two groups. The control group followed the standard treatment for diabetes. This involved taking the same or a similar dose of insulin at the same times each day, usually in the morning and evening. Volunteers in the control group also checked glucose levels, using either a urine test or blood test, two or three times each day. The rest of the volunteers were part of the experimental, or study, group. They adhered to an intensive diabetes therapy plan to achieve tight blood glucose control. This involved three or four daily injections of insulin or the use of an insulin pump, testing blood glucose levels four to seven times each day, and adjusting insulin doses to match exercise and food intake.

The results were astounding. The researchers found that after 10 years, practicing tight control reduced the risk of developing diabetic eye disease (retinopathy) by 76 percent. Among individuals who already had early signs of eye disease before entering the trial, intensive management slowed the progression of retinopathy by 54 percent. Tight blood glucose control also reduced the risk of kidney disease by 50 percent and that of nerve disease by 60 percent. Study volunteers, who ranged in age from 13 to 39, were too young to develop many heart-related problems, but were monitored for some of the signs of cardiovascular disease. The study found that those on intensive management had a 35 percent lower risk of developing high cholesterol levels, a major contributor to heart disease. Before the DCCT, many people with diabetes thought that complications would progress no matter what they did. After the DCCT, we know that way of thinking is wrong—keeping glucose levels in control does matter.

The DCCT also showed that intensive diabetes management has some drawbacks. People in the study practicing tight control had three times as many severe low blood sugar episodes compared to those on the standard treatment program. This happened because their overall blood glucose levels were much lower. And, those practicing tight control

Benefits of Tight Glucose Control Demonstrated by the DCCT

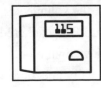

Keeping blood glucose levels close to normal reduces the risk of:

▪ Eye disease by 76%   ▪ Nerve disease by 60%
▪ Kidney disease by 50%   ▪ Cardiovascular disease by 35%

tended to gain more weight—an average of ten pounds more than those following a standard management plan. This is because they were no longer losing calories in the form of glucose in the urine. Their insulin regimen made their bodies more efficient at capturing and storing calories.

Is Intensive Management Right For You?

You may already be practicing tight control. Or you may firmly believe that you are doing fine without intensifying your diabetes management. Hopefully, you don't feel overwhelmed managing your diabetes on a day-to-day or meal-to-meal basis, which could cause you to ignore your blood glucose levels. But even if you have your diabetes under control and have settled into a manageable routine, you may not always like the idea of having your life dictated by a schedule. Maybe you can't take that 6 p.m. aerobics class because that's when you have to give yourself a dose of insulin and then eat. So the idea of taking on intensive diabetes management, with even more blood glucose tests and more injections of insulin, may seem out of the question. But the truth is, intensive diabetes management may actually give you more freedom, not less.

For people with type 1 diabetes, and many people with type 2 diabetes, your schedule and activities are often dictated by when you took your last dose of insulin or when your next one is due. But the idea with intensive management is that, by monitoring frequently, you can make adjustments in your insulin dose to accommodate variety in your eating and activity patterns. Thus, by learning how to interpret your monitoring results and predict the effect your food and activities will have on your blood glucose level, you can learn to adjust your insulin doses to get greater flexibility in day-to-day living.

Here's a simple example of how it works.

To keep his blood glucose levels predictable, Jerry was used to eating the same thing for breakfast and lunch and injecting a certain dose of insulin before breakfast and another fixed dose of insulin before dinner. At dinner, he never knew what he might be having, so sometimes his blood glucose was really high in the morning, and sometimes he even had lows overnight. Jerry decided to tighten up his control. But, instead of teaching himself to eat the same thing every night for dinner, he decided to learn how food and insulin and exercise increased and decreased his blood glucose levels. He started taking shots and testing four times a day, instead of two. Over several weeks, Jerry learned to predict how much his blood glucose would go up when he ate certain foods. He also learned how much his blood glucose would go down if he added an extra unit or two of insulin, or when he rode his bicycle to work. After a few months, Jerry found he was able to eat at different times, or eat more or less food, and still get similar blood glucose readings because he increased or decreased his insulin dose to suit particular meals. Jerry was able to add variety to his daily eating habits and get even better control.

Adapting to an intensive management program does not happen overnight. You will need lots of help. Do not attempt to tighten your glucose control without first consulting with your health care team. This is because not everyone is a candidate for intensive diabetes management. To have the best chance at success, you need:

■ to have a history of good diabetes self-care

■ to be committed to the idea of improving your blood glucose control

■ education about diabetes self-management techniques; for instance, you may need to learn to use an insulin pump

■ to understand the benefits and risks of tightening your glucose levels

■ to be willing to communicate often and honestly with your health care team

■ supportive health care team, family, friends, and coworkers

■ the ability to pay for the extra test strips, insulin pump (if used), and additional education.

Reaching your goal of tighter blood glucose levels will require commitment on your part. If you find that diabetes interferes with living the kind of lifestyle you would like, you may be more likely to stick with the program. When you and your health care team decide to forge ahead, they will probably recommend that you attend classes or a series of personal training sessions to learn how to adhere to an intensified care plan and how to make adjustments in your diet, exercise, and insulin regimen.

Intensive diabetes management is an approach that can benefit almost any person with diabetes. For years, women with type 1 or type 2 diabetes who were planning a pregnancy and women who developed gestational diabetes have been advised to follow an intensive diabetes management plan. This is because of the particular importance of keeping sugar levels as close to normal to avoid problems in the development and growth of the baby.

Who Can Sign Up

Potential candidates for intensive diabetes management include:

■ Healthy adults with type 1 or type 2 diabetes

■ Adolescents and older children who understand the risks and benefits

■ Women with diabetes who are pregnant or who plan a pregnancy

■ Patients who have had or will have kidney transplantation for diabetic nephropathy

These candidates also need to show their health care team that they want the best diabetes management possible through their efforts at diabetes self-management.

There are some people for whom intensive diabetes management is not safe. For instance, due to the fact that tighter blood glucose levels bring a higher risk of severe hypoglycemia, intensive insulin therapy in children is risky. Severe hypoglycemia can interfere with normal brain development, which is not complete until the age of seven. So, tight control for children under the age of about seven can be especially dangerous. Intensive diabetes management in children requires extreme caution and a doctor's close supervision.

Lowering blood glucose levels to normal by intensive diabetes management is risky for the elderly. This is because of the increased risk for hypoglycemia. During episodes of very low blood sugar, older people can be more prone to heart attacks and stroke. In addition, people over age 70 who begin an intensive therapy program may find that the potential benefits are not worth the effort and risk. The idea behind intensive therapy is to prevent complications that may take years to

Poor Candidates for Intensive Diabetes Management

 Your health care team may discourage you from aiming for near-normal blood glucose ranges if you:

■ have a history of severe hypoglycemic episodes or hypoglycemia unawareness

■ are younger than age 7 or older than age 70

■ have cardiovascular disease, angina, or other medical conditions that can be aggravated by hypoglycemia

■ have severe complications of diabetes

■ have conditions such as debilitating arthritis or severe visual impairment that would functionally limit intensive management

■ have drug or alcohol abuse problems or are unable to make reasonable decisions about your everyday diabetes management.

develop, and people of advanced age may not survive long enough to fully realize the benefits.

Intensive diabetes management may not be appropriate for people who are already experiencing severe complications of diabetes. For people with marked vision loss or end-stage kidney disease, tight control is unlikely to provide any noticeable benefit to the kidneys or the eyes. Although intensive therapy can slow down or prevent the development of complications, there is no evidence to date that it can reverse the process.

Other health conditions can make intensive therapy unsafe. For example, individuals with coronary artery disease, irregular

No, Thanks, I'm Intense Enough Already

 Even if you decide not to participate in an intensive diabetes management plan, there are still several simple things you can do to improve your blood glucose levels. They include:

■ Eat about the same amount and type of carbohydrate every day, at about the same time in relation to when you take your insulin or oral diabetes medication dose.

■ If a blood glucose test shows a level higher than your target range, take action. Take a supplemental dose of lispro or regular insulin, skip a snack, or if meal time is coming up, eat less than usual. Getting extra exercise can also help some people.

■ Increase your dose of lispro or regular insulin (or plan to get some extra exercise) when you know you'll be eating more than usual. Take less insulin if you plan to eat less than usual. Discuss in advance your plans to make adjustments with your health care provider.

■ If you feel like you're having low blood glucose, test. If you are low, eat 15 grams of carbohydrate, and retest 10 to 15 minutes later. If you're still low, repeat: eat 15 grams of carbohydrate and retest. This will keep you from causing your blood glucose levels to go too high after a low.

■ Save some of your day's calories (100 to 200 of them) for a bedtime snack. This helps you avoid going too low overnight or going too high in the morning as a result of treating your overnight low. A protein snack works for some people.

heart beats, cerebrovascular disease, angina, or other types of heart disease may not be suitable candidates for intensive therapy. Anyone requiring medications, such as beta blockers, that may make it more difficult to detect hypoglycemia may be at higher risk when trying to achieve tight control. Also, people with emotional disorders or alcohol- and drug-abuse problems and those who are unwilling or unable to commit the effort to achieve tight control are not advised to attempt intensive management. People with limited hand agility, such as brought on by severe arthritis, or who are blind may have a difficult time meeting the demands of intensive diabetes management.

Education

The idea of embarking on an intensive diabetes management plan may seem a little overwhelming. There is a lot to remember. But keep in mind that it is an ongoing process. You can't learn it overnight and no one expects that of you. Your health care team is there to help you. You'll have many questions as you begin. How many units of insulin should I take if my blood glucose is a little high? How should I change what I eat at my next meal? It will require trial and error and probably several calls to your team members as you develop the confidence to make some of the adjustments on your own. Ultimately, you will need to make these adjustments on your own, if intensive diabetes management is to work best for you.

Talk to your health care team members about the best way to approach intensive therapy. Maybe your local ADA chapter, community hospital, or health care team offers classes in intensive management. Or maybe your diabetes educator wants to arrange several one-on-one sessions to teach you what you need to know to make the program work for you. Whether you enroll in formal classes or arrange several individual sessions with your diabetes educator, check to see if the following subjects will be covered:

■ nutritional guidelines and the effect of food on blood glucose control

■ insulin action and dosage adjustment

■ measuring the effects of exercise

■ blood glucose and urine ketone monitoring and interpretation of the results

■ ways to help you change your lifestyle and adjust to a new management style.

Choosing Goals

The idea behind intensive diabetes treatment is to maintain tight control over blood glucose levels. If you decide that intensive management is for you, you will want to choose blood glucose goals as close to those of people without diabetes as is reasonable and safe for you. It's a group decision that you, your health care team, and your family need to make together.

For people without diabetes, blood glucose levels rarely go over 140 mg/dl, even after eating a meal. Their bodies take care of it for them. When your after-meal blood glucose level is higher, you'll need to take action to lower it: by injecting more insulin or compensating (with food or insulin) at the next meal time. But 140 is not the magic number for everyone. Your target range may be a little higher (if you live alone) or lower (if you've just found out you're pregnant). What suits an otherwise healthy young adult with recently diagnosed type 1 diabetes may be very different than for an elderly person with type 2 diabetes who has coronary artery disease or severe retinopathy. And an eleven-year-old with working parents who spends lots of time alone may have different needs still. There are many factors to consider in setting your personal goals, including:

- your age
- how long you've had diabetes
- the type of diabetes you have
- the frequency and severity of hypoglycemia
- your lifestyle and occupation
- other medical conditions
- how much support by family and friends you get
- your personal motivation for diabetes self-management.

One piece of information that came out of the DCCT is that even if you set goals that seem reasonable, you may not reach them. The DCCT goals for people in the intensive management group were to have near-normal blood glucose levels before (70 to 120 mg/dl) and after (under 180 mg/dl) meals and at bedtime. Most people just couldn't consistently reach these goals. Even with highly motivated patients and health care team members, it was difficult to keep blood glucose levels close to those found in people without diabetes. So, the appropriate goals for blood glucose levels for people with diabetes are often less ambitious than those set in the DCCT (see the table below).

Goal setting must be done carefully. You'll want to see how close to near-normal you can get without too much hypoglycemia. But if your body just can't cooperate, even after a few months of hard work on your part, you'll need to set different goals. Otherwise, you'll get discouraged. And remember

Blood Glucose Goals

	Time of test	Person without diabetes	Person with diabetes
	Before meals	Less than 110 mg/dl	80 to 120 mg/dl
	Before bedtime	Less than 120 mg/dl	100 to 140 mg/dl

this: The DCCT proved that any improvement in lowering blood glucose levels will definitely gain you real benefits.

Another way to measure blood glucose control is to measure glycated hemoglobin (HbA1c). Many doctors use laboratories that measure HbA1c, but your doctor may measure total glycated hemoglobin or something else (see Chapter 3; if your doctor does a test other than the HbA1c, ask him or her to convert your test result so you can compare it with DCCT results, and be sure to ask your doctor what the normal range is for the lab performing the test, as it may vary from lab to lab). In the DCCT, HbA1c measurements were taken to know how well the subjects in the intensive treatment group were doing with overall control. Despite being unable to consistently reach the daily blood glucose goals, they lowered their HbA1c values dramatically. This improvement was seen after about six months of intensive management. They were reaching for normal (nondiabetic) HbA1c values of below 6%; almost half reached this target at least once during the study. However, only five percent of the people stayed around 6%; most had HbA1c around 7%. This is a reasonable goal for most people with diabetes. The risk for nephropathy and retinopathy increases as HbA1c goes up.

Type 1 Diabetes

If you have type 1 diabetes, you will need to use multiple daily injections of lispro or regular insulin or an insulin pump for intensive diabetes management. You may also find that combinations of lispro or regular and NPH or regular and ultralente work for you. For lots more information on the insulin pump, see Chapter 4.

You will need to set a target range for your blood glucose levels, say between 70 and 140 mg/dl. If your blood glucose levels fall below 70 mg/dl or rise above 140 mg/dl, then you'll need to take action to increase or decrease them. For example, if glucose levels are too low, you'll need to treat yourself for hypoglycemia, unless you're about to eat a meal. If levels are too high, you'll need an extra dose of insulin. It will be the same routine when you test before bedtime. If your results are under 100 or over 140 mg/dl, you'll need to take action: a little more food or insulin, respectively, may be in order. Make sure to ask your doctor whether supplemental doses of insulin are the best way for you to deal with high blood glucose levels (especially at

Diabetes: Myth or Fact?

"Intensive diabetes management means I'll have lots more hypoglycemic reactions."

This, unfortunately, turns out to be true. When you've worked out a plan that narrows your range of blood glucose highs and lows, you're always closer to low than you were on standard diabetes therapy. Your room for "error" becomes much narrower. This isn't a good reason to avoid intensive management, however, unless hypoglycemic reactions would aggravate other health conditions.

To deal with this fact, you need to become expert at telling when to pull out the meter and do a test. Just as you'd make an adjustment when you're too high, so you'll need to treat your hypoglycemia when you're too low. The secret to keeping hypoglycemia from turning you away from tight control is to prevent severe reactions. Act early, think clearly, and avoid letting your low level go so low that you give up control.

Here's a sample chart for treating hypoglycemia. It's based on your blood glucose test result. This chart gives an average: in general, each 5 grams of carbohydrate raises blood glucose about 15 mg/dl. After treating, your blood glucose goal is about 120 mg/dl. You'll need to figure out how much 5 grams of carbohydrate raises your blood glucose level.

If your blood glucose is:	Eat this much carbohydrate:
Under 40 mg/dl	30 grams
40 to 50 mg/dl	25 grams
51 to 60 mg/dl	20 grams
61 to 80 mg/dl	15 grams
Over 80, but have symptoms	5 to 10 grams

bedtime) and how much you should take. If you take too much insulin, you could put yourself at risk for hypoglycemia.

Of course, the goals mentioned above are guidelines only. You should discuss your needs with your health care team to arrive at goals that will work for you. Goals may change over the course of your intensive management. For instance, you could find it harder and harder to detect oncoming hypoglycemia. This would call for increasing your target range and perhaps new training at recognizing your symptoms.

You'll be encouraged to test your blood glucose often: at least as often as you inject insulin (or take your bolus dose via pump) and sometimes more. You could be testing seven times a day: before your three meals, after each meal, and before bedtime. You may even test at 3 a.m. once or twice a week. For instance, you will not want your blood glucose level to fall below 65 mg/dl during the night. But if you have experienced several severe hypoglycemic reactions, you may want to aim for a higher overnight blood glucose level. Talk with your health care team to find bedtime and overnight goals that are right for you. Every bit of testing gives you more knowledge of how your body reacts to food, exercise, and insulin (and stress or illness). Once you've settled into a comfortable routine, you may be able to do fewer tests. Testing so much may be the hardest part of intensive diabetes management.

Type 2 Diabetes

For twenty years, over 5,000 participants took part in the United Kingdom Prospective Diabetes Study to learn if intensive management helped people with type 2 diabetes avoid complications, too. The results were released in 1998, and they are clear: not only do people with type 2 diabetes following an intensive regimen experience fewer microvascular complications, but if they control their blood pressure, they significantly reduce their risk of virtually all cardiovascular and microvascular complications. That means far fewer strokes, heart attacks, and problems with atherosclerosis, as well as improved circulation to the legs and feet, which helps reduce problems with neuropathy.

One of the treatment goals of the UKPDS' intensive therapy group was a fasting plasma glucose of less than 108 mg/dl, and participants were on combination therapies of either two diabetes medications or a diabetes medication and insulin. For this group, the study found that:

■ microvascular complications decreased by 25%
■ over 10 years, the average HbA1c dropped from 9.1% to about 7%
■ for every percentage point decrease in HbA1c, complications were reduced by 35%, heart attacks were reduced by 18%, and diabetes-related deaths were reduced by 25%
■ tight blood pressure control reduced the risk of stroke by 44% and the risk of heart failure by 56%.

What do all these numbers mean? Intensive control of blood sugar and blood pressure can significantly reduce your risk of diabetes complications.

The blood glucose goals for a person with type 2 diabetes who wants to pursue intensive diabetes management are not much different than for those with type 1 diabetes. Almost all people with diabetes can gain benefits from keeping blood glucose ranges close to those of people without diabetes. But the way those of you with type 2 diabetes go about reaching for your blood glucose goals may differ from someone with type 1 diabetes. It will still take a bit of trial and error to figure out what works best for you.

It's possible that you can achieve tight glucose control by becoming more determined to meet your eating and exercise goals. If you take oral diabetes medication or control your diabetes by diet alone, perhaps adding a once-a-day insulin injection would help. A small-scale study showed that people with type 2 diabetes came close to achieving near-normal blood glucose levels when a shot of insulin at dinner or bedtime was added to their therapy. Ask your health care team whether starting insulin will open the door to improving your blood glucose control.

If you already take oral diabetes medications or insulin, you may need to take a more aggressive approach. Your therapy might even be similar to that of a person with type 1 diabetes who is pursuing intensive diabetes management. If you are on pills, you may need to switch to insulin. If you take insulin once or twice a day, you may need to increase to three or four shots a day. You will definitely need to test your blood glucose levels several times a day regardless of your medication schedule.

Whatever methods you and your health care team choose for intensifying your diabetes management, your goals should be tailored to your particular needs. For instance, if you are overweight, you'll want to watch out for weight gain that can accompany better control. Adding an extra workout a week may be just enough to counteract the fact that you're not losing as much glucose in your urine anymore. If you also are just learning to treat low blood glucose levels, you'll want to follow a treatment schedule and do extra testing to make sure you're not adding more calories than you need to get blood glucose up into the normal range. The method for most effectively dealing with low blood glucose revealed by a glucose test is to eat 15 grams of carbohydrate (see list on page 163), wait 10 to 15 minutes, and test your blood glucose again. A result in the normal range means you've successfully treated your low blood glucose. If you're still low, repeat your treatment and test again.

Pregnancy and Gestational Diabetes

Getting and keeping tight blood glucose control is especially important during pregnancy. If newly developed diabetes is left untreated, or if blood glucose control is poor, several problems can develop for both mother and baby. However, having well-controlled blood glucose levels decreases the risks to mother and baby to the same level as women without diabetes. This is why intensive diabetes management is recommended for mothers-to-be with diabetes.

Women with diabetes are encouraged to plan their pregnancies. It's critical for you to have blood glucose levels as close to normal as you can before you get pregnant. Too much glucose in the blood in the first two months of pregnancy, while the baby is developing its nervous system and body parts, can cause birth defects. It also increases your risk of miscarriage. You'll want to have your blood glucose levels under control before you get pregnant. It's important to take care of your general health, too. Pregnant women with diabetes are more likely to develop high blood pressure, hypoglycemia, and a temporary worsening in the complications of diabetes, including retinopathy, if their blood glucose levels are not well controlled. Blood glucose goals for you are likely to be even tighter than for people who are not pregnant. Tight premeal blood glucose levels for you may be 60 to 105 mg/dl. Ideal after-meal blood glucose levels might be 100 to 120 mg/dl. Your target average blood glucose level over the day might be in the 70 to 100 mg/dl range.

Gestational diabetes shows itself a little more than halfway through the pregnancy. The baby is mostly developed and puts its energy into getting bigger. If you have too much glucose in your blood, the baby will take in the glucose and grow too big. Delivering a baby too large for its age is dangerous for baby and mother. For this reason, you will need a nutrition plan. About three-quarters of women with gestational diabetes can control blood sugar levels by diet. Exercise can also be a big help in lowering blood glucose levels. Some women need the help insulin gives. Your doctor may recommend starting to use insulin if your fasting blood glucose levels go over 105 mg/dl or your levels two hours after eating are over 120 mg/dl.

Because you are aiming for very tight control, your risk of hypoglycemia will increase. Make sure you can recognize early warning symptoms of low blood glucose. Test your blood glucose level often. When low, follow guidelines that will help you avoid overtreating it. Take 15 grams of carbohydrate (see the list on page 163), wait 10 to 15 minutes, and retest your blood. If you are still low, repeat this treatment. You want to avoid letting your blood glucose go any higher than your target range.

Striving for these tight target blood glucose levels requires extra effort and diligence and discipline. You may find motivation in knowing that by maintaining very tight blood glucose control, you can ensure good health for both yourself and your baby.

Intensive Management Techniques

How do you go about achieving tight control? Your tools are insulin and insulin delivery, oral medications, food, exercise, and blood glucose monitoring. Learning to use these old friends in new ways takes some education and practice.

Insulin Regimens

Maintaining tight glucose control if you use insulin means more than simply taking extra insulin. In fact, you may not increase the total amount of insulin you take at all. What does change is how you deliver it. You'll need to decide when to take it and how much to take to effectively cover your meals and your background (basal) glucose levels. You'll need to plan your insulin therapy to cover you throughout the day and night. The goal is to mimic the natural secretion of insulin from the pancreas as much as possible. The pancreas continually secretes a low level of insulin at all times and secretes higher levels when there is more glucose in the blood, includ-

Elements of Intensive Management

- Testing blood glucose levels 4 or more times each day
- Three or four daily insulin injections or the use of an insulin pump
- Adjusting insulin doses according to food intake, exercise, and blood glucose levels
- Following a diet and exercise plan
- Frequent office or phone visits with your health care team (once care routine is established).

ing after a meal. Therefore, in planning your insulin regimen, you may want to have low levels of insulin around at all or most times with more available at meals. But just how do you do that? By taking several doses of lispro or regular insulin or combinations of fast and slower-acting insulins or by using an insulin pump.

If you decide not to use an insulin pump, you will have a schedule that includes three or more insulin doses each day. For example, you might take one injection before each meal and another before bed. You might want to inject an intermediate or long-acting insulin at bedtime and a short-acting insulin before each meal. There are different ways to do this (see the insulin plans in Chapter 4). Your plan will give you the opportunity to make adjustments during the day. If you are exercising after lunch, you might want to reduce the amount of your noontime insulin dose. If you are going out to a fancy dinner where you know you'll be eating more than usual, you may want to take a little more insulin. Your diabetes educator can help you learn how to adjust your insulin doses.

You may want to try an insulin pump. The pump is usually worn on a belt clip or in a pocket and delivers insulin via tubing through the needle or catheter. With a pump, you keep a

Insulin Distribution

 One formula that some people find helpful as a starting point for deciding how to distribute insulin throughout the day is:

- 40 to 50% total insulin as the basal dose
- 15 to 25% before breakfast
- 15% before lunch
- 15 to 20% before supper
- 0 to 10%, as needed, to cover a bedtime snack.

needle or catheter fixed in one position for a couple of days to provide insulin to your body continuously. Insulin pumps are programmed to deliver a steady supply of buffered lispro or regular insulin throughout the day. This is the basal infusion rate. You will program your basal infusion rate; it may change over the course of a day, delivering more when you need it (in the early morning hours when insulin resistance is high) or less at other times. When you need a burst of insulin to cover meals (the bolus infusion), you'll instruct the pump to deliver it. The amount may change depending on your blood glucose level and what you plan to eat. (For more about pumps, see Chapter 4.)

Your doctor will help you determine your starting insulin doses for either injections or the pump. For instance, for people with type 1 diabetes who are within 20 percent of their ideal body weight, the total daily insulin dose needed for intensive therapy is 0.5 to 1.0 units per kilogram of body weight. That means if you weigh 127 pounds (1 kilogram equals 2.2 pounds), you would take about 29 to 57 units of insulin each day. You would be at the high end of the range if you were insulin resistant and at the lower end of the range if you were very sensitive to insulin. About a third to a half of your total daily dose would provide your basal insulin level, and the rest would be used to cover meals.

Whichever formula or calculation you use, you will most likely have to make adjustments as you find the schedule that best suits you. For instance, if you are pregnant, your total daily insulin dose will go up as you gain weight and develop more insulin resistance. Your insulin dose may even triple during the course of your pregnancy.

You will probably have to make small adjustments throughout the day to accommodate your meals and activities. If monitoring shows that your blood glucose levels are too high, you need to take extra insulin, or reduce the amount of carbohydrate in your next meal. Generally, 1 unit of insulin will lower blood glucose levels by about 50 to 100 mg/dl. You need to find out what is true for your body. You can also adjust your insulin intake to account for changes in meal patterns. In general, 1 unit of insulin will cover 10 to 15 grams of carbohydrate. You also need to find out if this is true for you.

It may be worth the effort. You will no longer have to keep a rigid schedule. The short-term benefits include, for example, going to a birthday party and eating cake (see the next section) or jogging an extra mile while keeping your blood glucose under control. Keeping complications at bay is the long-term benefit. Make sure to talk to your health care team about creating a starting plan and then making adjustments as your needs change.

Diet

The food you eat plays a big role in intensive diabetes management. In the past few years, the guidelines for food choices for people with diabetes have broadened to include more previously "forbidden" foods. This fits in well with intensive diabetes management, where you can adjust your therapy to suit your preferences. For instance, the new guidelines acknowledge that including modest amounts of simple sugars in your diet is not harmful.

For example, a reasonable goal would be to derive 10 to 20 percent of all your calories from protein and less than 10 percent from saturated fat. The remaining calories should be divided between carbohydrates and monounsaturated fats. In addition, 20 to 35 grams per day of fiber and less than 3000 milligrams of sodium per day are recommended. Discuss your needs and preferences with your nutritionist to devise a plan that works for you.

For more information on healthy eating, see Chapter 8.

If You Use Insulin. You should work with your health care team, especially your dietitian, to arrive at an eating plan:

■ Start with a meal plan that takes into account your usual food intake. Your meal plan should have about the same number of calories, types of food, and meal timing that you are already used to.

■ Follow an insulin schedule that follows your usual patterns of meals, exercise, and sleep.

■ Time your insulin doses to match your meal times. Your insulin should peak at the same time blood glucose levels from your meal are also peaking. By monitoring your blood glucose levels, you can adjust your insulin doses to suit your needs.

■ Work with your health care team to explore "what if" situations and develop contingency plans that will guide you as you make adjustments in eating, exercise, and insulin patterns.

With these strategies in mind, you and your nutritional counselor can come up with a meal plan that uses a simple system for quantifying or keeping track of food intake. For example, you may find it easier to draw from a list of measured food exchanges. This will make it easier to match insulin doses to total food intake. It will probably take a few months for you to get used to matching your food intake with insulin dose to achieve the target blood glucose levels.

Once you have established the ideal insulin dose for each type of meal, you can practice predicting what insulin doses will match your food intake. You'll need to have lots of practice estimating your insulin need in terms of the amount of carbohydrate you eat and adjusting for changes in food intake and exercise. The next step is to learn to calculate and take extra doses of short-acting insulin when your blood glucose is higher than your target range. This is how you begin to fine-tune your diet and make adjustments in your insulin doses as desired.

Then, you might want to learn to count carbohydrates. This technique allows you the maximum variety in your eating plan. It is based on calculating your personal carbohydrate to insulin ratio. This gives you a good idea of how your body uses the insulin you inject to process the carbohydrate you eat. Ask your dietitian for instruction on carbohydrate counting.

It will take a while before you feel like you've mastered these food and insulin adjustments, but in the long run they pay off. They will buy you greater flexibility in your activities and meals while keeping your blood glucose levels under better control.

If You Are Pregnant. One technique for keeping blood glucose levels steady and low throughout the day is to distribute your total daily calories as follows:

- 10 to 15% of calories at breakfast
- 5 to 10% of calories at a mid-morning snack
- 20 to 30% of calories at lunch
- 5 to 10% calories at a mid-afternoon snack
- 30 to 40% of calories at dinner
- 5 to 10% of calories at a bedtime snack.

This plan keeps carbohydrate intake low in the morning, when insulin resistance is high. Eating less carbohydrate than is normally recommended is another technique for keeping blood glucose levels low. When pursuing these options, it's important to have the input of your health care team. They may recommend urine ketone testing every day to alert you to problems that can come from a lower-carbohydrate diet.

If You Need to Lose Weight. Intensive diabetes management can create a weight gain. Your nutritional plan should include the following strategies:

■ You and your health care team, especially your dietitian, should review your normal eating habits, including total calories, types of food, and how much fat and carbohydrate you eat.

■ You may be advised to distribute the food you eat throughout the day so that you don't eat too many calories or carbohydrates at one sitting. This can help even out glucose levels.

■ You may be advised to eat fewer calories each day. Your health care team can help you decide how many calories this should be.

■ If you're not exercising regularly, you need to start. This will help counteract the better job your body is doing at capturing and storing glucose, as your control improves.

■ You'll need to be careful not to over treat the lows that are more common in intensive diabetes management. Follow the guidelines for doses of carbohydrates given on page 212 of this chapter.

Coping

As you embark on an intensive approach to diabetes management, you may find that you need more support and encouragement in adjusting to the new routines. The people in the intensive management group of the DCCT needed lots of help and had 24-hour access to their health care team. Sometimes you might just need someone to talk to, to discuss common problems, air your concerns, or just ask simple questions. Sometimes it will help to know that someone cares and understands what you are going through. You can look to several sources for the support and encouragement you will need.

Your health care team, a special friend or family member, a religious organization, or diabetes support group are all potential sources of support.

You may find that you seek different kinds of support from different people. Friends and family may provide you with the encouragement you need to affirm your commitment to the intensive approach. Maybe you need someone to reassure you when you fall short of your goals, a cheerleader to help you get back on track. You may also need technical support—someone to answer your questions as they arise and assure you that you are doing the kinds of things you think you should be doing. Are you making the right treatment decision? You might also need financial support or help with locating financial resources. Your health care team can help you in these areas. And you might just want someone to commiserate with. Look to support groups to find others with whom to share stories, to let you know that you're not alone and that the extra effort is really worthwhile.

Chapter 8:
Healthy Eating

Food and blood glucose levels are intimately linked. Knowing what's in the food you eat, the calories, carbohydrates, protein, and fat, will make it easier for you to control your blood glucose levels. Eating healthy is a gift you give yourself, for your diabetes and your overall health.

Sharon was diagnosed with type 1 diabetes when she was 4 1/2 years old. Getting her on a regular insulin schedule was a real challenge. After a few months, she and her parents had worked out a manageable blood testing and injection schedule, and Sharon didn't seem to mind too much. The bigger problem was with food. Getting any four-year-old to eat healthy foods is hard enough. How would they ever get Sharon to adhere to a diabetes diet? And soon her fifth birthday would be coming up. Sharon's parents were concerned that she would forever be missing out on many of the joys of childhood—birthday parties, holiday dinners, and baking cookies—which all seemed to work against her meal plan.

Adam had always had a problem keeping his weight under control. And since he retired last year, he'd gained a few more pounds. Now he and Sarah were about to celebrate their 40th wedding anniversary with a Caribbean cruise. But last month he was diagnosed with type 2 diabetes. His doctor thought he could control his condition through diet. But how could he ever stick to a diet while on a cruise? Should he call it off?

Nancy was thoroughly enjoying her second pregnancy. She exercised every day—walking or swimming—and ate a fairly balanced diet. She did give in to temptation and have a Dove Bar every afternoon, but it didn't seem to cause any problems. The baby was active and gaining weight at a steady pace, and she was right on target in her weight gain. But a routine glucose test during her 24th week showed that she had gestational diabetes. Would the baby be all right? She had already given up coffee and alcohol. Now, she would have to give up the Dove Bars. Could she stand 3 months without any sort of special treat?

For many people with diabetes, food is a very big problem. Being diagnosed with diabetes often means that you need to change your eating habits. The millions of us who have ever tried a "diet" know exactly how hard it is to change how we eat. The lore of diabetes is filled with food myths, starting with what causes diabetes. Have you ever been told that eating too much sugar gives you diabetes? (See Chapter 1, page 14, to dispel this myth.) And the good-hearted people in your life may often remind you that you're not supposed to eat sugar (also untrue; see the Diabetes: Myth or Fact in this chapter). Most people need help knowing what's true and what's not about diabetes and food. Your time and money will be well-spent if you decide to get some eating education from a registered dietitian or a certified diabetes educator.

The truth is, healthy eating for a person with diabetes is no different than healthy eating for a person without diabetes. It's just a matter of eating a wide variety of foods and a balanced amount of carbohydrates, proteins, and fat. It doesn't mean you have to give up all sugars or special treats. You just have to make sure you account for the carbohydrate, fat, and calories in your total meal plan for the day. Nancy may be able to have a Dove Bar, Arthur can go on a cruise, and Sharon can attend birthday parties and even have cake like the other children. Ask your doctor, dietitian, or diabetes educator for your individual guidelines. They may suggest you make up for special treats by eating less of something else, exercising a little longer, or taking an added amount of insulin.

People without diabetes may not notice the immediate effects of scarfing down an extra doughnut at breakfast—other than a need to loosen the belt a little. But if you have diabetes, you have to take extra care to make sure that your calorie and carbohydrate intake throughout the day is in the range to keep your blood glucose levels under control. Your meals must be carefully balanced with your insulin doses, oral medication, and physical activity to avoid highs and lows in blood glucose levels. It's a little extra work, but nothing out of the ordinary for a healthy eater. And the best part is that by eating more nutritious meals, you will improve your overall health. An unhealthy diet can contribute to heart disease, some cancers, and hypertension.

What's in a Healthy Meal Plan?

Don't think of your meal plan as a "diet. " Because if you are on a diet, it's easy to go off your diet. And once off, it's even easier to stay off. "Well, I've already blown my diet for today, so another slice of cheesecake won't hurt," you might think. But that will only make matters worse. Instead, think of your meal plan as a new way of eating. But in planning for that new way of life, make sure you work with your dietitian to develop a plan you can stick with. If your goal is to lose pounds, a low-calorie diet may look good on paper, but if you can't follow it, it won't do any good.

In working out your nutrition plan, your dietitian or diabetes educator should work with you to achieve your goals. If you have type 2 diabetes and are overweight, maybe you want to shed a few pounds. Or maybe you want to achieve tighter blood glucose control through careful meal planning. If you have type 1 diabetes, you may want to learn to balance food intake with insulin schedules. Or you may want to find out how your diet fits in with intensive insulin therapy.

Once you, your doctor, and dietitian decide on your diabetes management goals (see Chapter 2), you will need to work out a meal plan. If there are certain foods you absolutely can't stand, make sure to tell him or her. If there are certain foods you can't do without, make your wishes known. You might be able to include your favorite treat in your meal plan—if not every day, then occasionally. Your nutrition counselor can help you learn to make allowances for certain foods in your meal plan.

Just what is involved in devising a healthy meal plan? A helpful food plan will make it easier, not harder, to control blood glucose levels. Your eating plan should:

■ include foods you like
■ take your daily activities and schedule into account
■ be flexible
■ help you keep your blood glucose levels within your target range
■ help you reach and maintain a healthy weight
■ help prevent diseases and conditions, such as heart disease, high blood pressure, and cancer, which are linked to diet.

Variety Through the Food Pyramid

The best approach to healthy eating is to eat a wide variety of foods. This goes for everyone, whether you have type 1, type 2, or gestational diabetes—and even if you don't have diabetes. No single food group can provide you with all the nutrients your body needs. Your body requires nutrients to repair and replace proteins, tissues, and cells throughout your body and to keep you rolling along. Your body needs three important nutrients to do this: protein, carbohydrate, and fat, as well as vitamins and minerals. Various combinations of these nutrients are found in different foods. So, by eating a variety of foods, you are sure to get all the nutrients you need. This is much better than taking vitamin supplements, because nature combines the needed nutrients in food in a way that your body can best use them.

Where can you find the nutrients you need? Good sources of carbohydrates (starches and sugars) are cereals, grains, pasta, bread, fruit, vegetables, legumes, and milk products. Protein can be found in meat, milk products, poultry, eggs, and fish. There is also a smaller amount of protein in grains, bread, nuts, and vegetables. You can find fat in meat, milk products, oils, and nuts.

Just about all foods provide your body with energy. The amount of energy they provide is measured in calories. Any foods that are not used as energy are stored as fat in your body. The trick is to try to balance the total number of calories you take in with the total number you burn up. Carbohydrates and proteins provide about the same amount of energy, 4 calories per gram. Fats provide more than twice that amount, 9 calories per gram. So if you are trying to keep your weight under control, you are better off eating proteins and carbohydrates rather than high-fat foods. A high-fat diet can also put you at greater risk for developing heart disease and certain cancers.

Think of the foods you eat as part of a food pyramid. At the top, or apex, of the pyramid are fats and sweets. Eat small amounts of these foods. Lower down on the food pyramid are beans, meats, eggs, and dairy foods. You can eat slightly more of these foods, but still be careful that they are not the mainstay of your diet. Vegetables and fruits are near the base of the pyramid, and cereals, grains, pastas, and breads are at the base. Choose most of your foods from the carbohydrates, fruits, and vegetables at the base of the pyramid. These foods are loaded with nutrition, providing easily used energy, lots of fiber, vitamins, and minerals. They also tend to be lower in calories than those foods at the top of the pyramid.

Carbohydrates

Carbohydrates include sugars, such as sucrose, fructose, and lactose, and large, complex molecules, such as starch. In the body, most carbohydrates get broken down into glucose, a sugar that is the body's main source of energy. Starches are made of many glucose molecules linked together. Sugars

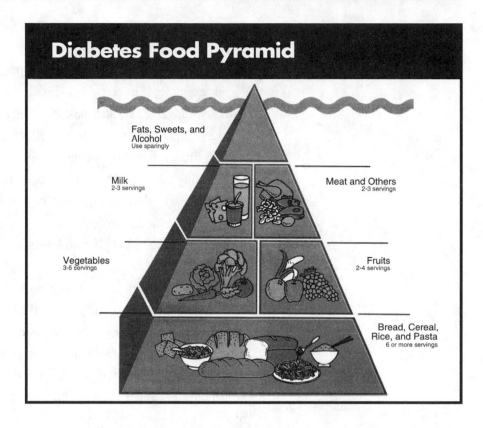

Diabetes Food Pyramid

Fats, Sweets, and Alcohol
Use sparingly

Milk
2-3 servings

Meat and Others
2-3 servings

Vegetables
3-5 servings

Fruits
2-4 servings

Bread, Cereal, Rice, and Pasta
6 or more servings

have only one or two molecules, of which one may be glucose.

Starches are found in vegetables, grains, cereals, and breads. Sugars occur naturally in some foods (fruits, vegetables, and milk, for instance) and are added as a sweetener to others (such as cakes, candy, and soft drinks). Everyone is encouraged to eat starches because they provide the most nutrients per calorie. These nutrients include vitamins, minerals, and dietary fiber. Processing, however, can remove many of these beneficial nutrients, so choose foods that have had a minimum of processing, such as bread made from whole grains.

Contrary to popular belief, whether a carbohydrate is a sugar or a starch has no effect on how fast glucose gets into the blood. What does matter is:

■ how much carbohydrate you eat at a meal

■ the way the food is prepared

■ the combination of foods eaten at a particular sitting.

For example, if a cookie made with sugar has 12 grams of carbohydrate and a cookie make with an artificial sweetener has 12 grams of carbohydrate, the effect on the blood sugar will be similar. Fat slows down the absorption of food. Therefore, adding fat to a carbohydrate food during preparation or at the table will slow digestion of the carbohydrate and delay the effect on blood glucose level.

By measuring blood glucose levels one and two hours after your meals, you can get a feel for how different foods and patterns of eating affect your blood glucose levels. You most likely will begin to think about your total carbohydrate intake and how it changes your blood glucose levels. If your goal is to eat a certain amount of carbohydrates each day or at a particular meal, you may find that if you eat too many sugary foods, you'll only get to eat a few of the more nutritious—and often more filling—starchy foods.

Calorie-free sugar substitutes do not raise blood glucose levels because they don't contain any carbohydrates. These include artificial sweeteners such as aspartame (Nutrasweet), acesulfame-K, and saccharin. Some sugar alcohols, which serve as sugar substitutes, have calories and are absorbed into the blood. These include sorbitol, mannitol, and xylitol. They are usually absorbed more slowly than glucose and usually cause a smaller rise in blood glucose levels than do glucose or sucrose. But beware. If you eat these sweeteners in large amounts (more than 20 to 50 grams, or 2/3 to 1-2/3 ounces in a day), you may experience intestinal distress and diarrhea.

Get in the habit of reading the labels of all the foods you eat. You may be surprised. Many foods that have low-calorie sweeteners in them, such as diet desserts, often contain starches, other sugars, fats, and proteins. These substances contribute calories and can cause blood glucose levels to rise.

Also, watch out for low-fat and no-fat items. Often these products have ingredients added as bulking agents, which can affect blood glucose levels. Many of these ingredients

The Carbohydrate–Blood Glucose Connection

 Very little of the fat and protein you eat becomes glucose. Instead, the lion's share of the glucose in your blood after a meal comes from the carbohydrate in your food. As the carbohydrate is broken down into glucose and absorbed, the amount of glucose in your blood goes up.

Different kinds of foods produce different amounts of blood glucose. There are several reasons for this:

■ First, some foods contain more carbohydrates per serving than others. One popcorn cake has 8 grams of carbohydrate, 1/2 cup of kernel corn has 11 grams of carbohydrate, and 1/2 cup of creamed corn has 21 grams of carbohydrate. The more carbohydrate you eat at a meal, the higher your blood glucose level goes.

■ Second is how fast the glucose is freed from the food. Carbohydrates come in several forms that take various amounts of time to break down. Food that stays in bigger pieces, like kernels of corn, breaks down more slowly than smaller pieces, like the bits in creamed corn. Cooked food digests faster than raw food. Food that contains liquid (the corn) digests more quickly than dry food (the popcorn cake). Food that digests slower will release the carbohydrate into the blood more slowly. Your blood levels of glucose may not rise as high.

■ Finally, combination foods, those that contain carbohydrates plus other nutrients such as fat, take longer to digest. This is why it's a bad idea to depend on ice cream or a candy bar to treat low blood glucose. Your blood levels of glucose may not rise until later than you expect, because of the fat in these foods.

are modified forms of carbohydrate that are used as emulsifiers or bulking agents. For example, maltodextrin and polydextrose can be found in products such as sugar-free, nonfat yogurt or low-fat pudding or ice cream. Maltodextrin is digested like a carbohydrate and provides 4 calories per gram. Polydextrose for the most part passes through the body, so it only has 1 calorie per gram. Maltodextrins, because they are absorbed, have some effect on blood glucose level, whereas polydextrose has very little effect. You should be aware that even if a product is labeled as low calorie, low sugar, or sugar-free, it may contain substances that deliver glucose to the blood. It can be difficult understanding what some of the ingredients are. Ask your dietitian what ingredients to be on the lookout for.

Protein

Proteins are used as replacement parts in the body. They are not used for energy unless there are not enough carbohydrates and fats present. Eating protein is an important part of any healthy diet. However, too much of a good thing can be bad, and Americans often eat much more protein than they need. People who have kidney problems or nephropathy may be advised to limit the amount of protein they eat.

Meat, poultry, milk products, and eggs are all good sources of high-quality protein, but they also come with cholesterol and saturated fat. Seafood is a good source of protein, and most kinds of seafood are lower in saturated fat and cholesterol than meat.

You can also find protein in legumes, grains, and vegetables. Nuts are laden with fat, but most nuts do not contain saturated fat (coconut is an exception). Vegetables, grains, and legumes are low in fats and saturated fat, contain no cholesterol, and have other nutrients as well. (Cholesterol is only found in animal products.)

Tip: Artificial sweeteners let you enjoy the sweet taste of sugar without its calories and without raising your blood glucose levels. One packet gives the same sweetness as two teaspoons of table sugar. Artificial sweeteners are okay for everyone, young or old, except that pregnant or breastfeeding women should not use saccharin and people with phenylketonuria should not use aspartame.

Diabetes: Fact or Myth?

"When I found out I had type 2 diabetes, I said 'no' to sugar. No more sugar in my tea, no more cakes, cookies, or pies, and no more jelly on my toast. I even switched from my favorite brand of peanut butter because it had sugar in it."

These efforts most certainly have made for a healthier diet. But now it turns out, you probably didn't have to go to such extreme measures.

Sugar has long had a bad reputation, especially among people with diabetes. People used to think that eating sugar would cause blood glucose levels to rise much more rapidly than eating other types of carbohydrates, such as bread or potatoes. So although bread and potatoes were okay to eat, pure sugar or sugar-laden treats were considered taboo.

It turns out that sugar's bad rap is not entirely deserved. Researchers are now finding that sugars, such as fruits and sucrose, and starches, such as bread and potatoes, are digested at the same rate. That means that all carbohydrates will raise your blood glucose levels equally fast. What does seem to matter in how quickly your blood glucose levels rise is the other foods you eat in combination with carbohydrates and how the food is cooked. Foods that include fat are digested much more slowly.

You can include foods that contain sugar in your diabetes meal plan. As long as you account for the calories and carbohydrate content of the sugar you eat, it won't hurt your blood glucose control. But that doesn't mean you should go hog wild over sugar. You still have to count sugar as a carbohydrate, but it has little nutritional value. And what you make on the peanuts, you lose on the bananas, so to speak. If you start including lots of sugary items in your diet, you won't be able to eat as much of the nutrient-rich carbohydrates such as grains and cereals that your body needs to keep you healthy. But you can include some sugar in your diet, in moderation.

Your dietitian can help you decide how to count sugar in your meal plan. For example, if you plan on having a piece of cake for dessert, you might want to skip the roll you normally have at dinner time. You may want to also talk to your doctor about whether you need to adjust your insulin dose to deal with extra carbohydrates in your meal plan.

Skinny Meat

There are several ways you can reduce the fat in meat:
- Broil, roast, grill, steam, or poach instead of frying.
- Cut off all visible fat before or after cooking and remove the skin from chicken and turkey.
- Chill meat broth and drippings so the fat rises and solidifies. Then it can be skimmed off the top before serving or making gravy. You can also use this method to reduce the fat in canned or homemade broths and soups.
- Buy lean cuts of meat. Ask your butcher to tenderize them through mechanical means rather than with chemical additives.
- Try quick-cooking methods such as stir-frying meat that you have marinated using tiny amounts of oil or dressing with lots of seasoning to enhance juiciness and flavor.

For example, a 1/3 cup serving of cooked kidney beans has 3 grams of protein. So does 1/2 cup of corn. Both of these count as 1 Starch Exchange in a typical meal plan based on food exchanges. One-half cup of cooked nonstarchy vegetables, such as carrots, broccoli, or zucchini, gives you 2 grams of protein and counts as 1 Vegetable Exchange.

Fats and Cholesterol

Everyone needs a little fat in their diet to make sure their bodies function properly. Fats are used to rebuild the membranes that protect the cells in your body and to help the cells in your body send signals. Fats are also stored and used as energy reserves. But fat can clog up blood vessels and increase your chances of developing heart disease and stroke. Many Americans eat too much fat. For healthy living, you are better off trying to limit the amount of fat, especially saturated fat, that you eat each day.

Cholesterol is a kind of lipid substance that your body makes on its own. It is used to make and repair the cell membranes in your body. It is also used to make many of the steroid hormones such as estrogen and testosterone that your body needs. But too much cholesterol in the blood can hurt you. It can clog your arteries and cause heart disease and stroke. In addition to the cholesterol your body makes on its own, the cholesterol and saturated fats that you eat can also raise blood cholesterol levels. Trying to keep your blood cholesterol levels down can be tricky.

Harvey was a good candidate for a heart attack. He already knew he had type 2 diabetes. He was about 50 pounds overweight and was doing his best to watch his carbohydrate intake. But, when he visited his doctor for a checkup last year, he found that his cholesterol level had skyrocketed.

He decided to cut down on the cholesterol in his diet by avoiding eggs and not eating red meats. But, his cholesterol levels were about the same. As his dietitian explained, eating less cholesterol is one step to reducing blood cholesterol but is not beneficial if the saturated fats in the diet are not also reduced. She recommended switching to low-fat dairy products and leaner cuts of meat to reduce Harvey's intake of cholesterol and saturated fat. After several months of using skim milk and low-fat cheeses instead of the high-fat varieties he was used to, Harvey saw his cholesterol levels start to come down.

How do you know how much fat is in the food you eat? Sometimes it can be difficult, especially when you are eating out. For foods you buy and prepare yourself, check the food labels. The Nutrition Facts section on food labels tells you how much fat, saturated fat, and calories from fat are in one serving. If you are cooking a meal or dish with lots of ingredients, try to add up the fat and calories from each ingredient and divide by the number of servings. If you are eating out, many restaurants, particularly chain and fast food restaurants, now provide nutritional information on request. If you are uncertain about any foods, ask your nutrition counselor for an estimate. At the end of the day, add up all the calories from fat from the labels on the foods you've eaten and any other hidden fats in foods without labels. This will give you the total of daily calories

Figuring Out Fat

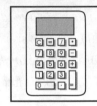 If you need to limit your fat and cholesterol intake, try not to eat more than 300 milligrams of cholesterol a day. Less than 30 percent of your total calories each day should come from fat (with less than 10 percent from saturated fats). If you find that you've eaten too much fat or cholesterol on one day, eat less for the next couple of days.

Here's an easy way to figure out how much fat to eat each day. First, decide on the number of calories you eat in a day. Let's say you eat 1,800 calories a day. Drop the last number, so 1,800 becomes 180. Now divide by 3. The answer is the number of grams of fat you can eat each day and still end up eating less than 30 percent of your total calories from fat.

from fat. Divide this by the total calories you've eaten for the day and multiply by 100. This will give you the percent of total calories from fat.

Hidden Fat. Be careful when you find cookies marked as "sugar-free" or other desserts marketed specifically for people with diabetes. They may be sugar-free, but more than 60 percent of their calories can come from fat. You will find saturated fat in all animal products such as butter, whole milk, half-and-half, and meat fat. The vegetable products high in saturated fats are palm oil, palm kernel oil, cocoa butter (chocolate), coconut oil, solid shortening, and partially hydrogenated oils. Often these fats are found in mixes for pancakes, biscuits, cookies, crackers, cakes, and some snack chips.

Preferred Fats. Not all fats are created equally. You also help your heart by making sure the fats you do eat are, for the most part, not saturated. Unsaturated fats (monounsaturated and polyunsaturated) are found mostly in plant foods and are liquid at room temperature. Saturated fats are usually solid at room temperature. Corn, cottonseed, sunflower, safflower, and soybean oils are all polyunsaturated, whereas, olive and

Healthy Oils

Spend your fat calories wisely. Opt for fats that are unsaturated, and avoid saturated fats.

Saturated fats (avoid these):	Polyunsaturated fats:	Monounsaturated fats:
■ bacon and bacon grease	■ corn oil	■ avocados
■ butter	■ cottonseed oil	■ canola oil
■ cocoa butter (chocolate)	■ margarine	■ nuts— almonds,
■ coconut oil	■ mayonnaise	cashews,
■ cream cheese	■ safflower oil	hazelnuts,
■ lard	■ salad dress- ings	macadamias,
■ meat fat	■ soybean oil	peanuts, and
■ palm oil	■ sunflower oil	pistachios
■ solid shorten- ing		■ olive oil
■ sour cream		■ peanut butter

Cutting Down on Fat and Cholesterol

The following simple steps can help keep dietary fat and cholesterol in check:

- Choose lean cuts of meat. Look for descriptions such as loin, round, lean, choice, and select.
- Remove visible fat from meats and skin from poultry, preferably before cooking.
- Choose fish and skinless poultry and lean meats.
- Try to limit your portions of lean meat, fish, or poultry to 3 ounces per meal—about the size of a deck of cards. One half of a skinless, boneless chicken breast is about 3 ounces of meat.
- Avoid fried foods.
- Limit the number of eggs you eat to four per week.
- Use a nonfat cooking spray to cook pans and cooking utensils to prevent sticking.
- Select reduced-fat or fat-free dairy products, such as salad dressings, baked goods, luncheon meats, soups, and dairy products.

canola oils are monounsaturated. You should decrease saturated fat intake to less than 10 percent of calories and select the rest of your fats from food with mono- or polyunsaturated fats. Choose margarine that has vegetable oil as its first ingredient rather than a partially hydrogenated oil. Hydrogenation makes an oil solid and spreadable, but it also makes the fat more saturated, which is less healthy. Hydrogenated margarine has 0.6 grams of saturated fat per teaspoon and butter has 2.5 grams per teaspoon.

Vitamins and Minerals

People with diabetes have the same requirements for vitamins and minerals as people without diabetes. If you are eating a variety of foods, rich in vegetables, fruits, cereals, and grains, then you are most likely getting all the vitamins and minerals you need. Large doses of micronutrients have not been shown to help diabetes or blood glucose control. In fact, large doses of some vitamins, especially those that are fat soluble, can be harmful. If you think you may not be getting all the vitamins and minerals you need, check with your dietitian before you resort to vitamin supplements. A few changes in your food choices may correct any nutritional deficiency.

If you are thinking about becoming pregnant or are pregnant, you have slightly different nutritional needs. You may need more vitamins than normal. Check with your dietitian or doctor to see if you are getting all that you need in your diet (see below).

Salt

Many people with diabetes, especially those with type 2 diabetes, may also have to watch their blood pressure. High blood pressure can increase the risk of heart disease and stroke. And in some people, too much dietary salt can increase blood pressure. So, if you tend to have high blood pressure, your health care team may suggest reducing your salt intake.

But what does that mean? Just stop shaking table salt on your food? That's part of it, but it may sometimes be difficult to figure out where all the salt in your diet is coming from. Many foods contain salt or another ingredient high in sodium, the element in salt that influences blood pressure. Sometimes it's rather obvious, because the foods taste salty, such as pickles and bacon. But there can be hidden salt in many foods, such as cheeses, salad dressings, cold cuts, canned soups, and fast foods. Even most peanut butters contain added salt. Take the salt shaker off the table, read labels to get an idea of salt or sodium content, and try other flavorings such as herbs and spices to make your food tastier. Remember, as is the case with fat, a little salt goes a long way.

Diabetes: Myth or Fact?

"People with diabetes can't drink alcoholic beverages."

Not true. If you have good control of your blood glucose levels, it is unlikely that an occasional alcoholic drink at mealtime will harm you. In fact, a recent study published in *JAMA* showed that light to moderate alcohol intake is associated with reduced risk of death due to coronary heart disease for people with type 2 diabetes. The key is to drink moderately and don't drive after drinking. Moderate drinking is defined as no more than one drink a day for women and two drinks a day for men. One drink is 12 ounces of regular beer, 5 ounces of wine, or 1-1/2 ounces of 80 proof distilled spirits. Remember that:

■ Alcohol contains calories, almost as many per gram as fat. If weight control is a critical part of your diabetes treatment plan, then the extra calories from alcohol need to be carefully evaluated. Generally, alcohol is substituted for fat calories, with one drink equal to 2 Fat Exchanges or 90 calories.

■ Alcohol can affect blood glucose level, most often causing a very low blood sugar when consumed on an empty stomach. People who use sulfonylureas or insulin should drink alcohol only with meals.

■ The signs of hypoglycemia (no matter what the cause) are very similar to the signs of inebriation. There is the risk that people will think you are intoxicated if they smell alcohol on your breath, and they may not consider the possibility that you have very low blood sugar and need help quickly.

■ Some people have hypoglycemia unawareness, a lack of symptoms of low blood sugar. Drinking alcohol increases their risk of hypoglycemia.

■ Some medications, including diabetes medications, require limits on alcohol use.

■ If you have health problems, such as pancreatitis, high triglyceride levels, gastric problems, neuropathy, kidney disease, or certain types of heart disease, you may be advised to abstain from alcohol.

Be aware that alcohol can affect your motivation to do even simple tasks, from folding laundry to monitoring your blood glucose levels. It's important for anyone not to drink so much alcohol that you lose sobriety. But it's even more important for someone with

Diabetes: Myth or Fact? (continued)

diabetes to remain sober. You need to be able to think clearly enough to monitor your blood glucose levels and to know what to do should they drop too low. If you are drinking, make sure to tell a friend what to do in the event of very low blood glucose. Your friend should be prepared to take action even if you are not able to cooperate.

Medical Nutrition Therapy: Your Meal Plan

Keep in mind that a healthy meal plan for you is just a healthy meal plan. You don't have to worry about following some strange diet involving weird foods that no one else in your family will want to touch. You will be developing a healthy living strategy that will benefit all the members of your household. Often, family members will not even realize that they are following a "diabetes meal plan."

Although your entire household will probably be part of your new eating strategy, you will most likely be the one setting the nutritional goals. Your doctor and dietitian may recommend certain goals, but it is up to you to choose the ones you can live with and then see that they are carried out. The more you are involved in developing your meal plan, the more your nutritional action plan will reflect your needs, tastes, preferences, and lifestyle—and the more likely you are to succeed.

After first consulting with your physician, you will most likely set up a visit with your dietitian to develop your mealtime strategy. You may feel that you don't really need a dietitian. Maybe you've seen sample meal plans recommended for people with diabetes that look easy enough to follow. But remember, your meal plan is not a short-term diet that you can follow for a few weeks only to drift back to old patterns. You will be developing a new way of eating that will stay with you throughout your life. Having a plan you can live with is a must. Your dietitian or diabetes educator can help you tailor a meal plan to suit your tastes. And as lifestyle changes occur, you can remodel your meal plan to suit these changes. Even if you are an old hand at planning meals, products change and you can change. Maybe now that the kids are grown, you decide to train for a half-marathon, join an over-40 soccer league, or plan a trip down the Nile. All of these events will change your dietary goals and most likely, you will need a new approach.

A dietitian can help you learn any of these approaches to managing your food choices:

- counting calories
- counting fat grams
- counting carbohydrate grams
- counting sodium milligrams
- counting food exchanges
- tightening your blood glucose control
- changing your eating habits
- meeting specific nutritional goals (for instance, keeping protein intake low or eating vegetarian).

A dietitian with experience in diabetes care can help you develop new ways to look at food. You might want to get a better sense of matching your carbohydrate intake to your insulin doses to keep your glucose in balance. Or maybe you'd like to know how to maintain blood glucose control on a vegetarian diet. Or perhaps you would like to lose weight. Your dietitian can help you figure out:

- how many calories you should try to eat each day

■ how many grams of carbohydrates you can eat each day and still keep your blood glucose levels within your target range

■ how many grams of fat you should eat if you want to keep your fat intake to less than 30 percent (including only 10 percent saturated fat) of calories

■ new ideas for breakfast, lunch, dinner, and snacks

■ how to adjust your meals (or medications) for exercise

■ foods to have on hand to treat hypoglycemia

■ how to manage your diabetes when you travel across time zones

■ how to handle changes in eating on sick days.

To get started, or to try a new approach, you may want to try out some meals that are already measured and counted for you. These can be found in the ADA's *Month of Meals* series of books. At first, trying to figure out how to match your food choices to these guidelines may seem overwhelming. But try to keep in mind that developing a workable meal plan takes time and a little trial and error.

Shopping Wisely

Sorting out all the various food claims as you make your way through the grocery aisles may at first require a little detective work. What do they mean by low fat? Is this a food that I can easily accommodate in my meal plan, or is it going to be loaded with lots of extras (like added sugars that will throw my carbohydrate count out of whack)? Once you and your dietitian have set daily goals for calories, fat, saturated fat, cholesterol, and carbohydrate, as well as fiber and sodium, you will find information about all of these nutrients on every food label. Reading food labels may seem daunting at first, but your dietitian can help you understand what to be on the lookout for.

As you shop, the easiest way to compare packaged foods is to look at the Nutrition Facts panel. As shown in the sample label from a can of chili with beans, you'll find the serving size, the number of calories per serving, and the calories from fat. (Pay special attention to the serving size. A bag of potato chips may not seem all that bad in terms of calories and fat content until you realize that the bag you just gulped down actually contained three and a half servings, not one.) Below this information and on the left are the actual number of calories, grams of fat, cholesterol, sodium, carbohydrate, and protein in one serving. On the right, you will find the % Daily Value. The % Daily Value tells you how much of the total daily intake you use up when you eat one serving of this food. These numbers assume that you are eating 2,000 calories each day. The actual percentages may be higher or lower depending on how many calories are in your diet. If you are eating less than 2,000 calories, you will be using up a greater percentage of your daily intake. If you are eating more than 2,000 calories each day, you will actually be using up a lower percentage of your daily intake for each serving as listed.

The chili label below shows that if you are on a 2,000-calories-a-day meal plan, a cup of chili gives you:

Nutrition Facts

Serving Size 1 cup (235 g)		Servings Per Container 2	

Amount Per Serving		Vitamin A 35%	Vitamin C 2%
Calories 260 Calories from Fat 72		Calcium 6%	Iron 30%
	% Daily Values	*Percent Daily Values are based on a 2000-calorie diet. Your Daily Values may be higher or lower depending on your calorie needs.	
Total Fat 8g	13%		
Saturated Fat 3g	17%		
Cholesterol 130mg	44%		
Sodium 1010mg	42%	Ingredients: water, beef, tomatoes, beans, modified food starch, chili powder, salt, sugar, flavoring.	
Total Carbohydrate 22g	7%		
Dietary Fiber 9g	36%		
Sugars 4g		1 Starch Exchange, 3 Lean Meat Exchanges, 1 Vegetable Exchange	
Protein 25g			

- 8 grams of fat (3 grams are saturated fat)
- 72 calories from fat
- 13 percent of your recommended fat allowance for the day.

Eating the whole can (2 servings) would give you 144 calories from fat or 26 percent of your daily fat limit. Is this too high? Should you avoid this chili? The answer depends on what you eat with the chili and at other meals during the day. Even 2 cups of chili as an entree for your evening meal would not be out of line if you accompanied it with a salad with reduced-fat or fat-free dressing, a whole-grain roll or bread, and fruit or fat-free frozen yogurt for dessert. Most important is that you do not garnish the chili with high-fat foods such as cheddar cheese and sour cream or eat it with tortilla chips or cornbread. With careful planning, the chili meal can be kept under 30 percent of your daily fat calorie allowance. Of course, your other meals and snacks should not exceed 60 percent of your recommended daily fat intake.

Along with fat, you should consider the carbohydrate content of foods. One serving of this chili provides 22 grams of carbohydrate or 7 percent of the total carbohydrate you are trying to eat each day. Under the heading "Total Carbohydrate" is 4 grams of sugars. These include both the sugar naturally present in the tomatoes, as well as the added sucrose. All sugars—whether added or naturally present—are listed in the Nutrition Facts. This means that the lactose in yogurt and the fructose in fruit juice show up as sugars on the labels, even though they occur naturally.

The chili does not provide much of your daily quota for carbohydrates. Even if you eat 2 cups of chili, you have only 14 percent of the recommended intake. The low-fat choices of salad, bread, and fruit or frozen yogurt suggested above help. They are rich sources of carbohydrate, providing 35 grams and another 12 percent, bringing the total carbohydrate in the meal to 26 percent of the recommended daily intake.

Health Claims. Food manufacturers can only make health claims on food labels that are supported by scientific research. Some of these valid claims that you might see on packages include the relationship between:

- calcium and osteoporosis
- fiber-containing grain products, fruits, and vegetables, and cancer
- fruits and vegetables and cancer
- fruits, vegetables, and grain products that contain fiber—particularly soluble fiber—and the risk of coronary heart disease
- fat and cancer
- saturated fat and cholesterol and coronary artery disease
- sodium and hypertension
- folate and neural tube defects.

Other Claims. Manufacturers also make claims about the nutritional value of their products. Sometimes it can be a little confusing. What's the difference between low-calorie or "lite?" What is "natural?" Here's what some of those claims really mean:

- **Calorie-free** means that the product has less than five calories per serving or other designated amount (make sure to note the size of the serving).
- **Low calorie** means 40 calories or less per serving.
- **Light** or **lite** means that the food has one-third less calories or 50 percent less fat than the foods it is being compared with, usually the full-calorie version of the same food.
- **Less** and **reduced** (as in fat or sugar) mean that the food is at least 25 percent lower in calories or other ingredients compared to the full-calorie or nonreduced version. When these words are used on a label, the actual percentages must also be included, for example, "50 percent less salt" or "fat reduced by 25 percent."

- **Cholesterol free** means that the food must contain less than 2 milligrams of cholesterol and 2 grams or less of saturated fat per serving.
- **Low cholesterol** indicates that a given serving contains 20 milligrams or less of cholesterol and 2 grams or less of saturated fat per serving.
- **Low fat** means that a food must have 3 grams or less of fat per serving. For example, although vegetable oils contain no cholesterol, they are 100 percent fat. Vegetable oils are still preferable to butter or lard because they have less saturated fat. But a tablespoon of vegetable oil still has about 14 grams of fat and the same 126 calories found in a tablespoon of butter or cream.
- **Fat-free** means that a food has less than 0.5 gram of fat per serving.
- **Low saturated fat** means that a food has 1 gram or less of saturated fat per serving and not more than 15 percent of its calories from saturated fat.
- **Low sodium** foods contain 140 milligrams or less of sodium per serving and per 100 grams of food. Ordinary table salt (sodium chloride) is not the only source of sodium. It is also found in monosodium glutamate (MSG), sodium bicarbonate (baking soda), and sodium nitrate and occurs naturally in some foods.
- **Very low sodium** means that a food contains 35 milligrams or less of sodium per serving and per 100 grams of food.
- **Sodium-free** or salt-free items have less than 5 milligrams of sodium per serving.
- **Light in salt** means that the food has 50 percent less sodium than the regular version.
- **Sugar free** means that the item has less than 0.5 gram of sugar per serving.
- **Dietetic** has no standard meaning. It indicates only that something has been changed or replaced. It could contain

less sugar, less salt, less fat, or less cholesterol than the regular version of the same product. For example, if you look at a package of "dietetic" cookies you might find that they are low in sodium but are not low in calories or sugar, as you might be led to believe.

- **Natural** has no specific meaning except for meat and poultry products. Here it means that no chemical preservatives, hormones, or similar substances have been added. On other food labels the word "natural" is not restricted to any particular meaning by government regulation.

- **Fresh** can only be used to describe raw food that has not been frozen, heat-processed, or preserved in some other way.

Healthy Shopping. Here are some tips for buying foods that will fit in with your healthy living plan. Try to choose foods that are rich in vitamins, minerals, and fiber and low in fat and cholesterol. Keep in mind that the ingredients list on all food labels is in order of greatest amount by weight. That is, those ingredients that make up the largest percentage of the product are listed first and those that make up a smaller percentage of the total are listed last.

- **Bread.** Look for low-fat varieties that list whole grains as the first ingredient on the label.

- **Cereal.** Choose brands that list whole grains first on the label and contain (per serving):
  - 3 or more grams of dietary fiber
  - 1 gram or less of fat
  - 5 grams or less of sugar.

- **Crackers and snack foods.** Look for whole grains listed first on the label and 2 grams or less of fat per serving (5 to 12 crackers). Consider pretzels or plain popcorn (air-popped, with no cheese or butter, 2 grams fat or less per serving) as low-fat snacks. Check sodium content per serving. Try to keep it under 400 milligrams per serving.

Tip: Cooked oatmeal is an inexpensive, healthy cereal.

Tip: Try using nonstick vegetable cooking spray for cooking and cut back on oil. Use seasonings and condiments that add flavor but not calories to your meals. Try the good taste of fresh herbs for added flavor.

- **Rice, pasta, and whole grains.** Choose converted, brown, or wild rice of any type. Look for unfilled fresh or dried pasta, preferably made with whole-grain flours. Try to avoid pastas that also contain eggs and fat.
- **Frozen desserts.** Choose varieties that contain 3 grams or less of fat per 4-ounce serving (1/2 cup). Look for low-fat frozen yogurt or low- or fat-free ice cream. Try frozen fruit juice bars with fewer than 70 calories per bar. Avoid foods made with cream of coconut, coconut milk, or coconut oil, which are high in saturated fat.
- **Milk.** Choose:
  - Fat-free or 1 percent milk—they're lower in fat
  - Buttermilk made from low-fat milk
  - Low-fat and fat-free yogurt, artificially sweetened or unsweetened.
- **Cheese.** Look for fat-free and reduced-fat cheeses with 6 grams of fat per ounce or less. Try:
  - Fat-free mozzarella and low-fat Farmer's cheeses
  - Fat-free or low-fat ricotta cheese
  - Fat-free or 1 percent fat cottage cheese.
- **Red meat.** Beef, veal, and pork are labeled by animal, body part, and type of cut: for example, "pork loin chops." Meat is graded based on its fat content. Prime is highest in fat and Choice, or Select, is lowest in fat. Choose lower fat grades of meat, such as Select, and lean body parts, such as beef—round or sirloin, pork—tenderloin, and lamb—leg.
- **Luncheon meat.** Look for lean or 95 percent fat-free meats (by weight) with:
  - 30 to 55 calories per ounce
  - 3 grams of fat or less per ounce.
- **Poultry.** Breast meat is the leanest of all. Removing the skin before cooking cuts fat by 50 to 75 percent and cholesterol by 12 percent. When turkey or chicken is used to make salami, bologna, hot dogs, and bacon, they

Tip: Ask your butcher to cut 4-ounce servings of raw meat. On cooking, it will shrink to a 3-ounce serving size.

Tip: Look for ground turkey that is less than 7 to 8 percent fat by weight (36 percent or less of its calories from fat). Often the fatty skin is ground in with the meat giving it a higher fat content.

can be high in fat. Look for those that are 30 percent fat or less.

■ **Seafood.** Supermarkets offer a wide variety of seafood. Buy fresh fish or shellfish. Look for clear eyes, red gills, shiny skin, and no "fishy" smell. Shrimp is usually shipped frozen to preserve freshness. Choose canned fish packed in water or with the oil rinsed off. Look for low-sodium products.

■ **Vegetables.** Fresh and frozen vegetables are the most nutritious per bite. Drain and rinse canned vegetables to reduce sodium content.

■ **Fruit and fruit juice.** Choose fresh, frozen, or dried fruit, preferably without added sugar. Look for 100 percent pure fruit juice. Fruit juices made from concentrate can come fresh, canned, bottled, or frozen. Check labels of brands that say "made with 100 percent juice" or "juice drink." These drinks may list other ingredients. Look for "no sugar added." Check the Nutrition Facts.

■ **Margarine and oil.** Choose:
   ■ Olive, canola, soybean, safflower, sesame, sunflower, or corn oils
   ■ Brands with vegetable oil listed first on the label
   ■ Brands that contain 1 gram or less of saturated fat per serving (usually one tablespoon)

■ **Salad dressings.** Try reduced-calorie and fat-free types.

■ **Sour cream and cream cheese.** Try fat-free or light sour cream or cream cheese. As an alternative to sour cream, consider using fat-free or low-fat yogurt either plain or flavored with chives, herbs, and spices.

■ **Soup.** Choose low-sodium, reduced-fat varieties. In preparing cream soups, use fat-free or low-fat milk or water.

■ **Cookies and cakes.** Choose brands that contain 3 grams or less fat per 100 calories. Angel food cake is made

Tip: Some fat-free cookies have more calories than the original recipe because of added sugar. Avoid palm, coconut, and hydrogenated oils.

without fat and has no cholesterol. Other cakes can be made without cholesterol by using egg substitutes but usually not without fat. Some substitute applesauce or nonfat yogurt for oil. Many cake mixes now include directions for low-fat and low-cholesterol variations.

Eating Out

Going out to eat is a part of today's lifestyle, and there is no reason to avoid it just because you have diabetes. However, as for anyone, it is important that you know what you are eating. You may want to consider calling restaurants in advance to ask about menu options. When you do dine out, keep the following in mind:

- If you don't know the ingredients in a dish or the serving size, don't be afraid to ask.
- Try to eat portions similar to what you would eat at home. Don't feel a need to clean your plate just to get your money's worth. Some restaurants allow you to order smaller portions at reduced prices. If larger portions are served, put the extra in a "doggie bag" even before you begin to eat. Or share your meal with your dining companions.
- Ask that no butter or salt be used in preparing your meal.
- Ask that sauces, gravy, salad dressings, sour cream, and butter be served on the side or left off altogether.
- Choose broiled, baked, poached, or grilled meats and fish rather than fried. If food is breaded, peel off the outer coating to get rid of the extra fat.
- Try asking for substitutions, such as low-fat cottage cheese, baked potato, or even a double portion of vegetables instead of French fries.
- Ask for low-calorie items, such as low-calorie salad dressings or broiled, steamed, or poached fish, instead of fried, even if they are not listed on the menu.

■ Plan ahead. Ask your health care team for guidelines for adjusting your insulin dose to account for changes in your meal plan.

Problem Solving

Without a doubt, special circumstances are likely to come up from time to time. Disruptions in your schedule, occasions to overindulge, holidays, and parties are inevitable. Here are some tips to help you deal with those situations.

Eating Later Than Usual. If you can't change the timing of your insulin dose, eat a piece of fruit or a starchy, low-fat snack from that meal at your usual mealtime. Even if you are not taking insulin, you may need a snack if your meal is later than usual. Just make sure to take account of it in your overall daily tally. Always carry snacks with you. You never know when you might get stuck in traffic or delayed at work. If you plan to go out for brunch, eat an early-morning snack. Then, use your lunch-time meal plan and what is left of your breakfast allotment. If dinner is to be very late, have your bedtime snack at your normal dinnertime. If you are taking insulin, you will need to adjust your short-acting doses to account for these changes. If you are not sure how to do this, talk to your health care team.

Eating More Often Than Usual. At holidays, it may seem like you're around food all day long. To deal with this, try dividing your total food for the day into snack-size meals. Then you can spread the food out a little more than usual while nibbling throughout the day without going over your allotted amounts.

Eating More Food Than Usual. Sometimes going to parties, having friends visit, or just dining out may tempt you to overeat. And you are bound to eat a little more than you should on occasion. Overeating may make you feel guilty. But don't overstress yourself with guilt. Swings in blood glucose levels are inevitable from time to time—even if you never vary your foods. Instead, think about using your other blood

> **Tip:** Instead of eating until you are full, eat until you are no longer hungry.

Traveling

 Problems are likely to arise while you're traveling, even with the best-laid plans. What if your train breaks down or your meal service is delayed on your flight? Follow these hints for smoother travels:

■ Don't take your mealtime insulin unless you are sure that you can follow it with food.

■ Carry an emergency snack pack that contains a nutritious and somewhat substantial snack, for example, crackers and cheese or peanut butter, granola bars, peanut butter, or dried fruit and nuts. Also carry some form of quick-acting glucose (hard candy or glucose tablets) in case of low blood sugar.

■ If you are changing time zones, talk to your health care team about adjusting the timing of your meals, exercise, and insulin doses.

■ Consider intensive diabetes management if you want to vary your mealtimes on a daily basis. This could be in order if you do a lot of traveling or your schedule is unpredictable.

■ When you're on the move, keep your medications or insulin, as well as injecting and glucose testing supplies, with you at all times.

glucose management tools. Do a little more exercise than usual either before or after the event.

Eating Disorders

Eating disorders occur in people with diabetes just as they do in the general population. Some researchers believe that individuals with diabetes may have an increased risk for eating disorders because they have to pay constant attention to what they are eating. Unfortunately, in our society, the self-worth of many people comes from having a "perfect" body. Some people resort to extreme measures to get or stay thin.

There are two main eating disorders, anorexia nervosa and bulimia. Each has a distinct set of warning signs. People with anorexia refuse to eat in order to stay thin. Their perception of their body is often out of tune with reality. Even very thin women sometimes perceive themselves as being overweight. People with bulimia will often eat normal or even excessive amounts of food and then purge the food by inducing vomiting or taking laxatives. Both disorders stress the body and deny it the necessary nutrients.

People with diabetes and eating disorders are likely to have more episodes of ketoacidosis (type 1 diabetes) and hypoglycemia, and their glycated hemoglobin levels tend to be higher. And because their blood glucose is not under very good control, the risk for diabetes complications, such as neuropathy, is also much greater.

A disorder similar to the common eating disorders has been found in women with diabetes who use insulin. These women intentionally reduce or omit insulin doses in an attempt to lose glucose and calories in the urine. As in other eating disorders, people who use insulin manipulation for weight loss have poorer diabetes control and more emotional problems.

If you have an eating disorder or are omitting insulin for weight control, you need professional help. Eating disorders are serious and can lead to death. Please talk to someone with whom you feel comfortable discussing your feelings. Ask your doctor to recommend a mental health counselor who can work with the other members of your health care team. Your team will work with you and your family to help you understand your disorder and how to control it. It may help you to join a support group. Talking to others who have similar problems can help you feel understood. They can also offer valuable tips for controlling the disorder.

Losing Weight

People with type 2 diabetes are more likely to be overweight and are therefore more likely to benefit, in terms of diabetes care, from weight loss. If you are overweight, losing weight is one of the single greatest steps you can take to bring your diabetes under control. Often people with type 2 diabetes who are initially prescribed insulin or oral medications find that once they lose weight, they can control their blood glucose through diet alone. But anyone can, from time to time, need to lose weight—even people with type 1 diabetes. The exception to this is women during pregnancy, a time when losing weight is probably not healthy.

If you are beginning to follow a healthy eating plan, you are probably already well on your way to losing weight. Talk to your dietitian about your weight loss goals and set up a realistic plan for trying to achieve those goals. But don't try to lose too much weight too quickly. You want to develop a new lifestyle plan that you can continue with throughout your life.

Are You Obese? More than 75 percent of all people with type 2 diabetes either are or were obese at one time or another. But what is obesity? In medical terms, obesity refers to anyone who weighs more than 20 percent over his or her ideal body weight. But what is an ideal or healthy weight for you? Your physician can help you determine what weight you should shoot for. There is a chart of generally recommended body weights on page 7 in Chapter 1. Your healthy body weight depends on many factors, including your age, height, and bone structure.

Also, how much you should weigh can also depend on how much muscle and how much fat you are carrying around. Because muscle weighs more than fat, you could weigh more than someone with a similar build, but still be at a healthier weight. And the same weight of muscle and fat can have very different health consequences. Muscle earns its keep by burning calories, but fat is stored energy. It accumulates when your food intake exceeds the amount of energy your body needs for growth, repair, and physical activity.

The Body Fat–Insulin Resistance Connection. Extra food that your body doesn't need is stored in fat cells as triglycerides. The size and number of fat cells increases with increased body fat. Having too much fat, especially on the upper body, decreases your body's ability to use insulin. This is called insulin resistance. Being overweight and overfat also strains your pancreas, and it has a harder time making the insulin your body needs. So, by getting rid of excess body fat, you can improve your sensitivity to insulin. This will help you get your diabetes under better control. See Chapter 5 for more about achieving blood glucose control.

Controlling Your Weight. Your biggest challenge may be motivating yourself to lose weight. Your best approach is a combination of exercise and a healthy diet. No one plan works for everyone. Some people find it easier to restrict their calories. Some find it easier to exercise a little harder. Whatever your approach, a cornerstone will be to develop a lifetime plan of healthy eating and regular exercise. It helps to have some people to cheer you on: your dietitian, physician, family, and friends. Your dietitian will discuss possible approaches, which can include:

■ a nutritionally sound, calorie-restricted, low-fat meal plan designed to achieve a slow gradual weight loss over several months
■ increased physical activity, daily or several times a week
■ behavior modification through a goal and reward system.

The most important thing you can do to achieve weight loss is to discuss your goals with your physician or dietitian and set realistic expectations. Don't agree to an eating plan you know you won't stick with. It will only backfire, and you could end up gaining weight instead of losing it in the long run. A steady loss of 1 pound per week or less is a safe and effective means to reach your goal.

If you use insulin or an oral diabetes medication for blood glucose control, you need to monitor your blood glucose levels as you lose weight. Your doctor will want to reduce the dose of your medication as weight loss improves your diabetes control. If you have episodes of hypoglycemia, you need to treat them with food, and this will add calories to your meal plan and slow down your weight loss. Call a member of your health care team if you start to have more frequent low blood sugar reactions so they can advise you on decreasing your insulin or oral diabetes medication dose.

Setting up a healthy weight loss plan is not much different than a healthy eating plan for someone who doesn't need to lose weight. You will need to eat fewer calories than you are used to. You will still want to eat a variety of foods and include a lot of fruits, vegetables, and grains. But you won't necessarily have to eat less food. One simple—and healthy—way to lose weight is to cut down on the fat in your diet. Each gram of fat in your diet provides twice as many calories as a gram of protein or carbohydrate. To get started, think about substituting some of the fat in your diet with these low-fat, nutrient-rich foods:

- **Bread**. Bread, especially whole-grain varieties, is one of the best foods for losing weight. It's filling, low fat, and nutritious. Good, fresh bread doesn't need any topping. Stick with whole-grain breads, English muffins, bagels, and pita bread. Steer clear of muffins and crackers, which often have a lot of added fat.

- **Pasta.** Like bread, pasta is filling, versatile, and nutritious. Whether you make your own or buy prepared noodles, avoid those made with eggs and added fat. You can make a good-tasting pasta with semolina flour and water.

- **Other grains.** Try wheat, rice, bulgur, millet, couscous, and barley. Or get adventurous and go for quinoa and amaranth. They can be used as additives in soups and casseroles, topped with vegetables, or as dishes in their own right.

- **Beans.** Beans are high-fiber, low-fat protein sources that can be used in soups and casseroles, combined with rice, used as a salad topping, or eaten by themselves.

■ **Potatoes.** The potato is an ideal diet food—as long as you don't load it with butter or sour cream. It has lots of fiber and vitamins and no fat. Try topping a baked potato with a tablespoon of fat-free yogurt or sour cream or low-fat cottage cheese. Sprinkle with herbs for added flavor. Steamed vegetables or salsa make great toppings for a baked potato.

■ **Dark, leafy vegetables.** Spinach, chicory, sorrel, Swiss chard, and even dandelion and turnip greens are rich in vitamins with no fat. The darker the color, the more vitamins the vegetable usually has.

■ **Cruciferous vegetables.** Broccoli, cabbage, bok choy, Brussels sprouts, cauliflower, and kale are rich in vitamins and high in antioxidants, substances that may protect against heart disease and certain cancers.

■ **Fruits.** Most fruits, especially those high in vitamin C, such as grapefruit, oranges, and papayas, are good for weight loss. Skip avocados—they're full of fat.

■ **Fat-free milk.** Fat-free milk and products made from fat-free milk have most of the fat removed, making it a good low-fat protein source.

As you plan your weight loss program, think ahead to keeping your new healthy weight. Many people are successful in losing weight only to find that the pounds creep back on in a year or two. What are the strategies of people who take it off and keep it off? Studies show that exercise is an important part of both taking the pounds off and keeping them off. People who keep lost weight off say that daily exercise is an essential part of their lifestyle. They also report eating more fruits and vegetables than before, a healthy habit they hung onto even after they went off their "diet."

Pregnancy

Whether you have diabetes before pregnancy or develop gestational diabetes during pregnancy, you will want to pay

Portion Control: Another Step Toward Weight Loss

■ Invest in a set of measuring cups and spoons and a food scale that weighs food in ounces or grams.

■ Serve yourself your usual portion. Now measure it. Is it more or less than you expected?

■ Weigh a piece of bread or a bagel. One serving of bread is one ounce. How does yours compare?

■ Try dividing and weighing portions of different meats and seafoods before cooking. One serving of meat is four ounces raw (three ounces after cooking).

■ Practicing portion control at home will help you estimate how much of your meal to set aside for a doggy bag when eating out.

special attention to the food you eat. Eating healthy during pregnancy really isn't all that different from a healthy diet for anyone. However, you will find that you and your growing baby require more nutrients than normal. For example, you will need more protein, calcium, iron, and vitamins while you are pregnant. Your appetite may increase, especially in the last months of pregnancy.

Ideally, you should talk to your doctor and dietitian before you decide to become pregnant, because good nutrition starts even before conception. For instance, your doctor or dietitian will advise you to take folate as a precaution against neural tube defects, which can occur early in the baby's development. Having tight blood sugar control before conceiving is another safeguard against birth defects. If you are overweight, your doctor may recommend a calorie-restricted diet before you conceive.

Once you are pregnant, your dietitian, your diabetes doctor, and your obstetrician can assess your dietary needs and help you develop a meal plan that you can follow throughout your

Recommended Dietary Allowances for Women Between the Ages of 25 and 50

	Pregnant	Not pregnant
Protein (grams)	60	50
Average calories	2,500	2,200
Vitamin C (milligrams)	70	60
Vitamin B$_6$ (milligrams)	2.2	1.6
Folate (micrograms)	400	180
Calcium (milligrams)	1,200	800
Magnesium (milligrams)	320	280
Iron (milligrams)	30	15
Zinc (milligrams)	15	12

From the National Research Council, 1990.

pregnancy. They will need to take into account your overall health and nutritional status. You'll need to know:

■ how many calories you should aim to eat each day
■ whether you will need a vitamin supplement
■ how you should divide your daily calories and carbohydrates between meals and snacks
■ goals for your blood sugar readings throughout the day.

Your dietitian and doctors can also help you ease into making lower-fat food choices if controlling weight gain is one of your goals. If you are suffering from nausea, your dietitian can help you avoid this by incorporating snacks at certain

Tip: You may be advised to eat a small breakfast because blood glucose is more likely to be high first thing in the morning.

times. If you are taking insulin, you will also want to talk to your physician and dietitian about adjusting your insulin doses to match the changes in your diet. As your pregnancy proceeds, insulin resistance increases, and you'll need more insulin. You and your dietitian and doctor may also want to discuss the use of caffeine, alcohol, and artificial sweeteners during pregnancy. Unless you have special needs, it is safe to use the artificial sweeteners aspartame and acesulfame-K during pregnancy. You need to avoid saccharin during pregnancy and breastfeeding.

Chapter 9:
Keeping Fit

A healthy, active lifestyle is a lifetime plan. Get off on the right foot by starting with a thorough preexercise exam and fitness testing. Then ask for an exercise prescription. That way, you'll have an exercise plan that will meet your individual needs.

L arry was a self-described couch potato. He worked 10 to 12 hours a day and the last thing he wanted to do when he got home was to go jogging. All he wanted was to do was sit down with a nice cold beer and relax. But since he was diagnosed with type 2 diabetes 3 years ago, his doctor, wife, and kids were after him to start an exercise program. But how would he ever find the time?

Charlotte was in the middle of training for her first marathon. She had run track in high school but wanted to do a marathon before starting college in the fall. But in the middle of her fourth week of training, she was diagnosed with type 1 diabetes. Would she be able to do the marathon? Would she even be allowed to run at all?

Diabetes or no diabetes, regular physical activity improves your overall health and helps protect you against heart disease. It can increase your energy level and help you lose weight or stay at a healthy weight. And because exercise clears glucose from the blood, if insulin is available, it fits nicely into a diabetes care program. The benefits of regular exercise sound almost too good to be true. But this is one miracle cure that really lives up to its advertising. And the more researchers study the benefits of regular exercise, the better the news gets.

One great benefit of regular exercise, especially aerobic exercise, is that it improves your heart, lungs, and blood vessels (your cardiovascular system) and protects against heart disease and stroke. It does this by strengthening your heart and circulatory system. This is important for anyone, but especially for people with diabetes, who are at greater risk for developing hardening of the arteries (arteriosclerosis) and other types of cardiovascular disease. Active movement, the kind that makes you breathe a little deeper and gets your heart pumping, improves the flow of blood through your blood vessels. Exercise helps to decrease blood cholesterol and increase levels of "good" high-density lipoprotein (HDL) cholesterol in the blood. Not only that, exercise removes glucose from your blood, both while you are exercising and for several hours afterward. For people who treat their diabetes with insulin, this could mean that you can use less insulin or eat more on the days you work out. For people with type 2 diabetes, a regular exercise program combined with a healthy diet could mean that you can control your diet without the use of insulin or oral agents, or that you can get by with less medication.

Regular exercise improves both physical health and mental outlook. It can help you lose weight and body fat and increase muscle tone and strength. For women, exercise, especially weight-bearing activities, can help preserve bone mass and prevent osteoporosis. It offers stress relief, too. Exercise may not be a cure-all, but it can be the next best thing.

Exercise Will Do You Good

Your individual response to regular exercise may include any of the following:

- ■ lowering of blood glucose levels
- ■ improvement in insulin sensitivity
- ■ lowering of glycated hemoglobin levels
- ■ decreased triglyceride levels
- ■ increased HDL (good) cholesterol
- ■ improvements in mild-to-moderate hypertension
- ■ burning more calories
- ■ conditioning of the cardiovascular system
- ■ increased strength and flexibility
- ■ improvements in your attitude, your sense of well-being, and your quality of life.

Before You Begin . . .

You may be an old hand at fitness like Charlotte who's just been diagnosed with diabetes. Or perhaps you have been living with diabetes for a while like Larry and want to start an exercise program or make changes in your existing program. Either way, a visit with your physician and other members of your health care team is in order. If you haven't done so recently, you should have a complete history and physical examination. You will also want to talk to your registered dietitian about adjusting your eating plan and your doctor about adjusting your insulin or oral diabetes medication to keep your blood sugar levels well-controlled. And you may want to talk to both your doctor and an exercise physiologist about finding an activity that's right for you.

Your doctor will want to make sure that you don't have health problems that may keep you from exercising safely. Most likely, your doctor will test for evidence of retinopathy and cardiac disease and any problems with kidney or nerve function. If you have any of these problems, it doesn't necessarily mean you can't exercise. Any damage these complications have caused needs to be considered, and perhaps repaired if possible, before you start working out regularly. For instance, you may need laser surgery to stop the advance of retinopathy. Even after laser surgery, you may be advised to avoid certain activities or to take certain precautions. Talk with your doctor and ophthalmologist about what activities are safest for you.

By the time you've finished talking with your health care team about your exercise plans and the results of your exercise tests are in, you should be able to answer these questions:
- How often should I exercise? What times of the day are best for me?
- How long should my exercise sessions be?

■ How hard should I exercise?

■ Should I stick to the same routine each time, or can I vary the length and intensity of my workouts?

■ How should I monitor how hard I exercise? Should I count my heart rate? What heart rate should I aim for? How often should I monitor?

■ Are there any types of exercise I should avoid?

■ Are there symptoms (for hypoglycemia or heart disease) that I should watch out for?

■ What special precautions should I take?

■ Do I take less insulin or change my injection site before I exercise?

Do I Need an Exercise Specialist?

 If your doctor wants you to have exercise testing before you start an exercise program, but doesn't perform exercise testing, you'll need a referral to a doctor, an exercise physiologist, or a wellness program that does.

If you are over 35 or have heart disease, you'll need a treadmill stress test that includes an electrocardiogram. This will test how a workout affects your heart activity and blood pressure. It can also help detect "silent" heart disease. You will be asked to walk on a treadmill while your blood pressure and heart function are monitored.

Exercise physiologists—people trained to study the effects of physical activity on the body—run a variety of tests to determine your fitness level. In addition to running a treadmill stress test to find out how much exercise you can do, they'll measure your strength, flexibility, and endurance and the percent body fat. Together with your doctor, the exercise physiologist can help write an exercise "prescription" just for you.

Many hospitals and universities have wellness programs for people with diabetes or rehabilitation programs for people who've had heart surgery or a stroke. These programs offer stress tests by exercise physiologists and a full range of exercise options to get you started in a medically supervised environment.

- How do I modify my meal plan?
- Will oral agents affect me differently if I exercise?

Exercising Safely

The best rule of thumb for a safe workout is to listen to your body. You should not have too much fatigue, pain, or shortness of breath. Doing too much too fast can lead to injuries or even life-threatening situations. And if you are injured, this could prevent you from doing anything at all. But how much is too much?

A good workout session should include 5 to 10 minutes of warm-up exercises and gentle stretching. Follow this with at least 20 to 30 minutes of aerobic activity. The aerobic activity should rev you up and get your heart pumping and blood flowing but should not be so intense as to cause shortness of breath, weakness, or intense pain. One easy guideline to remember is that, during your workout, you should still be able to carry on a conversation with your workout partner. Follow the aerobic activity with 5 to 10 minutes of cool-down exercises and stretching. Regular aerobic exercise, which keeps your body moving, benefits your heart, lungs, and muscles. It is the best way to burn calories and get rid of fat. Stretching increases your flexibility. To see improvement, you'll need to work out at least three to four times per week. You might want to alternate days of aerobic activity with days set aside for strengthening activities for muscle toning. For more intense workouts, you might want to alternate resting days and workout days. But, some people find it easier to control blood sugar levels by keeping a similar exercise routine each day.

Regular aerobic exercise has a double benefit. Not only does it burn calories while you are working out, it also increases your body's rate of metabolism for some time afterward. That means even after you have finished your

Diabetes: Fact or Myth?

"You know I can't overdo it. I have diabetes. Exercise might make my complications worse."

Have you convinced yourself that you're just too fragile to exercise? Diabetes is no longer an acceptable excuse for a student to miss out on sports, so why are you still using it? People with diabetes have climbed mountains, run across America, and won tennis, biking, and swimming championships. They have also participated in college and professional team sports at the highest level. Certainly you can find a way to stay fit.

There are circumstances where diabetes complications might restrict your choice of activity, but they are few:

■ If you have autonomic neuropathy that affects your heart rate and blood pressure control, you may need to avoid certain aerobic activities.

■ If you exercise with untreated proliferative retinopathy and without the guidance of an ophthalmologist and your doctor, you are threatening your vision.

■ If you are on dialysis, you can benefit from a gradually progressing exercise program.

■ If you have hypertension or heart disease, try aerobics. Avoid exercises that involve pushing against an immovable object (like a wall) or isometric exercises, where you keep your muscles contracted.

■ If you've had an organ transplant, you need to exercise. Antirejection drugs often cause weight gain and muscle wasting. Try aerobic and strength training once your doctor gives the okay and you are ready.

So, hit the pavement for a brisk walk! Get back in the business of fitness!

workout, your body is still burning more calories than it would if you hadn't worked out at all. The effect depends on the intensity of your workout. It can last for 15 minutes after a walk or for several hours after a hard racquetball match. And if you do exercises that increase your muscle mass, over time you will be burning more calories in everything you do.

That's because muscle burns many more calories than does fat tissue.

But overdoing exercise or cutting back too much in the calories you eat can be dangerous for you. If you want to lose weight, the best approach is to reduce the fat in your diet, aim for a moderate reduction in calories, and incorporate a regular exercise program into your daily routine.

Warm-Up Phase

Always warm up before any physical activity. Move slowly at first, using low-intensity, easy movements. Once your muscles are warm, gentle stretching is recommended—but no bouncing. If you stretch when your muscles are cold, you may injure them, so always warm up first. For example, if you are following a walking program, walk at an easy or comfortable pace for about 5 to 10 minutes, then stop and do some stretching. Resume walking, and gradually increase the pace. Continue to increase the intensity of the workout until you reach the aerobic phase. For a running program, you could also start out by walking, then stretching. Then try a brisk walk or an easy jog to take you into the aerobic phase.

Aerobic Phase

This is the fun part. During the aerobic phase, you rev up, keep your body moving, and get your heart pumping. Your muscles will require more oxygen during this phase. This makes your heart beat faster and your lungs breathe deeper to deliver the oxygen through your small blood vessels to the muscles that need it. During this phase, your heart rate should be kept higher than normal for about 20 to 30 minutes.

If you are starting a new exercise program, you may not be able to sustain aerobic activity for very long. That's okay. Try 5 to 10 minutes at first, and gradually increase the aerobic phase. Or try going a full 20 minutes,

What's My Target?

The simple calculation below shows you how to determine your target heart rate range, based on your age. This calculation does not work for people with autonomic neuropathy that affects their heart rate or people who take medications that affect heart rate. Your doctor or exercise physiologist can advise you on the target zone that is right for your condition. To determine this, your doctor may suggest that you have an exercise stress test.

1. Measure your heart rate while at rest. To do this, count the number of beats your heart makes in 1 full minute the first thing in the morning, before you get out of bed. Begin counting the first beat as zero. This is your resting heart rate (HRrest).

2. Determine your maximum heart rate (HRmax) by subtracting your age from 220: 220 – age = HRmax.

3. Subtract your resting heart rate from your maximum heart rate to determine your maximum heart rate reserve (HRmax reserve). HRmax – HRrest = HRmax reserve.

4. Multiply HRmax reserve by 0.5 and 0.7 to determine 50% and 70% of your heart rate reserve. When added to your resting heart rate (HRrest), this gives you the lower and upper limits of your heart rate during an aerobic workout. For example, if you are 40 years old, your maximum heart rate is 180 (220 – 40 = 180). If your resting heart rate is 75, you would have a heart rate target range of 128 to 149 (see below), to be working at 50 to 70% of your aerobic capacity.

Example:

	Lower Limit	Upper Limit
HRmax – HRrest	180	180
	– 75	– 5
HRmax reserve	105	105
× % intensity	× 0.5	× 0.7
%HRreserve	53	74
+ HRrest	+ 75	+ 75
Target HR	128	149

Be careful! This calculation does not take into account any of your specific health conditions or medications. Check that your doctor agrees that the target heart rate you've calculated is safe for you.

but if you get winded or overtired, slow down but don't stop. Walk in place or go at a leisurely pace, but just keep moving. Then when you regain your breath, start in again. Eventually, you will be able to go the full 20 to 30 minutes. Just listen to your body and slow down when you have to. If you know you don't have to kill yourself every time you exercise, it can make it less daunting. And an easy workout is better than none at all. Sometimes once you get going, you will feel better and will go the whole way. However, if you start an aerobic workout and feel increasingly worse, slow down. If you think you are having a low blood glucose reaction, stop and test your blood. If this is not possible, treat your symptoms and test as soon as you can.

Cool-Down Phase

Never stop exercising abruptly, no matter how tired you are. Keep your legs and arms moving at a relaxed pace. Walk around, step side to side, walk in place, or try some easy kicks, but avoid bending over so that your head is below the level of your heart until you have cooled down. This "cool-down" allows your heart rate and breathing to slow gradually as your movement slows. Afterward, stretch out your muscles again while they are warm. You will be able to stretch much more freely than in the warm-up phase.

Keeping Pace

In her 1976 book, *Women's Running*, Dr. Joan Ullyot described her husband's reaction to her new-found interest in running. She was a self-described "cream puff" before she decided to take up running in her 30s. After a few weeks at her new hobby, she came in from a particularly exhilarating run and told her husband, an avid runner and long-time marathoner, how much she enjoyed it. "You enjoy it?" her husband asked. "Then you must be doing something wrong!"

Unfortunately, too many people, like Dr. Ullyot's husband, have the idea that if it's exercise it's got to be too much work, and if it's not work, it can't be exercise. "No pain, no gain," seems to be the prevailing attitude. But the truth is, exercise can give you a good workout, with all the benefits to your

Safety Guidelines for Exercise

- Know your blood glucose level before, during, and after you exercise.
- Carry a fast-acting source of carbohydrate with you, such as glucose gel or tablets, a soft drink, or raisins, in case of low blood sugar.
- Try to exercise with a friend or, when you exercise alone, let people know when you are going out, where you will be, and when you will be back.
- Warm up and cool down each time you work out.
- Remember to replace body fluids. Start your workout well watered. If you are engaging in aerobic exercise for more than 30 minutes, drink water during the workout. Water is the best fluid replacer.
- Carry visible diabetes identification and money for a phone call. If convenient, consider carrying along a cellular phone.
- Use well-fitting footwear and check your feet every day and after each exercise session for redness, infected cuts, or open sores.

body—and still be fun. The trick is to pick an activity that you enjoy and do it at a pace that is comfortable for you.

A good workout should be invigorating and slightly challenging, but not miserable. If you find that you are uncomfortable the whole time, stop for a few minutes and take a rest, cut back the intensity, or find a new activity. Consider taking up a recreational sport or activity to get in your exercise. Listen to what your body is telling you. If you are in agony, you're not going to stick with that activity, and you are certainly not going to make it a lifetime habit.

The key to a safe and effective workout is to find the pace that is best for you. This is the heart rate that is best for aerobically conditioning your heart and lungs. Once you know this, you can gear your workouts to get your heart rate into the target range.

Exercise and Your Blood Glucose Level

Glucose is the fuel that muscles use to keep you going. You know that the glucose from the food you eat makes its way into the blood. This is what you measure when you do a blood glucose test. But glucose can also be found in your muscles. Your muscles keep plenty of glucose, stored as glycogen, ready to use for energy.

When you first start exercising, your body uses the glucose stored in your muscles and liver as glycogen for fuel. When these stores of glucose run low, your muscles recruit the glucose from your blood. So, during exercise, your blood glucose levels can fall. After you stop exercising, your body replenishes the stores of glucose in the liver and muscle cells. This can further lower blood glucose levels even hours after you have stopped exercising. Because of this, if you exercise in the evenings, you leave yourself vulnerable to hypoglycemia while you sleep. Even though regular exercise can be a good tool for lowering blood glucose levels, it also puts you at risk for hypoglycemia. This is why monitoring blood glucose levels before and after exercise works to keep you in the game. Exercise-induced hypoglyccmia is a concern for people who take insulin or a sulfonylurea. Whether taking metformin puts you at risk for exercise-induced hypoglycemia is questionable.

Besides directly affecting blood glucose levels, exercise can also affect the action of insulin. It's a fact that the body absorbs insulin differently from one day to the next. Similarly, exercise can affect insulin absorption. By increasing the flow of blood throughout the body, exercise speeds up how fast the insulin you inject gets to work. Injecting into an arm or leg that's then involved in exercise can speed up insulin absorption. So, a given amount of insulin can have different effects from one day to the next, especially if there are differences in your physical activity routine. This makes it doubly important to check your blood glucose levels when you exercise.

For people with type 2 diabetes, especially those who are controlling blood glucose levels through diet and exercise alone, big swings in blood glucose levels do not usually occur during exercise. However, if you have type 2 diabetes and are taking insulin or a sulfonylurea, your blood glucose levels may drop too low during or after exercise. Like people with type 1 diabetes, you will want to be careful to avoid hypoglycemia. If you are beginning an exercise program or have just been diagnosed with diabetes, it would be smart to monitor your blood glucose levels just to make sure they aren't falling too low.

Guidelines

Everyone (with or without diabetes) should follow the general recommendations for a safe and effective workout, outlined above. This means taking time to warm up and cool down and aiming for an appropriate target heart rate range. People with diabetes, especially type 1 diabetes, must also take extra care to make sure that blood glucose levels do not swing too wildly. This is true not only during the activity, but also up to 16 to 24 hours later, as blood glucose is used to replenish glucose stored in muscle tissue.

Type 1 Diabetes

The way that exercise affects blood glucose levels in people with type 1 diabetes can be a little complicated. Not only do

Tip: Check your blood glucose level before you exercise. If your blood glucose level is less than 100 mg/dl before you exercise, have a snack that has at least 15 grams of carbohydrate, such as a piece of fruit or 3 graham crackers. Then test 15 to 30 minutes later. Don't start exercising until your blood glucose level is over 100 mg/dl.

you have to worry about blood glucose levels getting too low, you also have to make sure they don't get too high. Having the right amount of insulin on board will help you get the most benefit from your workout or play time. So, take the time to learn how to predict your insulin and food needs by testing in all types of situations. This will buy you the right to enjoy all manner of aerobic and strengthening exercises open to you.

During mild to moderate exercise that doesn't last too long, your blood glucose levels are likely to fall during and after exercise. This is because the glucose in your blood is being used up faster than your liver can produce glucose. This is one of the positive benefits of exercise. But if you exercise for longer periods, or if you didn't have much glucose in your blood to begin with, you could have an episode of hypoglycemia. If you exercise on an empty stomach, you'll probably need to snack during or after your workout so your blood glucose levels don't drop too low during or after you are exercising.

If you exercise vigorously, or if you have not injected yourself with enough insulin, you could experience the opposite effect. A high blood glucose level can go even higher because of exercise. Sometimes during vigorous exercise, the nerves signal the liver to release stored glucose. This can result in a rapid rise in blood glucose levels. These increases can occur even with exercise of moderate intensity if your insulin levels are low. In this situation, then ketones can be produced, and ketoacidosis can result. That's why it is important to check blood glucose levels both before and after exercising to make sure your glucose levels aren't going too high or too low.

If you are exercising vigorously or for long periods, think about testing during the exercise. You may also want to consider eating a snack during the workout. Try snacking on something that is low in fat and has 20 to 25 grams of carbohydrate. If you are really going at it, you may need to repeat this snack every 30 minutes. How much food you need

Tip: If your blood glucose is over 250 mg/dl, test your urine for ketones. If you show moderate or large ketone levels, this means you do not have enough insulin. You will need another injection. Do not exercise until ketone levels return to negative or trace amounts.

depends on what you ate before you began exercising, how hard you are exercising, and what your insulin levels are. When in doubt, test your blood glucose.

It's never a good idea to exercise within an hour of your last injection of short-acting insulin. The insulin will be starting to work and your blood glucose levels can fall faster if you're also exercising. Know the action times of your specific insulin(s). Consider what type of insulin you are using and the timing of your injections, exercise, and meals. Try not to exercise when insulin is working its hardest unless you have eaten.

You'll also want to consider where you inject your insulin. That's because insulin can be absorbed much more rapidly if

Avoiding Exercise-Induced Low Blood Glucose

■ Exercise 1 to 3 hours after a meal. This is when your blood glucose is elevated.

■ Try not to exercise when your insulin injection is peaking. If you use only Regular insulin, this would mean to avoid exercising within the first one to two hours after injecting it. Remember that exercise increases blood flow, which speeds up how fast your insulin goes to work.

■ If your exercise is going to be of moderate to high intensity or you're going to be working out at a more moderate intensity but for a longer time than usual, think about decreasing the insulin dose that will be working while you exercise.

■ Know your own blood glucose response to different types of exercise. Learn this by monitoring often, before, during, and after exercising.

■ Test your blood glucose twice before you exercise, 30 minutes apart, to know whether your blood glucose level is stable or dropping.

■ You may need to eat during or after exercise if you work out hard or for a long time (an hour or more).

■ Know that you may need extra food for up to 24 hours after exercising, depending on how hard and how long you exercised.

it is injected close to muscles that are being exercised. The longer you wait between injecting insulin and working out, the less you have to worry about choosing your injection site. Talk to your doctor or diabetes educator about the kinds of exercise you like to do and the best places to inject your insulin. Also, discuss the timing of your insulin injection, meals, and exercise. Perhaps you can time these events so you won't have to worry about where you inject insulin.

You may need to know which way your blood glucose level is heading, especially if you are about to start an activity in which you can't easily "pull over." If you are about to go scuba diving or wind surfing, testing your blood glucose level midstream may not be very convenient. Try testing 1 hour, then 30 minutes before you start. If your tests show that your blood glucose level is coming down, even if you are still in a safe range, you may want to have a snack to keep it from going any lower. Also, keep in mind when your insulin is peaking.

If you suspect a low blood glucose reaction coming on, **stop exercising at once.** Take some form of fast-acting sugar. Don't fool yourself into thinking you can last just 5 minutes longer. Always keep some form of glucose handy just in case you need it while exercising. This can be a soft drink or fruit juice, which will provide sugar and replace water. Or you can use glucose tablets, raisins, or hard candy.

Be on the lookout for hypoglycemia not only while you are exercising, but up to 24 hours later. Keep monitoring your blood glucose levels to prevent very low blood glucose.

Type 2 Diabetes

Regular exercise can be an important part of the management plan for people with type 2 diabetes. Many people with type 2 diabetes find their blood glucose levels are much easier to control every day if they exercise regularly. This is because regular exercise increases insulin sensitivity and lowers insulin resistance. And regular physical activity,

Tip: Testing your blood glucose levels is a great idea, even if you're not at high risk for hypoglycemia. You'll get a kick from seeing just how much exercise can reduce your blood glucose level. So, try testing before and a little bit after your workout.

How Do I Keep Motivated?

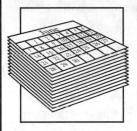 It will take several months for your new, more active lifestyle to become a habit. In the meantime, try these strategies for sticking with it.

■ **Schedule your workout and stick to your schedule.** It's as important as any other appointment in your day.

■ **Find a workout partner.** On those days when you're tempted to skip your workout, your partner will probably be ready to go. It helps to have a commitment to someone else.

■ **Cross-train.** This means having different activities in your exercise bag of tricks instead of doing the same thing every time. Twice a week, you may lift weights; three days a week, you may take an aerobics class; once a week, you may play tennis. This keeps your interest level up and your risk of injury down. By building up your fitness in many areas—strength, flexibility, and aerobic capacity—you'll protect yourself from overuse of any one group of muscles.

■ **Set realistic, specific goals.** Don't expect to lose a lot of weight or run a mile without stopping right away. Set both long-term ("I plan to lose 15 pounds this year") and short term ("I plan to exercise four times this week") goals.

■ **Reward yourself for sticking with it.** Do an easier workout one day a week, like a yoga session. Don't skip the hot tub or steam room if you really enjoy them after your workout. Buy a new pair of workout shoes.

■ **Track your progress.** Record noticeable changes like your energy level, the way your clothes fit, and the amount of medication you take.

combined with a balanced, calorie-restricted diet, leads to weight loss—which further lessens insulin resistance.

If you have diabetes complications or other health concerns, you need to be careful. Be sure to consult with your doctor before starting an exercise program. However, be assured that anyone can benefit from some form of exercise, as long as it doesn't increase your risk of injury. For example, just increasing some daily and familiar activities, such as walking and climbing stairs, is an excellent start. Or consider a mild weight-lifting program to increase your strength. You can start strength training using very small weights or no weights at all. Ask your health care team about working out with elastic bands or with isometric exercises.

If you take insulin, you'll need to follow precautions to prevent low blood glucose, just like people with type 1 diabetes. See the section above about type 1 diabetes, and follow those guidelines for reducing insulin or adjusting medications. You'll probably want to try to avoid treating low blood glucose with extra snacks, but talk to your doctor and diabetes educator about what's best for you. If you take oral diabetes medications, you won't need to worry too much about exercise lowering your blood glucose levels to the point that you have severe hypoglycemia. However, exercise-induced hypoglycemia can occur, so it pays to know what to look for and how to treat it. People who treat their type 2 diabetes by meal planning and exercise rarely suffer from hypoglycemia.

If you are cutting back on calories to lose weight, exercise will speed up your progress. Review your meal and exercise plans with your health care team to be sure you are getting enough vitamins and minerals and you are replacing fluids lost during exercise. If you are on a very-low-calorie diet (fewer than 800 calories per day), your doctor should be closely monitoring your activities and overall health. Follow your doctor's instructions about exercising.

If you have difficulty getting around, are obese, or are recovering from heart surgery or stroke, talk to your doctors and an exercise physiologist about the best way to begin your exercise program. You'll need to start slowly and build up gradually. Consider joining a wellness or rehabilitation program, or see what kind of program your insurance will cover. The exercise specialists at these types of programs will create an exercise plan that avoids worsening any health problems you have.

Exercise and Pregnancy

If you're a regular exerciser with type 1 or type 2 diabetes, pregnancy is no excuse to stop working out, but you may need to lower your workout intensity. If you have gestational diabetes, you need to know that exercise lowers your blood glucose level, and so is considered an effective part of your treatment plan. Staying physically fit during your pregnancy will help you prepare for the work of labor and baby care that lays ahead. Exercise can also moderate your weight gain, increase your strength and stamina, and lower your anxiety level.

Exercise during pregnancy does pose some risks. You'll need to consult with your diabetes doctor and your

Tip: Some good exercises during pregnancy are swimming or aerobics classes held in the pool, walking, and stationary bicycling. Discuss with your doctor what exercises are safe for you.

Keep Your Workout Safe During Pregnancy

- Work with your health care team to develop a glucose testing regimen.
- Drink plenty of fluids before, during, and after you exercise.
- Warm up before and cool down after you exercise.
- Keep the strenuous part of your workout no longer than 15 minutes.
- Keep your heart rate under 140 beats per minute while you exercise (this is about 23 beats in a 10-second pulse count).
- Keep your body temperature under 100° F. Ask your doctor about hot tubs or steam rooms.
- Avoid exercises that involve:
    - lying on your back after your fourth month of pregnancy
    - straining or holding your breath
    - jerky movements or quick changes of direction
- Stop exercising if you feel lightheaded, weak, or very out of breath.
- Ask your obstetrician to show you how to feel your uterus for contractions during exercise. These contractions can be a sign you're overdoing it.

obstetrician about what types of workouts you want to do. They will consider your medical history. One thing you definitely should not do is start a new, strenuous exercise program while you're pregnant. This is especially true if you weren't a regular exerciser before pregnancy. However, you'll probably be able to begin a new program of low-intensity exercises.

Blood glucose control is very important before and during your pregnancy, for both your health and that of your baby, and you will be aiming for tight control. So, you'll need to be extra watchful for low blood glucose levels caused by exercise. Your glucose level can go very low very quickly. Frequent blood glucose monitoring will be your way to keep watch on hypoglycemia. Chances are, you'll be testing a lot more than normal anyway. Many women aiming for tight control measure their blood sugar level seven or more times a day.

Finding an Exercise That Works for You

There is no single perfect exercise. But there are some types that burn more calories, some that are particularly good for developing strength and flexibility, and others that are especially good for improving your cardiovascular system. Every exercise also has its downside or even risks. For people with heart disease or diabetes, some of the risks of particular types of exercise are important to know. The trick is to find an activity that is good for you, and of course fun, but one that won't worsen any of your complications or lead to new problems.

Certain activities should certainly be avoided by people with health problems.

■ People with untreated proliferative retinopathy should avoid any activity before their retinopathy is treated. Then get your doctor's okay to exercise.

■ If you have peripheral neuropathy, exercises that traumatize the feet, such as running, jogging, and high-impact aerobics, should be avoided. You may also be at a higher risk for injuring soft tissues and joints because you may not be able to feel when you've overstretched or overdone it.

■ If you have been given a diagnosis of autonomic neuropathy, you should not exercise until your doctor and perhaps an exercise specialist have given you the okay. Your body may not be able to compensate for the exertion of exercise. You may be at high risk for dehydration and low

Foot Care: The Agony of the Feet

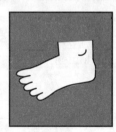

If you're an adult, you'll need to pay attention to foot care. Most children and teens with diabetes don't need to think too much about foot complications.

■ Check your feet daily for any red, irritated areas, blisters, corns, calluses, or ingrown toenails. If you detect a problem, take care of it right away. Don't expect it to get better on its own.

■ Well-fitted shoes are worth their weight in gold. They will help keep problems from starting in the first place. Shoes should feel comfortable right away. Don't count on breaking them in.

■ If you have neuropathy or decreased sensation in your feet, you can't always trust the way shoes feel as you try them on. You may need to consult your podiatrist or a professional shoe fitter (a pedorthist) to get a correct fit.

■ You may want to try special socks designed with extra cushioning for exercise. In truth, any good athletic sock that is made of a blend of cotton and synthetic material will provide warmth and cushioning and will absorb perspiration away from your skin. Start each workout in a clean pair of socks.

blood pressure. Your aerobic capacity—the ability of your heart, lungs, and blood vessels to support your muscles while they work—and your ability to achieve maximum heart rate may also be limited by neuropathy, so you may have to stick to activities of low intensity, such as walking. You will also need to choose a method other than counting your heart rate to measure workout intensity.

■ If you are pregnant, avoid strenuous activities and those that are jarring, especially during the last months.

Walking

Walking is probably the best, safest, and least expensive form of exercise. It can fit into almost anyone's schedule and can be integrated into other events and activities. If you have to drive a half-mile to the post office, you may as well walk and squeeze in a workout. The only investment you need to make is in a comfortable pair of shoes for walking. In exchange for this—and extra attention to foot care—you get an exercise that conditions the cardiovascular system, the lungs, and the muscles of the arms, legs, abdomen, lower back, and buttocks.

Walking can be especially invigorating if you move at a brisk pace and travel over hilly terrain. Walking is a life-long activity, and it is a good way to ease into a more active lifestyle. It is especially good if you are newly diagnosed with diabetes or are not used to exercising. Maybe you are a little afraid that exercising too vigorously will throw your blood glucose levels out of whack, just when you thought you had things under control. After walking for a while, you will develop the confidence, stamina, and fitness level to try other activities.

Start walking for 5 or 10 minutes and gradually increase your time. You don't necessarily have to set mileage goals. Work on lengthening the time you spend walking and eventually your mileage will increase. At the beginning it may take

Tip: Try on shoes in the afternoon, when foot size tends to be a little bigger, while wearing your workout socks. Wear new shoes for short periods at first. Check your feet for red, irritated areas. You may need extra padding in some areas of the shoe to prevent friction.

Counting Cals

Counting the calories you're burning is one way to keep track of your fitness efforts. The numbers of calories burned shown here are for a 150-pound person working out at an average intensity. If you weigh more or work out harder, you'll burn a few more calories. But remember, exercise has more benefits than just burning calories.

Activity	Notes	Calories burned in 30 minutes*
Walking at 4 miles/hour	Works the lower body; include some hills	135
Jogging at 5 miles/hour	Run on soft surface; use well-padded shoes	240
Swimming, leisurely	The crawl uses the whole body	200
Bicycling, leisurely	Works the lower body	200
Ice skating	Nonstop at a moderate pace	235
Low-impact aerobics	Nonstop at a moderate pace; include arms	170
Advanced aerobics	Nonstop at high intensity	240
Tennis, doubles	Keep moving	200
Tennis, singles	Keep moving	270
Golf	Carry your clubs and walk the course	150

*Based on metabolic expenditure units given in Ainsworth BE et al.: *Med Sci Sports Exercise* 25:71–80, 1993.

you 30 minutes to walk a mile. An experienced walker can walk a mile in 10 to 12 minutes. A pace of 4 miles per hour or 15 minutes per mile is a good goal to work toward, if you are motivated by keeping track of your time and mileage. However, for many people, paying too close attention to the pace destroys the joy of the activity. Walk at a pace that is both enjoyable and invigorating for you. Some people find that walking with hand weights makes for a more challenging workout, but first check with your physician or exercise physiologist.

Jogging/Running

Some people would rather jog or run than walk. You get a more intense workout in less time than walking. But jogging is tougher on your joints and feet because each step pounds the foot with three to five times your body's weight. Make sure that you discuss your running or jogging program with your doctor before you start.

To reduce the chances that you'll get injured or drop out of a walking/jogging/running program, take the time to develop your leg and foot muscles. If you are trying to progress from walking to running, try this: Start walking your normal route or distance. Walk for a few minutes, then try jogging. Jog for as long as you feel comfortable. If you start to feel winded or uncomfortably out-of-breath, switch to a brisk walk. Don't stop, but keep walking. When you have regained your breath, jog for a little bit. You may find that eventually you will be able to jog the whole distance. Of course, you may want to stick to a combination run-walk or you may want to alternate some days running and some days walking. Do what feels good for you.

Avoid jogging on concrete—it's too hard; try the track at a nearby school or a park instead. Buy a pair of well-padded running shoes and replace them before they wear out. They should be comfortable from the first time you put them on. If you start to develop any persistent pain, especially in your joints, don't risk further injury. Rest, take a few days off, or try walking instead.

Strength Training

Strength training with weights is not just for Mr. Universe wannabes. Anyone, old or young, male or female, who wants more strength and endurance can benefit. Well-toned muscles can help in all your daily activities, whether it's carrying groceries, climbing stairs, doing laundry, or changing a flat tire. Strength training can also help prevent osteoporosis and build muscle, even in elderly people. This is important because as people get older, they tend to lose muscle mass and tone. Even people in their 80s and 90s can greatly increase strength through weight training. Another benefit of weight training is that well-toned and larger muscles burn more calories even when you are doing absolutely nothing. So, a regular weight-lifting program can help you lose fat and

Safe Strength Training

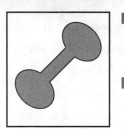

■ Talk to your doctor before starting any weight-lifting routine. For some people, lifting weights will increase the risk of worsening diabetes complications.

■ Always do some sort of aerobic exercise, such as walking, jogging, jumping rope, or jumping jacks for 5 or 10 minutes to warm up before lifting weights. Cool down after lifting.

■ Don't hold your breath while lifting. Instead, breathe in when lowering weights and breathe out when lifting.

■ Exercise with a partner or trainer, who can help you if something goes wrong.

■ Always allow at least a day's rest between workout sessions, or alternate upper body training one day with lower body training the next.

control blood glucose levels in the long run, both during and in-between workouts. It may also help reduce the risk of heart disease.

There are several approaches to weight training. It can be as simple as lifting a small set of hand weights in your living room. Or you may want to join a gym or health club where you will have access to a whole array of weight machines and exercise equipment. Most weight training programs involve sets of weight lifting exercises. Each set consists of a series of repetitions. When you first start, do just one set each session. Eventually work your way up to three to six sets each session. As you become stronger, you will also find that you can lift more weight. Then add more weight, a little at a time. Muscles become stronger by lifting heavier loads. Your training program should be tailored with your goals in mind:

■ If you just want to increase your endurance, then choose a weight that you can lift only 15 to 20 times. Rest for a few minutes between each set of repetitions (reps).

■ If you want to build both strength and endurance, choose a weight you can lift only 8 to 12 times. Rest for a few minutes between sets of reps.

■ If you are geared toward competitive weight lifting, you might want to maximize your strength by lifting only 2 to 6 times. Rest for a few minutes between sets of reps.

The Best of the Rest

Try yoga to increase your flexibility. Try aerobics classes, especially if you like to dance. Try a trial membership at a health club convenient to your home. You could try out their machines to see if there are any you would use at home. You could rekindle your love of tennis, squash, or volleyball. Make an aerobic challenge out of washing the windows or sweeping the deck. When it comes to your fitness, the old saying "use it or lose it" is true!

Chapter 10: Diabetes Complications and Prevention

A long, healthy life with diabetes is possible if you avoid complications of diabetes. The key is the same for every single complication: controlling blood glucose levels.

red went to the doctor because he was having problems with his vision. He didn't expect a diagnosis of diabetes. It was bad enough that he would have to change his diet and start insulin, but he would also need eye surgery. He read that complications arise after living with diabetes for years. It hardly seemed fair that he had retinopathy even before he knew he had diabetes. He wondered what else might be wrong with him.

Elaine was only 16 when she was diagnosed with diabetes. Everyone had told her to take care of herself and she did everything she was told. But back then, they didn't have glucose meters and insulin pumps. Now she was in her 30s and started to experience numbness in her legs. It just wasn't fair. She had done all the right things.

It's possible that you view your diabetes care from two perspectives: the "close-at-hand" and the "far away." The close-at-hand might be things like daily blood glucose monitoring, making wise food choices, and reaching next month's fitness goal. And, if you're like most people with diabetes, the far-away category contains diabetes complications: They are something to consider, but not dwell on.

But the truth is, the more you think now about the complications of diabetes and ways to prevent them, the better off you will be. The best way to reduce your risk of getting diabetes complications is to keep your blood glucose levels as close to normal as possible. Doing this not only helps your faraway picture look brighter, your close-at-hand experiences with diabetes will be more rewarding.

The tell-tale signs of diabetes complications usually don't appear until after many years of having diabetes. That's why, if you're between 12 and 30 years old, you can wait until you've had diabetes for five years to have a comprehensive dilated eye exam—unless, of course, you're having vision problems. Teenagers would do better to keep up good blood glucose testing habits rather than do daily foot exams. Foot problems due to diabetes are much more common in adults with poorly controlled blood glucose levels. Women with gestational diabetes do not need to worry about developing eye, kidney, or nerve problems from diabetes.

Warning Signs of Diabetes Complications

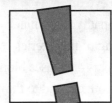 Anytime you "just don't feel right" and can't explain it, you need a discussion with your doctor. Waste no time in telling your doctor if you notice:

- vision problems, like blurry or spotty vision or flashes
- unexplained, overwhelming tiredness
- discomfort in your leg with walking
- numbness or tingling in hands or feet
- chest pain that comes on when you start to exert yourself
- cuts or sores that stay infected or take a long time to heal
- constant headaches, which may be a sign of high blood pressure.

However, some people have the unpleasant experience of having diabetes complications come on rather suddenly after diagnosis. Or they find that complications are present at diagnosis. This is more likely if you're diagnosed with type 2 diabetes. The signs of type 2 diabetes may be so subtle that you may have had a problem with high blood glucose levels for quite a while without ever realizing it. The damage was occurring even before your diagnosis. Maybe it was a diabetes complication, like problems with your vision, that brought you to the doctor in the first place. Because of your symptoms, your doctor tested your blood glucose levels and diagnosed diabetes.

The Glucose Connection

Almost all of the complications of diabetes are caused by having too much glucose in the blood. Think about how sticky your fingers feel when you get maple syrup on them. A major problem—and the cause of many health problems associated with diabetes—is that the small blood vessels that carry blood throughout the body get clogged up. Blood can't get to where it needs to be. This causes problems with circulation and leads to eye disease (retinopathy) and kidney damage (nephropathy). Too much glucose can speed up the normal hardening of the arteries (atherosclerosis) that occurs as you age. This decreases blood flow to the heart, which can cause a heart attack, and to the brain, which can cause a stroke. Too much glucose can also damage nerve cells and delay, change, or halt the electrical messages that your nerve cells send throughout your body.

But the good news is that we know why these problems happen to people with diabetes, so we know how to go about preventing them. The Diabetes Control and Complications Trial (DCCT) and the United Kingdom Prospective Diabetes Study (UKPDS) showed that keeping blood glucose levels as close to normal as possible can help prevent or slow the progression of many of the complications of diabetes. The DCCT examined more than 1,400 people with type 1 diabetes for 10 years, and the UKPDS studied people with type 2 diabetes for over 20 years. Those people who kept their blood glucose levels as close to normal, or nondiabetic, levels as possible ended up with less eye disease, less kidney disease, and less nerve damage.

The volunteers in the DCCT's tight control group had to test their blood more often—4 to 7 times each day—and follow more complicated schedules for injecting insulin. They had to stay in close touch with their health care team. Their health care teams had to be available for support a lot more often than usual. But their hard work paid off. They cut their risk for developing these complications by more than 50 percent. For example, those who kept their blood glucose under tight control had 76 percent less eye disease, 60 percent less nerve damage, and 35 to 56 percent less kidney damage than the study group who used less intensive insulin therapy. For more information about the DCCT, the UKPDS, and tight control, see Chapter 7.

Even if you decide that intensive diabetes management is not for you, any improvement you can make in lowering your blood glucose levels will benefit you. The less time you spend with too much glucose in your blood, the lower your risk for developing diabetes complications. Your goal is to help your body use the glucose you take in as efficiently as possible. If you use insulin, controlling blood glucose levels involves matching insulin doses to your food intake and exercise. If you use oral diabetes medications, the technique for controlling blood glucose levels is similar, but fine-tuning is harder. And for everyone with diabetes, watching your carbohydrate intake and getting regular physical activity help your body get the glucose into your cells where it can produce the energy you need.

Even if you already have some of the complications of diabetes, it's not too late to improve your glucose control. Most conditions can be helped by improving blood glucose control, even if they have already developed. And all diabetes complications can be treated. At the very least, you can keep many complications from getting worse by keeping your blood glucose under control and taking other steps to healthier living. So, if you are already following a healthy living plan—exercising regularly and eating nutritious foods in healthy portions, for example—you're already on your way to preventing complications.

Besides Controlling Glucose, You Can . . .

Quit Smoking

The role of smoking in causing lung disease is well known. But smoking causes other problems that are especially harmful for people with diabetes. Over time, smoking damages your heart and circulatory system by narrowing your blood vessels. When blood flow to cells is restricted, the cells in your body can die. This damage can lead to heart disease, impotence, and amputation. Coupled with too much glucose in the blood, the effect can be devastating. If you smoke now, talk to the members of your health care team about methods that can help you quit.

Eat Healthy Foods

Your doctor or dietitian has most likely suggested a meal plan low in fat and cholesterol with lots of whole grains, fruits, and vegetables and a moderate amount of protein. Maybe you have even been advised to cut down on salt, if you have high blood pressure. By eating wisely, you can reap benefits far beyond keeping your blood glucose under control. You can also reduce your risk of cardiovascular and kidney disease. And learning healthy eating habits is contagious. Your family will benefit, too.

Control High Blood Pressure

High blood pressure, or hypertension, puts a strain on your body, especially your heart, blood vessels, and kidneys. You can lower your blood pressure by losing weight, exercising, and limiting the amount of alcohol you drink. For some people, limiting salt intake helps lower blood pressure. Your doctor may also prescribe medication to keep your blood pressure down.

Exercise Regularly

Exercise helps people with diabetes in several ways. It can delay or help stop cardiovascular disease. It can help clear glucose out of your blood, so that cells can use it for energy. This lowers blood glucose levels and may lower the amount of insulin you need. And it can give you an emotional boost that can help you be more motivated to control your blood glucose. For people who are overweight, exercise helps in weight reduction, and losing weight lowers your insulin resistance. Exercise just helps your body work better, like a well-

Diabetes: Myth or Fact?

"I give up. It's just not worth the trouble. No matter what I do, I'll get diabetes complications."

Unless you've been dealt an incredibly poor genetic "hand," this is a diabetes myth. Blood glucose levels are at the root of this disease, so it makes sense that keeping blood glucose levels as close to normal as possible will stop or slow down diabetes complications from occurring. People studying diabetes and seeing patients with diabetes have suspected this connection for decades. But it took the Diabetes Control and Complications Trial and the United Kingdom Prospective Diabetes Study to prove it.

You are not predestined to get debilitating diabetes complications. It's true that one study found that, after 20 years of diabetes, 95 percent of the people in the study had some evidence of retinopathy. Early retinopathy can be successfully treated without impairing vision. But, there's always the genetic wild card. Like diabetes, heart disease and high blood pressure run in families. If you have genes that make you more susceptible to, for instance, poor circulation, your body might react more to the effects of too much blood glucose. Do high blood pressure, obesity, or cardiovascular problems occur in your family? These are health conditions that are worsened by high blood glucose levels. If health problems that are aggravated by the effects of diabetes are in your family gene pool, you have even more reason to work hard at getting near-normal blood glucose levels.

oiled machine. See Chapter 9 on working with your doctor to design an exercise program that is safe for you.

Dealing With Complications

Despite your best efforts, you may some day develop complications from diabetes. Factors you can't control—your age, race, and genetic makeup—can affect your risk of developing complications.

Diabetes Care Schedule

✔ **Every 3 months**   ■ **Regular visits to your doctor:** if using insulin or if on intensive insulin therapy*

✔ **Every 6 months**   ■ **Glycated hemoglobin test (such as HbA1c)**

■ **Regular visits to your doctor:** if not using insulin*

✔ **Every year**   ■ **HDL/cholesterol:** for average reading; more often if high levels are being treated

■ **Kidneys:** microalbumin measured

■ **Eyes:** examined through dilated pupils

■ **Feet:** more often in patients with high risk foot conditions (neuropathy, vascular disease)

✔ **Every 2 to 3 years**   ■ **HDL/cholesterol:** if last reading indicates very low risk

*Depending on your individual health.

If you have been taking steps to prevent complications, you may feel cheated if you develop a diabetes-related health problem. You may have many of the same feelings you had when you were first diagnosed with diabetes—anger, fear, guilt, or denial. You may feel overwhelmed that on top of dealing with diabetes and the ordinary stresses of everyday life, you now have new health problems to contend with. You may feel tired of having worked so hard to prevent complications, only to have them develop anyhow.

But there are treatments for diabetes complications, and they are getting better all the time. So be sure you are getting up-to-date information on treatments and prevention. Ask your doctor and other members of your health care team—don't rely on hearsay from friends and relatives who may not be up on the latest.

The remainder of this chapter is in sections that explain some of the most common complications of diabetes, with emphasis on ways to prevent and treat them:

- cardiovascular disease
- retinopathy (eye disease)
- nephropathy (kidney disease)
- neuropathy (nerve disease)
- infections.

If you are interested in information about blood lipid abnormalities, look in the section on cardiovascular complications. If you want information about amputation, see the section on infections. If you need information about impotence or sexual problems, see Chapter 11.

Cardiovascular Disease

There are several kinds of cardiovascular disease, and they are all due to problems in how the heart pumps blood or how blood circulates throughout the body. Blood flows through the blood vessels in your body to deliver

Your Risk, In General: Cardiovascular Disease

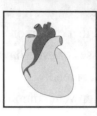

People with diabetes are:
- 2 to 4 times likely to get heart disease
- 5 times more likely to have a stroke than people without diabetes
- Cardiovascular disease causes more than half of the deaths in older people with diabetes.

all the oxygen, glucose, nutrients, and other substances needed to run your body and keep your cells alive. When blood can't get to cells and tissues, they can become damaged or die.

Most of the cardiovascular complications related to diabetes have to do with a blockage or slowdown in blood flowing throughout the body. Diabetes can change the chemical makeup of some of the substances found in the blood, and this can cause the openings in blood vessels to narrow or to clog up completely. This is called atherosclerosis, or hardening of the arteries, and diabetes seems to speed it up.

Blood vessels can become clogged in several ways. If there are too many lipids in the blood, such as cholesterol and triglycerides, they can cling to the walls of the blood vessels. Diabetes changes the number and makeup of proteins that deliver lipids to cells. But if you achieve good glucose control, these so-called lipoproteins will return to normal and do their job of delivering blood lipids to cells. Blood lipids can also accumulate if you eat too much fat and cholesterol. And if there is also too much glucose in the blood, these lipoproteins can become extra sticky, and blood vessels are even more likely to clog. That's why it is important to eat a balanced diet if you have diabetes. By keeping your glucose levels under control and limiting fat intake, you can prevent the clogging of your blood vessels. Diabetes can also affect the platelets in your blood, which play a role in blood clotting. Diabetes can cause blood platelets to churn out too much of a substance that causes blood to clot, and this can also cause blood vessels to narrow.

When blood vessels narrow or clog due to cardiovascular disease, the blood supply to the heart, brain, and other tissues and organs can be restricted. If blood to the heart is slowed for a time, it can cause chest pain known as angina. Angina is not itself a disease, but it can give a warning that something is slowing the flow of blood to the heart. A complete stoppage of blood is a heart attack. When the blood flow to the brain is cut off, this can cause a stroke. Blockages in the arteries of the legs can cause leg pain known as intermittent claudication.

Hypertension

Hypertension, or high blood pressure, can also contribute to cardiovascular disease. Hypertension itself usually has no symptoms. If you have it, you probably won't even realize it unless you have your blood pressure taken at your doctor's office. Hypertension is especially common among people with type 2 diabetes. Nearly 60 percent of people with type 2 diabetes also have high blood pressure. Hypertension in people with type 1 diabetes can be a sign of kidney disease.

If you have hypertension, your heart is forced to work harder than usual. This extra stress can damage the lining of your arteries. If this goes untreated for a long period, a type of fatty tissue called artheroma can form. This can cause your arteries to narrow or become completely blocked. Even by itself, hypertension can damage small blood vessels and capillaries, especially in the eyes and kidneys. If you have hypertension on top of diabetes, there is an even greater chance that your arteries may become clogged. The risk of further damaging tissues and further aggravating cardiovascular disease increases dramatically if you have both hypertension and diabetes.

Prevention

There are five things you can do to prevent cardiovascular disease:

- control blood glucose levels
- stop smoking
- eat low-fat foods

Blood Lipid Abnormalities

 Abnormal blood lipid profiles are quite common in diabetes, especially type 2 diabetes. Blood lipid abnormalities, obesity, and type 2 diabetes seem to go hand in hand. That has led researchers to ask whether blood lipid abnormalities are the result of obesity, and ultimately, type 2 diabetes. If you and other family members have severely high levels of blood fats, you may have a lipid disorder that is not related to diabetes. This condition needs to be evaluated and treated.

High levels of LDL cholesterol (bad cholesterol) and triglycerides can usually be lowered by:

- losing weight
- keeping blood glucose levels under control
- increasing physical activity
- eating a healthy low-fat, high-fiber diet.

All of these steps will help control your diabetes and will also bring down blood fat levels. To help change your eating habits, your best bet is to visit a dietitian.

In some cases, medications are needed. If you are prescribed drugs to lower blood lipids and cholesterol:

- watch carefully for changes in your blood glucose levels; even if you have type 2 diabetes, you may have to monitor your blood glucose level several times each day
- start new drugs one at a time, if possible; some medications can interfere with the breakdown, absorption, and removal of other medicines
- know that many kinds of medications are used to treat high blood lipid levels, and that side effects may occur; report anything unusual to your doctor.

■ avoid high blood pressure

■ exercise.

All of these actions will help keep your large blood vessels wide open for blood to flow to all your vital organs, and you will lower your risk of developing cardiovascular disease dramatically. Some people with hypertension may also find that cutting down on salt in the diet can also improve high blood pressure, which in turn can help prevent cardiovascular disease.

Treatment

If you develop cardiovascular disease, the five preventive measures listed above can still help you. Even if you are treated for cardiovascular disease, taking preventive steps can slow or stop the progression of the disease. A low-cholesterol, low-fat diet is especially good. And increasing the amount of fiber-rich foods you eat can further lower your levels of cholesterol and triglycerides (the blood vessel clogging culprits). Your doctor may also recommend that you take a "baby" aspirin each day.

But sometimes, prevention alone isn't enough, especially if you have had cardiovascular disease for a while. If your blood vessels are already blocked or significantly narrowed, your physician may recommend surgery to remove the blockage. Or you may be prescribed medication to reduce blood clotting, to lower cholesterol levels, or to reduce high blood pressure. Angina can also be treated by both preventive and surgical steps. The goal is to increase the amount of oxygen going to the heart.

Several different surgical procedures are now commonly used to physically remove the blockages of blood vessels. **Balloon angioplasty,** while not performed as often as it used to be in people with diabetes, is a procedure that uses a balloon at the tip of a long tube. The surgeon inserts the tube into the blocked artery and then inflates the balloon. This opens up the blocked vessel. A metal stent, or ring, may be left in place to help the blood vessel stay open. **Arthrectomy** is another kind of minor surgery used to open blood vessels. With this technique, a surgeon bores a hole through a blocked blood vessel. Laser surgery can also be used to melt away blockages with an intense beam of light. All of these surgeries can remove smaller blockages and require little recovery time.

A more severe blockage calls for more serious surgery. Surgeons can create a detour around the blocked artery through arterial bypass surgery. Maybe you already know someone who has had a single, double, triple, or even quadruple bypass surgery of the heart. Surgeons can construct one, two, three, four, or even more detours, if there are multiple blockages. To do this, surgeons remove a part of a larger artery from the chest wall or from a vein in the patient's leg and attach it above and below the blocked blood vessel. Now, instead of running up against a wall, blood can flow around the blockage and through the new blood vessel.

Intermittent claudication, or leg pain, is not a nerve problem but a sign of a circulatory problem. It can be relieved by exercise, quitting smoking, drug therapy, and surgery similar to that for blocked heart arteries. Strokes are usually treated by a combination approach. Normalizing blood glucose and blood lipid levels and blood pressure, helping the person recover mental and physical abilities, and giving drugs that reduce blood clotting are all effective common approaches. Sometimes surgery is needed.

People with cardiovascular disease are advised to get more exercise and eat a low-fat diet. Because of diabetes, you'll also need to add controlling blood glucose levels, and perhaps losing weight, to your recovery strategies.

Retinopathy

One common complication of diabetes is retinopathy, a disease of the retina, the light-sensing region of the inner eye. The retina acts like a miniature "movie screen" in the back of your eye, on which the images you see are projected. Retinopathy is caused by damage to the blood vessels that supply blood to the retina.

You probably won't even notice diabetic retinopathy when it first begins. Only a doctor can detect the changes in blood vessels found in the early stages of disease, during an eye exam. And early detection is the key to keeping this disease from interfering with your vision. Detected early enough, retinopathy can be slowed or stopped altogether.

Retinopathy is more common in people with type 1 diabetes, but people who have had type 2 diabetes for many years can also develop it. There are two major forms of retinopathy. In one type, called nonproliferative (or background) retinopathy, blood vessels can close off or weaken. When this happens, they leak blood, fluid, and fat into the eye. Although this

Your Risk, In General: Retinopathy

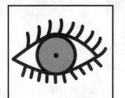

- People with diabetes are 4 times more likely to become blind than people without diabetes.
- After 15 years of diabetes:
  - 97 percent of people using insulin showed some signs of retinopathy
  - 80 percent of people not using insulin showed some signs of retinopathy.

can lead to blurry vision, it does not cause blindness, unless there is leakage in the macula, the area of the retina near the optic nerve.

Nonproliferative retinopathy can progress to a more serious, although less common, form of eye disease called proliferative retinopathy. This occurs when new blood vessels sprout, or proliferate, in the retina. This may seem like a good thing, but the new vessels don't grow in the way they should. Instead they grow out of control. They are fragile and rupture easily during exercise or even while sleeping, especially if you have high blood pressure. When this happens, blood can leak into the fluid-filled portion of the eye in front of the retina. This can block the light coming into the eye and impair vision. In addition, scar tissue can form on the retina. The scar tissue often shrinks, and when that happens, it can tear the layers of the retina apart. This damages your eyesight, because images look as though they are being projected onto a sheet flapping in the breeze. Glaucoma, or high pressure within the eye, occurs more often in people with diabetes. If spotted early on, glaucoma can be treated.

Retinopathy can also cause swelling of the macula of the eye. Because the macula is that central portion of the retinal that allows you to see fine detail, when it swells, vision can be impaired and blindness can result. This condition is know as macular edema.

Prevention

There are two reliable ways to lower your risk of impaired vision from retinopathy. First, get a yearly eye exam from an eye doctor once you reach the age of 30. You should also have your eyes examined each year if you are under age 30 and have had diabetes for 5 or more years. Your doctor should examine your eyes through dilated pupils. The early detection of any eye problems is critical to keeping your vision.

The other thing you can do is keep your blood glucose levels as near to normal as possible. The DCCT found the most striking results of tight control in preventing retinopathy. In that study, people with type 1 diabetes who maintained tight glucose control reduced eye damage by 76 percent. By practicing tight control, whether you have type 1 or type 2 diabetes, you can significantly reduce your chances of developing retinopathy or of having your retinopathy worsen.

Treatment

The best way to treat proliferative retinopathy, oddly enough, is with light—an intense beam of light called a laser—using a procedure called photocoagulation. An ophthalmologist aims the laser beam at the retina. This creates hundreds of tiny burns in the retina. These burns will destroy abnormal blood vessels, patch leaky ones, and slow the formation of new fragile blood vessels. If you have the more serious form of retinopathy, proliferative retinopathy, or macular edema, photocoagulation can usually prevent blindness.

Photocoagulation may not be for everyone, however. It may not work if the retina has bled a lot or has detached. In these cases, a surgery called a vitrectomy can remove the excess blood and scar tissue, stop bleeding, replace some of the vitreous humor—the clear jelly-like substance that fills the eye—with salt solution, and repair the detached retina.

If you need either of these procedures, choose an ophthalmologist who specializes in retinal disease and who has had patients with diabetes. Don't put off visiting your eye doctor. The earlier you get treated, the greater your chances of preventing blindness or further eye damage.

If laser treatment or vitrectomy do not restore vision, low-vision aids can often help people regain the ability to read the paper, do paperwork, or watch TV. You may also need to consider diabetes equipment for those with vision loss. See Chapter 4 for insulin injection tools and Chapter 6 for meters and blood testing tools for those with vision loss.

Nephropathy

Your kidneys are your body's filter units. They work 24 hours a day to rid your body of the toxins that your body makes or takes in. Toxins from the blood enter the kidneys by crossing the walls of small blood vessels along its border. In people with nephropathy, these tiny blood vessels, called capillaries, are unable to filter out the impurities in your blood. They become blocked and leaky at the same time. As a result, some of the waste products that should be removed stay in your blood, and some of the proteins and nutrients that should remain in your blood are lost in the urine. When your doctor checks out your kidneys, he or she will test your urine for signs that you are losing valuable protein. Symptoms of kidney disease usually occur after much kidney damage has already been done and may be subtle: fluid buildup, sleeplessness and tiredness, vomiting, or weakness.

When you first develop diabetes, your doctor may find that you have an excess of protein in your urine. This is usually a temporary condition. Unchecked hypertension and a period of

Your Risk, In General: Nephropathy

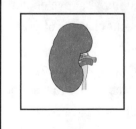

■ People with diabetes are 20 times more likely to get end-stage renal disease than people without diabetes. End-stage renal disease means kidney failure.

■ One-third of people with type 1 diabetes and 10 to 20 percent of people with type 2 diabetes develop kidney disease after 15 years of diabetes.

hyperglycemia before diagnosis could contribute to this condition. But the more obvious symptoms of kidney disease take a long time to appear. The kidneys have so much extra filtering ability that noticeable problems will not appear until 80 percent of the kidney is damaged.

Not everyone with diabetes develops nephropathy. Severe kidney damage is more common in people with type 1 diabetes than in those with type 2. However, kidney damage can also result from high blood pressure, and many people with type 2 diabetes also have hypertension. Years of high blood pressure can damage the delicate filters in the kidneys, leading to less efficient removal of waste products from the blood. The good news is that there are steps you can take to reduce your risk of nephropathy.

Prevention

The most important thing you can do to prevent kidney damage is to keep your blood glucose levels under control. The DCCT showed that people who kept tight blood glucose control reduced their risk of kidney disease by 35 to 56 percent. Another important step you can take is to keep your blood pressure under control. If your blood pressure is too high, the delicate capillaries in your kidneys can become damaged. Two things that you can do to avoid high blood pressure are to keep a healthy body weight and to eat less salt. If kidney damage is advanced or if you cannot reduce your blood pressure by following these steps, your doctor may prescribe drugs to lower blood pressure.

Treatment

The earliest sign of kidney disease is finding small amounts of protein in the urine (microalbuminuria). Your doctor will check your urine for this regularly. If you have this early sign of nephropathy, your doctor will advise you to tighten up your blood glucose control. In the DCCT, people with microalbuminuria who were in the tight control study group cut their risk of progressing to a more serious stage of kidney disease in half. To reap this benefit, these study participants kept a glycated hemoglobin level of 8.1% or lower. You will need to control hypertension, if you have it. You may also be advised to begin a diet low in salt. A special type of blood pressure medication, called an angiotensin-converting enzyme (ACE) inhibitor, is usually prescribed, even if blood pressure is normal. ACE inhibitors decrease the rate of progression of kidney disease.

If your kidney disease is more advanced, you'll need to do more than control your blood glucose. A low-protein diet is often recommended. When the kidneys are failing, they are no longer able to do their job of filtering out toxins from your body. This condition is known as **end-stage renal disease.** At this point, the only two treatment options are dialysis and kidney transplantation. Both remedies are ways of replacing the kidneys.

Dialysis is a way of using a machine to artificially do the job that the kidneys are no longer able to do. There are different types of dialysis, but they all accomplish the same thing— removing toxins from the blood. One type of dialysis, called hemodialysis, removes the blood from an artery (usually in the arm), filters it through a machine, and returns it to a vein. If you need hemodialysis, you will most likely go to a dialysis treatment center three times a week for 2 to 4 hours. Or you may be able to have a trained caregiver come to your home to provide hemodialysis.

The other type of dialysis is called peritoneal dialysis. Here, instead of using a machine to filter the blood, the abdominal cavity, or peritoneum, serves as the filtering site. A solution called a dialysate is poured through a small tube into the abdomen, where it is allowed to sit and collect waste products. Waste products from the blood are exchanged in the peritoneum. After a few hours, the dialysate, which now contains the wastes, is drained out of the abdomen. This process can be performed manually by letting gravity carry the dialysate into the cavity and drain it out again. Or, a machine can carry out the exchange, usually overnight.

Transplantation is usually more effective than dialysis. A new kidney functions as well as your old ones did before disease. However, it depends on the availability of a kidney and requires taking drugs that suppress the immune system to prevent rejection of the new kidney. A genetically near-identical donor is desirable, but not essential. A relative may be willing to donate a healthy kidney or a kidney may become available from someone who has just died. People often go on dialysis while waiting for a transplant.

Transplantation has its drawbacks also. It is major, expensive surgery and requires good cardiovascular health. The drugs you must take to prevent immune rejection of the new kidney may put you at a greater risk of developing infections. And the new kidney will face the same pressures as the old ones did. Without good prevention and good blood glucose control to keep the kidney healthy—and sometimes even with prevention—the new kidney may fail, too.

Neuropathy

Your body's nervous system controls virtually everything you do, every move you make. From moving your muscles and digesting your food to breathing, blinking, and thinking, the nerves in your body serve as your body's electrical circuits. They are the wires that send and receive signals from your brain that tell other cells to do what they need to do. Unfortunately, too much glucose in your blood over long periods can damage your nervous system.

Diabetes usually doesn't impair the brain and spinal cord (central nervous system). But the nerves in the rest of the ner-

Your Risk, In General: Neuropathy

■ After 25 years of living with diabetes, at least half of people have neuropathy.

■ Autonomic neuropathy occurs in 20 to 40 percent of all people with diabetes.

vous system can get damaged. They may be unable to send messages, send them at the wrong times, or send them too slowly. And because the nerves send signals to so many places in your body, nerve damage can cause a range of effects. Maybe you have pain in your hands and feet or thighs and face. Or perhaps you are having trouble with digestion or bladder or bowel control. You may even become impotent, if you are male, or experience other types of sexual dysfunction, even if you are female. Many people with diabetes experience a loss of sensation or feeling or find that their muscles are weak. All of these conditions could be caused by diabetic neuropathy. However, these conditions could also have other causes not related to diabetes or blood glucose levels, so be sure to see your doctor about any symptoms. Often the symptoms of diabetic neuropathy come and go or are severe for only a short period. Good blood glucose control can help you avoid or improve these symptoms. Neuropathy is more likely to affect people who have had diabetes for a long time or whose glucose control is poor.

No one really knows for sure why high blood glucose causes nerve damage. It may be that proteins coated with glucose cause direct damage. Or high levels of glucose may upset the chemical balance inside nerves. Or the blood supply to nerves may be cut off or constricted and nerves may not receive the oxygen they need. Single nerves can also get squeezed by the tissues surrounding them.

Prevention

Good blood glucose control is an important step in preventing nerve disease. The DCCT showed that people with type 1 diabetes who practiced tight control reduced their risk of neuropathy by 60 percent, compared to those who controlled blood sugar levels by standard treatment. Keeping blood vessels healthy will protect the nerves they supply. Nerves need a constant blood supply to function properly. It's also important to exercise regularly, stop smoking, and eat healthy meals. Nutritious food, rich in vitamins and minerals, helps keep the nervous system in prime working condition. Alcohol is a direct toxin to nerves, so try to keep alcohol intake to a minimum.

Types of Neuropathy and Treatment

There are many types of nerve damage; our nervous systems are so complex. It's often hard to decide exactly what type of neuropathy a patient has. Complicating this is the fact that high blood glucose levels can hurt nerves in two ways: directly, and by slowing down or stopping their flow of blood. Sometimes it's hard to know whether a problem is caused by nerve damage or by circulation problems.

Distal Symmetric Polyneuropathy. This type of neuropathy can strike the nerves in many parts of your body. It can affect the arms, hands, legs, or feet on both sides of the body. It can make you feel numb, or you could lose the sensitivity to temperature or to the position of your limbs. Or, you could feel shooting or stabbing pains, burning, tingling or prickling, or muscle weakness. If you are feeling any of these symptoms, be extra careful to wear comfortable shoes and check your feet every day. Because of a loss of feeling, you could step on something and injure your foot without even realizing it. This could lead to infection.

Treatment. If you practice good blood glucose control, the pain of distal symmetric polyneuropathy often vanishes after a few months or a year. Your doctor can help by suggesting exercises and by prescribing oral medications and surface creams to rub into painful areas. A cream containing capsaicin, an extract of hot peppers, often works for people who don't benefit from traditional treatments.

Focal Neuropathy. This is a rare condition due to damage to a single nerve or group of nerves. It may develop when the blood supply to a nerve is shut off due to a blockage in the blood vessel that supplies the nerve. Or it could result from a nerve being pinched. Focal neuropathy can injure nerves that sense touch and pain as well as nerves that move muscles. Fortunately, it is not usually a permanent condition. It usually goes away within 2 weeks to 18 months, once better blood glucose control is achieved.

Carpal tunnel syndrome, a type of focal neuropathy, is seen more often with people with diabetes than in the general population. It occurs when the median nerve of the forearm is squeezed in its passageway, or tunnel, by the carpal bones of the wrists. The syndrome is three times more common in women than in men. It can cause hand tingling, burning, and numbness. This can make you drop things you are holding without even realizing it. Suspect carpal tunnel syndrome if you have tingling in your hands or fingers that goes away when your arms are relaxed down at your sides. Carpal tunnel syndrome is often treated with splints, medication, or surgery to remove the pressure on the nerve.

Autonomic Neuropathy. Some of your nerves control parts of your body that you don't move voluntarily. These are called autonomic nerves, and when they become damaged, autonomic neuropathy can result. Autonomic neuropathy can take many different forms:

- Your stomach and gut muscles can slow down or become less efficient at emptying, leading to nausea and vomiting, constipation, or diarrhea.

- Nerves to the bladder can become damaged, causing muscle weakness and an inability to completely empty the bladder. Because urine can then stay in the bladder for long periods, you can develop urinary tract infections.

- Men may find that they cannot have an erection even though they may still have sexual desire.

- Women may experience vaginal dryness and a decreased sexual response.

- Autonomic neuropathy can also affect blood pressure. You may find yourself feeling lightheaded or dizzy when you stand, because of a drop in blood pressure. Or when you exercise, your blood pressure may go way up.

- Nerves to the skin may cause too much or too little sweating or very dry skin.

- Nerves to the heart may fail to speed up or slow down your heart rate in response to exercise. So, it's important to get a check-up before starting any exercise program. If your heart rate doesn't respond as it should to your exertion, you won't be able to use a standard method, like counting your pulse, to find your target heart rate during and after a workout.

Treatment. Different types of autonomic neuropathy call for different treatments. If you have digestive problems, patience and some trial and error are in order. For example, you may have to try changing your eating habits. Maybe eating small frequent meals instead of large ones or soft or liquid foods may help. Your doctor may prescribe medications, such as cisapride or metaclopramide, that can help you empty your stomach. There are other medications that can treat constipation or diarrhea.

Incontinence, or urine leakage, can be treated with training in bladder control and timed urination by a planned bladder-emptying program. Rather than waiting until your bladder feels full, you could try urinating by the clock—say every hour or every two hours. Men sometimes find it helpful to urinate sitting down. Applying pressure over the bladder may also be helpful. If these steps don't work, your doctor may prescribe oral medication. Or you may have to resort to using a catheter or having surgery. Fecal incontinence (passing stool involuntarily) is treated in a similar way, with medicine for diarrhea and biofeedback training.

If you are experiencing a sudden drop in blood pressure when you stand up, several treatments may help. If you drink alcohol or take certain medications, such as diuretics, stopping them may help. However, don't stop taking any medication without first talking to your doctor. Your health care team may advise you to take medications for low blood pressure, raise the salt content of your diet, or change your sleeping position. However, low blood pressure in itself is not unhealthy. It only becomes a problem if it makes you dizzy or disoriented. Try to stand up more slowly and avoid staying still for long periods to prevent fainting. When you get up in the morning, sit of the edge of the bed for five minutes before you stand up. For information on specific sexual problems, see Chapter 11.

Sometimes neuropathy can trigger a cascade of diabetes-related complications. For example, many people who have had diabetes for a long time develop a condition known as Charcot's foot. This disorder usually affects weight-bearing joints, such as the ankles. It may start with a loss of feeling and thinning of bones in the feet. This can lead to a painless fracture. Because the injury doesn't cause pain, it can go unnoticed and untreated. You may continue walking on the fracture, making matters worse. Muscle shrinking (atrophy) and joint damage can occur and add to the damage, which can become severe enough to deform the foot. The key to treating Charcot's foot is early nonweightbearing. This involves keeping weight off the joint and wearing special footwear. If you notice any swelling in a joint, especially in your ankle or foot, see your doctor right away.

Infections

Having too much glucose in your blood can foul up many of the functions of blood, including the immune system. Having high blood glucose levels can put you at greater risk for infection. The white blood cells attack the invading bacteria, viruses, and fungi that can cause infections. An excess of glucose makes the immune cells less effective. This can keep them from reaching and killing their targets—the invading microorganisms that cause infection. To make matters worse, some of the invading pathogens feed on the extra glucose in the blood, making infection even more likely. People with diabetes tend to have more infections everywhere: in their mouth and gums, lungs, skin, feet, and genital areas and in the incision areas after major surgery.

Other complications of diabetes can add insult to injury. When neuropathy affects the bladder, the bladder is more likely

Your Risk, In General: Infections

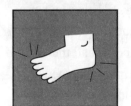

- Although the rate of kidney infection is about the same in people with or without diabetes, people with diabetes are twice as likely to need to be hospitalized to treat the infection.
- About 40 percent of people with type 1 diabetes older than 19 have gum disease.
- Recurrence of tuberculosis was found to be 5 times more common in Native Americans with diabetes compared to those without diabetes.

to be infected. Neuropathy can make you unaware that you need to urinate, which can lead to bladder infection. If neuropathy affects your arms, legs, or feet you may be less likely to notice a cut or burn, because you will not feel pain. Left untreated, even minor skin abrasions can sometimes lead to infection.

There are several reasons why your legs and feet are prone to infection:

- neuropathy numbs legs and feet, making you unaware of injury and infection
- injury opens the door to infection
- diseased blood vessels slow blood flow to the legs and feet, impairing the healing process
- high blood glucose disables the body's immune cells, the white blood cells.

It doesn't matter where in the body an infection happens to start—the gums, vagina, skin, or feet—an infection can be prevented or treated with better blood glucose control and antibiotics. There are other steps you can also take to prevent some of the more common types of infection.

Prevention and Treatment

Bacteria love to feast on the areas between your gums and teeth. To prevent gum disease, or periodontitis, you need to be extra vigilant about brushing and flossing daily. Have your dentist clean your teeth every 6 months. If bacteria set in, they can destroy the bone in your tooth socket. This can cause sores on your gums. If gums are inflamed, or infected, they will pull away from the teeth and jaw bone, and the situation can get even worse. Bacteria will multiply in the newly created gap. The teeth may even become loose and fall out. If periodontitis is severe, your dentist may need to scrape the plaque from your teeth and remove tissue from around the root of the tooth, which can sometimes require surgery.

Many women with diabetes also find that they are susceptible to vaginal yeast infections. This is due to the yeast Can-

What's a Foot Ulcer?

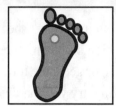

The word **ulcer** probably brings stomach problems to mind. But foot ulcers are more common in people with diabetes than stomach ulcers.

An injured or infected area of the bottom of the foot can develop an ulcer. Ulcers are more likely to occur when circulation to the foot is poor and blood glucose levels are not well controlled. Foot ulcers are serious business. If you discover that you have a foot ulcer, you need to see your doctor that day.

In untreated ulcers, layers of the skin and foot tissue are gradually destroyed by infection, creating a hole. The hole may go as deep as the bone and infect the bone, too. You'd be surprised at how quickly this happens. When infection is very deep, a part of the foot, or even the entire foot and leg, may need to be removed to save the person's life. So, don't underestimate the importance of daily foot care, especially if you have any loss of feeling in your feet.

dida albicans, which flourishes in a moist environment nourished by high levels of glucose. Candidiasis is annoying but not risky. To prevent yeast infections, in addition to improving blood glucose control, wear only all-cotton underwear and avoid pants and panty hose that restrict the flow of air. If you think you have a yeast infection, make sure your doctor agrees with your diagnosis before you treat it. Yeast infections are characterized by a burning, itching sensation in the vaginal area, often accompanied by a thick white discharge. But it is easily confused with other conditions. After diagnosis, you can probably treat the yeast infection yourself with a nonprescription antifungal cream.

Your feet deserve special attention. No matter how much you weigh, pound for pound, your feet carry a heavy load. Because they are vulnerable to injury, you must check them every day. This is doubly important if you have neuropathy, because you may not feel pain due to an injury or abnormality, such as shoes that don't fit correctly. Check your feet every day for ulcers, calluses, corns, or other visible problems. See your doctor if you have any concerns. You can take action to prevent foot infection. See Chapter 3 for pointers on good foot care.

Keeping blood flowing to your feet is an important aspect of foot care. To do this, take steps to lower high blood pressure and cholesterol levels. Take regular walks, or get some form of sustained exercise daily. If you are smoking, try your hardest to quit. Ninety-five percent of all amputations are in smokers.

If a foot or leg infection goes out of control, a surgeon may need to remove part of the foot or leg to save the rest of it from being infected. Amputation is traumatic, but it does not mean you can't live a normal lifestyle. It's not even the end of walking. The surgeon will remove as little of the limb as possible to make walking as easy as possible. After the limb heals, you will most likely be fitted with a prosthesis. Today, prosthetic limbs are lighter and more comfortable than the clunkier models of the past. Some have springs that allow you to even be able to run and jump.

Chapter 11:
Diabetes and Sex

At several different times in your life, you are bound to have concerns about how diabetes affects your sexual health. Even though it may be tough to voice what's bothering you, turn to your health care team. They can help you pin down the problem and improve how you feel.

Most people would rather have a tooth extracted than discuss their sex life with a doctor or nurse. But, the truth is that diabetes can affect your sexual performance, your choices of birth control, and how you respond to the aging of your reproductive system. It is worthwhile to open the lines of communication with your health care team. Rest assured, there are answers to your questions and ways of coping with any problem you might face.

For men with diabetes, the major concern is impotence—worry about becoming impotent or anxiety about how to treat it if it happens. Men and women both may share concerns about birth control and safe sex. For women with diabetes, sexual problems may include poor vaginal lubrication and pain during intercourse or diminished sexual desire and problems achieving orgasm. In addition, women need to deal with the effects of sex hormones on blood glucose levels, throughout the menstrual cycle and as they go through menopause. Women with diabetes have extra challenges as they prepare for pregnancy and carry a growing baby. Don't face these important issues alone just because they concern your sexual life. Sex is a part of each of us as humans and belongs in a healthy life.

Glucose Control and the Estrogen Cycle

Menstruation

Andrea had been living with type 1 diabetes since she was a teenager and had been doing reasonably well. Last year, she decided to try to tighten up her blood glucose control. Through hard work, she mastered balancing her insulin doses to her meal plan and exercise routines but noticed that things became more difficult about a week before her period. Her blood glucose levels were much higher than normal, even though she was careful to do everything she always did to control them. Her doctor suggested that she might be eating more than she thought during these times, but she knew this wasn't true. What was happening?

At first, you think you're just imagining it. You're going along, and everything seems fine. You're in good spirits, eating well, getting regular workouts, and your blood glucose levels are right on target. Then, for some unexplained reason, everything seems out of whack. Maybe your blood glucose levels are too high. Or maybe they're too low. Then you check the calendar. Oh, yeah—it's that time of the month.

If you have trouble keeping your blood glucose levels in check just before your period starts, you are not alone. A survey of 200 women with type 1 diabetes showed that in the week before their periods, 27 percent had problems with higher-than-normal blood glucose levels and 12 percent had lower-than-normal blood glucose levels. Another study revealed that among women under the age of 45 who were hospitalized for diabetic ketoacidosis, half were within several days of starting their periods. And a survey of more than 400 women revealed that nearly 70 percent experienced problems with blood glucose control premenstrually. The problem was more common in women who considered themselves to suffer from the moodiness associated with premenstrual syndrome, or PMS. Just what proportion of women have problems with keeping their blood glucose under control before menstruation is uncertain. Many studies are based on surveys conducted after the fact and do not control for exercise and eating patterns.

Sex Hormones and Insulin Resistance

From the onset of menstrual cycles until menopause, every month a woman's reproductive system revolves around the all-consuming task of ovulation—releasing an egg ripe for fertilization. The follicular phase of the menstrual cycle begins the day your period starts and lasts for about 12 to 14 days until you ovulate, or release the egg. During the early part of this stage of the cycle, the female sex hormones estrogen and progesterone are at their lowest levels. Another hormone, follicle-stimulating hormone, is produced, which turns on estrogen production. This causes the ovary to release an egg midway through the cycle. After egg release, the luteal phase takes over. A second pituitary hormone, luteinizing hormone, triggers the ovary to produce estrogen and progesterone. These hormones cause the lining of the uterus to thicken, in preparation for a possible pregnancy. If fertilization does not occur, the ovary stops making estrogen and progesterone. The sudden loss of estrogen and progesterone cause the shedding of the uterine lining, and menstruation occurs.

It's the high levels of estrogen and progesterone that seem to wreak havoc with blood glucose control in some women about a week or so before menstruation. Researchers aren't exactly sure why, but they have some clues. Insulin works by binding to receptor proteins that sit on the surface of cells. After insulin binds, it sets off a "relay race" within the cell that in the end allows glucose to enter the cell. When levels of progesterone and other progestin hormones are high, it affects insulin action within cells. This leads to temporary extra insulin resistance—the cells no longer respond to insulin the way they should. The result is that blood glucose levels may be higher than normal.

In other women, however, higher than normal estrogen levels may actually increase sensitivity to insulin by improving insulin action. When this occurs, the increased insulin action can lead to blood glucose levels that may be lower than normal.

Not all doctors and researchers agree that estrogen and progesterone can cause changes in insulin action and blood glucose levels before menstruation. Some studies have shown no differences in blood glucose levels throughout the menstrual cycle. Other doctors acknowledge that problems in controlling blood glucose levels do occur, but think that premenstrual syndrome (PMS) is to blame. Some women experience bloating, water retention, weight gain, irritability, depression, and food cravings, especially for carbohydrates and fats. If you have a tendency to give in to these food cravings, this could also be contributing to poor blood glucose control before your period.

Steps to Staying in Control. If you suspect that your blood glucose levels are affected by your menstrual cycle, there is a way to find out for sure. If you are already charting your blood glucose levels on a daily basis, look over the past few months. Mark the date that your period started for each month. Do you see any pattern? Are your blood glucose levels higher or lower than normal during the week before your period? If you are not recording your blood glucose levels, now may be a good time to start.

If you find that your blood glucose levels go out of control on a monthly basis, there are some steps you can take to get things back on track. Changes in blood glucose levels could be due to PMS or they could be due to insulin resistance, or both. You probably already know whether you get PMS routinely. Probably, some months are worse than others. Along with charting your blood glucose levels, think about charting your PMS symptoms. Note your moodiness, bloating, fatigue, cramps, food cravings, or weight gain. It will also help your detective work to note how you are feeling throughout the month, not just before your period. Maybe you feel tired or irritable more often than you think. The important thing is to be honest about how you are feeling and see whether you can detect any sort of pattern.

If you have abnormal blood glucose readings—either too high or too low—around the time you get your period, and you think it may be due to PMS, first try to control the symptoms of PMS:

■ Stick with your meal plan as closely as possible. Be especially careful to limit your salt intake, which causes bloating. Use pepper, fresh or powdered garlic, cayenne, or scallions to add some zing to food.

■ Eat at regular intervals, as much as possible. This will keep your blood glucose levels from swinging too much. Large blood glucose swings could contribute to some of the emotional and physical symptoms of PMS, which may in turn make variations in blood glucose levels worse.

■ Cut back on alcohol, chocolate, and caffeine. They can affect both your blood glucose levels and your mood.

■ Try to exercise regularly. Many women find that regular exercise diminishes mood swings, prevents excessive weight gain, and makes it easier to control blood glucose levels.

These measures may not be enough. You may need to make temporary changes in the days before your period begins in how you handle food and physical activity, and perhaps medication. Try making changes one at a time, so you know which one is the most effective in getting you some relief.

If your blood glucose levels tend to rise about the time you expect your period:

■ Add some extra exercise to help bring down high blood glucose levels by clearing some glucose from your blood.

■ Try to avoid eating extra carbohydrates. Keep a handy supply of fresh veggies—celery, radishes, cucumbers, for example—and dip them in fat-free salsa.

■ If you use insulin, ask your doctor about gradually increasing your dose. This should be done in small increments so that insulin levels are higher the last few days of your cycle, when blood glucose levels normally rise. One to two additional units of insulin may be all it takes. Success will require a little trial and error to figure out what insulin dose is right for you. As soon as menstruation begins, estrogen and progesterone levels drop. When this happens, return

Predicting Ovulation

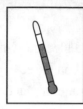 If your periods are irregular, you can learn to predict when they occur. Then, you'll know when to start your "preperiod" diabetes management routine.

■ Ovulation prediction kit: Available over the counter in most pharmacies, these tests can tell you when you ovulate based on a simple urine test. However, they are costly.

■ Basal body temperature: Take your temperature for two minutes each morning before you get out of bed. A chart of these temperatures from month to month will show a pattern. Your body temperature is relatively constant. But, just before ovulation, there is usually a dip of 0.5 to 1.0 degrees. At ovulation, body temperature can rise 0.5 to 1.5 degrees. When you notice the rise in temperature, you know that you are ovulating. Mark this date on your calendar. After ovulation, your body temperature will remain elevated until a day or two before your period, when it decreases. Among women with irregular periods, the interval between menstruation and ovulation can vary, but the interval between ovulation and the next period is usually constant—about 14 days. Using this method, you can predict when your next period will occur, even if you are irregular.

■ Vaginal secretions: Although this varies a lot between women, immediately after menstruation, you probably secrete very little fluid and your vagina is relatively dry. As you approach ovulation, you may begin to secrete some vaginal fluid. It will probably be wet, but not too sticky. When ovulation occurs, the secretions become very sticky, with the consistency of egg whites. With training, some women can use their vaginal secretion to tell when they are ovulating.

to your usual dose of insulin to lower your risk of hypoglycemia.

If you have a tendency toward low blood glucose before your periods:

■ you may want to reduce, but not eliminate, the amount you exercise.

■ Try increasing your carbohydrate intake. But don't make the mistake of eating junk food. Add healthy, low-fat foods to your diet.

■ If you use insulin, ask your doctor about gradually decreasing the amount of insulin you take a few days before your period starts. Again, trial and error will help you determine what dose change is right for you. A decrease of one or two units of insulin may do the trick.

If your periods are irregular and your blood glucose swings are unpredictable, first try to chart your ovulation to see whether you can tell when your period will come. If that does not work and you are taking insulin, you may want to try intensive diabetes management, perhaps with an insulin pump. With training, this may give you the flexibility you need to deal with changes in blood glucose levels on a daily basis.

Menopause

Rita had type 2 diabetes. She had learned to deal with it but was now going through menopause. Her doctor suggested hormone replacement therapy, but she just wasn't sure. What were the risks? She had heard that these hormones could cause cancer. And how would it affect her diabetes and the blood glucose control she had worked so hard to achieve?

Menopause is a process, not an event. It proceeds slowly, often lasting 5 to 10 years. It begins when your body slows down its production of estrogen and progesterone, the hormones that set the stage for pregnancy. Ovulation and menstruation become irregular. Some months you may ovulate and have a period, other months you may not. It can begin before you turn 40, but many women continue to menstruate well into their 50s or 60s. The average age for most women having their last period is 51.

If you have finally figured out how to control your blood glucose levels through a combination of meal planning, exercise, and oral diabetes medications or insulin, you should realize that menopause can throw your diabetes management plan out of balance. That's because you may have learned to adjust your plan around your normal hormonal fluctuations. And the hormones that keep your menstrual cycle going—estrogen and progesterone—can also affect blood glucose levels. In some women, high levels of progesterone and other progestin hormones may decrease the body's sensitivity to insulin. High levels of estrogen tend to improve insulin sensitivity. As you start the transition of menopause, you'll want to pay close attention to the effects it will have on your blood glucose control.

Many women find that they gain weight or become more sedentary as they proceed through menopause. This can increase the need for insulin or oral medication. To fight the fat that often accumulates during middle age, be sure to keep your meals full of nutritious, low-fat foods. And try to maintain or increase your level of activity. This can be a time of life when you are free from some of the responsibilities you had when you were younger. Start a walking program, join a health club, or think about taking up a sport or hobby that you've always wanted to try.

Facing New Risks. Without so much progesterone circulating through your body, you may have greater insulin sensitivity. That's good news. But losing estrogen can increase your insulin resistance. And lack of these hormones can also cause other changes, some of which can worsen diabetes complications.

Having diabetes increases your risk for heart attack and stroke two to four times above that for people without diabetes. Estrogen protects against cardiovascular disease. So, as your supply of estrogen wanes, up goes your risk a little further. In the years after menopause, women without diabetes develop the same risk of heart attack as men. If you also have diabetes, your risk for heart attack and stroke can zoom to twice that of a man without diabetes.

How estrogen offers women some protection against heart disease is not known for certain. It may increase blood flow to the heart and other organs. But we do know that without estrogen, your total cholesterol levels tend to rise and your levels of "good," or HDL, cholesterol tend to drop. Poor blood glucose control can make this situation even worse by contributing to increased total cholesterol levels. Keeping your blood glucose and cholesterol levels in check with healthy eating habits and regular exercise can help. And many women also find that hormone replacement therapy works for them.

Estrogen also helps to maintain strong bones. As estrogen levels fall, your bones can lose some of the minerals that hold them together. This can lead to osteoporosis, a condition in which bones are brittle and easily broken. Eating calcium-rich foods, taking calcium supplements, and partaking in regular weight-bearing exercise, such as walking, can help. Again, hormone replacement therapy can lower your risk of osteoporosis. Your doctor may want to prescribe other medications as well to combat osteoporosis.

Many women with diabetes find they are more prone to vaginitis and yeast infections once they enter menopause. Yeast and bacteria can irritate the vaginal lining if they grow out of control. They thrive in warm, moist places with a good supply of food (glucose). Even before menopause, you are more likely to develop yeast infections if your blood glucose levels are frequently too high. After menopause, the risk increases. That's because estrogen normally nourishes and supports the vaginal lining. Without it, yeast and bacteria have an easier time growing uncontrolled. Here are some suggestions for preventing vaginal infections after menopause:

■ Keep your blood glucose levels under control

■ Bathe regularly to keep fecal bacteria from entering the vagina

■ Consider hormone replacement therapy

■ Some doctors also recommend eating low-fat yogurt on a daily basis. The idea is that the bacteria found in yogurt will help battle yeast in the digestive tract and will prevent vaginitis. Look for yogurt that contains "active cultures."

Hormone Replacement Therapy. You may have a hard time trying to decide whether to undergo sex hormone replacement therapy. It is a complicated issue. On one hand, estrogen can decrease the risk of heart disease, stroke, osteoporosis, and vaginitis. On the other hand, it can increase the risk of breast cancer and uterine cancer. When estrogen and progesterone are administered together and in the correct doses, the risk of cancer of the uterus or endometrium is not increased. Many studies indicate that the risk of dying from heart disease for postmenopausal women is much greater than the risk of developing cancers caused by hormones. However, research on this very important issue is ongoing; not all questions are answered.

Your doctor may suggest hormone replacement therapy after your first hot flash. Hormone replacement therapy can continue for the rest of your life. There are different types of hormonal treatments available. The most common plan is to take estrogen every day and progesterone during the last 10 to 14 days of the cycle. Progesterone protects against cancer of the uterus or endometrium. Some hormone replacement regimens call for taking estrogen and low-dose progesterone every day. Some treatments also include small amounts of testosterone, which helps improve bone mass and may improve sex drive.

For some women, estrogen and progesterone replacement can cause frequent or irregular bleeding, even after menopause is complete. Sometimes, bleeding occurs at the start of treatment and disappears as therapy continues. Along with the protection these hormones can give you, you must also deal with potential effects on blood glucose levels. There is evidence that estrogen replacement increases insulin sensitivity. Adding a progestin hormone may counteract this. Blood glucose testing will help you figure out the effects.

Whether you decide to use hormone replacement therapy is up to you. Many factors can influence your decision. If you have a personal history of breast or endometrial cancer or blood clotting problems, you probably should not receive sex hormone replacement therapy. If you have a family history of breast cancer or have had uterine fibroids or fibrocystic breasts, you should know that hormone replacement therapy increases your risk for also developing these problems. On the other hand, if you have a personal or family history of heart disease or osteoporosis, hormone therapy may definitely be in order. Talk to your health care team, including your gynecologist, about whether your health situation warrants hormone replacement therapy.

Menopause is a normal, natural process. As a woman with diabetes, you need to play an active role in your overall health care throughout menopause and beyond. You have more at stake going through this stage in life than do women without diabetes. As with other issues related to your sexual health, it's important that you feel comfortable discussing concerns freely with your doctor and other health care team members.

Graying Gracefully

After menopause, if you are on hormone replacement therapy, add these tests to your diabetes care plan of blood glucose control, regular exercise, a healthy eating plan, and a responsive health care team. Any tests that give abnormal results should be repeated more frequently.

■ Have your glycated hemoglobin tested four times a year. This test tells you how well you are controlling your blood glucose levels over the long term.

■ Have your blood lipid and cholesterol levels checked four times a year. The progesterone in hormone replacement therapy can sometimes cause blood cholesterol levels to rise.

■ Have yearly eye exams and kidney function tests.

■ Have a yearly mammogram to detect breast cancer.

■ Have a yearly Pap smear and gynecologic examination to detect cancer of the cervix, uterus, endometrium, and ovary.

Birth Control

Practicing birth control and safe sex are important for anyone, but they are especially important for people with diabetes. Erratic blood glucose levels can interfere with the normal development of a growing baby. If you do not have well-controlled blood glucose levels when you become pregnant, your baby may have up to a 1 in 4 chance of developing a major birth defect. Also, the risk of spontaneous miscarriage may double in early pregnancy when blood glucose levels are high. You greatly increase your chances for a healthy child when you plan your pregnancy and achieve blood glucose control that is as near to normal as possible before you conceive. The only way to accomplish this goal is by choosing and using the effective form of birth control that is best for you.

For Women

Women with diabetes have the same birth control options as other women. The pill, intrauterine device (IUD), and barrier methods such as the diaphragm plus spermicide, sponge, and condom are all ways to reduce the risk of unplanned pregnancy **when used correctly**. The rhythm method, in which women predict ovulation and avoid intercourse during fertile times, is not a sufficiently reliable method of birth control for women with diabetes. Sterilization may be an option if you never want to become pregnant, because it is nearly impossible to reverse.

Many birth control methods work by altering hormone concentrations. The methods of birth control that rely on hormones, such as birth control pills and the IUD that releases progesterone, can affect your blood glucose levels. Birth control methods that don't rely on hormones are not likely to change your blood glucose levels. Which method you choose will depend on your own personal and family health history and your individual situation. If you have any special concerns, be sure to bring them up with your health care team.

Birth Control Pill. Oral contraceptives are the most popular and effective birth control method available. But whether the pill is right for you depends on many factors.

The three major types of birth control pills on the market today are monophasic, triphasic, and progesterone-only. Monophasic pills contain a fixed amount of estrogen and progesterone that are taken throughout your cycle. Triphasic pills contain doses of estrogen and progesterone that vary every seven days. Progesterone-only contraceptives contain only progesterone and are also available in an injectable form as Depo-Provera and in implantable capsules as Norplant. Before committing to the long-lasting injectable or implantable forms, you may want to try a progesterone-only pill, which you can stop at any time, to see how it works for you. The progesterone-only pills can affect your blood glucose levels if you are on insulin, so monitor carefully. If you have type 2 diabetes, the progesterone-only pill can cause you to need insulin treatment.

Studies of short-term (one-year) use in women with diabetes who use insulin indicate that monophasic or triphasic birth control pills are safe. However, there is no data indicat-

Pill Precautions

 If you use the pill or other hormonal contraceptives:

■ Test your blood glucose levels frequently, especially during the first couple of months after beginning a pill regimen. Some women need to slightly increase their insulin dose. By keeping good records, you and your health care team can decide whether you need to make changes in food, activity, or insulin dose.

■ Have your glycated hemoglobin, blood pressure, cholesterol, and triglyceride levels checked three months after you go on the pill, and then as scheduled by your doctor.

ing how safe they are for long-term use. If you are over 30 and smoke, or have a history of heart disease, stroke, high blood pressure, or peripheral blood vessel disease, the pill may be too risky for you. If you develop high blood pressure while on the pill, your risk of retinopathy and kidney disease will also increase.

If you are healthy and have type 1 diabetes or type 2 diabetes treated with insulin, there's no reason why your diabetes should stop you from using an oral contraceptive. If you've found that your insulin sensitivity varies at certain times of the month, being on a monophasic pill may even help smooth out blood glucose control. By providing a steady dose of hormones, they are effective in keeping blood glucose swings to a minimum. Triphasic pills contain varying amounts of hormone and could result in changes in your insulin needs. However, you may not find this to be a major problem or may learn to adjust insulin accordingly.

Oral contraceptives can raise insulin resistance in some women. For this reason, women with type 2 diabetes treated with oral diabetes medications or by meal planning and regular exercise can expect to have a more difficult time keeping blood glucose levels in control while taking an oral contraceptive. Discuss your options with your doctor.

IUD. The IUD is a small T-shaped object that is placed into the uterus by a physician. One kind contains copper and another contains progesterone. You may be told that IUDs will increase your risk of vaginal infections because of diabetes. This is true for the progesterone-containing IUD, but the copper-containing IUD has not been shown to increase this risk. The IUD is often an appropriate type of birth control for older women who have finished having children, because the IUD is put in place for a year or more at a time. When properly inserted and retained, IUDs are about 97 percent effective in preventing pregnancy. Talk with your doctor—some do not prescribe IUDs for women with diabetes.

Diaphragm. The diaphragm is a shallow rubber cup that, when inserted and placed properly, fits tightly over the cervix, the entrance to the uterus. You coat the diaphragm with spermicidal jelly before inserting it. The diaphragm acts as a barrier to prevent sperm from entering the uterus. The diaphragm must be kept in place for at least 6 hours after intercourse but needs to be removed shortly after that. Its ability to prevent pregnancy depends on the user's ability to place the device correctly. Because of this, you should have your gynecologist fit your diaphragm and show you how to place it properly and check that it is covering the cervix. Effectiveness increases with experience.

Sponge and Cervical Cap. The sponge, also a barrier method of birth control, contains sperm-killing gel. You place it in the vagina over the cervix before intercourse. Like other barrier methods, the sponge works most effectively when inserted correctly and left in place for the proper amount of time.

The cervical cap is a small barrier device that fits tightly over the cervix to prevent sperm from entering the uterus. It is used with spermicidal jelly. It has been linked to abnormal Pap smear results.

Female Condom. This is another type of barrier method that has been developed for women. It is a larger type of condom that is inserted into the vagina before intercourse and is removed afterward, taking the sperm with it. It can also help protect against sexually transmitted diseases.

Sterilization. If you are sure you never want children or don't want any more children, you may want to consider tubal ligation. In this surgery, doctors tie off the fallopian tubes. This prevents eggs from reaching the uterus. Done correctly, this method is 100 percent effective in preventing pregnancy. In very rare cases, a fertilized egg may reach the uterus, resulting in pregnancy, or may grow outside the uterus, resulting in an ectopic pregnancy that requires surgery. You'll need to be certain about your decision to be sterilized, because it is nearly impossible to reverse.

For Men

Although the choices are more limited, men also have options for birth control. The most popular is the condom, a thin sheath of rubber that fits over the penis before intercourse. It prevents the sperm from entering the woman's vagina. When used correctly and in conjunction with a spermicide, the condom is about 88 percent effective in preventing pregnancy. The condom should be put on before intercourse and can be removed soon afterward. A distinct advantage to condom use is that it also helps prevent the spread of several sexually transmitted diseases, including gonorrhea, chlamydia, and AIDS.

Men who are certain they do not want to father any or any more children can opt for a vasectomy. This is a simple procedure that prevents the release of sperm into the seminal fluid. When the man ejaculates, the semen contains no sperm, but men still experience the full pleasure of intercourse. However, it is very difficult and expensive to reverse a vasectomy, and you'll need to be certain about your decision to have a vasectomy. Some men opt to store some of their sperm before vasectomy for possible in vitro fertilization or artificial insemination, should they decide they want children at some later time.

Sexual Performance

Problems with sexual performance can have either physical or psychological roots. Sometimes a small physical problem can snowball into a large worry for you. Don't let things go for too long. If you are having any problems related to sexual fulfillment, try talking to your doctor about them, to rule out any physical cause. If you don't

Avoiding Lows After Sex

 Having sex is exciting, and sometimes even a great workout. If you use insulin, you need to be watchful for low blood sugar after sex.

■ Test your blood glucose first: This may slow you down a bit, but it's better than having to deal with severe low blood glucose later

■ Eat just before or right after active sex, just as you would if you were exercising

■ Consider having a snack before going to sleep for the night

■ If you use an insulin pump, you may want to unhook during lovemaking to avoid going low; how long you can keep the pump off without an injection depends on how active you are while off the pump.

feel comfortable talking with your doctor or other members of your health care team, perhaps you need to find a doctor or health care professional with whom you do feel comfortable discussing personal matters.

Your doctor will evaluate your concerns and sort physical causes from psychological causes. There are many physical factors that can result in sexual difficulties, starting with medications. If your sexual problem appears to be due to a physical cause, your doctor may suggest that you visit a gynecologist or urologist. If stress or anxiety is contributing to your problem, a visit with a mental health professional may be in order. Depression, which is more common in people living with a chronic disease such as diabetes, can contribute to problems with sexual fulfillment and performance.

Women

Problems with sexual fulfillment are not unique to women with diabetes. Most women at one time or another experience some sexual problems. Women with diabetes don't appear to have more problems than those without diabetes. However, you may experience trouble with vaginal lubrication and yeast infections if you have a hard time keeping your blood glucose levels in control.

One of the more common complaints of women with diabetes is poor vaginal lubrication. Low sex hormone levels, such as those occurring after menopause, can cause your vagina to be dry and easily irritated. This in turn can result in pain during sexual intercourse. First, talk to your doctor or gynecologist to see whether this could be due to a hormonal problem. If so, you may want to consider estrogen replacement therapy. This often improves vaginal lubrication. It can be taken in pill form or as a patch, injection, or vaginal cream or ring. Make sure your doctor diagnoses the problem. Don't try to do it yourself or use over-the-counter products that contain estrogen. If you have gone through menopause and have risk factors that prevent hormone replacement therapy, a special vaginal moisturizer or a water-based vaginal lubricant may help (including a new slow release form in the vaginal ring), but discuss your choice with your doctor first.

Diabetes rarely damages the nerves that control orgasm. However, long periods of high blood glucose levels can lead to damage of other nerves that control the blood flow to sexual organs. These problems can interfere with the ability of the vagina to expand and lubricate with sexual arousal.

■ If you have severe nerve damage, it is possible that you have lost some sensitivity to touch around the genital area. This in turn can diminish sexual pleasure. Some women find that a gentle touch or a hand-held vibrator on or around the clitoris can help them reach orgasm more easily. Others are helped by oral stimulation from their partner.

■ Some women are hindered by poor bladder control. This is also called neurogenic bladder. To avoid problems brought on by this condition, be sure to empty your bladder before and within 30 minutes after intercourse. This can also help prevent bladder infection. To help prevent or lessen the problems due to the loss of sensation and neurogenic bladder, try to achieve good blood glucose control. Loss of sensation and neurogenic bladder can develop when glucose levels are left uncontrolled.

■ Women with end-stage kidney disease may have problems with sexual desire.

■ Some medications can interfere with your desire for sex and ability to reach orgasm, including antidepressants, tranquilizers, and opiate pain relievers.

■ And if you have limited mobility or have lost a limb due to diabetes, talk to your physical therapist. He or she should be able to suggest ways to be comfortable during sex.

If you are unable to find a physical basis causing your problem, perhaps psychological issues are at work. Like many people without diabetes, day-to-day concerns and more deeply rooted issues can interfere with an active sex life. You may worry about being unattractive or be overwhelmed with anxiety about money, children, or stress at work. Learning how to identify your anxieties and voice concerns, especially with your partner, are communication skills a psychiatrist, psychologist, or licensed social worker can help you learn. Perhaps your doctor can recommend a mental health counselor who is familiar with the kinds of concerns women with diabetes have.

Men

Paul had been diagnosed with type 2 diabetes a few years ago. He had been pretty good about keeping his blood glucose levels in check, but had recently been traveling quite a bit. Maybe he wasn't exercising very often or maybe he was eating out too much, but he also noticed that he had put on a few pounds. But the worst part was the effect on his sex life. For the past several months, it had become increasingly difficult to sustain an erection. And he had been unable to achieve an erection the last dozen or so times he attempted sexual intercourse. Now he had just given up trying.

Among men, the diagnosis of diabetes brings with it the fear of erection problems, or impotence. But, are problems with erections really more common in men with diabetes than men without diabetes? Because so many men suffer in silence, unwilling to approach a doctor for help, it's difficult to count how many men with and without diabetes actually have a problem. What we do know is that:

■ Erection problems are age related. It is primarily a problem of men in their 50s, 60s, and older. And diabetes is more common in people in this older age-group. This is one reason why you hear that there is a relationship between diabetes and erection problems.

■ Men with diabetes develop erection problems 10 to 15 years earlier than men without diabetes.

■ Fifty to sixty percent of all men with diabetes over the age of 50 have some type of erection problem.

Impotence, or an erection problem, has a range of severity. The numbers about impotence count all types, from occasional impotence to complete impotence. Complete impotence occurs much less often. So, just what is impotence? Being impotent means that all, most, or some of the time, the penis fails to become or stay hard enough for sexual intercourse. If, on occasion, you fail to maintain or achieve an erection, you're not impotent. You are also not impotent if you experience a decrease in sexual desire, have premature ejaculation, or if you fail to ejaculate or reach orgasm. If you are impotent, you can't achieve or maintain an erection. However, many of these other problems can also occur with impotence.

Erection problems can be caused by either physical or psychological factors. The most common cause in men with diabetes are physical problems that result from blood vessel- and nerve-related complications. If you have experienced neuropathy or cardiovascular complications of diabetes, you may also be at risk. The way to reduce your risk is to maintain blood glucose control. Keeping blood glucose levels as close to normal as possible will help you avoid nerve damage and blood vessel and kidney disease. In addition, you should quit smoking, decrease your alcohol intake, and keep blood pressure controlled. Psychological factors, depression in particular, are common culprits in men with diabetes.

Figuring out why erection problems occur can be difficult. Because sex involves a joining of mental and physical factors, pinpointing the problem takes some time. Sexual desire begins in the brain and signals are sent through the nervous system to the blood vessels to trigger an erection. The male sex hormone testosterone is also involved in sexual desire and achieving erection.

Hearing so much about erection problems can create a fear that contributes to psychological impotence. And if you know that you are at increased risk because you have diabetes, you may even expect it to happen. For instance, you may be unable to have an erection if you feel pressured to perform. Sometimes, a one-time failure to maintain an erection can create fear and anxiety that can eventually lead to psychological impotence. Worry and stress can decrease your brain's response to testosterone. However, because your nerves and blood vessels are in working order, you might have erections at night when you don't even realize it. Most healthy men have several erections each night when they sleep. Your doctor should be able to test whether you are having erections in your sleep. This may reassure you that you'll be able to recover your ability to have erections.

Although psychological impotence often comes on rather suddenly, erection problems caused by physical problems usually comes on slowly and gets worse with time. Early symptoms of physiological impotence include a less rigid penis during sexual stimulation and when you wake up. Over time, men with physiological impotence may not be able to sustain firm erections long enough to enjoy sexual intercourse.

One of the most useful ways to distinguish between medical and emotional erection problems is to monitor your sleeping erections. When you're asleep, you're not as bothered by emotional factors, so a firm erection indicates you're medically okay. This monitoring can be done in a sleep lab or with a take-home monitor.

Some of the side effects of diabetes can directly cause trouble. Blood vessel damage is a common cause of erection problems in men with diabetes. When blood flow to the penis is reduced, the penis no longer can become erect. A frequently used test for this is an ultrasound study of the penis. Sound waves are used to measure blood flow through the arteries and veins. Another test involves injecting a drug or mixture of drugs into the penis to cause an erection. The drug is injected in such a way that it bypasses the penile nerves. If the injection causes you to have an erection, damaged blood vessels are not the cause. If you don't have an erection, it means there may be some damage or problems with your blood vessels.

Nerve disease is also a culprit. When the nerves that signal the penis are damaged, erection can be impaired. Your doctor may decide that the nerves in your penis need to be checked and may refer you to a urologist.

Because erection problems can also, in rare cases, be caused by low amounts of testosterone, your doctor may also want to measure your testosterone level. If it is too low, your problem may be caused by a hormonal problem not related to diabetes.

Also be aware that certain medications can cause temporary difficulty. Make sure that your doctor knows about all the medications you are using—even over-the-counter remedies. Drugs frequently used to treat high blood pressure, anxiety, depression, and peptic ulcers can all be factors. If you have signs of trouble and suspect that it may be related to a new medication you are using, let your doctor know. But don't stop taking any medicine without first talking to your doctor. Smoking and alcohol consumption can also contribute to erection problems.

Treating Impotence. If your erection problems have a physical basis, there are several treatments available. In choosing a treatment, find one that is most compatible with the needs and desires of both you and your partner.

One option is to induce erection by injecting a form of the drug alprostadil directly into the penis. This induces a penile erection that lasts about 30 minutes to one hour. Side effects include bruising and prolonged erection. Some men also develop scarring in the penis, which occasionally results in a permanent curvature during erection. There is a suppository form known as muse that can be inserted in the tip of the penis 5 to 10 minutes before sex.

Another drug available for treatment is called sildenafil (Viagra). Viagra can be taken in pill form and stimulates and maintains an erection for 30 to 60 minutes after being swallowed. Talk to your doctor about other drug therapies, including apomorphine and phentolamine.

Another treatment uses a vacuum pump to create an erection. This method requires an understanding partner and a willingness to interrupt lovemaking. A cylinder is placed around the penis. A small vacuum pump pulls air out of the container, creating a vacuum. This causes blood to flow into the penis, triggering an erection. To maintain the erection, the container is removed and replaced with a rubber band. This provides an erection for about 30 minutes. The rubber band can cause bruising if kept on for more than 30 minutes.

Doctors can also surgically implant pump devices called penile prostheses into the penis to produce erections. Your best bet is to visit a urologist with experience in this type of implant. Be sure to ask about the risks, which can include infection and the need for further surgery in case of instrument failure.

Testosterone injections can be prescribed if a low hormone level is the problem. These are usually given every 3 to 4 weeks. Patches are also available. Older men are at risk for prostate cancer and should never take testosterone unless they have abnormally low levels and they have been evaluated for prostate cancer.

If your impotence is due to psychological factors, your best bet is to work with a therapist who knows how to deal with sexual issues. Even if fear of impotence somehow interferes with your sex life, consider seeing a therapist. If, like most men, you have experienced or worry about impotence, confronting your fears may be the best thing you can do to improve your sex life.

All the treatments for impotence have risks or drawbacks. You may decide to seek no treatment. Some men and their partners choose to live with the condition and express their sexuality without benefit of treatment.

Pregnancy

In the past, it was very common for women with diabetes who became pregnant to experience serious problems, such as miscarriage, stillbirth, or a baby with birth defects. Today, it is very common for women with diabetes—either type 1 or type 2—to have safe and healthy pregnancies. Although women with diabetes and their unborn children face some risks because of diabetes, these can be kept to a minimum through excellent blood glucose control, before and during pregnancy, and careful obstetrical care. For this reason, all women with diabetes need to plan ahead **before** becoming pregnant. You will need to achieve excellent blood glucose control before conceiving.

Before You Become Pregnant

When you decide to start a family, the first step is to meet with your health care team to consider the specific challenges you face. You may be concerned that your baby could develop diabetes. You may be worried for your own health. Your glucose control may be an issue: The mother's glucose control is directly related to the risks to the growing baby. It's important to get a good idea of how much extra work and expense may be involved before you become pregnant.

Genetics. Whether you are a potential mother or father with diabetes, you may have concerns about your child someday developing diabetes. The best time to assess the genetic risk of your child developing diabetes is before you get pregnant.

Type 1 diabetes is caused by an autoimmune attack on the pancreas that destroys the insulin-producing cells. A child born to a parent who has type 1 diabetes is at slightly greater risk of developing type 1 diabetes than children of parents without diabetes. But the risk is different depending on whether it is the mother or father who has diabetes. Researchers have identified genes that could play a role in developing type 1 diabetes. But it is not yet clear what percentage of children who inherit a "diabetes" gene go on to develop diabetes or what environmental factors are also involved.

If a baby is born to a mother who is age 25 or older and has type 1 diabetes, that baby has a 1 percent risk of developing diabetes. This risk is not much different from that of a child born to parents without diabetes. If the mother is younger than age 25 at the time the child is born, the risk increases to about 4 percent. If the father has type 1 diabetes, the risk for the child of developing diabetes is about 6 percent. Each of these risks is doubled if the parent with type 1 diabetes developed it before the age of 11. If both parents have type 1 diabetes, the risk is not known but is probably somewhat higher.

Development of type 2 diabetes seems to depend on both genetic and lifestyle factors. Type 2 diabetes tends to run in families. Habits that contribute to obesity and diabetes, such as poor eating habits and inactivity, also tend to run in families. Research on families with type 2 diabetes shows that you can inherit genes that increase your tendency to develop type 2 diabetes. Families can be classified as "insulin resistant" or

Diabetes: Myth or Fact?

"My sister with diabetes had a baby, and it nearly killed her. It's just not a safe thing to do."

Women with diabetes can and do have healthy babies all the time. It doesn't cost them their lives or health, either. The survival rate for pregnancy is no different between women with and without diabetes, as long as the woman with diabetes takes care to practice tight blood glucose control and treats any diabetes complications early. And chances are excellent that her baby will be just as healthy as a baby born to a mother without diabetes.

Women who avoid prenatal medical care or ignore their blood glucose control will have problems with their health and the health of their baby. Poor glucose control early in the pregnancy may cause miscarriage or improperly formed organs in the baby. Poor control later in the pregnancy puts the mother at risk for hypertension and preterm labor as well as possible worsening of preexisting diabetes complications. Babies who get too much glucose later in pregnancy grow too large and have problems at delivery.

Pregnancy puts stress on any woman's body. This is why it is so important that you and your health care team keep a close watch on your health before and throughout your pregnancy. And here's the other side of the coin: When groups of women with type 1 diabetes who have been pregnant are compared to groups of women with type 1 diabetes who have never been pregnant, about the same number of women in each group show signs of diabetes complications. So, being pregnant doesn't seem to raise your risk of getting complications over your lifetime.

With self-monitoring of blood glucose levels and improved techniques for early detection and treatment of complications such as retinopathy and nephropathy, women with diabetes have entered an era of expanded possibilities. Don't let old-fashioned thinking stop you from working toward having a healthy baby, if that's your goal.

"insulin sensitive." This suggests that some families may be particularly prone to developing type 2 diabetes.

If you have a family history of type 2 diabetes, it may be difficult to figure out whether your diabetes is due to lifestyle factors or genetic susceptibility. Most likely it is due to both. You may be able to guess whether obesity due to overeating and a sedentary lifestyle have contributed. Just because you may have a tendency toward developing type 2 diabetes does not mean that insulin resistance cannot be reversed. Weight loss and exercise programs are effective in preventing type 2 diabetes even in the face of genetic susceptibility.

Studies of twins have shown that genetics play a very strong role in whether a person develops diabetes, especially type 2 diabetes. If you are concerned or have questions about the likelihood of having a child with either type 1 or type 2 diabetes, consider talking with a medical geneticist or genetic counselor. These health care professionals are trained to assess the contributions of genetic and environmental factors in causing many diseases, including diabetes. They will know the results of the latest diabetes and genetics studies and studies to prevent diabetes in high-risk individuals.

Mother's Health. Before becoming pregnant, you'll need a thorough physical exam. Your doctor will be looking for any problems that could jeopardize your health or that of your baby. These problems include high blood pressure, heart disease, kidney disease, nerve disease, and eye disease. If you have any of these complications, they should be treated before you attempt to conceive. Even kidney transplant recipients who are otherwise healthy have had babies. Your doctor should also take a blood sample to measure glycated hemoglobin, which tells how well you are controlling your blood glucose levels over time, and thyroid function, if you have type 1 diabetes.

In rare cases, diabetes-related problems may be serious enough that it's safer to avoid pregnancy. If you have uncontrolled high blood pressure, cardiovascular disease, kidney failure, or crippling gastrointestinal neuropathy, examine your options carefully. Pregnancy can make these conditions worse, or they can lead to related problems, such as stroke or heart attack.

If you have had diabetes for more than 10 years and have any signs of heart disease, such as chest pain on exertion, your doctor may also suggest an electrocardiogram. Your doctor should also look for signs of nerve damage. If the nerves that control heart rate or blood vessel opening and narrowing have been damaged, this can affect how your heart and blood pressure will respond to the physical stress of pregnancy. Neuropathy can also affect how well your body nourishes you and your growing baby, so let your doctor know if you have had persistent problems with nausea, vomiting, or diarrhea.

Your prepregnancy exam should also include a look at your kidneys. In women with poor blood glucose control and untreated kidney disease, kidney function can worsen during pregnancy. Fortunately, pregnancy does not appear to have long-lasting effects on kidney function. If you have kidney problems, you and your doctor have to be prepared for a potentially more difficult pregnancy. This can include problems with edema (swelling) and high blood pressure. If you have been treated with angiotensin-converting enzyme (ACE) inhibitors for kidney disease or high blood pressure, your doctor will change your medication. ACE inhibitors taken during pregnancy can cause kidney problems in the baby.

Also, before becoming pregnant, have an ophthalmologist examine your eyes, especially the retina—that part of your eye that senses visual images. To do this, the eye doctor will look at your retinas through dilated pupils for damage caused by diabetes. Untreated diabetic retinopathy may worsen during pregnancy and should be treated until it has stabilized before

Tip: The ideal health care team for your pregnancy includes your diabetes doctor, an obstetrician experienced and interested in treating pregnancy complicated by diabetes, a pediatrician interested in the care of infants of mothers with diabetes, and a registered dietitian. You will also want to include a diabetes educator experienced in teaching people how to achieve tight blood glucose control.

you become pregnant. Make sure you continue to get your eyes examined throughout the pregnancy.

Glucose Control. Although birth defects occur in 2 to 3 percent of all babies born to women without diabetes, they occur in 6 to 12 percent of babies born to women with diabetes with average blood glucose control. Problems include abnormalities of the central nervous system, heart, and kidneys. Although these risks cannot be eliminated, they can be lowered to those of mothers without diabetes by keeping your blood glucose levels as close to normal as possible.

Why is well-controlled blood glucose important **before** conception? It's important to build the habits that lead to excellent blood glucose control and to make sure that your diabetes management plan will work for you. This takes some trial and error as well as patience. But you will want the glucose levels in your body to be as favorable to your developing baby as possible. All the baby's major organs are formed during the first 6 to 8 weeks of pregnancy, making it especially important for you to have excellent glucose control in place before the baby is conceived. In one study, women who started their program of tight control before conception lowered their baby's risk of birth defects to only 1 percent, compared with 10 percent in babies of mothers who began intensive diabetes management after conceiving.

Before you become pregnant, you will need to make a commitment to achieve the best blood glucose control you can. Meeting this goal will probably mean intensifying your daily diabetes care. If you have type 1 diabetes, you will begin or fine-tune a regimen of several insulin injections each day or switch to insulin pump therapy. If you have type 2 diabetes, using oral agents for blood glucose control during pregnancy is not recommended. Your doctor will probably advise you to begin insulin therapy. Many women with type 2 diabetes who in the past have controlled blood glucose levels without medication find that they need to use insulin to achieve excellent blood glucose control during pregnancy.

Your blood glucose control will be assessed with glycated hemoglobin measurements. When your glycated hemoglobin and day-to-day blood glucose levels are at their best, you and your health care team should make a decision about stopping birth control. It might also be helpful for you to record your basal body temperatures (see box above on predicting ovulation) so that your doctors know when you conceive. This will be useful for decision making later in pregnancy.

Expenses. Having a baby is a major financial investment for any parent. Your pregnancy will include the added expenses involved in tight blood glucose control. But, it used to be worse: Before self-monitoring of blood glucose, a woman could easily spend half of her pregnancy in the hospital, with a bill of more than $40,000. Now the major expenses are fetal monitoring and blood glucose testing instead of hospitalization and loss of salary.

Before you conceive, make sure you are prepared to cover the following:

- You will need to see both your obstetrician and your diabetes doctor frequently—perhaps every week or every two weeks for most of your pregnancy. Achieving excellent blood glucose control means learning to make adjustments in insulin dose based on blood glucose values. This takes time and practice and lots of support from your health care team.
- Your health care should include nutrition counseling with a registered dietitian. You may want to learn techniques such as carbohydrate counting or insulin dose adjustment.
- You'll need extra blood glucose tests to make sure your glucose control is staying within your target ranges. Many pregnant women do seven or more tests each day. Test strips are the big expense in testing.

■ You may need to do ketone testing each day. This will protect you against surprise ketoacidosis as well as starvation ketoacidosis, which can occur when carbohydrate intake is very limited. This means buying more ketone strips.

■ If you have controlled your type 2 diabetes with oral diabetes medications, you'll need to switch to insulin before you become pregnant. Oral diabetes medications may cause birth defects. This means spending money on syringes and insulin, plus training in insulin use.

Once You Are Pregnant

Blood Glucose Control. You and your health care team will need to choose blood glucose goals for you during pregnancy. The goals given in the box are an example. Your blood glucose target ranges need to be personalized to your health and your lifestyle.

In the first trimester, your goals should help you minimize the risk of birth defects or miscarriage. In the second and third trimesters, the goals will help to prevent your baby from growing too large. If you have trouble reaching these goals, or if you have frequent or severe hypoglycemia, you need to revise your goals with the help of your health care team.

To meet these glucose control goals, women with type 2 diabetes may need to use insulin during pregnancy. So may

Sample Target Blood Glucose Ranges During Pregnancy

You'll need individualized blood glucose goals. Talk with your doctor about target ranges that meet your needs. For instance, your first trimester goals may be a little higher.

■ Before meals: 70 to 100 mg/dl

■ One hour after meals: 110 to 130 mg/dl

■ Two hours after meals: 90 to 120 mg/dl

■ Middle of the night (2 to 3 a.m.): 60 to 120 mg/dl

many women with gestational diabetes. It is common for women who use insulin to find that they need to increase insulin dose over the course of the pregnancy to maintain excellent glucose levels. You may also have to make adjustments in the kind of insulin you take and how often you inject it. Usually, the amount of insulin you take increases with each trimester, because the hormones of pregnancy, which increase in effect over time, create more and more insulin resistance. Some women need to increase their insulin dose by as much as two or three times, especially in the last trimester. This is normal and does not mean that your diabetes is getting worse. You and your doctor need to decide together when and how to make any changes in your insulin schedule or dose.

Food and Exercise. Your eating habits are likely to change during pregnancy to help you control blood glucose levels. And you also will want to make sure that you are eating foods that provide adequate nutrition for you and your baby. You will need to schedule a special visit to your dietitian even before you become pregnant. In general, choose nutritious foods that play a part in any healthy eating plan (see Chapter 8).

Your dietitian will help you tailor your calorie needs to your recommended weight gain. A weight gain of 22 to 32 pounds over the 9-month period is normal. Women who are underweight to begin with may be advised to gain more. And women who are already overweight may be advised to limit their weight gain to 15 pounds. You will probably be advised to check your urine for ketones each morning to be sure you are getting the proper amount of carbohydrate and insulin.

Eating five or six small meals a day may help your efforts to stabilize blood glucose swings. This eating pattern may also help with morning sickness, a feeling of nausea, when the stomach is empty. It is not limited to mornings and can occur day or night, often accompanied by vomiting. If you have morning sickness, there are some dietary steps you can take to feel better.

Help With Nausea

- Eat dry crackers or toast before rising
- Eat small meals every 2-1/2 to 3 hours
- Avoid caffeine
- Avoid fatty and salty foods
- Drink fluids between meals, not with meals
- Take prenatal vitamins after dinner or at bedtime
- Always carry food with you

It can help to keep some starch, such as Melba toast, rice or popcorn cakes, or saltines or other low-fat crackers close at hand. Eat if you become nauseated. You can prevent early morning nausea if you eat a protein and carbohydrate snack at bedtime, such as cheese and crackers or half of a sandwich.

It is important to maintain physical activity during pregnancy, as long as your overall health permits it. Fitness prepares you for the physical stress of labor and delivery and the busy days that follow. Your doctor and obstetrician may recommend that you continue with any exercise you were doing regularly before pregnancy. Now is not the time to take up any new, strenuous activities. See the section on exercising during pregnancy in Chapter 9.

Glucose Monitoring. Your doctor will probably encourage you to test several times each day. If you take insulin, you may start out monitoring before meals only in the first trimester and add after-meal tests during the second and third trimesters. If you have type 2 or gestational diabetes and are controlling it through meal planning and regular exercise, you will be advised to test more frequently than you are used to.

Times for blood glucose testing include:
- once before each meal

- one to two hours after each meal
- at bedtime
- during the middle of the night, around 2 a.m.

If you take insulin and are successful at achieving lower overall blood glucose levels, you will be more likely to have episodes of very low blood glucose. While pregnant, your early warning symptoms of hypoglycemia may change. Many pregnant women develop hypoglycemia unawareness (see Chapter 5). You may have less shaking and sweating and more rapid development of drowsiness or confusion. So, it's very important for you to monitor frequently to know whether you are close to being low. There is no evidence that hypoglycemia is dangerous for the baby. But, a hypoglycemic episode can be dangerous for the mother-to-be. In addition to testing before and after exercise, always test your blood glucose before you drive. Be prepared for severe low blood glucose by carrying a glucagon kit and training several people you see daily how to use it (see Chapter 5).

Obstetrical Care. Because of diabetes, you'll need more frequent visits to your obstetrician, perhaps every two weeks for most of your pregnancy. Your obstetrical care needs to include screening for neural tube defects early in pregnancy (around weeks 15 to 20) by measuring the concentration of alpha-fetoprotein in your blood. You'll need an ultrasound test for birth defects during the second trimester and several more ultrasound tests to follow the baby's growth. This is when it's helpful to know when your baby was conceived. Your doctor may recommend daily fetal movement monitoring. Also, fetal heart rate monitoring during the last 6 to 8 weeks of pregnancy helps ensure your baby's well-being. These tests will assist your doctor in deciding when you should deliver your baby.

Birth

In the past, babies born to women with diabetes tended to be oversized. This problem, called macrosomia, was the baby's response to having access to extra amounts of glucose from the mother's blood. To reduce the risk of delivery problems or stillbirth, these babies were usually delivered before or during the 37th week of a 40-week pregnancy. Now, because more women with diabetes maintain tighter blood glucose control and special tests are available to monitor the baby's health more closely (such as fetal heart rate monitoring), most women can deliver close to their due date.

Macrosomia is less common, but it's still difficult to completely prevent it. Even with frequent monitoring and tight glucose control, sometimes the baby is too large or the woman's pelvis is too small for a safe vaginal delivery. Trying to deliver a too-large baby vaginally can result in shoulder damage or respiratory distress in the baby. In this case, a cesarean section (C-section) is performed. Your chances of avoiding a C-section are increased by practicing good blood glucose control.

Your doctor will be on the watch for elevated blood pressure throughout your pregnancy. This can indicate preeclampsia, a serious condition that occurs more often in women with diabetes. Preeclampsia may also lead to early delivery, often by C-section.

Labor is work, and usually you will not be allowed to eat. But your blood glucose levels still need to remain close to normal (under 120 mg/dl), so you will be monitored frequently during labor. You will probably get an intravenous catheter (IV) so that fluids or calories can be given as needed. You can be given insulin either as injections or through the IV. Many women don't need insulin during active labor.

Because of diabetes, your baby will be closely watched for certain conditions. He or she is at risk for hypoglycemia and will be monitored for blood glucose in the first 24 hours after birth. Jaundice is also common and may require therapy with lights. If your baby was delivered early or is very large for his or her age, your pediatrician will also watch for respiratory problems.

Diabetes: Myth or Fact?

"Because I had gestational diabetes, I might get diabetes when I'm older."

This it true. Gestational diabetes is a temporary form of insulin resistance that usually reveals itself about halfway through the pregnancy. This is when the hormones of pregnancy create extra insulin resistance. Women who get gestational diabetes somehow are unable to physically overcome this extra resistance to insulin. Either their pancreas is not able to make the additional insulin that is needed or their body's cells become less efficient at taking up glucose from the blood.

Because their body reacted to this stress in this way, women who have had gestational diabetes can get diabetes again. They have a 2 in 3 chance of developing gestational diabetes again. Also, their risk of developing type 2 diabetes 5 to 15 years after they had gestational diabetes rises to between 40 and 60 percent, compared with about a 15 percent risk in the general population. If she's obese, a woman's risk of getting type 2 diabetes after having gestational diabetes rises to a 3 out of 4 chance. Women who have had gestational diabetes can reduce their risk of ever developing diabetes closer to a 1 in 4 chance by keeping a healthy body weight (see Chapter 1), with plenty of regular exercise.

After Delivery

If you have type 1 diabetes, after delivery your blood glucose levels should be checked regularly to find out when you should start taking insulin again. You may require less insulin for the first 3 to 7 days. If you have type 2 diabetes, you may not need insulin at all during this time. You will probably be able to resume your prepregnancy diabetes management plan soon after your baby is born, except that you cannot use oral diabetes medications if you are breastfeeding.

The postpartum period may be one of unpredictable blood glucose swings. Your hormones and body chemistry are in flux. You are recovering from a major physical challenge. And you are probably exhausted from around-the-clock feedings. That's why follow-up visits with your diabetes doctor are especially important. If you find that keeping good blood glucose control poses a greater challenge, try not to get too discouraged. Don't let good habits fall by the wayside. Talk to your doctor or other members of your health care team if you are having any special problems. Your baby needs a healthy mother!

If you had gestational diabetes, your blood sugar levels will most likely return to normal after delivery. Nevertheless, your doctor should test you for diabetes between 6 to 8 weeks after your baby is born. A few women continue to have diabetes after they deliver. Also, the early postpartum glucose tolerance test will help determine your risk of getting diabetes later in life. You will be at greater risk for developing diabetes than women who never had gestational diabetes. If your postpartum test reveals a higher than normal blood glucose level, but not diabetes, your risk of developing diabetes in the next 5 years is high, and you need to exercise and reach a healthy body weight. You should also have your blood glucose level checked every 6 to 12 months to detect any increases as early as possible. Even if your postpartum glucose tolerance test is normal, you have a higher risk for someday developing diabetes. You need to have your blood glucose tested on a yearly basis. You also need to remind all doctors prescribing drugs to you that you had gestational diabetes. Some drugs, such as steroids or oral contraceptives, can raise your blood glucose levels just as pregnancy did.

If you can muster up the energy and desire for sex, don't forget that you can become pregnant again soon after you give birth. Even if you have not had a period, you can still ovulate. And breastfeeding does not necessarily prevent you from becoming pregnant. So, before you resume having intercourse, be sure you are using effective birth control.

Although virtually every aspect of your life may seem turned on its head after the birth of a new baby, the four basic management tools remain the same: insulin or oral diabetes medication (you should not use oral diabetes medications while you are breastfeeding), blood glucose monitoring, meal planning, and exercise. Exercise may be the last thing you are thinking about after the baby is born. But as soon as you feel well enough and you have your doctor's okay, a daily walk may make you feel better. Set it aside as a little time for yourself.

Highs and Lows. It's a wonderful idea to stick with the blood glucose testing habits you formed while you were pregnant. Hormonal changes, emotional shifts, irregular sleep patterns, and fatigue may hide or change your symptoms of high or low blood glucose. You may find it hard to tell the difference between "after-baby" blues, such as unexplained crying or moodiness, and low or high blood glucose. Fatigue, feeling spacey, weakness, or forgetfulness can be caused by both high and low blood glucose and by physical and emotional changes. If you're not sure, play it safe and test.

With a new baby depending on you, it's critical to guard against hypoglycemia. Test often; if you feel hypoglycemia coming on, treat it right away, whether or not you can test. Keep sugared items such as glucose tablets, hard candy, or regular soda handy in several rooms. Make sure that those around you know how to spot your signs of low blood glucose; teach them what you want them to do if you don't seem like yourself. Keep a glucagon kit on hand.

If you have had hypoglycemia unawareness in the past, be vigilant not to let your blood glucose get too low when you are alone with your baby. Get help with middle-of-the-night feedings, or make it a habit to eat a snack then. Take care to test before you get into the car to drive. Don't nap or sleep on an empty stomach. Remember that your best protection is still frequent blood glucose monitoring, appropriate insulin doses, and regular snacks and meals.

Having a new baby can affect your diabetes care habits, especially if you have other children to care for. You may find that your baby's unpredictable schedule and your own erratic sleep patterns make it difficult for you to eat or snack when you need to. But good timing of meals is critical to your diabetes control. Although your baby's screams may tempt you otherwise, don't put your infant's feedings before your own dietary needs. Taking good care of yourself is important for both you and your baby.

Breastfeeding

The ideal food for your baby is your own breast milk. An added bonus is that babies who are breastfed for at least three months have a lower incidence of type 1 diabetes. Although breastfeeding can complicate your blood glucose control, don't let it prevent you from nursing. The extra energy your body uses to make breast milk can cause your blood glucose levels to swing. Some women find that it is a little easier to keep blood glucose levels from going high during the weeks or months they're nursing. You can eat a little more and still use less insulin. You also need to watch out for low blood glucose.

You may want to schedule another visit with your dietitian if you are breastfeeding. Your hunger level may change, and you may need some help trying to balance your meals and your baby's meals with any exercise routine or insulin regimen.

Throughout the time you breastfeed, continue testing your blood glucose level often. And make sure you have a source of fast-acting sugar, such as glucose tablets or orange juice, handy while breastfeeding. When your baby is ready to nurse during the day, eat your own snack or meal, plus a glass of water or low-fat milk, as you feed your infant. It helps to have the snack or meal portion ready so you don't have to prepare your food while the baby is waiting to be fed. Snacking or eating this way provides your body with fluids and helps prevent low blood glucose. During nighttime feedings, have a snack yourself. Otherwise, you might find you have low blood glucose or trouble waking up the next morning, especially if you have been up several times in the night.

Chapter 12: Coping with Diabetes

Many people with diabetes feel blamed or criticized for their efforts at diabetes care. When someone you care about has diabetes, simply listening to how he or she feels about living with diabetes can be the most loving act.

eanne was sailing along, enjoying life. She had just turned thirty, started a new job, and bought a horse, all in the last two months. She lived for the thrill of cantering her horse across the hills and through the woods almost every day. But then one day after a long ride she felt dizzy and collapsed in the barn. She was rushed to the hospital and that's when she found out she had diabetes. She always thought diabetes affected older, sedentary people, but she was young and active. It just wasn't fair. Now her doctor told her she had to cut out all the foods she liked, stop smoking, eliminate her Friday afternoon margarita, and, worst of all, stop riding. She felt angry and was determined to show everyone that she could live just fine without all these stupid rules.

Hilda, a 60-year-old widow, had just retired from nursing. A few months later, her youngest daughter got married. She thought she would enjoy the peace and quiet, but instead she just didn't feel quite right. During her yearly medical exam, her doctor told her she had diabetes. As a former nurse, she knew all about diabetes, but never thought it would happen to her. Even though she knew how to manage diabetes, she couldn't help feeling alone, helpless, and down in the dumps. She just couldn't motivate herself to do what she knew she had to do.

When you found out you had diabetes, you were probably given a lot of new information about how to manage the disease. You were told you would have to change your lifestyle, your eating habits and your daily activities. You may have been prescribed new medications. And most likely you were told how to test your blood glucose on a regular basis.

Having all this thrown at you at once can be overwheming. In the midst of trying to sort out all the new information, you may have also experienced many different feelings. Maybe you denied the seriousness of the disease, and tried to shrug it off. Maybe you felt imperfect, or somehow flawed. Or perhaps you felt angry, and wanted to find something or someone to blame. Maybe you felt sad, blue, or out of sorts. Diabetes can cause feelings of depression and isolation, wreak havoc with your self-esteem, and cause you to be stressed out. You may have experienced many different emotions as you tried to come to terms with the disease.

Most likely, you put some of those feelings aside as you tried to absorb the new medical information and adapt to your new lifestyle. Once the shock of diabetes wears off, however, it is important to begin to pay attention to your feelings.

Dealing with Your Feelings

Some of the emotions you experience as you deal with diabetes may make you feel bad. But some feelings may actually be useful in helping you come to terms with your new lifestyle. For example, denial can be part of nature's way of letting the news of diabetes sink in gradually. Even anger can be an ally in dealing with diabetes if you channel your energy in a direction that helps you take charge of your condition.

The key to dealing with your emotions is to understand your feelings without trying to suppress or deny them. Some emotions might require immediate attention and others may just have to run their course. Some people find that it helps to indulge their feelings for a little while, to sit around feeling sorry for themselves for a week or two before mustering up the wherewithall to meet the problems head on. But the better you understand your feelings, the easier it will be to come to terms with diabetes.

Beating Denial

If your first reaction to the news that you have diabetes was to try not to think about it, to wish it would go away, to tell yourself you would deal with it later, or to convince yourself that the doctors don't know what they are talking about, then you may be experiencing denial. Denial is not necessarily a bad thing. It can help you adjust to living with diabetes. By putting your emotions on hold, you can better deal with the

Food for Thought

If you're having trouble knowing where to start talking about living with diabetes, try out this series of questions. They will help you identify how you feel and take steps toward feeling better.

■ What part of living with diabetes is the most difficult or unsatisfactory for you?

■ How do you feel about this situation?

■ How would this situation have to change for you to feel better about it?

■ Are you willing to act to improve this situation for yourself?

■ What steps could you take to bring yourself closer to where you want to be?

■ Can you pick out one thing that you can do to improve things for yourself?

shock of absorbing all the new instructions and medical information. By pretending you don't have diabetes or that diabetes is not that big of a deal, you can avoid feeling overly stressed out, angry, or depressed while you begin to fathom all the changes that lie ahead.

However, if you stay in denial for too long, you run a greater risk of neglecting your health and not taking care of your diabetes. This can cause emergency situations to occur in the short term and can also lead to serious problems in the long term. You may be tempted to keep your old routine, or pretend that you can eat the way you used to, but the sooner you make changes, the better off you will be.

Diabetes is a manageable disease if you keep your blood glucose under control. By doing this you can avoid many of the debilitating complications of diabetes such as eye disease, kidney disease, heart disease, stroke, and infection. But it is up to you to take charge of your diabetes aand make those changes that will ensure a long and healthy life. No one can make that decisoin for you.

Breaking out of denial may take some work. It may help to talk to other people with diabetes about how they manage. You might consider joining a support group, joining a chat room or newsgroup on the internet, or seeking counseling.

If you feel overwhelmed, talk to your doctor or diabetes educator. It may help to take on just a little bit at a time. Don't try to change everything all at once. Think about just watching your diet or learning how to monitor blood glucose for a few weeks before you dive into an exercise program. Talk to your doctor or diabetes educator about how you can approach your diabetes management in small steps.

Denial and other feelings such as guilt and anger are a part of living with diabetes for many people. They may come and go as life changes and as diabetes changes over the course of a lifetime. Sometimes you need reassurance that you have some of the same concerns as everyone else.

Controlling Anger

When you find out you have diabetes or during the course of adjusting to diabetes, you are likely to experience feelings of anger. You may feel that life is treating you unfairly. You might start to feel angry once you have gotten over denial. Or you may find that feelings of anger coexist with feelings of denial, depression, or anxiety. You may find yourself feeling angry when confronted with some of the problems brought on by diabetes. Or you may find that you flare up in situations that have nothing to do with diabetes.

All of these feelings are a natural reaction to dealing with a difficult condition. Anger is common as you adjust to diabetes. It is normal to feel angry over something you feel you can't control. If you find that months after developing diabetes, you regularly feel an unusual amount of anger or hostility that you can't control, then you may need extra help in dealing with your anger.

A good way to deal with anger and other bad feelings is to recognize the feelings, realize they are normal, and find ways to channel your energy that will help you take charge of your diabetes.

Start by recognizing your anger and take responsibility for it. Don't blame an angry outburst on someone else or an unrelated situation. At the same time, accept that it is okay to feel angry.

Next, start to keep track of your angry episodes and the events that trigger your anger. Keep notes or a journal if possible. After a few days or even weeks, sit down and review your observations. Try to figure out if there is any sort of pattern. See if there are any particular situations or people that make you angry. Does your anger typically occur after sitting in a traffic jam for an hour? Or does it occur when people start to ask you about your diabetes? Try to figure out what situations tend to make you angry.

Sometimes just identifying the triggers may be enough to help you come to terms with your anger. You may also need to avoid those situations that cause you to become angry. If you find yourself getting hot under the collar everytime your spouse nags you about your blood glucose, don't wait until things build up to an angry outburst. In a calm moment, explain that it bothers you. Make a deal that you will test your blood glucose at certain times if he stops nagging.

You may discover that you have angry feelings because you haven't completely come to terms with your diabetes. If this is the case, think about joining a support group, talking with other people, or seeking the help of a professional counselor.

You can let anger eat away at you and make you miserable, or you can think of it as unharnessed energy. Use that energy to do something positive. Your anger may be telling you that you are due for a change in your life. Educate yourself about diabetes and become your own health advocate. Try testing your blood glucose whenever you feel an episode of anger coming on. Or go for a walk to calm yourself down. By taking positive steps to bring your anger under control, you can take charge of your diabetes care.

Handling Stress

People with diabetes, as well as doctors and researchers, have long suspected that stress can affect blood glucose control. Although there is no clear evidence that stress alone can cause any disease, it is possible that it can bring on or worsen symptoms in someone already headed for disease.

Stress is a double-edged sword for people with diabetes, as with many chronic diseases. Stress may contribute to the symptoms of the disease and the disease itself can trigger stress. How to best handle diabetes and its associated stress is different for everyone. But you may find diabetes-related stress similar to how you experience stress in general.

Diabetes can churn up real, imagined, or expected stresses in all of us. It can make you feel as though you can no longer control your own body, making you feel helpless and out of control. It can cause anger and lead you to question, "Why me?" You may also find yourself in denial ("this can't be happening to me"), depression ("I feel sad and hopeless") or helpless ("I can't cope with this"). It can also lower your self esteem and lead you to think there is something wrong with you.

To manage your stress, it may be helpful to first recognize how you act when you are stressed out. Do you anger easily and take your feelings out on others? Do you cry easily or become depressed or withdrawn? Perhaps you feel emptiness or apathy. Maybe you reject help from those close to you or demand unrealistic attention from them. Maybe you come down too hard on yourself.

If you tend to get overanxious or lash out when under stress, tell yourself to slow down and take things in stride. Delegate responsibilities and carve out time for yourself. If you tend to internalize stress, remind yourself that diabetes is not your fault and that you can take positive steps to deal with your condition. Learn how to relax (see page 369).

Some of the following stress-management strategies might work for you.

- Find someone to talk to when something is bothering you.
- Join a support group.
- Form a discussion or networking group on any topic or activity that interests you.
- Join a team sport.
- Take up a new hobby, learn a musical instrument, or join a dance class.
- Consider a career change.
- Think about the things you have always wanted to do and never had a chance—and do them!
- Exercise—join a health club, sign up for an aerobics class, or just take a walk every day.
- Engage in volunteer work.
- Sign up for a class that interests you.

■ Read a book you've always wanted to read.

■ Take a vacation or even a night away.

■ Get a babysitter to give you some extra free time.

■ Train for a short fun run or walk-a-thon.

Recognize that everyone has choices in life and you make your own choices. Pace yourself. Avoid excessive behavior. Make it a point to identify the things that stress you out and devise ways to deal with them. You may not be able to control traffic jams, an angry boss, or a crying baby, but you do have

Progressive Muscle Relaxation

■ Close your eyes and breathe slowly and deeply.

■ Start with the muscles in your face, working your way down to your feet and toes.

■ Inhale. Raise your eyebrows. Tense them. Hold for a count of 3. Relax your eyebrows. Exhale.

■ Inhale. Open your mouth and eyes wide. Then close your mouth and eyes tightly. Squeeze. Hold for a count of 3. Relax your eyes and mouth. Exhale.

■ Inhale. Bite down on your teeth. Hold for a count of 3. Relax your jaw. Exhale.

■ Inhale. Pull your shoulders up. Hold for a count of 3. Relax your shoulders. Exhale.

■ Inhale. Tense all the muscles in your arms. Hold for a count of 3. Relax your arms. Exhale.

■ Inhale. Tense all the muscles in your chest and abdomen. Hold for a count of 3. Relax your chest and abdomen. Exhale.

■ Inhale. Tense all the muscles in your legs. Hold for a count of 3. Relax your legs. Exhale.

■ Inhale. Tense all the muscles in your feet. Curl your toes. Hold for a count of 3. Relax your feet. Exhale.

■ Inhale. Exhale any tension that may be lingering in your body. Breathe in energy. Take several more deep, slow breaths. Enjoy the relaxation.

■ Gradually open your eyes.

some control over the way you react to these situations. Try to find healthy ways to deal with feelings of loneliness, low self-esteem, anger, and other uncomfortable emotions.

Dealing with Depression

If you are like most people, every now and then you probably feel a little down in the dumps. But if you feel sad, blue, or have feelings of hopelessness or despair that last for more than a few weeks, you may have clinical depression.

Depression is more common in people with diabetes, occurs more frequently, and lasts longer, compared with the general population. Depression can occur anytime—when you are first diagnosed or after you have been dealing with diabetes for years. Depression can coexist with other feelings, such as denial, anxiety, or even anger. If you experience any of the following, you may be depressed:

- you no longer find pleasure in activities you once enjoyed
- you have trouble falling asleep at night or wake up once you have fallen asleep
- you feel tired during the day
- you no longer enjoy eating the foods you once liked
- you find yourself eating more or less than you used to
- you either gain or lose weight
- you have a hard time concentrating
- you have a difficult time sitting still
- you cannot seem to make even the most trivial decision
- you experience feelings of guilt or a lack of self-worth
- you feel that everyone else would be better off without you
- you entertain thoughts of suicide or think of ways to hurt yourself

If any of the above symptoms apply to you or if you have been feeling sad or hopeless for more than a few weeks, talk to your doctor or health care provider. There may be an obvious physical reason for your feelings of depression—a change in medication or poor blood glucose control, for example.

If your doctor cannot find any physical causes, you may be referred to a mental health professional. Seeing a mental health professional does not mean there is something wrong with you as a person. It simply means that you may have a medical problem that affects your emotions.

You may see a psychiatrist, psychologist, psychiatric nurse, licensed social worker, or other mental health counselor. Your counselor may recommend psychotherapy, antidepressant medication, or both. Many people find successful relief from depression from a combination of the two. If antidepressants are in order, you will need to see a psychiatrist or other medical doctor. Many emotional problems are caused by chemical imbalances in the brain and antidepressants can help you get back on track.

It is important to recognize the symptoms of depression and seek help right away. When you feel depressed, you are less likely to take care of yourself and this could worsen your diabetes. Unfortunately, when you feel depressed, you probably feel even less motivated to seek help. But this is the best thing you can do to get your life and health back on track.

Controlling Anxiety

Everyone feels nervous or anxious from time to time, especially in a stressful situation. This is normal, and often, even helpful. Anxiety is a normal survival mechansim that can help you get through a difficult situation. If you are face to face with a man-eating bear or have to give a lecture before 1,000 people, for example, feeling a little anxious can help you get through the ordeal. But if you find that you feel nervous or anxious in situations that are not stressful to most people or if your anxiety is so intense and long-lasting that it interferes with day-to-day living, you may need extra help. When you are anxious, it is not so much a problem that your worries are unfounded, but your worries may be more intense, frequent, or last longer than the situation calls for. Feelings of anxiety can coexist with feelings of depression.

If you experience any of the following, you may have an anxiety disorder:

- you feel restless, irritable and have difficuty concentrating much of the time
- you tend to be overly worried or overly concerned about even the most trivial things
- you feel tired or easily fatigued
- you have problems sleeping
- your muscles feel tense or you experience frequent headaches

If your worries or concerns are beginning to interfere with daily living or prevent you from enjoying the things you once enjoyed, it may be time to seek help. First, try talking with your doctor. Your anxiety could have a physical cause. Your doctor may want to check your records of blood glucose control. Poor blood glucose control could be triggering your feelings of anxiety.

If your doctor cannot determine a physical cause, you may be referred to a mental health counselor. Through medication, counseling, or a combination of both, your mental health counselor may help you find a way to control your feelings of anxiety. Once you overcome your feelings, you are on your way to better care of your diabetes and better health in general.

Boosting Your Self-Esteem

It is much easier to meet life's challenges with a good dose of self-esteem. But, unfortunately, diabetes can gnaw away at your self-esteem, which in turn makes it even more difficult to deal with the disease. You do better in your work, studies, and personal relationships when you have a high sense of self-worth. And you are more likely to go after what you want out of life when you feel good about yourself.

It is more difficult to feel good about yourself when you have a chronic disease like diabetes. But it is important to try. Blood glucose levels can affect your mood, appetite, energy or fatigue level, sense of well-being, and control over your life. Some people with diabetes have low self-esteem because they blame themselves for having the illness. Or they think less of themselves because they feel different. This can happen whether you are a child, a teenager, or an adult. Some people even wonder if there is some negative factor that singles them out for this disease.

An important step is to try to develop and maintain a positive self image. Realize that even the most successful people have to deal with some kind of limitation, whether real or perceived. Emphasize your good qualities and give yourself a break, even if no one else does. Recognize that you are your own best friend and you have to live with yourself for the rest of your life. Strive to be the kind of person you want to live with. The only thing that can hinder your self-esteem is how you feel about yourself.

When you are feeling good about yourself, write down a list of all your strengths and positive qualities. When someone pays you a compliment, add it to the list. Then on days when you are feeling down, take out the list and remind yourself of what a great person you are. If you have trouble coming up with things to put on the list, ask those around you who like and love you for help. Often your friends and family are quicker to recognize your strengths than you might be. You might even enlist the help of someone close to read the list to you when you are feeling particularly low. It might also help to engage in an activity you are good at to remind yourself of what a wonderful person you truly are.

Taking Charge

The trick to taking charge of your diabetes is to learn to assert yourself and to feel good about the choices you make. When you assert yourself, you can communicate better with others and achieve better control over your diabetes. If you are unable to assert yourself, you might find it difficult to talk about your diet or how much time you need to take care of your diabetes. Or you may be reluctant to have your needs interfere with those of the people around you. But it is risky to downplay your diabetes to be accepted socially. With or without diabetes, you are bound to have a conflict with anyone you are in close contact with—your health care team members, your family, or your coworkers. And you are more likely to resolve any misunderstandings or developing tensions if you assert yourself and make your needs or position understood. Often conflicts arise not out of differences of opinion but out of gaps in communication.

Try out these assertiveness skills which can help in the workplace, in social situations, and at home with the family:

- **Learn to say "no."** A simple "no, thank you" communicates to yourself and to others that "I respect myself enough to act in in my own best self-interest and I respect you enough to know that you will understand."
- **Maintain courtesy.** Courtesy is the cornerstone of effective and assertive communication. It relays the assumption that you will treat your needs and those of others equally and that neither will suffer at the other's expense.
- **Be direct.** Direct communication while maintaining courtesy is as important as saying no at the appropriate time.
- **Watch others.** Other people project signals that will help you decide how to act with them.
- **Meet your own needs.** Hypoglycemia is the most urgent situation in which you must be assertive. Don't put off

treatment because you are afraid of offending someone you are interacting with.

■ **Be firm.** It is important to be firm with both yourself and others. Decide that you need to avoid certain foods. If pressured to join in, explain your decision directly to others. Prepare your companions in advance about your diabetes and your needs.

■ **Maintain self-respect.** If you respect yourself, you will have no qualms about being assertive in explaining your situation ahead of time and asking for help should the need arise.

To fully take charge of your diabetes, you must also be self-motivated and disciplined. This does not come easily. Only discipline and self-motivation can allow you true freedom. It may seem unliberating to be tied to a particular meal plan or insulin regimen. But realize that if you stick to your program, you can fully participate in all the other things life has to offer.

Taking charge of your diabetes involves several key steps. Once you accept your diabetes, you can stop wasting energy denying it and channel the energy toward managing your condition. Also, you eventually need to accept responsibility for making your own choices. Only you can control your diabetes and you alone make the decisions to manage your diabetes. In the long run it serves no useful purpose to blame others for your condition. Your friends and family can help, but only you can take charge of your disease. You will also need to choose to maintain a healthy lifestyle. Since your diabetes affects other people in your life, make it a positive influence. And positive diabetes care requires that you delay your rewards for the appropriate time. You might have to put off having something you want to eat now, because it helps you stay healthy. Finally, realize that if you balance your meal plan, exercise, and medication in response to your monitoring results, you can have flexibility in your routine and lifestyle.

You have many choices. You can think of diabetes as a challenge or a limitation. You can remain strong and wise and in charge of your disease or you can remain unhealthy. The choice is yours and it makes all the difference.

Is depression more common among people with diabetes?

Your Emotions and Diabetes

Some studies say that depression is more common, that it recurs more frequently, and that it lasts longer among people with diabetes than in the general population. Whether you believe this applies to you probably depends on whether you think "depression" is having the occasional "blues" or if you use the more clinical definition of chronic feelings of hopelessness. Everybody, diabetes or no diabetes, goes through periods of feeling down, along with low energy and not caring to be involved in things going on around them. Depression is serious when these feelings go on for long periods, perhaps for weeks, and you don't feel better.

If your blood glucose control goes down the tubes, you may also experience some of these feelings. Having high blood glucose for a long stretch brings on fatigue and sleepiness. It can sap your energy and keep you from getting involved with activities. So, in addition to the fact that having to deal with diabetes day in and day out can give you the blues, poor blood glucose control can add to the blues. Can you see why people with diabetes might report feeling depressed often?

Can diabetes affect my sense of self-worth?

Having a chronic disease like diabetes can make it harder to feel good about yourself. You may feel "damaged," just because of diabetes. Being different can make the teenage years even more painful than usual. It may reassure you to remember that all of us deal with limitations.

A number of problems with diabetes care can be traced back to how you really feel about yourself. Ask yourself whether it is worthwhile to take care of yourself. How do you show yourself respect? If you do it by making healthy choices that show how capable you are of taking care of yourself, others will respect your needs, too. If you need to do a blood glucose test right now, do it. Don't be worried about asking others to wait for you while you test.

CAN STRESS AFFECT BLOOD GLUCOSE CONTROL?

Yes. There are really two ways to look at how stress affects blood glucose control. One way is to examine the effect of stress on how you take care of yourself. If you find that you sometimes react to stress by overeating, drinking extra alcohol, or zoning out in front of the television, then stress can alter your self-care and therefore also alter your blood glucose levels.

Second, stress affects your body's hormone balance. Your body produces powerful hormones in response to a difficult or "fight or flight" situation. These hormones get your body ready for quick action by breaking down stored forms of glucose into blood glucose. This sends your blood glucose levels up. If you have type 1 diabetes, you probably don't have enough insulin on board to cover the higher glucose levels. If you have type 2 diabetes, your levels are likely to remain too high due to insulin resistance. Your body also releases stress hormones in response to situations like illness or surgery. This can even happen if the "threat" isn't serious, but a nagging worry, like being late for an appointment.

CAN STRESS CAUSE DIABETES?

A stressful lifestyle doesn't cause diabetes. However, for someone already headed in that direction, it can push them along a little faster. Perhaps you've heard stories of people whose diabetes began after a stressful experience, such as a severe illness or a car accident.

In type 1 diabetes, the immune system mistakenly destroys the insulin-producing cells of the pancreas. This is a process that usually takes many months, perhaps even years, before enough cells are lost so that diabetes starts. A person on the way to getting type 1 diabetes makes less and less insulin. A stressful experience increases the need for insulin. So, the insulin demands brought on by a stressful experience could overwhelm the body's ability to produce insulin. The ability to mask the diabetes any longer could be lost.

In type 2 diabetes, the body stops responding normally to insulin. As this happens, the ability of the pancreas to make enough insulin decreases. Adding stress-produced hormones, which create more resistance to insulin, to this scenario could bring on the first symptoms of diabetes.

WHY DO MY FEELINGS CHANGE SO QUICKLY? IS IT BECAUSE OF DIABETES?

Trying to meet the never-ending demands of life with diabetes can make anyone feel frustrated, or up one minute and down the next. It's easy to feel cheated when you've met your end of the bargain by doing the tests and following your eating plan, but blood glucose levels aren't doing what they should. Maybe you need a good listener. One of the most supportive things your loved ones can do is listen to how you feel. They may be tempted to solve your problems for you, but they help the most when they can just listen to you express how you feel about living with diabetes.

If you suspect that your feelings change quickly because of changes in your blood glucose level, consider doing some investigative testing. Quick, large changes in blood glucose level can change your emotions. You can feel fine one minute, and the next be sad, mad, or frustrated. If your mood swings are related to blood glucose fluctuations, talk to your health care team.

Keeping your emotions tucked inside you may lead to psychological problems. Let the people close to you who want to support you listen to how you feel. If you need more help dealing with mood swings, consider seeing a psychologist or other mental health counselor.

Chapter 13: Diabetes and Family Life

Diabetes affects all family members. It can be tough to balance the needs of everyone, but with practice, families can cope and even grow closer together.

*E*ver since he had been diagnosed with type 2 diabetes two years ago, Richard had a hard time staying on track. He tried to watch his diet and he was pretty good about eating the right amount of carbohydrates. But he still needed to lose about fifty pounds. He knew he was eating too many fatty foods, and he couldn't resist a bag of potato chips, which his wife seemed to always have around. To Richard, that seemed to be a big part of the problem. His wife never really understood that he needed help in sticking to his diet and making healthy living a part of his life. If anything, she seemed to be undermining all his efforts....

Stacey had always managed her type 1 diabetes almost effortlessly. She was an exercise fanatic and had always been very diligent about eating the right foods and sticking to her insulin and eating schedules. But the demands of family life were getting to her. It was okay when the kids were little. She still called all the shots. But now her three kids were in school and life was full of their activities. Driving them between ballet class, soccer and softball practice, and piano lessons was taking its toll. Her husband was often late getting home from work, so it all fell to her. Now she was having a hard time sticking to her schedule, making sure she ate at the right times, and taking her insulin when she should. Last week she'd had a close call—an insulin reaction while driving her kids to soccer. They were running late, and she didn't have enough time to grab a snack....

Balancing Family Demands and Diabetes

*L*ife is tough enough. Whether you are married, have children or grandchildren, live with your parents, or have just struck out on your own, it's difficult enough to balance all the stresses of modern life. Work, school, financial matters, child rearing, retirement, or divorce are all hard enough to deal with without the additional burden of diabetes. If it were just you living alone, you could eat what you want, when you want, and you could fit exercise into your own schedule. But if you live with others, you are going to have to work them into your overall diabetes management plan. Even if you live alone, friends and family still enter into the picture. You need their support and understanding, but don't forget that they may need a little help, too. To be successful at managing your diabetes, you will need your family's cooperation. It's important that you feel that you are not alone in meeting the challenge of learning to live with diabetes.

How Diabetes May Affect Your Family

Maybe at first it seems as though you should be able to handle things okay. After all, your family can't hold your hand and watch you do everything, can they? It is still up to you to monitor your blood glucose, right? Maybe, but having diabetes is bound to affect your family. First of all, family life can be demanding. You can't tend to your two-year-old screaming for a cookie if you're in the middle of giving yourself an insulin shot. Your partner may begin to resent having you test your blood glucose and take insulin at dinnertime instead of helping prepare dinner. And sex can lose some spontaneity if you have to eat a snack just when the mood is striking.

Much of diabetes revolves around a schedule. And if your family is not used to adhering to a tight schedule, there will be adjustments that have to be made—either by you or your family members. And if your family is used to running a tight ship—soccer practice at 4:45, homework at 6:15, dinner at 7:00, and baths at 7:45—you are going to have to carve out pieces of time to tend to your diabetes care. Even if you don't have children, you and your spouse may be used to eating dinner at a certain time. And that may require some changes depending on your insulin or exercise schedule. Probably the best way to approach this is to enlist their support right away. Hold a family meeting and explain how important it is to coordinate insulin doses, exercise routines, and meals. Ask for suggestions as to how your new schedule might fit into the family routine.

Finding out you have diabetes may upset the delicate balance of your juggling act. You may already feel stretched to the limit. Planning meals, testing your blood glucose, and taking insulin will all take extra time. You may have to sit down with your day calendar and try to figure out how to best fit it all in. Maybe your spouse will have to pitch in a little more and pick up the kids from school or daycare a few times a week. (Remember that vow about "in sickness and in health?") Maybe the kids can help cook dinner a few nights a week. Or maybe it's time to hire that cleaning service you always dreamed of. Don't be afraid to acknowledge that you can't do it all and something is going to have to give. It may require other family members to do a little more or it may mean enlisting some outside help. But don't try to take on more than you can handle. That can just add more stress, which could make your diabetes even more difficult to control.

Scheduling might not be the only change in order. Maybe you decide you have to eat differently. If your family is used to evening meals at the local fast food joint, this may have to change. Ideally, your family will go along with your new eating habits. But without diabetes affecting them personally, they may be unwilling or lack the willpower to make drastic dietary changes. Again, open communication is the best approach. Try to find out what healthy foods they are willing to eat. Explain that you are not going on a diet and are not going to force them into spartan eating conditions. But eating better foods might be a boost for everyone. The key is getting their input. No one likes to be forced into doing something they don't like to do. Also, although your family may agree to better food choices for the most part, they may still need an occasional junk-food fix from time to time. If this gnaws at your willpower, ask them not to flaunt it in front of you. It's hard to stick to a new routine when temptation is staring you in the face.

There will be other changes as well. Maybe you need to exercise more. Ideally, your family will join in, walking or jogging alongside of you. If not, ask them to at least encourage your efforts. Try to plan family activities that involve some form of exercise—walking the dog, a nature walk, or a bicycle trip to the corner store. The more you can get your family involved in your exercise program, the easier it will be for everyone.

And with diabetes, there are bound to be mood changes. Maybe you get a little cranky when your blood sugar is low. Maybe your partner is getting a little tired of having to nag you all the time to watch your meal plan. And maybe you are getting tired of the nagging. Learn to talk about your feelings and try to establish open channels of communication. Sometimes you'll be cranky because of the diabetes, and sometimes you might just feel cranky because of life's demands. Learn to work with your family members to talk about how you are feeling and what to do about it. Maybe you just need a snack or maybe you need to go for a walk. Or maybe your spouse or children need a little break. Recognize when there is a problems and talk about solutions.

Finally, your family has to know what to do should an emergency arise. Make sure they understand the signs of hypoglycemia. Give them blanket permission to override your protests, in case you lose your sensibility. Often people with diabetes having a low blood sugar reaction will deny there is a problem even though they may be in dangerous state. Make sure your family can recognize the signs and knows how to deal with it even though you may be denying that anything is wrong.

What Your Family Can Do

Sometimes problems arise among family members when they don't really understand the disease. If your teenager is grumpy because he has to wait for you to take an insulin shot before you drive him to the mall, it may be because he doesn't understand how important it is to adhere to your schedule. And if your spouse is waving potato chips under your nose when you are trying to cut back, she may not understand the importance of diet in controlling diabetes. Many people think that it is as simple as taking insulin a few times a day, and that will make the disease go away.

As a first step, each family member needs to understand what diabetes is, how it is controlled, and how to handle those rare emergencies. There is lots of help available. Books, magazines, pamphlets, libraries, support groups, on-line message boards and chat rooms, and medical professionals can all be of assistance. Try to get your family members to go with you to some of your medical appointments. By keeping a running list of questions or issues with which they may be concerned, they can get answers to their questions firsthand. Family members should also try to attend diabetes education classes, either with you or on their own. The more information they have, the more they can help you and learn to integrate your diabetes management plan into the daily family routines.

Your family can also help with your eating plan. For many people, this is the most difficult adjustment to make after being diagnosed with diabetes. You will have to change the foods you eat and when you eat. It will help you tremendously if the members of your family also change their eating habits. Your family may object to eating a special diet and may resent being confined to a certain eating schedule. But eating well for diabetes is not really a special diet, it just means eating sensibly. Whether you have diabetes or not, eating large amounts of sugar, fats, and salt isn't good for anyone.

Exercise is also important for diabetes control, and your family can help with that. Exercise benefits everyone, not just those with diabetes. So consider some activities that you can do together. Maybe an evening family stroll or bicycle ride might add to the quality of life for all family members.

Depending on your family, you can expect different responses to your diabetes and different levels of enthusiasm for helping you achieve your diet and exercise goals. Some may partake wholeheartedly, looking at this as a team effort. Other families or family members may resent having restrictions imposed upon them when they aren't even sick. You need to find the approach that works best for you. In some situations, you may have to go it alone. Your family may be reluctant to join in on your diet and exercise plan. But if you show them that by following a healthy living plan you are not starving to death, just eating healthy foods, they may eventually join in. And if they see how rewarding and fun exercise can be, they may be more likely to try it themselves.

Finding Other Sources of Support

Without the support of your family, it may be more difficult for you to make the changes you need. You may need to look elsewhere for an extra boost, to get things on track.

American Diabetes Association (ADA). One place to start is your local chapter of the American Diabetes Association. Check the Resources section at the end of this book for the ADA chapter nearest you.

Many ADA chapters sponsor support and educational groups that you can join. These groups can help you deal with the emotional part of living with diabetes. By participating in these groups, you can meet other people with diabetes and health care experts. Whether you are seeking more information about the disease or are just want to talk to people who share your feelings, an ADA support group may be just the thing.

In addition to support groups, ADA chapters can mail you a free packet of information on request. They can also answer any questions you may have about the disease or some of the practical issues in managing diabetes: health care, health insurance, and referrals. And they may be able to point you to a diabetes education program. They also have several books, magazines, and publications available that may help.

Health Clubs. You might also consider joining a health club. Although this is a source you may not have thought of, developing a diabetes management program really means developing healthy living habits. And people who actively participate in the local health club or fitness center may share similar diet and fitness goals, whether they have diabetes or not. There, you can probably have access to a personal trainer who can be a tremendous help in achieving your fitness goals. You might also meet other people with diabetes who are following a similar routine for health and fitness.

Counseling. Sometimes, despite the help of support groups, and even with a supportive family, you might need extra help. Coping with diabetes and all of the feelings that go along with it is not an easy process. Adjusting to diabetes when you first find out about it is probably the most difficult. But there are bound to be times down the road when you will need extra support. Maybe your friends and family will be enthusiastic cheerleaders at the beginning, but as time goes on they may forget how much you need their help. Or new issues may arise during the course of your life or the course of your disease.

Whatever your situation, you may want to consider psycho-therapy or some form of individual or group counseling for those times when you need a little extra help. It might help you to sort out any difficulties you may be having to work with a professional and objective source of support. A professional psychotherapist can help you examine your problems. Depending on your individual needs, you may want individual, marriage, or family therapy.

You might seem a little put off by the idea of psycho-therapy. Maybe it conjures up negative images or maybe you think seeing a psychotherapist indicates that there is something wrong with your mental state. Nothing could be further from the truth. Psychotherapy is a healthy way of helping normal people deal with some of life's difficult problems.

Psychotherapy involves an ongoing conversation between you and your therapist. Your therapist will help you explore your thoughts and feelings and examine how you interact with others and the decisions you make. Your therapist may encourage you to tell your story, starting from the beginning. This may help you find a new perspective on the problems in your life and discover the patterns in your actions. He or she may also offer suggestions that may help you see the situation from another person's viewpoint and may help you find new ways of coping.

One of the most important aspects is to find a therapist you trust. You should feel comfortable with your therapist and feel that he or she is supportive. It often means finding the right personality match. Someone who works well with one person may not necessarily be compatible with someone else. So don't be too discouraged if the first therapist you see doesn't fit your needs. You may need to talk to several before you find one that feels right.

Living with diabetes means adjusting to the complex inter-play between family relations, personality, emotions, lifestyle habits, and blood glucose control. The key to psychotherapy is the desire to make changes in your behavior. Therapy will help you learn to take the initiative and necessary action to take control of your diabetes as well as the conflicting emotions that go along with it.

Group Therapy. While some people benefit most from the one-on-one encounters with a therapist, others gain more from weekly group therapy sessions. And many people find the combination of approaches to be a double benefit. These groups can foster mutual support, encourage camaraderie, and help combat the depression and isolation that often goes along with a diagnosis of diabetes. Sometimes talking things out with other people helps you to find fresh solutions.

There are many types of settings and formats for group therapy. Some meet in hospitals, clinics, community agencies, and even in therapists' private offices. Group therapy should include a trained therapist, a careful selection of group members, and a social structure that includes rules for behavior. All psychotherapy groups share the principle that talking about feelings, ideas, and experiences in a safe respectful atmosphere increases self-esteem, deepens self-understanding, and helps a person get along better with others.

The group setting gives each member a chance to see how others react to their feelings about diabetes and observe how they incorporate diabetes into family, work, and play. Group therapy has special advantages for people with diabetes. It can help you:

- learn that you are not alone
- discuss deeper feelings, worries, and concerns that you may never dreamed of discussing anywhere else
- discover new approaches to old problems
- explore who you are and who you are not
- reduce stress, which in turn may lead to more stable blood glucose levels, eating patterns, and exercise patterns

Don't Forget Your Partner

If you have diabetes, you know that it can take an emotional toll. But you're not the only one who may feel the stress. Your family members, especially your partner, is likely to share in the burden. If you shut out your partner completely, he or she may feel isolated and helpless. They may feel a need to "rescue" you and resent being left by the wayside. But if you shift too much of the burden to your partner, he or she may resent having to spend too much effort trying to help you and feel that you should be doing more to help yourself. Many spouses dislike being put in the position of parent or nursemaid.

Your mate may worry when you don't make the effort to eat properly, monitor your blood glucose levels, or exercise regularly. He or she may fear the consequences of what will happen, either in an emergency situation or down the road, when you neglect your health. Maybe you feel that your spouse is nagging too much. Maybe your spouse feels that you are deliberately undermining his or her efforts to support you. However you are feeling, it is important for both of you to realize that nobody is perfect. And often many of these feelings are due to love, concern, stress, or fear. It is important to acknowledge that these feelings—any probably many other conflicting emotions—do exist. Try to share them honestly when neither of you is feeling pressured or stressed out. By sharing your feelings and communicating openly, you and your partner may be drawn closer together rather than driven apart.

You might need help learning to communicate. Admitting to this is a sign of strength, not a weakness. Confide in your friends. Speak with your spiritual counselor. Consider seeking the help of professional counselors who are trained in coping strategies for people with chronic disease. Your health care professional or ADA chapter may be able to help you find the skilled professional you need to talk to.

And finally, don't forget to lighten up. Humor can help you get through stressful times. Laughter helps lighten the load, relaxing us in the process.

Diabetes and Children

*J*enna and Drew were just like any other brother and sister. Sometimes they fought, but most of the time they got along fine. Then Jenna, at the age of 10, was diagnosed with type 1 diabetes. Now all the attention was on her, it seemed to eight-year-old Drew. Everything from family meals to outings seemed to revolve around Jenna. Their parents, Gail and David, couldn't understand why Jenna and Drew weren't getting along anymore. Drew was getting whiny and demanding. Why couldn't he cooperate at a time when they needed it most?

Any kind of change can upset the family dynamic. How you treat your children and how they interact with each other can be influenced by many factors. And having a child diagnosed with diabetes is a big change that is likely to affect the entire family in ways you never thought possible. At a time

Suggestions For Family Members

Caring about someone who has diabetes offers special challenges in addition to the usual ones. Here's how you can help.
- Get an education in diabetes care.
- Be supportive, but don't take on the role of caretaker.
- Help those you love keep the rules, not break them.
- Lend a sympathetic ear.
- Be flexible and open to new ways of eating and spending free time.
- Plan for emergencies.

when you, your child, and other children are probably fearful about what the future holds, you will likely be confronted with feelings of anger, resentment, and jealousy. At a time when you are trying to gather medical information and help your child manage his or her diabetes, it is difficult to keep all the family relationships running smoothly at the same time.

If you have a child with diabetes, your top priority will be to help your child manage the disease while trying to live as normal a life as possible. You will also want to help the rest of the family make a smooth transition into accepting the changes that are inevitable.

Dealing with Your Child's Diabetes

The first step in helping your child manage his or her diabetes is to learn all you can. Other chapters in this book and internet resources are a good starting point (see the Resources section at the end of this book for ideas). You will also want to talk to your child's doctor and diabetes educator. Try to schedule an appointment that is long enough so that all your questions and concerns can be addressed. In general, you will want to know how to test your child's blood glucose, how to give insulin, and how to figure out an insulin injection plan. You will also want to know the extent to which your child should be expected to take responsibility for her own care. If your child is only two years old, it is unrealistic to expect her to give herself insulin or test for blood glucose, but if your child is ten, she may very well be capable of testing herself and giving herself insulin shots. In doing your research and helping your child develop a treatment plan, don't forget that every child is different. What works for one child may not work for your child. Your job is to find out how your child experiences diabetes and what you can do to help.

After you meet with your child's doctor, you will also want to meet with a diabetes educator. A diabetes educator can help you coordinate your child's overall diabetes management plan. This includes balancing your child's meals with her insulin schedule and physical activities. You will also want to meet with a dietitian and work out a healthy eating plan. Make sure to take into consideration your child's likes and dislikes. Your child will not stick to an eating plan that is full of foods she doesn't like. Your child should not feel that having diabetes means having to eat differently than anyone else. All kids should be eating healthy food, whether they have diabetes or not. In fact, you will help your child and your family if you eat the same foods. Don't prepare one dish for the rest of the family and a special diabetic meal for your child with diabetes. Also, talk to your child's dietitian about ways to include special treats into your child's meal plan. Make sure to involve your child in the meal planning and ask her what special foods she would like to include in her eating plan.

Also talk to your child's teachers and school officials or daycare providers about any special needs your child will have. (For more on diabetes at school, see page 423.) Once you and your child figure out the daily routine and work out ways to deal with special events and circumstances, you will both feel better about living with diabetes.

Dealing with Your Own Feelings

When you first find out your child has diabetes, you may be overwhelmed with feelings of shock, disbelief, sadness, anger, or even guilt. It can seem so unfair. You may experience self-doubt as you wonder whether you can give your child the care she needs. With all the stresses in your life and all the demands on your time and energy, it may seem that you just won't be able to handle it all.

If you feel overwhelmed, just relax and take a deep breath. Once you learn enough about diabetes, you will soon realize that your kid can live a normal life, just like any other kid. All it takes is a little work as you figure out how to balance your child's meals with insulin injections and physical activities. You may find that your child takes it all in stride and that the hardest part may be coming to terms with your own feelings.

Don't forget that your child is looking to you for guidance. Your attitude will have a direct impact on how your child sees herself and how she comes to terms with her new lifestyle. If you accept your child's condition in stride, so will your child. If you react with anxiety, apprehension, and fear, so will she. It may not be easy, but try to maintain a sense of calm. Deal with diabetes in a matter-of-fact way. Don't downplay your child's fears or concerns, but address them in a straightforward fashion. The more both you and your child know about diabetes, the more relaxed you will both be.

If you are overly anxious and concerned about your child's diabetes, your child will sense your fear. Don't try to do everything for your child. Let your child have some say in her diabetes care plan. Let your child assume some of the responsibility with taking care of her diabetes. But at the same time make sure your child doesn't skip blood tests or insulin doses. You may feel you are doing your child a favor by giving her a break every now and then, but you will do your child great harm if you let her diabetes care slide. A missed insulin shot or blood test could end up triggering an emergency situation such as diabetic ketoacidosis (DKA). You will want to treat these procedures as givens with no exceptions and no questions asked. As soon as your child sees that these are non-negotiable duties, she will be less likely to try to get you to let her off the hook. If you don't provide the discipline, your child will learn that she doesn't have to pay attention to her diabetes care. The best way to establish good diabetes care habits for life is to set the pattern early so that they become a way of life.

Dealing with the Rest of the Family

If you have more than one child, getting your child with diabetes on track is bound to cause some tension in the family. Siblings may feel jealous of the child with diabetes, because of all the attention that she is getting. On the other hand, siblings may give your child with diabetes too much attention and your child may feel like her siblings are bugging her too much. She may feel that everyone is breathing down her neck. Even if she doesn't have siblings, she may not welcome the extra attention.

The best way to deal with diabetes in the family is to treat it openly, but without any cause for alarm. Explain what is happening to other family members and ask them to be patient as you work things out. Try to schedule special times with those children who may feel left out, or try to give them a role in the overall care of your child with diabetes. A sibling could help record blood glucose readings, for example. In general, you will want to treat your child's diabetes as a simple fact of life and nothing to get alarmed about. Once your child and her siblings come to accept diabetes as a normal part of your family routine, feelings of anger and jealousy should subside. However, if you continue to experience family turmoil months after the initial diagnosis, you might want to consider family counseling. Talk to your child's doctor and diabetes educator for help in finding a family counselor, if necessary.

Your Child's Changing Role

Just how much you can expect your child to handle with respect to her diabetes care will change as she matures and will depend on her personality. If your child is an infant or toddler when diagnosed, you will be completely responsible for your child's care. But you can and should still keep her involved. You will have to see that your child gets her shots at the right time and you will have test her blood glucose and evaluate the test results, but you can give your child a voice. Let her pick the injection spot or the finger to poke. This is a good way for your child to get used to having a say in her care. It will help her to develop a sense of responsibility about her diabetes care as she grows older.

If your child is in preschool, you are still responsible for making sure she is eating according to the plan you have worked out together, conducting blood tests whenever necessary, and taking the right amount of insulin at the right time. But there is nothing wrong with letting your child begin to take over some of these tasks. Many three-year-olds can do their own finger pokes. By age 12 or even earlier, most can take their own insulin. Your child can manage this even sooner with an insulin injection aid, such as Inject-Ease. Your child may also have good luck with an insulin pump. This can give her much greater flexibility and independence. As your child matures during this period, it is essential that she learn to take responsibility for her own behavior, because she will often be with friends or at school and out of your watchful field of vision.

Adolescence is bound to provide the greatest challenges to both you and your child with diabetes. Even if you are June Cleaver, there will be times when your child resents you and blames you for all the ups and downs of diabetes. This is a normal part of becoming independent and would happen whether or not she had diabetes. She may try to rebel by neglecting her diabetes care. The best way to handle this stage is to educate yourselves about diabetes care together and allow your child to participate in treatment decisions. Your child may try to deny her diabetes in an effort to fit in and appear just like everyone else. She may try to skip insulin doses, ignore meal plans, and even falsify glucose readings. But the best way to fit in and lead a normal life is to keep blood glucose levels under control and stick to the plan as much as possible. A bout of severe hypoglycemia or DKA is one sure way to make your child feel like an outcast. Make sure she understands the consequences of neglecting her diabetes care. Ultimately, it is up to your child to take responsibility for her care. The more maturity she shows in handling her own care, the less you will have to nag her to stick to her diabetes care plan. You might suggest that your child visit a diabetes educator on her own. This may help her develop a sense of responsibility about diabetes care. When your child is treated more like an adult, she may act more like an adult. It is critical that she understand the importance of good diabetes care and recognizes that it is up to her to take charge of her care.

It is not uncommon for your teenager to feel depressed. Eating disorders, especially among girls, are common. One particularly dangerous type of eating disorder involves skipping insulin. This allows a person to eat and not gain weight. If you start to suspect that your child is developing an sort of coping problem, eating disorder, or behavioral problem, seek the help of a professional counselor immediately.

Handling Emergencies

Whether your child is a toddler or a teen, it is important that you, your child, and those close to her be aware of the signs that could signal a life-threatening situation. Severe hypoglycemia (low blood glucose) or hyperglycemia (high blood glucose) are both emergency situations. Hypoglycemia can affect the brain and lead to unconsciousness and coma. Hyperglycemia can lead to a life-threatening situation known as diabetic ketoacidosis. To prevent either situation, learn to recognize the warning signs, test blood glucose right away, and treat promptly. Talk to your child's doctor in advance about what you should do if your child's blood glucose levels fall too low or rise too high.

Hypoglycemia. Any time your child's blood glucose level falls below 60 mg/dL or whatever value your child's doctor suggests is too low, your child may have hypoglycemia. Sings of hypoglyccmia include nervousness, shakiness, sweating, irritability, impatience, chills, clamminess, rapid heartbeat, anxiety, light-headedness, and hunger. When hypoglycemia begins to affect the brain, your child may also appear sleepy, angry, uncoordinated, or sad. She may also experience nausea, blurred vision, tingling or numbness in the lips or tongue, nightmares, crying out during sleep, headaches, or strange behavior. In severe stages, confusion, delirium, personality changes, and unconsciousness can occur.

If your child is experiencing any of the symptoms of hypoglycemia, have her test her blood glucose right away. If you don't have time to test, treat anyhow. Usually, anything below 60 mg/dL requires treatment, but check with your child's doctor to see what valuc requires treatment for your child.

To treat hypoglycemia, give your child a fast-acting carbohydrate snack. This could be 2 to 5 glucose tablets, 2 tablespoons of raisins, half a can of regular (not diet) soda, 4 ounces of juice, or 5 to 10 jelly beans, lifesavers, or gumdrops. In general, you want to give your child 10 to 15 grams of fast-acting carbohydrate. Wait 10 to 15 minutes and test again. If her blood glucose is still low, give another dose of carbohydrate.

If your child is unable to eat or shows any signs of severe hypoglycemia (confusion, delirium, or unconsciousness), she needs emergency help right away. Call your doctor and/or call for emergency help. The quickest way to get blood glucose levels up is to give an injection of glucagon. Ask your child's doctor to show you how to give a glucagon injection and under what circumstances you should give it. This will require a doctor's prescription. Make sure your child wears jewelry identifying her as a person with diabetes at all times.

Hyperglycemia and Diabetic Ketoacidosis. If your child's blood glucose level rises too high, she could develop hyperglycemia and diabetic ketoacidosis. This is a life-threatening condition that requires immediate action. Symptoms of hyperglycemia include extreme thirst, dry parched mouth, and sleepiness or confusion. Your child may also have warm, dry skin with no sweating. If you notice any of these symptoms, have her test her blood glucose right away. If it is over 250 mg/dl, have her test her urine for ketones. If your child has moderate to high levels of ketones, call your doctor right away. Also call your child's doctor if your child has a lack of appetite, stomach pain, vomiting, feelings of nausea, blurry vision, fever, difficulty breathing, or a fruity odor on her breath. Call your child's doctor if your child has a blood glucose reading over 350 mg/dl whether or not there is evidence of ketones. If you are able to get in touch with your child's doctor, or if your child has a blood glucose reading over 500 mg/dl, take her to an emergency room right away.

Chapter 14: Diabetes in the Real World

Before you were faced with diabetes, did you know much about it? Most people don't. One of the tasks that comes with having diabetes is educating others in the workplace, the schools, and our society about what you need to live well with diabetes.

Okay, so you've finally figured out a diabetes management plan. You've sat down with your doctor and worked out an insulin injection plan. You met with your dietitian and figured out a sensible eating plan that works for you. You've even talked with an exercise physiologist, to come up with an exercise schedule that you can handle. This would all be very manageable, almost easy, if it weren't for one thing: the real world.

Sure, you could monitor your blood glucose 4 to 7 times a day, exercise once a day, eat specific meals on schedule, and give yourself insulin 2 to 3 times a day, if you had nothing else in the world to do. But most of us don't live a life of leisure. We work, go to school, take care of family, pursue outside interests, or tend to other responsibilities.

With everything else going on in your life, squeezing in a diabetes management plan may seem next to impossible. Whether you hold down a job or go to school, working your diabetes care into the rest of your day presents special challenges. And as if that weren't enough, you may have to brace yourself for the possibility that even if you do manage to balance the demands of work, school, and diabetes, you may face discrimination.

Fortunately, with the right planning, you can develop a new lifestyle that integrates your diabetes care plan with everything else you do. The better you plan and communicate with others around you, the better you will be able to take good care of your diabetes while still doing all the other things you have to do. And the better you are able to do this, the less likely you will be discriminated against.

Diabetes in the Workplace

Now that the kids were finally out of the house, JoAnn decided to return to nursing. She immediately found a position in the intensive care unit of the city's biggest hospital. She enjoyed working the night shift from 11 p.m. to 7 a.m. even though it meant keeping odd hours. But a few months after starting her new job, she was diagnosed with type 2 diabetes. She worried about whether she would be able to keep her diabetes in check while working such an erratic schedule.

Jason had just graduated from college. It had been quite an achievement, because he had been living with type 1 diabetes since his early teens. Nevertheless, he had learned how to maintain a reasonable schedule, attending classes, studying, working out at the gym, and even partying with his friends. And now he had landed an exciting sales job with a major pharmaceutical manufacturer. It would mean lots of traveling all over the country with occasional overseas visits, business luncheons, and cocktail parties. But how could he ever keep control of his diabetes with all that traveling and while keeping such crazy hours?

For Jason and JoAnn, new jobs and new schedules certainly mean big changes. Without a doubt, they will both have to make adjustments in their diabetes care routines. But they needn't worry about giving up the jobs they love. There's almost no job a person with diabetes can't handle. As teachers, cooks, doctors, nurses, electricians, engineers, athletes, and corporate executives, there's really no end to the types of work people with diabetes can master. But it hasn't always been this way. In the 1930s, if you had diabetes, you would have been turned down for any position in the federal government. And even as late as 1989, simply having a parent with diabetes would have kept you out of the military. But today, thanks to the Americans with Disabilities Act (ADA), which guarantees your rights in private employment, and the Federal Rehabilitation Act, which ensures your rights in federal government employment, there are more and more opportunities for people with diabetes. As long as you feel you are qualified and you have your diabetes under control, feel confident to go after any job you desire.

Maintaining Schedules

Of course, you'll have an easier time managing your diabetes if you have a regular work schedule. But if the job of your dreams means working the late shift or traveling all over the globe, diabetes shouldn't keep you from pursuing it. It just means you will have to make adjustments and be extra careful about monitoring your blood glucose levels. Diabetes doesn't have to dictate your schedule. If your employers or prospective employers are questioning your ability to manage a job with irregular work hours, explain to them how you are able to control your diabetes. Emphasize that you are in charge of your diabetes and the discipline you exercise in taking care of your diabetes is the same discipline and determination you will bring to the workplace.

Night Shift. Working the night shift poses a special problem if you have diabetes. You're not in sync with the rest of the world. While everyone else is eating breakfast, you're ready for your bedtime snack. And adjusting to conventional hours on your days off can also be a challenge. You may have to change the times and or doses of insulin you take. You may also find it helps to adjust your meal plan and exercise routines. Nevertheless, with careful planning and monitoring, you can make the adjustments so that your new routine works for you.

Let's say you're a nurse working the 11 p.m. to 7 a.m. shift at the local hospital. If you get home at 8 a.m. and plan to sleep through the day, you may have to change your morning insulin dose if you won't be eating lunch at noon. Otherwise, if you take the normal dose of insulin in the morning, you may develop hypoglycemia while you sleep. Your health care team can help you make changes, such as adding longer-acting insulin to your morning dose and eliminating shorter-acting insulin. Exactly how you modify your schedule will also depend on when you eat.

On the other hand, maybe it works better for you to stay up until noon and sleep through the afternoon and early evening. If that is the case, your normal morning insulin dose may work just fine. But you may have to make adjustments in your evening regimen. If your job calls for some nights on and some nights off, then you will need to test your blood glucose levels more often. This will allow you to fine-tune your schedule for more erratic hours. You may also need to use multiple injections or an insulin pump.

If you have type 2 diabetes and are not taking insulin, you may still have to make changes in your diet and exercise routine to accommodate an erratic work schedule. And if you are taking oral agents, eating at a particular time may make a difference. It may be as simple as making sure you eat a snack before sleeping or changing the times you eat and exercise. Whenever you are getting used to a new routine, you may find that more frequent blood glucose monitoring will help you decide how to best adjust your daily routine to keep your blood glucose levels in balance.

Erratic Hours. You may not work the graveyard shift, but you may have the sort of job that makes you keep odd hours. Perhaps a meeting with clients has you eating later than usual. Or your job may demand lots of traveling. Even in the most conventional job setting, there are probably going to be occasions when you're eating at a different time or exercising off-schedule. Whether it happens all the time or once in a blue moon, you'll need to learn how to make adjustments to accommodate changes in routine.

Whether you have type 1 or type 2 diabetes, the best way to figure out how to make adjustments for changes in routine is to monitor your blood glucose frequently. If you're going to eat a late lunch, try eating your afternoon snack at your normal lunchtime, and you'll be able to hold off for a while until you eat your full meal. If you take insulin, this might mean waiting to inject insulin until your full meal, because you still need to coordinate your insulin injections with your food intake. It will take a little trial and error, but by monitoring your blood glucose, you will soon figure out how to make the proper adjustments. If you do tend to keep a crazy schedule, consider an insulin regimen that allows for maximum flexibility.

Exercise can also be affected by an erratic schedule. If you are used to a lunchtime jog, but a noontime lunch meeting keeps you from your normal routine, adjustments may be in order. You may find that you can't eat as much as usual if you're not going to be exercising near mealtime. You can compensate by eating less, or, if you're taking insulin, injecting a little more insulin than usual. If you take that run later in the day, you may find it necessary to eat a larger snack than usual. Whenever changes in routine require adjustments in the way you normally manage your diabetes, be extra diligent about monitoring your blood glucose. And be sure to always keep a snack on hand.

Travel

In today's global marketplace, many jobs require travel. Whether you're circling the globe several times a month or riding the rails every now and then, you're bound to have changes in your daily schedule and routine. That doesn't mean you can't travel if you have diabetes. With a little advance planning, you can go anywhere and do almost anything. But there are a few things you should be aware of that will make your diabetes care that much easier.

Air Travel. If you are traveling by airplane, be sure to order a special meal in advance. Most airlines have special low-sugar, low-fat, low-salt, and low-cholesterol meals available on request. Most airlines require that you request special meals at least 48 hours in advance.

Mealtimes on the plane can be somewhat unpredictable. So don't inject your premeal insulin until you see the meal cart coming down the aisle. Bad weather, a bumpy flight, or air traffic can delay your meal. Make sure to take along extra snacks in case your meal is delayed. You may want to tell your flight attendant that you have diabetes, especially if you are traveling alone. That way, should any emergency arise, your airline crew will be prepared. And if there is a meal delay, he or she may be more willing to see that you get your meal as soon as possible.

Also be aware that air travel can be dehydrating, so it's a good idea to drink lots of water. Avoid alcohol because it can only add to dehydration.

Crossing time zones can sometimes be confusing. Should you be eating according to east coast or west coast time? If you are flying in the air, which time should you follow for injecting your next dose of insulin? In general, when you lose hours from your day (traveling from the west coast to the east coast), you may need to reduce or skip a dose of insulin. When adding hours to your day (traveling from the east coast to the west coast) you will probably need an extra dose of insulin. If you are uncertain of how to work your insulin and meals into your travel and business plans, take a copy of your itinerary and work schedule to your doctor. He or she may be able to suggest some sample routines to try.

Your health care team can help you adjust your intermediate- or long-acting and short-acting insulins for travel days. Exactly what you decide to do will depend on your meal schedule and plans for sleep or activity once you arrive at your destination. The best way to deal with uncertainty is to monitor your blood glucose more frequently while traveling.

Ground Travel. If you are traveling by automobile or other types of ground transportation, be extra careful that your insulin

Eating on the Run

Traveling can throw a monkey wrench in even the most well-thought-out eating plans. Here are some tips for eating while you are traveling.

■ Whether driving, flying, or riding the rails, keep snacks on hand in case your blood glucose levels start to drop. Nutritious snacks that travel well include cheese, crackers, fruit, and peanut butter.

■ In the event of an insulin reaction, keep glucose tablets, raisins, or other quick sources of sugar close at hand.

■ If you are traveling by plane, don't take your insulin until you get your meal—or see it coming. If you take your shot and then the meal service is slow, or if it is canceled because of a bumpy flight, your glucose levels can fall.

■ When you book your flight, order a special meal for people with diabetes. Not only is it better for you, but it usually tastes better because it is not mass-produced. Some railroad routes also have meal service available.

■ Talk to your doctor about adjusting your insulin and meal schedules when crossing time zones.

■ Check blood glucose levels more often than usual, even if you have type 2 diabetes. Eating different foods or following different eating and exercise schedules can affect your blood glucose.

■ When dining out, try to eat at off-peak hours. Or reserve a table in advance. Your meal is less likely to be delayed if the restaurant is not crowded.

is properly stored. Extreme temperatures—either hot or cold—may reduce the potency of your insulin. Even backpacks or cycle bags can get too hot in warm weather. Watch out for automobile glove compartments and trunks, which can often overheat. Most insulin preparations have added agents that prevent the growth of bacteria, so you don't need to refrigerate. But if you are traveling by car and there is a danger of overheating, keep insulin in an insulated container with ice, "Blue ice," a cool damp cloth, or some other cooling device. But don't let insulin freeze and never use dry ice to store it.

Exercising on the Road

You've got everything under control. You are exercising regularly and eating well. Then your boss decides to send you out of town at last minute's notice to meet with some prospective clients. How will you manage? Your days will likely be filled with high-calorie lunches and hours and hours of meetings. How will you ever find a gym, or even the time to exercise? Fear not. You may not be able to schedule a 2-hour session with your personal trainer, but here are a few suggestions to keep your exercise program on track.

■ Pack a pair of comfortable walking shoes and some athletic socks. It is easier to squeeze a brisk walk into a busy schedule than most other exercises and can be done in almost any locale. If your schedule is jam-packed with long meetings, try getting up a little earlier and squeeze in a walk after breakfast.

■ If you are attending a conference, wear dressy walking shoes instead of traditional business shoes. You'll be more likely to walk around the exhibit hall, walk outside to a restaurant or take a stroll in a nearby park if your feet aren't killing you.

■ Take along some exercise equipment when packing your bags. If space is tight, take a swim suit, running shoes, jump rope, exercise video, or light weights and resistance tubing.

Plan in Advance

The key to successful traveling, especially when you have diabetes, is careful planning. Think of all the contingencies that might arise or any particular needs that you might encounter and develop a plan in advance.

■ If you travel often, you may want to carry a letter from your doctor, preferably on letterhead stationary, stating that you have diabetes. Be sure the letter indicates that you must use insulin, syringes, and blood glucose monitoring supplies. This could come in handy, particularly if you go through customs or are a frequent airline traveler.

■ Keep a prescription for insulin from your doctor on hand in case you start running low while you are out of town. This is especially important if your travel plans are subject to frequent changes.

■ You can always look up your local ADA chapter in the white pages of the phone book if you're traveling in the United States. If you travel frequently to the same cities, keep list of local chapters on hand. This may come in handy if you need to know where to buy supplies or find a doctor in a pinch. If you are going overseas, write to the ADA for a list of International Diabetes Federation groups.

■ Wear a medical ID bracelet or necklace that says you have diabetes.

■ If you are traveling abroad, learn how to say "I have diabetes" and "Sugar or orange juice, please," in several languages so you can make yourself understood wherever you are.

■ If you are overseas and need medical attention—and you have a choice—think about contacting the nearest American consulate, American Express, or a local medical school for a list of English-speaking doctors.

■ To be safe, pack twice as much insulin and blood-testing equipment as you think you will need. Pack half in your carry-on luggage so you'll always have your supplies within reach.

■ If you find yourself running low on insulin while abroad, remember that insulin sold outside the United States is often less strong than the U-100 you are used to buying. If you buy insulin that is a different strength (U-40 or U-80), you must also buy new syringes to match the new insulin to avoid errors in dosing. If you use U-100 syringes for U-40 or U-80 insulin, you will be taking too little insulin. On the other hand, if you use U-100 insulin in a U-40 or U-80 syringe, you will be taking too much.

■ Don't get separated from your medical supplies. Get used to carrying a tote bag, fanny pack, or backpack with your insulin, syringes, meter, lancets, glucose gel or tablets, and some food.

■ Even if you are on a business trip, make sure to take comfortable shoes and clothes. If you'll be in sunny weather, bring sunglasses, sunscreen, and whatever else you need to be comfortable.

Carry-On Luggage Checklist

Make sure to bring twice as many supplies and medications as you need and pack half in your carry-on luggage. That way you won't get stuck high and dry if your luggage gets lost, or your trip is unexpectedly delayed or extended.

Medications
Insulin
Syringes
Oral diabetes medications
Glucagon kit
Glucose tablets or other sugar source
Snacks, such as dried fruit or crackers
Anti-nausea suppositories
Antibiotic ointment
Other prescribed medications

Blood testing equipment
Test strips
Lancets
Blood sampling device and a spare
Glucose meter
Alcohol wipes
Spare batteries for glucose meter
Cotton or tissues

If you are driving, you might be able to take a racquet and balls, golf clubs, skis, soccer ball, or even a bicycle.

■ Before booking your hotel, ask if they have a health club, swimming pool, or exercise room. Some hotels provide access to a nearby fitness center.

■ Check with health clubs in the area you are visiting to see if you can buy a few days of use. If you belong to a national health club chain, see if they have clubs in the city you are visiting.

Operating Heavy Equipment

If you operate dangerous equipment or even if you drive an automobile, it is important to test your blood glucose often. This is especially important for people who take insulin. An insulin reaction in either of these situations can result in serious injury to yourself and to others.

The federal government still does not allow people who take insulin to enter the armed forces, to pilot airplanes, or to drive trucks or buses on interstate routes. However, these policies are currently under review. It is possible that in the near future people with records of good blood glucose control may soon be able to work in these types of jobs.

If you drive, or operate heavy equipment, keep the following guidelines in mind:

■ Check your blood glucose level before you leave your house or start work. If it's low (70 mg/dl or less), treat it. Retest 15 minutes after your first test to be sure your blood glucose level is rising. Otherwise, it might not be safe to drive or operate equipment. If your glucose is not on the rise, treat again and wait until your blood glucose level is normal. Take along a snack in case the level drops later.

■ Always take along a fast-acting source of carbohydrate—raisins, glucose gel or tablets, or hard candy. If you feel even minor symptoms of low blood glucose while driving or operating dangerous equipment, stop and do a blood test. It is better to be a few minutes late or to take a little longer getting the job done than to risk an accident.

■ If you can't check your blood glucose and you feel hypoglycemic, stop what you are doing and treat the symptoms. Don't start driving or working until the symptoms pass. It's a mistake to think you can hold out until you get to wherever you are going or finish up the job.

Discrimination

 few years ago, David worked for a medical research university. He was told by his supervisor not to administer insulin at his desk or he would face *termination. David obliged, but resented that he couldn't take care of his diabetes the way he wanted. Eventually he found another job, but had to take a pay cut and give up some retirement benefits. He always wished he had stood up to his supervisor and stayed with the job he loved.*

Paula, who has been managing her type 2 diabetes for several years, was told that she would have to switch from working the day shift to a rotating shift schedule or face termination. This would wreak havoc with her diabetes care plan, but she doesn't want to lose her job.

Jon was enjoying the career he always dreamed of. He had just graduated from a prestigious military academy and was now serving as a second lieutenant in the U.S. Air Force. But after he started feeling dizzy on duty a few weeks ago, a medical exam revealed he has type 1 diabetes. His commanding officer put him on medical hold while his case is being reviewed by a medical board. He fears he will be discharged.

Today there are laws to protect against discrimination in the workplace. But, unfortunately, discrimination against people with diabetes still exists. Several years ago, people with diabetes were sometimes told outright they wouldn't be hired because of their diabetes. This may not happen today, but sometimes discrimination can be more subtle. Did you get passed over for a promotion because of your work performance or because your boss was afraid your diabetes might interfere with the added responsibilities? Did you fail to get that job offer because you weren't qualified, or because you told the employer you have diabetes? Sometimes it's hard to know. The best thing you can do to guard against discrimination in the workplace is to have a positive attitude, do the best job you can, and understand your rights.

In 1990, the Americans with Disabilities Act (42 U.S.C. §12101 et seq. [1990]) was signed into law. This law protects people with disabilities from being discriminated against. It covers all civilian employees who work for companies that employ 15 or more people. The Rehabilitation Act of 1973 provides similar protection for people who work for the federal government or who work for companies or contractors that receive federal funding. Under these laws, employers cannot discriminate against you if you are qualified for the job and carry out the work with reasonable accommodation by the employer. Although in principal employers are not allowed to discriminate, in practice some discrimination still occurs. Some employers, including the federal government, are slow to change workplace policies, such as blanket bans on hiring people with insulin-requiring diabetes, unless they are challenged in court. For example, the Merchant Marine Academy was ordered to reinstate a young man who had been discharged from the academy after developing diabetes when the student sued. In Toledo, Ohio, a young man admitted to the police academy was later turned down after he indicated during his physical exam that he had type 1 diabetes. He sued and provided the city's physician with medical records supporting the fact that his diabetes was well-controlled. Toledo now looks at potential employees with diabetes on a case-by-case basis.

The Federal Rehabilitation Act and the Americans with Disabilities Act require employers to give people with disabilities an equal opportunity. Perhaps you have been working hard to keep your blood glucose in control and to prove to yourself and to others that you are healthy. So it may be difficult to think of diabetes as a disability. But in this case, the definition can help defend your rights. The law defines a disabled person as one who:

- has a physical or mental impairment that substantially limits one or more major life activities, such as walking or seeing,
- has a record of such an impairment, or
- is regarded as having such an impairment.

Before these laws were passed, you may have been asked to list any medical conditions on a job application. The employer could then refuse to hire you based on this medical information. But, if you weren't hired, you might not always know whether it was because of your qualifications, a bad recommendation, or because of your diabetes.

The law allows an employer to ask an applicant for medical information only after making a job offer and only if this is done for all job applicants. Then an employer may withdraw a job offer only if, for medical reasons, the applicant cannot perform the tasks required for the job even if reasonable accommodations are made by the employer. An employer still has the option of hiring whomever he or she feels is best able to do the job. However, an employer can run into problems if he or she hires someone less qualified while refusing someone with better qualifications who happens to have diabetes or any other disability.

Once you have started working, an employer can only ask medical questions if they are job-related and consistent with the needs of the business. For example, if an employee falls asleep on the job, an employer may ask if a medical condition is the cause. However, if an employee doesn't look well, but is performing his or her job adequately, an employer may not ask whether there is a medical problem.

The laws require that employers try to accommodate people with disabilities. For example, employers may be required to build ramps or elevators to provide access for people who use wheelchairs. For people with diabetes, employers may have to allow workers to adjust their work schedule or take breaks for blood glucose testing so that they can keep their diabetes under control while on the job.

Fighting Back Against Discrimination

If you believe you have been discriminated against either in your job or while seeking employment, the best course of action is **first educate, then negotiate, and last, litigate**. Sometimes dealing with a discrimination problem is as simple as teaching people about diabetes. Many employers don't understand the needs or capabilities of people with diabetes. And sometimes they don't understand the laws that protect you from discrimination. By educating officials about your needs, limitations, and strengths and by informing them of your rights and their responsibilities, you can resolve many situations in which you suspect discrimination.

Sometimes education alone may not be enough. You may have to negotiate to secure your rights. Your negotiations may be more effective if you first seek legal advice. Seeking legal advice early will maximize your attorney's ability to help you. Negotiating involves listening to the concerns of those in the workplace with an open mind and offering solutions to the perceived problems. If your employer is unwilling to take the steps to resolve a problem, you might suggest a trial period in which you can show how your solution may benefit all involved.

If you have exhausted all avenues to educate and negotiate, and a problem persists, you may have no choice but to litigate. This usually begins by filing an administrative complaint with the appropriate agency. If you are discriminated against in your job or while seeking a job, you may file charges with the Equal Employment Opportunity Commission (EEOC). The EEOC provides free information booklets for the public and employers. Check the Resources section at the end of this book for more information.

If you think you have been discriminated against in your job, whether in hiring, firing, promotion, tenure, or other aspects, you can also file complaints with United States Attorney General. The Attorney General files lawsuits on behalf of citizens to stop discrimination. If a suit is decided in your favor, an employer may be forced to award you money, reverse the discriminatory decision, and pay penalties. If you then choose to bring a private lawsuit against the company later, money cannot be awarded. To decide on the best course of action, you may want to consult an attorney.

A successful job discrimination claim has to be based on fact, not just hearsay. It is up to you to prove that you have been discriminated against because of diabetes. The best evidence is a written statement from the employer or person who made the decision. Write to request a written statement saying why you weren't hired or promoted or were let go. There may be other reasons for the employer's decision and your attorney will need to know about them. Most likely, you will need an attorney's help in filing this claim.

However, if an employer is truly discriminating on the basis of your medical condition, he or she may not readily admit to it in writing. You may have to do some information gathering to substantiate your claim. Gather together materials such as the employer's job application form, policy manuals, or statements regarding the employer's position on equal employment opportunity and any rules or regulations cited by the employer as the reason you were dismissed or not hired. Save copies of the job advertisement or listing, the job description, and the job performance evaluation criteria.

You should also compile a list of potential witnesses, including work titles and how to contact them. Include some information about their duties at work and how they would know about your situation. Finally, make a diary of events in chronological order.

Job Hunting

Not everyone looks askance at people with diabetes. So don't let the fear of discrimination in the workplace keep you from seeking out or reaching your career goals. But when seeking a new job, keep the following in mind:

To Tell Or Not to Tell . . .

Whether you tell your employer or fellow employees about your diabetes is completely up to you. There are reasons to tell—and reasons not to. Much depends on your particular job circumstances and the people involved. Here are some of the plusses and minuses.

Reasons to Tell

- Being open helps people to learn more about diabetes. You can help fight prejudice by showing that people with diabetes are just like everyone else. By not telling, you may be sending the message that you have something to be ashamed of.

- If you tell everyone, you no longer have to hide a big part of your life. And you don't always have to keep track of which people you have told and which you haven't.

- If you have had a hard time coming to terms with diabetes yourself, telling people about it may help you accept the condition yourself.

- If you take insulin or oral agents, you may be prone to low blood glucose reactions. This can make you confused and unable to help yourself. If people know you have diabetes, they can help you in the event of such a reaction.

- When you talk about your diabetes, other people can learn about the symptoms and treatment. As a result, people you know may seek early treatment if they suspect that they may also have diabetes.

- By telling people you have diabetes, you learn who your true friends and allies are. True friends will accept you for who you are. You probably don't want "friends" who would reject you just because you have diabetes.

Reasons Not to Tell

- You may want to maintain your privacy. Just as you wouldn't necessarily talk about how much money you make, you might not want to discuss your diabetes, which is just as personal.

- If you don't tell, you are less likely to lose a job promotion or job offer because of your diabetes. However, diabetes can be difficult to hide if you need to take breaks or leave a meeting to test or take insulin. Although laws protect against discrimination, it is not always easy to prove.

- Don't think of your diabetes as defect. It is a part of your life and who you are. Don't be shy about asserting your special needs in the workplace.

- Be prepared by knowing your rights. Remember that employers are not allowed to ask about your health before deciding whether to hire you. Once the job has been offered, they can ask about medical conditions as they relate to the job as part of the employment physical examination.

- If you wait to disclose your diabetes until after the job has been offered, take a positive approach. Be sure to point out any awards you received in previous jobs. Let them know how many sick days you have taken. Describe your exercise routine, if you exercise, to stay in shape.

- During your physical exam, if required, present a truthful condition of your condition and how you control your diabetes. Don't try to change your plan immediately before any physical examination. Changes in routine can affect your control of your diabetes. Your company's doctor is probably not a diabetes specialist. Point out the steps you take to keep your diabetes under control.

If you are forced to change careers because of your diabetes, and you cannot afford retraining, don't despair. You can get training through State Departments of Vocational Rehabilitation. Your local ADA chapter can help you find the programs available in your state.

In time, popular thinking will catch up with what many know already: with good blood glucose control people with diabetes can do anything they're qualified for, from scuba diving to performing surgery.

Diabetes in the Military

If you think it is difficult dealing with diabetes in the private work force or even in the government, try taking on the U.S. military. While many working people choose to educate, negotiate, and then litigate, you may have little room

Sources to Contact in Case of Discrimination

- Your state's Human Rights Commission or Equal Employment Opportunity Commission. Most states have a commission charged with investigating discrimination.
- Your union representative. If your job requires union membership, your union may have an Employment Discrimination Office.
- Your state of local Department of Labor or Employment. There may be someone responsible for investigating job discrimination claims.
- Your state or local bar association. They may be able to help you find an attorney who handles job discrimination cases pro bono (at no cost to the client) or offers other legal assistance.
- Your local chapter of the American Diabetes Association. Some chapters have created a network of attorneys who will represent or help find counsel for people with diabetes who are being discriminated against in finding or keeping a job.

for negotiation in the military. Your primary concern will be holding on to your job.

A few years ago, you were not allowed to serve in the U.S. military if you had diabetes. You were not allowed to enlist if you already had diabetes or if your parents had diabetes. If you developed diabetes while serving, you were immediately discharged.

Today, things have changed somewhat. You are still not allowed to enlist in the military if you already have diabetes. If you develop diabetes while already serving, your fate is not so clear. The military will decide whether to let you continue serving depending on whether you have type 1 or type 2 diabetes, whether you require insulin or other medications, and the nature of your service duties.

Protecting Your Job With FMLA

In addition to the Americans With Disabilities Act and the Rehabilitation Act of 1973, there is another federal law that can help you and your family deal with diabetes in the workplace. The Family and Medical Leave Act (FMLA; 29 U.S.C. §2601 et seq. [1993]) was passed in 1993. This law allows workers up to 12 weeks of unpaid leave each year to care for their own serious illness or to help very ill family members. FMLA absences may be taken in a single 12-week stretch or in shorter intervals, such as one day off per week. Employers who normally pay health insurance premiums must continue to do so for an employee on FMLA leave.

The law applies only to those companies with 50 or more employees locally (within 75 miles of the workplace). To be eligible, employees must have been with the employer for at least one year and have worked 1,250 or more hours. In most cases, employees must give 30 days notice. Some high-level company executives—those who are in the top 10 percent salary range—may be ineligible for FMLA leave.

FMLA offers leave to care for:
- yourself
- your spouse
- parents
- step and foster parents
- minor children
- minor step and foster children
- adult children who are incapable of self-care

FMLA excludes leave to care for:
- unmarried partners
- in-laws
- siblings
- grandchildren
- grandparents

The military reviews all medical conditions on a case-by-case basis. If you are diagnosed with diabetes, you will first be reviewed by a medical board, which could consist of just one person—the doctor who diagnosed you. This board or physician would summarize your condition and other information, including how well you control your diabetes, and whether you have any complications. That summary is then referred to a Physical Evaluation Board (PEB), which consists of a physi-

Fighting Discrimination: A Success Story

 Ken Dugger had one goal in life: to become a federal agent. He began working toward that goal by winning an appointment to West Point Military Academy in 1980. He hoped to graduate and serve four years in the military before pursuing a career as a federal agent. But while at West Point, he was diagnosed with type 1 diabetes. He was discharged from West Point and told to forget about a military career.

Dugger earned a bachelor's degree in oceanography–marine geology and geophysics at the University of Washington in Seattle and landed a temporary job as a fire fighter with the U.S. Forest Service. It was a challenging job, classified as hazardous and arduous by the Forest Service. But he handled it. And it gave him the confidence to pursue the career he always wanted. He then applied for a position as a special agent with the Department of Treasury.

Dugger passed the written Treasury Enforcement Agent Examination and had his first interview with the Bureau of Alcohol, Tobacco and Firearms (ATF). He told ATF officials that he had type 1 diabetes and that it was well controlled. According to Dugger, he was tentatively offered a position with ATF, assuming his background check and medical exam were satisfactory. But within a month, ATF withdrew its offer.

Dugger then hired a lawyer, and through the Freedom of Information Act, found that his application was rejected because of his diabetes. With his lawyer, Dugger filed a complaint with the Equal Employment Opportunity Commission. Soon after, his position with the Forestry Service ended, and he was hired as a special agent with U. S. Customs Services in Los Angeles. His job involved undercover work in money laundering and drug-smuggling cases, and he performed special operations, arrests, and seizures at the Mexican border. Dugger earned superior performance evaluations, but Customs Services decided to pull him off hazardous work duty. So, Dugger filed a second complaint for this action in U.S. District Court against the U.S. Customs Service.

Dugger and his lawyers consolidated his two complaints. In between litigation and running the Long Beach Marathon, he kept his diabetes in good control. Dugger was hired as a special agent with the U.S. Environmental Protection Agency. In August 1994, seven years after he filed his initial complaint, the Treasury Department settled out of court. As a result, the Treasury Department no longer adheres to a blanket policy denying placement of qualified people who happen to have diabetes. All positions are now decided on a case-by-case basis, thanks to Ken Dugger and his persistence.

cian and two nonmedical officers. The PEB decides whether you can continue to serve, based on what you do. This step can take weeks or even months. The PEB then declares you either fit or unfit. If you are declared fit, you could return to your present duties or you could be reassigned. In either case, you will be given a profile stating that you have diabetes and listing any restriction you might have. For example, your profile might state that you cannot be assigned to areas that lack medical facilities. Your profile will also state that you require three meals each day. If you are declared unfit, you will be discharged. This decision can be appealed.

If you have been diagnosed with type 2 diabetes and you control it without medication, chances are you will be allowed to return to your unit as if nothing had happened. If you require insulin or oral diabetes medications, your fate will depend on the decision of the PEB. If you are diagnosed with type 1 diabetes, you could be discharged, or you could remain in the military but be restricted from worldwide deployment or combat. People with type 1 diabetes are generally not considered worldwide deployable. If you have the type of job that does not require you to be deployable, you have a chance of remaining in that position. But if you have a job that requires you to be deployable, you could face reassignment or discharge.

Diabetes at School

Megan had been diagnosed with diabetes as a toddler. Adapting to life with diabetes was difficult for her mother, Janet. But Megan seemed to take it all in stride. Under her mother's watchful eye, Megan eventually learned to test her own blood glucose and could give herself insulin injections. She could even sense when her blood glucose levels were falling too low. Janet was finally beginning to relax until she realized that Megan would be turning five this summer. That meant she would be entering school in the fall. Janet wasn't sure how Megan would handle her diabetes care plan in a school setting.

Nick had finally made the transition from elementary school to middle school. Instead of staying with one teacher all day, he switched classes every hour. He got to take cool classes like shop and woodworking, and even cooking, which he secretly liked. The best part was gym every afternoon. But then one day he passed out during gym class. That's when he was diagnosed with type 1 diabetes. He and his parents wondered how he would ever be able to deal with diabetes in his school setting. Where would he test? How would he know if his blood glucose were too high or too low? Could he eat the school lunches? What if he had to go to the bathroom during the middle of class? What would all the other kids say?

For Nick and Megan, as for all kids with diabetes, adjusting to diabetes in school can be especially challenging. This is true whether you have been living with diabetes and are entering school for the first time or changing schools, or are already in school and have been recently diagnosed with diabetes. You want to make sure your child is given the same opportunities as other children, but you also want to make sure that any special needs are met. And you don't want your child to feel like an outcast.

Communicate and Educate

The best approach to dealing with diabetes in the schools is to communicate openly with the school's administration and teachers and even with the kids in your child's class. Make sure your child's school staff understands what it means to have diabetes, how your child manages his or her diabetes, and what special needs your child with diabetes may need. Your child's school may already have a plan in effect to deal with the special needs of children with diabetes.

You should expect that your child should be able to:

■ Eat whenever and wherever necessary. This could include keeping snacks or glucose tablets close at hand.

■ Go to the bathroom or water fountain when necessary.

■ Participate fully in all extra curricular activities, including sports or field trips.

■ Refrain from physical activity when blood glucose levels are too high or too low.

■ Eat lunch on schedule with enough time allotted to finish eating.

■ Be absent more than the traditional limit.

■ Be excused for tardiness in case of a blood glucose problem.

■ Ask for assistance with blood glucose monitoring or insulin injections, if needed.

Usually, sitting down with your child's teachers and school administrators and discussing your child's needs is enough to ensure that they will be met. When schools are reluctant to accommodate a child's special needs, it is often because they have not been educated. It is your job as a parent to educate your child's school staff about your child's diabetes so that they understand that the needs of a child with diabetes are not unreasonable.

If your child is entering school for the first time, meet with the school principal several weeks before school starts. If your child is already enrolled in school but has been recently diagnosed with diabetes, meet with your school principal and your child's teachers as soon as possible, preferably before your child returns to school.

In your meeting with the school principal, discuss your child's need to test blood glucose, administer insulin or glucagon, or have a carbohydrate snack on hand for low blood glucose emergencies. Explain how your child must balance insulin, food intake, and exercise. Also explain the consequences of blood glucose levels that are too high or too low. Ask the principal about the school policies that might affect your child's diabetes care plan. Find out what time your child will be eating meals, whether there is a designated snack time, whether there is a nurse on duty to handle emergencies, whether the meals served at school are suitable for a child with diabetes, or whether there are any restrictions on your child's participation in school events or physical activities. Also discuss any other concerns you might have. If there are any problems with the school policies that might interfere with your child's well-being, bring them up at this time and ask whether any accommodations can be made.

Before your child starts school, or returns to school, also schedule a meeting with your child's teachers. In addition to meeting with your child's main classroom teachers, also talk to any special activity teachers. It is especially important to talk with your child's physical education teacher. In talking to your child's teachers, tell them that your child has diabetes and explain how your child cares for it. Describe the basics of diabetes and what it means to live with it. Several pamphlets available from the American Diabetes Association do an excellent job of explaining diabetes care in a school setting. For example, "Children with Diabetes: Information for Teachers and Child-Care Providers," is available on the ADA internet web site. Use the search function on the web site to find the pamphlet. You can then download the pamphlet onto your own computer or print it out. The ADA internet address is www.diabetes.org. If you or your school does not have access to the internet, call the American Diabetes Association at 1-800-DIABETES.

Make sure to tell your child's teachers that your child must eat a mid-morning and mid-afternoon snack each day. Tell the teacher what time those snacks must be eaten. Make sure the teacher understands that these snacks are not optional. This means that your child may have to bring snacks to field trips, assemblies, or other situations in which snacks are not traditionally allowed. Also ask your child's teacher what time your child will be eating lunch so you can figure out his or her insulin schedule. Whether your child eats at 11 a.m. or 1 p.m. could make a big difference in blood glucose levels. Also ask to be informed if there is any change in the scheduled lunchtime.

It is also important to discuss hypoglycemia with your child's teacher. Explain what happens during an episode of hypoglycemia and tell her what signs to look for in your own child. Ask that your child be allowed to test his or her blood glucose level whenever necessary, especially if hypoglycemia is suspected. Let the teacher know whether your child can test for blood glucose independently or whether he or she will need help from a teacher or nurse. Find out whether your child will test for blood glucose in the classroom or nurse's office and make sure this is acceptable to you. Your child's teachers should understand what blood glucose levels are too low for your child and how hypoglycemia should be treated. Give the teacher a supply of fast-acting carbohydrate snacks to keep on hand for your child. You might also give the school nurse a similar supply. Make sure the teacher understands that under no circumstances should your child be left alone if he or she has an episode of hypoglycemia. Even if your child is sent to the nurse's office, someone must go with your child. Fill out the Diabetes Care Guide shown on pages 432–433 for your child and give it to your child's teacher. This guide is also available on the internet for printing or downloading at www.childrenwithdiabetes.com/.

Your child's teacher should also know about hyperglycemia, or high blood glucose, and diabetic ketoacidosis. Explain to the teacher what hyperglycemia is and alert her to the danger signs of diabetic ketoacidosis (see page 400). Make sure both the classroom teacher and physical education teacher understand that your child should not exercise with a blood glucose level above 240 mg/dl. Exercise could trigger the release of stored glucose, making your child's blood glucose levels rise even higher. Your child may need more insulin with a blood glucose level in this range. Talk to your child's doctor in advance about what to do in this situation and pass this information on to your child's teachers. Anytime your child's blood glucose levels are this high, your child's urine should also be tested for ketones.

If possible, get yourself a pager. Make sure your child's teacher and the school nurse and administrator have your pager number. Have them send a page with your child's blood glucose level whenever it is out of the range of what you and your child's doctor think are acceptable. Also make sure the school has all your phone numbers (including your cell phone number) as well as your child's doctor's phone number and pager number.

If Discrimination Occurs

Once you have met with your child's teachers and school administrators and discussed your child's needs, it is very likely that the school will make an effort to accommodate your child. If your child's school receives any source of federal funding, the school administrators are required by law to make reasonable accommodations to meet the needs of your child. Two federal laws guarantee all students with disabilities a free and appropriate public education without discrimination. Section 504 of the Rehabilitation Act of 1973 (29 U.S.C. §794 [1973]) protects individuals with disabilities against discrimination in any federally funded program, including public school systems.

In 1975, the Education for All Handicapped Children Act was passed. This law was amended in 1990 and renamed the Individuals with Disability Education Act (IDEA; 20 U.S.C. §1400 et seq. [1990]). It guarantees "free appropriate public education, including special education and related service programming for all children with disabilities."

After you have discussed your child's needs with school administrators, the next step is to document how the school will accommodate your child. Whether or not you feel your child's needs are being met, it is important to document just what steps are being taken. The accommodation must be documented in either a Section 504 plan or in an Individualized Education Program (IEP) under IDEA. The difference between the Section 504 accommodation plan and the IEP is the process through which the plan is developed and implemented.

Your plan should accommodate those needs that you have already discussed with your child's teachers and administrators and any other needs that you can think of. Talk to your child's health care team while developing your plan. This could include making sure that the school lunch program meets your child's nutritional needs, that your child be allowed to keep snacks close at hand, that your child be allowed to test blood glucose levels during the day, that your child be given adequate time to eat meals, and that your child not be excluded from activities. Make sure to think through what things are important to your child's well-being and include those in the plan. In developing this accommodation plan, you have the right to expect that reasonable accommodations be made. You will probably get more cooperation from the school officials if you show a willingness to understand their concerns and to negotiate an agreement both parties are happy with. Try to encourage the attitude that you are all members of the same team, not adversaries.

If you feel that your child's school is not meeting your needs, you may have no choice but to take stronger action. Contact your attorney for help in deciding the best course of action. You may start by filing an administrative complaint with the Department of Education. Do not delay in getting legal help. Administrative appeal and other actions need to be started quickly, or you lose the ability to use them. You may need to be prepared to take your case to court.

Your Public School Rights

 Despite the fact that federal law prohibits discrimination of children with diabetes in public schools, many parents find that their children's needs are still not being met. In working with school officials to meet your child's needs, it helps to know your rights. You have the right to:

■ Request that your child be eligible for services.

■ Schedule a meeting with school officials to develop an Individualized Education Program (IEP) under the Individuals with Disability Education Act (IDEA) or a Section 504 accommodation plan. You have a right to bring experts to this meeting to better explain your child's diabetes management.

■ Develop an IEP or Section 504 plan to accommodate the unique requirements of your child. This plan should precisely set out the types of special services your child needs to receive.

■ Withhold signing a plan if it does not meet your child's medical needs. The law requires that all parties agree to the individual plan before it is established. Be reasonable, but stand firm if your needs are not being accommodated.

■ Be notified and review any proposed changes in your child's plan, be included in any conference or meetings held to review IEPs, and review and consider changes before they are implemented.

You're Not Alone

In the September 1995 issue of *Diabetes Forecast*, the American Diabetes Association published a questionnaire asking parents to comment on their children's experiences in the public schools. More than 446 parents responded. Most respondents (73 percent) reported negative experiences in their local schools. Although laws exist to protect children with diabetes from discrimination in the schools, it is clear that these laws are not being consistently implemented. According to the survey:

- 24 percent of parents reported that the school lunch program does not meet meal plan requirements.
- 22 percent said the school is inflexible with the time that lunch is served, and 17 percent reported that their child does not have enough time to eat.
- 24 percent said their children must take exams even when they are affected by high or low blood glucose levels.
- 23 percent reported instances in which a hyperglycemic child was left alone.
- 18 percent of students said that glucagon is not allowed in their school, and 15 percent are not allowed to treat a reaction in the classroom.
- 13 percent of children are not allowed to eat snacks in the classroom, and 14 percent are not allowed to go the bathroom or go to the water fountain when needed.

Guidelines for Caring for

1. **When to do a blood glucose check**

    a. She says, "I'm low," especially if during or after exercise.

    b. If she has symptoms of low blood glucose, including:

    ■ irritability

    ■ erratic responses to questions

    ■ sleepiness

2. **What to do based on your child's blood sugar reading**

    (this is an example only and should be adapted to your own child's needs)

    Under 60   Give two glucose tablets, followed immediately by food containing 30 grams of carbohydrates. If she doesn't respond or blood glucose levels do not rise within 10 minutes, telephone

    (mother) _____ at _____ or

    (father) _____ at _____

    for further instructions.

    61 to 100   Give one glucose tablet. If a meal or snack is within 30 minutes, she can wait. Otherwise, give her a snack including carbohydrates and protein, such as cheese crackers with peanut butter or cookies and milk.

    101 to 125   She is fine. If exercise is planned before a meal or snack, she must have a snack before participating. This includes recess.

    126 to 200   She's fine. She could feel low if she was previously high and is dropping.

    201 to 240   She is a bit high, but this is not uncommon for her, especially in the early morning. Be on the lookout for signs of hyperglycemia.

Guidelines for Caring for _____ (continued)

Over 240   Her blood glucose is too high. She must be given water or other non-caloric fluids. Allow bathroom use, if needed.

She needs to check her urine for ketones. If ketones are present, the parents or diabetes team should be called for advice. If moderate to large amounts of ketones are present, she may need emergency help immediately.

3. **When giving glucose, the following are roughly equivalent:**
   - Four ounces of fruit juice
   - 1/2 to 1 cup of milk
   - Two glucose tablets
   - One tube of Cake Mate cake decorating gel. If unable to swallow, place between the cheek and gums.
   - One-half can of soda (regular, NOT diet)
   - Two tablespoons of raisins
   - 6 jellybeans
   - 10 gumdrops
   - 5 to 7 lifesavers

Chocolate candy should not be used unless there is no other sugar source available. The fats in chocolate slow the absorption of sugar.

If the blood sugar remains low despite treatment and the student is not thinking clearly, the parents or diabetes care team should be called for advice.

Following an episode of hypoglycemia (low blood glucose), it can take several hours to fully recover. The student can return to the classroom, but may not perform at optimal levels.

Chapter 15:
Working with the
Health Care System

You need to be your own advocate, working with your diabetes care team, health insurance company, and hospital, in order to obtain the best possible care.

Elaine was in a dead-end job with a boss she couldn't stand. But the job had one big bonus: health insurance. She had been living with type 1 diabetes for 20 years and was starting to experience some of the complications. If she switched jobs and health care plans, she was afraid she would lose her insurance because of her preexisting condition or have to wait a year to be enrolled. She felt she had no choice but to stay in this miserable job forever.

Chuck had been living with type 2 diabetes for 10 years. He did a fairly good job of keeping his blood glucose levels under control. But now he was developing some back problems and his doctor suggested surgery. He wondered how the surgery would affect his blood glucose levels and whether his local community hospital could handle someone with diabetes. He had never really seen anyone besides his family doctor for his diabetes care and wondered whether he should find a hospital that specialized in patients with diabetes.

Medical care is expensive for everyone these days, making health insurance an absolutely must. Diabetes can make medical care extra expensive even if you have insurance. So getting the best coverage possible is critical, not only for your pocketbook, but also for your health. Because everyone has different needs and a different budget, it is important that you find the plan that works for you.

If you already have diabetes, you know how high health care costs can be. Not only do you have to pay for routine care, but you also have to be prepared for the unexpected. If you are like most people, you will need help paying for your care through some form of health insurance. If you are employed, you may receive health insurance through your employer. Or maybe you are insured through your spouse's employer. Or perhaps you are eligible for Medicare or Medi-caid. If you are on your own, you probably already know that finding affordable insurance can be tricky.

Throughout the course of your life, your career, and your diabetes, you should periodically evaluate your health insurance situation. Ask yourself if your needs are being met. If you are unhappy with your current situation, evaluate the options. But don't be too quick to jump ship. Any changes in your health insurance coverage requires careful evaluation. You need to make sure that any new situation will provide the coverage you need and that the new company is willing to insure you.

There may also be times when you want make changes in your life. Maybe you want to switch jobs, retire, get married or divorced, or move out of state. Each of these decisions can affect your health insurance coverage. So before you make a drastic change in your life, think about how you will continue to cover your health care expenses.

Health Insurance

The health insurance situation for people with diabetes can be discouraging. Under the current system in the United States, if you are new to a job or to retirement, you will discover that new health insurers consider diabetes a "preexisting condition." If you are changing jobs or insurance companies, you may be excluded from coverage for an extended period of time—from 6 months to up to 3 years. Or you may be charged higher premiums than people who do not have diabetes. Some insurance companies may even refuse to insure you. Others may offer you insurance, but refuse to pay any diabetes-related expenses. So, before you leave your old insurance—or the employer who is supplying it—be sure you have secured a new job and insurance.

Several efforts have attempted to revamp the nation's health care system. Although a previous attempt to institute a national health care plan that would make it easier for people with diabetes and other medical problems to receive health insurance failed to make it through Congress, with each new congressional session the political debate can take on a new flavor. The issue of affordable health care for all citizens is likely to be revived again and again.

Private Insurance

You can gain insurance in many ways. If you are employed or if your spouse is employed, you can usually obtain insurance from your employer. If you leave your job, you can purchase transition coverage known as COBRA, or through a conversion policy, or a stop-gap policy. Other options if you are not employed or recently terminated include individual coverage or pooled-risk insurance.

Ideally, your employer will cover all or at least most of the cost of your insurance. But many people are not covered through an employer. So if you are thinking about changing jobs, moving, or making other big changes in your life, it is critical to also consider how the change will affect your health care coverage. Don't ever get caught without insurance, even briefly. Insurance is like having an umbrella in case of rain. The day you forget your umbrella you can be sure it will rain.

Through Employment. You may have the option of joining a group policy offered by your employer. Group policies are usually open to all employees, regardless of their health. The Americans with Disabilities Act requires that if an employer grants insurance to one employee, it must make the same policy available to all employees. Employers with fewer than 15 employees may require health screening and a medical history. How much you will have to pay will vary from employer to employer. If you are lucky, your employer will pay all or most of the insurance premium for you. Many policies will also cover your spouse and children for an additional fee. Health care is considered a nontaxable expense, so if you pay a fee for health care coverage, you may have it deducted from your paycheck before taxes are taken out.

In Transition. If you are changing jobs or just striking out on your own for the first time, you may need insurance to cover you while you make the transition from school to work, from job to job, or from work to retirement. Fortunately, a federal law called the Consolidated Omnibus Budget Reconciliation Act (COBRA) may help you. Under COBRA, your employer must allow you to keep your health insurance policy with equal coverage for up to 18 months after you leave your job. You will have to pay for the coverage and may be charged up to 2 percent more than the rate the company was charging your employer. But this is almost always less expensive than paying for a new short-term policy independently. If you are disabled, COBRA coverage can be extended to 29 months. This legislation applies not only to employees but also to dependents, who can continue their coverage for up to 36 months. Recent high school or college graduates who have not yet secured their own insurance policies may be covered under this law while searching for a new job and during the exclusion period for any preexisting conditions imposed by many insurance companies.

Once you have been laid off or leave a company, you have 60 days to accept COBRA benefits. During that 60 days, employers must pay insurance bills incurred by employees and their dependents. However, employers with fewer than 20 employees, the federal government, and churches are exempt from COBRA. But if you are ineligible for COBRA or if your COBRA coverage runs out, you still have some other options.

Many states require employers to offer you a conversion policy regardless of your health or physical condition. (Fifteen states and the District of Columbia do not require this provision.) In most states, if an insurance company terminates a company's group plan, it is required to offer you a conversion policy as well. When you convert your policy, you remain with the same insurer, but begin paying for your own insurance. Conversion coverage is almost always more expensive than the group plan you may have been on while employed and it usually provides fewer benefits. However, it may be your only choice for coverage and is preferable to going without insurance. Once your COBRA insurance runs out or you leave your job, you have 31 days to accept or reject this type of coverage. So, if at all possible, explore all insurance options as far in advance as possible. For more information on COBRA, call the COBRA hotline at 202-219-8776.

Another avenue to explore is to purchase temporary short-term health care coverage on your own. This is known as a stop-gap policy and usually lasts for one year. It is designed for people between jobs. If you are considering this option, shop around with various insurance companies to get the best price for the most coverage.

The Health Insurance Portability and Accountability Act of 1996. This Act makes it easier for people with diabetes to get and keep their health insurance. According to the Act, insurers and employers may not make insurance rules that discriminate against workers because of their health. And all workers eligible for a particular health plan must be offered enrollment at the same price.

Insurers who sell individual policies must offer an individual policy without preexisting condition exclusions to anyone who 1) has had continuous coverage in a group plan for the previous 18 months, 2) is not currently eligible for coverage under any group plan, and 3) has used up COBRA coverage.

Another part of the Act helps you keep coverage when you change jobs. If you have had diabetes for more than 6 months and have had continuous coverage in an insurance plan, and then leave your job, you cannot be denied coverage by your new employer because of a preexisting condition.

If, however, you have been recently diagnosed, that is, up to 6 months ago, and you change jobs, your new employer may refuse or limit your health insurance coverage for 12 months. This is a one-time-only waiting period, and it can be reduced by the number of months you had continuous coverage at your previous job. For example, say you were diagnosed with diabetes while employed and covered by your employer's health insurance plan. Five months after the diagnosis, you change jobs. Your new employer may limit or deny your health insurance coverage for the remainder of the 12-month waiting period, or 7 months.

On Your Own. If you are self employed, unemployed, or do not receive health insurance as an employment benefit you may not be eligible for any form of group insurance. Finding an affordable policy under these circumstances may be difficult. But don't be tempted into forfeiting health insurance altogether. Having diabetes makes health insurance an absolute necessity.

Individual polices are contracts between individuals and an insurance company. Larger companies that enroll in group plans may insure everyone and offer lower rates, because everyone's risks are pooled. If the group is large enough, people with costly health care needs will be balanced out by people with fewer health care needs. But if you have a chronic condition such as diabetes, and you are seeking individual coverage, you are a known risk. Insurers will take your medical history into consideration when they decide whether to enroll you. If you are accepted, you can expect to pay hefty premiums.

Some states allow health insurance companies to offer bare-bones policies to small businesses and individuals. These policies cost 30 to 40 percent less than major-medical policies and provide fewer benefits. However, they may be of help to you.

Another alternative is to seek help through any professional or trade association to which you may belong. For example, the Student Nurses Association provides health insurance to nursing students and any dependents at a less expensive rate than either colleges or private companies. Check with your professional organization to see what kinds of insurance they may offer.

A Last Resort. If you have been turned down for insurance, you might want to consider "pooled risk" health insurance. This kind of insurance is offered by certain states to people who have lived in the state for 6 to 12 months and have been rejected for group or individual coverage. Although the coverage is good, the costs can vary widely among the different states that offer it. Most try to keep it affordable by placing limits on the premium. The cost will probably be higher than individual coverage, however. Some states have waiting lists to buy into the pool.

Blue Cross and Blue Shield Companies have traditionally been considered as the insurer of last resort. This is because they will insure anyone, regardless of health problems, especially people who live in states without pooled-risk insurance. However, only one-fourth of these companies now hold open enrollment periods during which anyone may apply for coverage. And many exclude preexisting conditions, such as diabetes, for a year or more, just as other insurance companies often do.

Types of Health Care

However you are covered, there are different agreements between insurers and doctors as to how services will be provided. Some employers may offer an array of health plans and service options. Other employers may have setteld on a single insurance company offering a single type of service. Some agreements limit your choice of doctors in exchange for a better-priced plan. This can be a problem, especially if you live far away from work and often, far from the available hospitals and doctors. The major types of plans are fee-for-service and managed care.

In the past, the vast majority of health insurance companies required you or your employer to pay a set premium each year and let you decide what doctors and hospitals to choose. In these **fee-for-service** plans, the insurance company pays for some or all of your medical care. Usually, you must first pay a small amount for your care as an out-of-pocket deductible. Once you have met your yearly deductible, your insurance company will take over and pay for the remaining expenses during the year, according to the particulars of your contract. Often, insurance companies will also require that you pay a portion of the cost of visits or health care (the co-payment), even after the deductible is met. However, most plans have a maximum out-of-pocket expense limit. Once you have paid a certain set amount out of your own pocket, they will pay for 100% of all expenses once that limit is met. When comparing policies, pay special attention to what you may have to pay as deductible, copayment, and out-of-pocket limits. Cheaper plans usually have higher deductibles, higher copayments, and higher catastrophic limits.

The great advantage of the fee-for-service plan is that you are able to choose your own doctors among a wide range of health care professionals and hospitals with whom your insurer is affiliated. The disadvantage is that preventive health care, such as a mammograms, pap smears, or well-child visits, are usually not covered.

Under **managed-care** plans, you or your employer pay a fixed premium and you receive a comprehensive care package, from routine office visits and preventive care to hospitalization. Your cost is lowest if you seek care from the network of participating in physicians and hospitals. Often, you are assigned a primary care practitioner by whom you must first be seen. You generally have no deductible to satisfy or paperwork to process. You also will not be expected to pay large out-of-pocket amounts for services. This allows you better control over your budget should unexpected illness or hospitalization occur.

The big disadvantage to managed care situations is that your choice of hospitals and doctors is often limited if you need anything other than emergency hospitalization. In an attempt to hold down costs, your insurer will carefully examine and approve what kind of tests and procedures you need to have done and when you need to see a specialist. Your primary care doctor will often serve as a gatekeeper in recommending what further care is needed for a particular problem. If you wish to see a health-care professional or have a test that is not approved, you may have to pay much of your bill and have your benefits reduced.

Health maintenance organizations (HMOs) are the best-known type of managed care health service. HMOs usually create a full-service health center by hiring or contracting with health-care professionals to work in their buildings. You must usually see someone under contract to or employed by the HMO to receive prepaid health care. The HMO makes arrangements for coverage of sickness or accidents when you travel outside the HMO's service area.

A **preferred provider organization (PPO)** is another type of managed care plan. Under this type of service doctors agree with an insurer (often Blue Cross and Blue Shield) to discount their fees. The doctors are then paid by the insurer. You may also be asked to pay a small fee when you visit. Under a PPO plan, you receive full coverage if you choose your doctor from among those who have joined the PPO. You usually visit that doctor in his or her private office. If you choose to use a doctor outside of this network, you may have to pay for most of the bill. Under some plans you may also lose benefits in the future as well.

Routine Care Coverage

Your insurance policy is a contract between you and the insurance carrier that outlines the services that it covers. Like any contract, you should read it carefully to make sure it provides for your needs. It may provide coverage for doctor's visits and annual or semi-annual physical exams. Some insurance companies will only provide partial coverage or will require a co-payment for each visit to the doctor. Others may not always cover routine physical examinations but will pay for a specific medical problem or medical emergency. Check to see that your carrier considers routine diabetes care part of the treatment for diabetes and provides coverage. Most insurers also cover durable medical equipment, such as glucose equipment, prescription drugs, and medical supplies. But read the policy to be sure. Often, purchases of prescription drugs and supplies can also require a substantial co-payment.

If your health insurance covers durable medical equipment, it should pay for a blood glucose meter, a fingerstick device, an insulin injector or syringes, and an insulin pump if prescribed by your physician as "medically necessary." Check your policy to see that none of these items are specifically excluded. Your physician will have to give you a thorough explanation in writing of why each of these items is necessary for you. This serves as your "prescription" for these items.

If your insurance covers prescription medications and/or medical supplies, it usually will pay for insulin, lancets, glucose meter strips, and insulin pump supplies, if you have a prescription for them. Whenever you have to buy medical supplies or equipment, it is a good idea to ask the company in advance what is covered. Be sure to record the name of the person who answers your questions along with the date, in case you need this information to appeal a denied claim.

In addition to visits to your primary care physician, find out if visits to other members of your health team are covered and under what conditions. Some carriers will provide coverage for routine physicals but will not cover visits to a dietitian, for example. You may recognize that treating your diabetes is a team effort, but not all insurance carriers have bought into the concept.

What You Should Know About Your Health Insurance Plan

When comparison shopping for health care insurance, ask yourself the following:

- Are visits to your primary care physician covered? Is there any limit on how many visits are allowed? How much will you have to pay per visit?
- Does the plan reimburse for diabetes education?
- Does the plan cover medical equipment and supplies? This is especially important if you inject insulin or self-monitor your blood glucose.
- Does the plan cover the services of a dietitian? Managing diet is critical for people with both type 1 and type 2 diabetes.
- What mental health benefits are covered? The services of a social worker or psychologist can help you through the rough spots in coping with diabetes.
- Does the plan cover the services of specialists, such as a podiatrist, eye doctor, or dentist, whose care is very important to people with diabetes?
- What medications are paid for? Is there a prescription plan to reduce costs? How often can prescriptions be refilled? Is a copayment required for each prescription?
- What kind of home health care coverage is included? Are there any limitations?

Medicare and Medicaid

I f you are over 65, disabled and unable to work, or have a very low income, you may have other insurance options. The federal insurance program **Medicare** covers a portion of hospital bills, doctor fees, and other expenses for people over the age of 65 and for some people with disabilities who cannot work. Even if you get Medicare, you may still have to pay for a large portion of your medical bills.

You can sign up for Medicare three months before the month of your 65th birthday. For more information, contact your local Social Security Administration office, listed under the United States Government listing in your telephone book. Bring your birth certificate when you apply.

Not everyone over the age of 65 is eligible for Medicare. For example, some people who have worked at state or local government jobs may not be eligible for Medicare. If you are unsure about coverage, contact your local Social Security Administration office.

If you have a very low income, you might be eligible for **Medicaid**, a federal and state assistance program. Medicaid regulations vary from state to state, so you will have to contact the Medicaid office in your state to find out whether you qualify. Also ask about what health expenses will be covered. If you have questions, a social worker can help you with this.

The health care provisions under Medicare and Medicaid are constantly changing as more decisions about distributing funds is put in the hands of the individual states. For more information about how these changes may affect you, contact your local Social Security Administration office.

Medicare and Benefits. There are two parts to Medicare: Part A and Part B. Part A helps to pay bills for medical care provided in hospitals, skilled nursing facilities, hospices (for people who are dying), and nursing homes. Medicare will not pay for custodial care provided in a nursing home or private home when that is the only kind of care needed. Custodial care includes help in walking, getting in and out of bed, bathing, dressing, eating, taking medicines, and other activities of daily living.

Part B helps to pay for health providers' services, ambulance services, diagnostic tests, outpatient hospital services, outpatient physical therapy and speech pathology services, and medical equipment and supplies.

Medicare also pays for blood glucose meters, lancets, test strips, and other supplies for the meter, whether you are on insulin or not. Your health care provider must certify in writing that you need all of these items to manage your diabetes. Make copies of your provider's written statement. Give a copy of it to your pharmacist each time you purchase these supplies so that it can be submitted along with your Medicare claim.

Medicare will not pay for diabetes pills, insulin, or syringes, but Medicare will pay for insulin pumps and the insulin used in the pump for people with type 1 diabetes. Medicare also will not pay for regular eye exams, prescription sunglasses or contact lenses, or routine foot care, such as nail trimming or removal of corns and calluses. Medicare will help pay for therapeutic footwear and shoe inserts, laser surgery for retinopathy, cataract surgery, kidney transplants, and dialysis.

Medicare may help pay for diabetes outpatient education if it is done by an approved program and prescribed by a health care provider. Medicare may also help pay for outpatient nutrition counseling services or dietitian services.

Most people covered by Medicare get Part A. You can get Part B by paying a monthly fee. Both parts have deductibles and coinsurance amounts that you pay. For more information on Medicare, call the Medicare Hotline at 800-638-6833. For a more detailed explanation of Medicare, ask for a free copy of *Your Medicare Handbook* from Social Security at 800-772-1213.

Medigap

Even in its present state, Medicare does not cover everything you will need for your diabetes care. To fill the gaps in your coverage, you can choose from the many so-called Medigap plans available from private insurance companies. These plans pick up some or most of the charges that Medicare won't cover. You cannot be denied Medigap coverage if you apply within 6 months of first applying for Medicare Part B. To be designated as a Medicare supplement policy, insurance policies must meet certain federal standards. If you are considering one of these plans, be sure to read the policy carefully and comparison shop before purchasing anything.

The booklet *Guide to Health Insurance for People with Medicare*, written by the National Association of Insurance Commissioners and the Health Care Financing Administration of the Department of Health and Human Services, is updated every year and is available through any insurance company. Ask for it, or call Social Security at 800-772-1213 to get it sent to you. It will be especially helpful in face of the changes that are likely to occur in Medicare. It contains the federal standards for Medigap policies and general information about Medicare.

When Your Claim Is Denied

It's bound to happen at one time or another. You have done all your homework and think you know just what is and what is not covered by your health insurance. So you may be surprised to someday receive a claim marked DENIED. To resolve the situation most fairly and efficiently, it will help if you have all the paperwork on hand to support your claim.

First, make sure you and your physician have filled out the claim form correctly. If this checks out, get the rest of your paperwork in order. When your claim is denied, you will receive an explanation of benefits from your insurance company, which should include a reason for the denial of your claim. If you do not understand the reason for the denial, you may want to call a company representative for a thorough explanation. Make sure to ask and record the name of the person to whom you are speaking. Understanding what the problem is may help you to better organize the papers and documents you need to support your claim.

To get your paperwork in order, make sure you have a prescription from your doctor for every piece of equipment you need, even if it does not require a prescription at the pharmacy. Sometimes, just submitting the prescription and receipt will provide the support to get your claim paid. Some companies may also want a letter of explanation from your doctor. Never send any original documents to your insurance company. Make copies of everything you plan to submit. Send in the copies and keep the originals. Send all pertinent paperwork by registered mail so that you have a record that they have been received.

Once you have received the statement telling you that your claim has been denied, you will have 60 days in which to appeal this decision. Your next step will be to write to the claims manager of your insurance company, explaining what is wrong. It helps to address the claims manager by name. Point out the items that have been denied payment and ask for a written response to your request. Give your address and phone number and that of your physician. Also, send your physician a copy of your appeal request for his or her records. State that you will call the insurance company on a certain date if you have not received a response by that time. On that date, call the claims manager and discuss your case. Two or three weeks is a reasonable period of time to wait.

Sometimes claims are denied for simple reasons. Maybe a clerk was unfamiliar with the newest equipment for diabetes care. Requesting an appeal moves the decision out of the clerk's hands and into those of people who should have greater familiarity with the latest blood meters, test strips, and other equipment. Even if you are denied again, don't give up! Request an insurance hearing.

Your state insurance department acts as a consumer complaint department. You can put pressure on the insurance company to respond to your request. If you work for a company that is self-insured, you should appeal directly to your personnel manager or to the head of the company first. Often they can easily remedy the situation. If the claim is still denied, write to the state labor department.

Most state insurance commissions have someone who handles complaints and will provide you with an opportunity for a hearing. This is where your paperwork is most important. When writing to the state commission, you should list

- the name of your insurance company,
- the coverage provided in your policy as you understand it, along with a copy of your policy,
- a description of what happened (this should include copies of all letters or details of phone conversations between you and the insurance company), and
- a specific request for a hearing to determine the insurance company's responsibility for payment.

An insurance hearing is like a court hearing in many respects. Both you and the insurance company will be allowed to state your case. You must also submit copies of all the documents you sent to the commission. Some people represent themselves, while others have lawyers. A decision may be made right away or within the ensuing few weeks. If you are dissatisfied with the decision, you still have the option of taking your case to small claims court.

Check with your local small claims court, because each system has a different way of handling cases. You can find a listing in the city or county government section of the telephone book. The judges there understand that most people represent themselves. The judge will want to hear your side of the story and see copies of your documents. If you want the help of a lawyer, contact your American Diabetes Association chapter. They may be able to help you locate one.

You can also seek the help of two organizations who will advise you of your situation: The National Insurance Consumer Helpline, operated by insurance industry associations, and the National Insurance Consumer Organization, a non-profit, non-partisan consumer organization.

Hospital Stays

No one likes to think about it. After all, a hospital stay means there is a medical problem. This can include anything from routine elective surgery to a life-threatening emergency. Once you are admitted to a hospital, you may feel that you are no longer in charge. All of a sudden, your daily routine is disrupted and you may have to face a recovery period that lasts from days to weeks or even months.

As unpleasant as it seems now, taking time to plan for how to handle hospital visits will pay off in the long run. You can take steps that will help get you the best possible care, whether you face an emergency situation or one for which you can plan ahead. Because, the truth is, the people who get the best care are the ones who take a proactive role in their health, are well informed, and know what questions to ask. By taking charge of your care and planning ahead, you can ensure that you will get the best care possible, should the need arise.

Plan Ahead. The first place to start is to learn something about your local hospitals. Which ones are accepted by your health insurance? Does your primary-care physician have privileges at a particular hospital? If he or she has privileges at several local hospitals, which is preferred? Are there advantages or disadvantages to a particular hospital depending on the situation?

There are three types of hospitals: city or county hospitals, private community hospitals, and hospitals that serve as teaching centers, usually affiliated with a medical school. But these types of hospitals are not mutually exclusive. A county or private hospital can also be a affiliated with a medical school or teaching center.

To learn about a hospital's general reputation, as well as its reputation for treating people with diabetes, talk to your primary care physician. Discuss the steps you should take in the event of an emergency and agree on which hospital to use. Ask your doctor where he or she would go or would send a family member. Or ask any friends, neighbors, or relatives

Getting Admitted

Here are some tips to keep in mind when you are checking into the hospital.
- Make sure the doctors and nurses are aware that you have diabetes.
- Tell them what medications you are taking for diabetes and any other medications you are taking, including any over-the-counter drugs you may be using. It helps to keep a list of these ahead of time, including how often you take them and in what doses.
- Explain any allergies or other conditions you may have, such as vomiting, that could affect the actions of medications.
- Speak up about any other medical conditions you may have, including complications of diabetes. High blood pressure may require special treatment before and during surgery. Heart disease medications may require adjustment.
- Tell them about any recent or frequent low blood glucose reactions. Bring your self-monitoring records with you.
- Tell them about your meal plan. Ask to see the hospital's dietitian and explain what type of meal plan you're on, including any special modifications such as less salt, less cholesterol, or less fat.

who have recent hospitalizations. You can also check with your local ADA chapter or diabetes support group for further input.

When evaluating the reputation of a hospital, try to find out the following:

- Are there endocrinologists on the staff?
- Does the hospital have diabetes education and dietitians with expertise in diabetes on the staff? Are they available to both inpatients and outpatients?
- Is there a diabetes education program within the hospital or affiliated with the hospital?
- What other types of support services are available to people with diabetes?

Ask your health insurance company which hospital services they will cover and for how much. Also many insurance companies require you to notify them in advance for any service, except emergencies, so they can pre-approve your treatment.

Facing Surgery

If you are facing surgery, it's perfectly normal to feel apprehensive, especially if you have diabetes. The good news is that with good care, people with diabetes recover just about as well as anyone. But blood glucose control can get out of hand around the time of an operation and diabetes can complicate recovery and prolong your hospital stay. That's why it's important that your diabetes is closely managed during your hospital stay. By taking an active role and by doing everything you can to ensure good diabetes control, you can help yourself recover on schedule.

The first question you will probably ask yourself is whether the surgery is necessary. This may not be possible in an emergency situation, but if your doctor recommends surgery, ask that doctor, as well as your primary care physician, the following questions:

■ Are there alternatives? What are the consequences of not having the surgery? If you are still in doubt, get a second opinion from a physician not affiliated with the physician who recommended the operation.

■ What is the risk involved? Feel free to ask questions. Even the most minor forms of surgery have some degree of risk. You have the right to have that spelled out in advance. If you want an explanation of tests or other procedures to expect, ask. Unanswered questions can produce anxiety.

■ Can you remain under the care of your primary care physician or a hospital physician who specializes in diabetes?

If at all possible, work with your physician to bring your diabetes under good control before you are hospitalized. This will improve your general health, which will help you withstand the stress of the surgery. In addition, it may help reduce the chances of infection and speed healing after the operation. However, don't panic if control of your diabetes is not where it should be. Often the condition that requires surgery can cause blood glucose levels to skyrocket. The hospital physicians and staff should be able to bring your blood glucose level into an acceptable range for the surgery. A carefully monitored insulin drip during surgery may be in order, especially if you normally rely on insulin injections. Ask your primary care physician to be by your side as much as possible. It's important for your surgeon and primary care doctor to be in contact and to agree on all treatments.

If you are scheduled for surgery, here's what you are likely to experience. The surgeon will meet with you at least once before your operation to explain the surgery and what to expect afterward. It's a good idea to have a list of questions ready for when your surgeon comes by. The anesthesiologist, who administers the anesthesia to keep you pain-free during surgery, will also visit you before surgery to tell you what to

Seeking a Second Opinion

You may want a second opinion when a doctor recommends surgery, long term medication, or other treatments that will drastically affect your lifestyle. Or, if you have a specific problem or needs that are not being addressed, a second opinion may also be in order—if your doctor says there is no known therapy or calls the condition incurable, for example. Sometimes insurance companies require a second opinion. Ask your insurer what costs for the recommended procedure are covered and whether they will cover the cost

of a second opinion. Also ask if they pay only if you see one of the consultants they recommend.

When seeking a second opinion, ask your physician or other doctor you trust. Look for a doctor who is board certified in the field in which you are seeking information, such as cardiology or surgery. Make sure to tell the physician you have diabetes. If the problem is diabetes-related, call your local ADA chapter for referrals. For non-diabetes problems, call the appropriate department of a major medical center or teaching hospital. Ask for the name of a specialist in the field.

Once you meet with the specialist, here are some things you may want to ask:

- What is the diagnosis and how was it determined?
- What treatments are available and which are most often used?
- Why do you suggest this particular treatment?
- What is the success rate of the treatment?
- Is the treatment reversible?
- What are the potential side effects and complications of treatment and how likely are they?
- Is the problem or treatment likely to affect my diabetes control?
- How long will I have to be in the hospital or undergo treatment? Will I need follow-up care?
- Are there hidden costs associated with this treatment, such as repeated blood tests, physical therapy, or postoperative nursing care?
- Is this an experimental treatment? Will I be participating in research?

expect and, sometimes, to offer alternatives. The nurses caring for you will also be able to answer questions or address concerns you may have.

After the operation, don't hesitate to ask for medication for pain or nausea. Short-term use of these medications does not interfere with blood glucose control.

Blood Glucose Monitoring in the Hospital

If you are managing your blood glucose levels successfully before entering the hospital, your physician will probably not want to tamper with your routine. But do expect the hospital staff to keep close tabs on your blood glucose levels. Lots of things can upset your blood glucose control: the stress of impending surgery, the condition making it necessary, and changes in your eating and exercise habits.

If you usually control your diabetes by diet alone, or diet plus oral agents, don't be alarmed if your physician decides to put you on insulin. It is most likely a temporary measure to keep things under control. Once the stress of hospitalization is over, you should be able to continue your normal routine.

For temporary insulin users, you may be given insulin injections several times a day. Or you may be given insulin intravenously. You may also receive glucose intravenously. The hospital staff will keep your blood glucose levels stable by checking your blood glucose frequently and making adjustments in either insulin or glucose flow.

Don't be surprised if your blood glucose levels are not within the same range that you normally shoot for. Your physician may want to keep them higher than normal to avoid the risk of hypoglycemia. This is unlikely to do you any long-term harm. If you feel the symptoms of either high or low blood glucose, tell the doctor or nurse right away.

For some operations, you will be able to eat right away. For others, you may require an IV feeding and may not be able to eat for several days. If this is the case, your blood glucose levels should be checked often.

Home Health Care and Nursing Homes

With an emphasis on shorter hospital stays, many people today are turning to home health care for a variety of reasons. Home health care services include nursing care and physical, respiratory, occupational, or speech therapy; chemotherapy; nutritional guidance; personal care such as bathing or dressing; and homemaker care. Home healthcare can include medical professionals who help you when you are bedridden with a long illness or housebound for a short period. They may provide blood testing or bring a nurse into your home to administer drugs and other treatments. Home health care workers include professionals, paraprofessionals (a trained aide who helps a professional), and volunteers.

Check with your health insurance plan or your company's benefits officer to see if home health care benefits are covered. Don't hesitate to ask the agency you are considering hiring how much they charge for each service and ask your insurance carrier what services will be covered. If you are covered by Medicare, some limited coverage may apply to you. These benefits apply only to those 65 or older or those under 65 who need kidney dialysis and/or transplants. Usually Medicare home health care benefits are restricted to the homebound and bedridden. Veterans Affairs, the military, and worker's compensation can be other sources of help for home health care.

If full-time care is needed, a nursing home is often the best option. If you are researching nursing homes, some good sources of help include:

- Private or public case management social workers
- Your local office on aging
- The county or state department of health
- Your primary care physician
- Your religious leader or pastoral counselor
- Local organizations for the retired or elderly

It is important that you visit prospective sites. It is also a good idea to talk to friends, family, neighbors, or coworkers who have family members in nursing homes.

Nursing homes can be very expensive. There are four possible sources of payment: private insurance, Medicare, Medicaid, and self-pay or private pay. Different facilities ask for different types of payments. It is important that you understand what you get for the required fees paid. The admissions coordinator should provide details of regular monthly charges and exactly what they do—and do not—include. Ask if there is something specific you should know about that is not covered.

As an alternative to nursing homes, many people are turning to assisted living communities. Many of these facilities are suitable for people who do not require full-time nursing care but who might enjoy the benefit of a medical staff and neighbors close on hand. There is a wide array of living situations, from communities that function much like individual apartment buildings, to individual units that provide nursing services, to full-time nursing centers. Check to see whether any of these facilities might meet your needs.

Glossary

autoimmunity: . . . . a condition in which the body's own immune system attacks cells of the body. This is the basis of type 1 diabetes, in which the immune system attacks the beta cells of the pancreas, and insulin is no longer produced.

basal insulin: . . . . intermediate- or long-acting insulin that is absorbed slowly and gives the body a steady low level of insulin. This mimics the body's natural low-level steady background release of insulin. Also used to describe the low-level steady background release of fast-acting insulin by an insulin pump.

beta cells: . . . . cells that make insulin. These cells are found in the islets of Langerhans in the pancreas.

blood glucose meter: . . . . a hand-held instrument that tests the level of glucose in the blood. A drop of blood (obtained by pricking a finger) is placed on a small strip that is inserted in the meter. The meter calculates and displays the blood glucose level.

bolus insulin: . . . . fast-acting insulin injected before meals that gives the body a quick rise in insulin levels. This mimics the body's natural after-meal release of insulin that stops the rise in blood glucose. Also used to describe the before-meal insulin dose given with an insulin pump.

calories: . . . . units that represent the amount of energy provided by food. Carbohydrate, protein, and fat are the primary sources of calories in the diet, but alcohol also contains calories. If all calories consumed aren't used as energy, they may be stored as fat.

carbohydrate: . . . . one of three major sources of calories in the diet. Carbohydrate comes primarily from sugar (simple carbohydrate) and starch (complex carbohydrate, found in bread, pasta, and beans). Carbohydrate is broken down into glucose during digestion and is the main nutrient that raises blood glucose levels.

cholesterol: . . . . a waxy, fat-like substance used by the body to build cell walls and make certain vitamins and hormones. The liver produces enough cholesterol for the body, but we also get cholesterol when we eat animal products. Eating too much cholesterol and saturated fat can cause the blood cholesterol to rise and accumulate along the inside walls of blood vessels. This is a risk factor for heart attack and stroke.

DCCT: . . . . the Diabetes Control and Complications Trial. This was a 10-year study sponsored by the National Institutes of Health. More than 1,400 people with type 1 diabetes were divided into two groups: those who aimed for near-normal blood glucose levels and those with standard goals. The study showed that tight blood glucose control reduces the risk of diabetic complications.

diabetes: . . . . a disease in which the body cannot produce insulin or cannot use insulin properly. It is characterized by high blood glucose levels.

endocrinology: . . . . the study of hormones at work in the body. Because insulin is a hormone, diabetes is a disease of the endocrine system. Many "diabetes doctors" are endocrinologists.

exchanges: . . . . the food groups used in the American Diabetes Association, The American Dietetic Association *Exchange Lists for Meal Planning*. There are six basic food groups: Starch/Bread, Meat and Meat Substitutes, Vegetables, Fruits, Milk, and Fat. Any food in a given group can be exchanged for any other food in that group in the appropriate amount.

fats: . . . . the most concentrated source of calories in the diet. Saturated fats are found primarily in animal products. Unsaturated fats mainly come from plants and can be monounsaturated (olive or canola oil) or polyunsaturated (corn or other oils). Excess intake of fat, especially saturated fat, can cause elevated blood cholesterol, increasing the risk of heart disease and stroke.

fiber: . . . . the parts of plants that the body can't digest, such as fruit and vegetable skins. Fiber aids in the normal functioning of the digestive system, specifically the intestinal tract.

gestational diabetes: . . . . diabetes that develops during pregnancy. The mother's blood glucose rises in response to hormones secreted during pregnancy, and the mother cannot produce enough insulin to handle the higher blood glucose levels. Although gestational diabetes usually goes away after pregnancy, about 60 percent of women who have had gestational diabetes eventually develop type 2 diabetes.

glucagon: . . . . a hormone produced by the pancreas that raises blood glucose levels. An injectable preparation is available by prescription for use in treating severe insulin reactions.

glucose: . . . . a simple form of sugar that serves as the body's fuel. It is produced when foods are broken down in the digestive system. Glucose is carried by the blood to cells. The amount of glucose in the blood is known as the blood glucose level.

glycohemoglobin or glycated
hemoglobin (HbA1c): . . . . describes the attachment of glucose to red blood cells. When blood glucose levels are high, the percentage of glucose attached to red blood cells increases. Doctors take blood samples to evaluate average blood glucose control over the past 3 to 4 months. One such test measures hemoglobin A1c (HbA1c).

health-care team: . . . . the group of health-care professionals who help patients manage diabetes. This team may include a physician, registered dietitian, and certified diabetes educator. (A certified diabetes educator can also be a physician, registered nurse, or registered dietitian.) Ophthalmologists, podiatrists, exercise physiologists, and other specialists can also be part of the team and may also be certified diabetes educators.

heart disease: . . . . a condition in which the heart cannot efficiently pump blood. Coronary artery disease is the most common form of heart disease. It occurs when the arteries that nourish the heart muscle narrow or become blocked. People with diabetes have a higher risk than the general population for developing heart disease.

hyperglycemia: . . . . a condition in which blood glucose levels are too high (generally, 140 mg/dl or above). Symptoms include frequent urination, increased thirst, and weight loss.

hypoglycemia: . . . . (or insulin reaction) a condition in which blood glucose levels drop too low (generally, below 70 mg/dl). Symptoms include moodiness, numbness in the arms and hands, confusion, and shakiness or dizziness. When left untreated, this condition can become severe and lead to unconsciousness.

immunosuppression: . . . . suppression of the immune system. People who receive kidney and pancreas transplants take immunosuppressive drugs to prevent the immune system from attacking the new organ.

impaired glucose tolerance: . . a condition diagnosed when oral glucose tolerance test results show that a person's blood glucose level falls between normal and diabetic levels. It isn't considered a form of diabetes, but people with this condition are at an increased risk for developing diabetes.

insulin: . . . . a hormone produced by the pancreas that helps the body use glucose. It is the "key" that unlocks the "doors" to cells and allows glucose to enter. The glucose then fuels the cells.

insulin resistance: . . . . a condition in which the body does not respond to insulin properly. This is the most common cause of type 2 diabetes.

intensive diabetes management . . . . a way of treating a person with diabetes who has the goal of achieving near-normal blood glucose levels. The approach involves using all available resources, including multiple daily injections of insulin, frequent blood glucose monitoring, exercise, and diet.

ketoacidosis or diabetic coma: . . . . a severe condition caused by a lack of insulin or an elevation in stress hormones. It is marked by high blood glucose levels and ketones in the urine, and occurs almost exclusively in those with type 1 diabetes.

ketones: . . . . acids produced when the body breaks down fat for fuel. This occurs when there is not enough insulin to permit glucose to enter the cells and fuel them or when there are too many stress hormones.

metabolism: . . . . term used to describe the body's capture and use of energy to sustain life. Diabetes is a metabolic disease because it affects the body's ability to capture glucose from food for use by the cells.

mg/dl: . . . . milligrams per deciliter. This is the unit of measure used when referring to blood glucose levels.

nephropathy: . . . . kidney damage. This condition can be life-threatening. When kidneys fail to function, dialysis (filtering blood through a machine) or kidney transplantation become necessary.

neuropathy: .... damage to the nerves. Peripheral neuropathy, which affects the nerves outside the brain and spinal cord, is the most common form of neuropathy. Peripheral neuropathy can damage motor nerves (which affect voluntary movement, such as walking) sensory nerves (which affect touch and feeling), and autonomic nerves (which affect bodily functions such as digestion).

obesity: .... an abnormal and excessive amount of body fat. Most obese people are significantly overweight. However, obesity also occurs in people who are not overweight, but have more body fat than muscle. Obesity is considered a chronic illness. It is on the rise and is a risk factor for type 2 diabetes.

oral diabetes medications or oral hypoglycemic medications .... medications taken orally that are designed to lower blood glucose levels. They are used by some people with type 2 diabetes and are not to be confused with insulin.

pancreas: .... a comma-shaped gland located just behind the stomach. It produces enzymes for digesting food, and hormones that regulate the use of fuel in the body, including insulin and glucagon. In a fully functioning pancreas, insulin is released through special cells located in clusters called islets of Langerhans.

protein: .... one of three major sources of calories in the diet. Protein provides the body with material for building blood cells, body tissue, hormones, muscle, and other important substances. It is found in meats, eggs, milk, and certain vegetables and starches.

retinopathy: . . . . damage to small blood vessels in the eye that can lead to vision problems. In background retinopathy, the blood vessels bulge and leak fluids into the retina and may cause blurred vision. Proliferative retinopathy is more serious and can cause vision loss. In this condition, new blood vessels form in the retina and branch out to other areas of the eye. This can cause blood to leak into the clear fluid inside the eye and can also cause the retina to detach.

receptors: . . . . molecules that often sit on cell surfaces and play a role in chemical "communication." For example, insulin cannot allow glucose to enter cells unless it first binds to the receptors on the cells and they respond properly.

stress hormones or counter-regulatory hormones: . . . . hormones released during stressful situations. These hormones include glucagon, epinephrine (adrenaline), norepinephrine, cortisol, and growth hormone. They cause the liver to release glucose and the cells to release fatty acids for extra energy. If there's not enough insulin present in the body, these extra fuels can lead to hyperglycemia and ketoacidosis.

sugar: . . . . a simple carbohydrate that provides calories and raises blood glucose levels. There are a variety of sugars, such as white, brown, confectioner's invert, and raw. Fructose, lactose, sucrose, maltose, dextrose, glucose, honey, corn syrup, molasses, and sorghum are also sugars.

sugar substitutes: . . . . sweeteners used in place of sugar. Note that some sugar substitutes have calories and will affect blood glucose levels, such as fructose (a sugar, but often used in "sugar-free" products), and sugar alcohols, such as sorbitol and mannitol. Others have very few calories and will not affect blood glucose levels, such as saccharin, acesulfame K, and aspartame (NutraSweet).

triglycerides: . . . . simple fatty acids found in both plants and animals. Vegetable oils contain triglycerides with unsaturated fatty acids and tend to be liquid at room temperature, whereas animal sources of triglycerides contain mostly saturated fatty acids and tend to be solid at room temperature.

type 1 diabetes: . . . . (or immune-mediated diabetes). A form of diabetes that tends to develop before age 30 but may occur at any age. It's usually caused when the immune system attacks the beta cells of the pancreas and the pancreas can no longer produce insulin. People who have type 1 diabetes must take insulin to survive.

type 2 diabetes: . . . . (or insulin-resistant diabetes). This form of diabetes usually occurs in people over the age of 40, but may develop in younger people, especially minorities. Almost all people who develop type 2 diabetes are insulin resistant, and most have a problem with insulin secretion. Some simply cannot produce enough insulin to meet their bodies' needs, and others have a combination of these problems. Many people with type 2 diabetes control the disease through diet and exercise, but some must also take oral medications or insulin.

UKPDS: . . . . The United Kingdom Prospective Diabetes Study. This was a 20-year study of over 5,000 people with type 2 diabetes. The study showed that people with type 2 who followed an intensive diabetes management regimen experienced fewer complications.

urine tests: . . . . tests that measure substances in the urine. Urine tests for blood glucose levels do not provide the timely information that is important in blood glucose control. Urine tests for ketones are very useful for monitoring diabetes control and are important in preventing ketoacidosis.

APPENDIX

Self-Monitoring Technique

Follow your meter manufacturer's instructions for best results. If you have problems, there should be an 800 number in the printed instructions that you can call for help.

Equipment:
- Lancet (blood-letting device)
- Clean test strip
- Cotton ball or tissue
- A watch or other timing device
- A blood glucose meter or color chart for matching

1. Make sure your hands are clean and dry. Soap or lotion on your hands can cause incorrect test results.
2. Puncture the skin of a finger, toe, or earlobe with the lancet. Most people use the side of a finger.
3. Squeeze out a large drop of blood.
4. Let the drop fall onto the pad of a test strip (or onto the sensor if your meter already has the test strip inside it). Wait the instructed amount of time for the test strip to develop.
5. Wipe excess blood from the test strip, if manufacturer's instructions say to. Then insert the test strip into the meter or compare the test strip to the chart on the vial. (With some meters, it is not necessary to wipe off the blood and a smaller drop of blood will do.)
6. Dispose of the lancet safely with your syringe needles.
7. Record your numbers.

Ketone Testing

Perform this test to check for ketones in the urine if a blood glucose test is 250 mg/dl or higher.

Equipment:

- Ketone test strip
- Cup or clean container for sample, if desired
- A watch or other timing device

1. Dip a ketone test strip in a urine sample, or pass it through the stream of urine.
2. Time test according to the directions on the package.
3. The strip will change colors if ketones are present. Compare test strip to package color chart.
4. Record the results.

Preparing Insulin Injections

Equipment:

- sterile syringe
- bottle of insulin
- alcohol swab, if desired, to clean the injection site or the insulin bottle

1. Wash hands.
2. Choose injection site.
3. Roll the bottle of insulin between your hands. (Regular insulin doesn't need to be rolled.) Don't shake it, because this makes air bubbles in the insulin. Air bubbles interfere with correct measurement of the units of insulin.
4. If desired, wipe the top of the bottle with an alcohol swab, then let the alcohol dry completely. Don't blow on it to dry it more quickly.
5. Holding the syringe with the needle pointing up, draw air into it by pulling down on the plunger to the amount that matches your insulin dose.
6. Remove the cap from the needle. Hold the insulin bottle steady on a table top, and push the needle straight down into the rubber top on the bottle. Push down on the plunger to inject the air into the insulin bottle.
7. Leave the needle in the bottle and the plunger pushed all the way in while you pick up the bottle and turn it upside down. The point of the needle should be covered by the insulin.

8. Pull the correct amount of insulin into the syringe by pulling back on the plunger.

9. Check for air bubbles on the inside of the syringe. If you see air bubbles, keep the bottle upside down and push the plunger up so the insulin goes back into the bottle.

10. Pull down on the plunger to refill the syringe. If necessary, empty and refill until all air bubbles in the syringe are gone.

11. Remove the needle from the bottle after checking again that you have the correct dose.

12. If you need to set the syringe down before giving your injection, recap and lay it on its side. Make sure the needle doesn't touch anything.

Mixing Insulins

Equipment:

- Sterile disposable syringe, the correct size for the total units of insulin
- Bottles of insulin
- Alcohol swab, if desired, to clean the injection site or the insulin bottle

1. Be clear on the amounts of each insulin and the total units you want. To find the total units, add the units of short-acting insulin to the units of intermediate- or long-acting insulin.

2. Wash your hands.

3. Roll any bottle of cloudy intermediate- or long-acting insulin between your hands. Don't shake it because this makes air bubbles in the insulin.

4. Draw air into the syringe equal to intermediate- or long-acting dose.

5. With the bottle upright on a table, inject the air into that bottle. Take out the needle without removing any insulin.

6. Draw air into the syringe equal to the dose of short-acting insulin and inject the air into the upright bottle of short-acting insulin.

7. With the needle still in the short-action insulin bottle, turn it upside down so that insulin covers the top of the needle.

8. Check for air bubbles on the inside of the syringe. If you see air bubbles, keep the bottle upside down and push the plunger up so the insulin goes back into the bottle.

9. Pull the correct amount of insulin into the syringe by pulling back on the plunger. If necessary, empty and refill until all air bubbles in the syringe are gone. Remove the syringe.

10. With the bottle of intermediate- or long-acting insulin held upside down, insert the syringe. (You have already injected the right amount of air into this bottle.)

11. Slowly pull the plunger down to draw in the right dosage of intermediate- or long-acting insulin. This will be the total units of the short- and intermediate- or long-acting insulins.

12. Do not return any extra insulin back to this bottle. It's now a mixture. Double check for the correct total amount of insulin. If incorrect, discard the syringe contents and start over.

13. Take the needle out of the bottle, recap, and lay the syringe carefully on a table without it touching anything.

Storing Insulin Mixtures

1. Only mix insulins made by the same company. For instance, don't mix regular made by Lilly with NPH made by Novo Nordisk.

2. If the mixture of insulin is stored in a glass or a plastic syringe, it will remain stable for 21 days under refrigeration.

3. Keep the prefilled syringes capped and in a vertical or oblique position with the needle pointing upward to avoid plugging problems.

4. Before injection, the plunger should be pulled back a little and the syringe tipped back and forth a few times to remix the insulin. Carefully push the plunger back to its original position, pushing air out of the syringe but not insulin.

5. NPH and regular insulins that are premixed by a manufacturer or that are mixed by you are stable and can be stored like any other insulin. There is no difference in action between a stored NPH-regular mixture and a fresh one.

6. Mixture of regular and lente insulins is not recommended except for patients already adequately controlled on such a mixture. The lente insulin delays the onset of action of the regular insulin in an unpredictable way. If regular-lente mixtures are to be used, always store the mixture for the same length of time each day.

Injecting Insulin

Equipment:

■ prepared filled sterile syringe

■ sterile cotton ball or gauze square, if desired, to cover the injection site for a few seconds after the injection

1. Choose an injection site with fatty tissue, such as the back of the arm, the top and outside of the thigh, the abdomen except for a 1-inch circle around the belly button, or the buttocks. Make sure the site and your hands are clean and dry.

2. Gently pinch a fold of skin between your thumb and forefinger and inject straight in if you have a normal amount of fatty tissue. For a thin adult or a small child, you may inject on a 45-degree angle.

3. Push the needle through the skin as quickly as you can.

4. Push the plunger in to inject the insulin.

5. Pull the needle straight out.

6. Cover the injection site with your finger or a dry cotton ball or gauze and apply slight pressure for 5 to 8 seconds—but do not rub. Rubbing may spread the insulin too quickly or irritate your skin.

7. Write down how much insulin you injected, the time of day, and the site you chose.

Reusing Syringes

1. Carefully recap the syringe when you aren't using it.

2. Don't let the needle touch anything but clean skin and your insulin bottle stopper. If it touches anything else, don't reuse it.

3. Store the used syringe at room temperature.

4. There will always be a tiny, even invisible, amount of insulin left in the syringe. So use one syringe with just one type of insulin to avoiding mixing insulins. For this reason, reusing syringes in which you have mixed insulins is not recommended.

5. Do not reuse a needle that is bent or dull. However, just because an injection is painful doesn't mean the needle is dull. You may have hit a nerve ending or have wet alcohol on your skin, if you use alcohol to clean the injection site.

6. Do not wipe your needle with alcohol. This removes some of the coating that makes the needle go more smoothly into your skin.

7. When you're finished with a syringe, dispose of it properly according to the laws in your area. Contact the city or county sanitation department for information.

Injecting Glucagon

1. A glucagon kit has a syringe filled with diluting fluid and a bottle of powdered glucagon. You must mix the diluting fluid with the powder before it can be injected. The instructions for mixing and injecting glucagon are included in the kit.

2. Inject glucagon in the same way and in the same parts of the body that you inject insulin.

3. If glucagon is mixed in a syringe but not used, you may refrigerate the capped syringe and use it for up to 2 days. Contact the manufacturer for more details.

4. The person with low blood glucose should respond to the glucagon injection in 15 to 30 minutes. If not, call emergency personnel.

5. The person will likely feel nauseated or vomit. So, keep the head elevated.

6. As soon as the person can swallow, offer regular soda, crackers, or toast.

7. Then offer a sandwich or protein snack.

8. Check blood glucose.

RESOURCES

For the Visually Challenged

American Council of the Blind
1155 15th Street NW, Suite 720
Washington, DC 20005
202–467–5081
800–424–8666
electronic bulletin board: 202–331–1058
e-mail: ncrabb@acb.org
Web site: http://www.acb.org
National information clearinghouse and legislative advocate that publishes a monthly magazine in Braille, large print, cassette, and computer disk versions.

American Foundation for the Blind
11 Penn Plaza, Suite 300
New York, NY 10001
212–502–7600
800–232–5463
e-mail: asbinfo@asb.org
internet: gopher.asb.org_5005
Works to establish, develop, and provide services and programs that assist visually challenged people in achieving independence.

American Printing House for the Blind
1839 Frankfort Avenue
P.O. Box 6085
Louisville, KY 40206
502–895–2405
502–899–2274 (fax)

800–223–1839
Concerned with the publication of literature in all media (Braille, large type, recorded) and manufacture of educational aids. Newsletter provides information on new products.

National Association for Visually Handicapped (NAVH)
22 West 21st Street
New York, NY 10010
212–889–3141
or
NAVH San Francisco regional office (for states west of the Mississippi)
3201 Balboa Street
San Francisco, CA 94121
415–221–3201
A list of low-vision facilities is available by state. Visual aid counseling and visual aids, peer support groups, and more intensive counseling are offered at both offices. Some counseling is done by mail or phone. Maintains a large-print loan library.

National Federation of the Blind
1800 Johnson Street
Baltimore, MD 21230
410–659–9314 (for general information)
800–638–7518 (for job opportunities for the blind)
Web site: http://www.nfb.org

Membership organization providing information, networking, and resources through 52 affiliates in all states, the District of Columbia, and Puerto Rico. Some aids and appliances available through national headquarters. The Diabetics Division publishes a free quarterly newsletter, *Voice of the Diabetic*, in print or on cassette.

National Library Service (NLS) for the Blind and Physically Handicapped

Library of Congress
1291 Taylor Street NW
Washington, DC 20542
202–707–5100
202–707–0744 (TDD)
800–424–8567 (to speak with a reference person)
800–424–9100 (to leave a message)
Encore, a monthly magazine on flexible disk (record), includes articles from *Diabetes Forecast*. It is available on request through the NLS program to individuals registered with the talking book program.

Recording for the Blind & Dyslexic (RFBD)

20 Roszel Road
Princeton, NJ 08540
609–452–0606
609–987–8116 (fax)
800–221–4792 (weekdays 8:30–4:45 EST)
Web site: http://www.rfbd.org
Library for people with print disabilities. Provides educational materials in recorded and computerized form; 80,000 titles on cassette. Registration fee of $50.00 includes loan of cassettes for up to a year.

The Seeing Eye, Inc.

P.O. Box 375
Morristown, NJ 07963-0375
201–539–4425
201–539–0922 (fax)
e-mail: semaster@seeingeye.org
Web site: http://www.seeingeye.org
Offers guide dog training and instruction on working with a guide dog.

For Amputees

American Amputee Foundation

P.O. Box 250218
Little Rock, AR 72225
501–666–2523
501–666–8367 (fax)
Offers peer counseling for new amputees and their families. Provides information and referral to vendors. Sponsors Give-a-Limb program. Has local chapters. Maintains a list of support groups throughout the United States. Publishes newsletter.

National Amputation Foundation

38–40 Church Street
Malverne, NY 11565
516–887–3600
516–887–3667 (fax)
Sponsor of Amp-to-Amp program in which new

amputee is visited by amputee who has resumed normal life. A list of support groups throughout the country is available.

For Finding Long-Term or Home Care

National Association for Home Care (NAHC)
228 7th Street SE
Washington, DC 20003
202–547–7424
202–547–3540 (fax)
Web site: http://www.nahc.org
Free information for consumers about how to choose a home care agency. Call and leave address or send a self-addressed, stamped envelope.

Nursing Home Information Service
c/o National Council of Senior Citizens
8403 Colesville Road, Suite 1200
Silver Spring, MD 20910
301–578–8800, ext. 8839
301–578–8999 (fax)
Information on selecting and paying for a nursing home and choosing other long-term care alternatives.

For Finding Quality Health Care

American Association for Marriage and Family Therapy
1133 15th Street NW, Suite 300
Washington, DC 20005-2710

For marriage and family therapists in your area, send a self-addressed, stamped envelope to the attention of Mr. Johnson.

American Association of Diabetes Educators
444 North Michigan Avenue
Suite 1240
Chicago, IL 60611
312–644–2233
312–644–4411 (fax)
800–832–6874
Referral to a local diabetes educator.

American Association of Sex Educators, Counselors, and Therapists
P.O. Box 238
Mount Vernon, IA 52314-0238
For a list of certified sex therapists and counselors in your state, send a self-addressed, stamped, business-size envelope (you may request lists from more than one state).

American Board of Medical Specialties
47 Perimeter Center East
Suite 500
Atlanta, GA 30346
800–776–2378
Record of physicians certified by 24 medical specialty boards. Only certification status of physician is available to callers. Directories of certified physicians organized by city of medical practice and alphabetically by physician names are available in many libraries.

American Board of Podiatric Surgery
1601 Dolores Street
San Francisco, CA 94110
415–826–3200
415–826–4640 (fax)
Referral to a local board-certified podiatrist.

The American Dietetic Association
216 West Jackson Boulevard
Suite 800
Chicago, IL 60606
312–899–0040
312–899–1979 (fax)
800–366–1655 Consumer Nutrition Hot Line;
9–4 CST, M–F only
Information, guidance, and referral to a local
dietitian.

American Medical Association
515 North State Street
Chicago, IL 60610
312–464–4818
Web site: http://www.ama–assn.org
Referral to your county or state medical society,
which may be able to refer you to a local
physician.

American Optometric Association
243 N. Lindbergh Boulevard
St. Louis, MO 63141
314–991–4100
314–991–4101 (fax)
Web site: http://www.aoanet.org\aoanet
Referral to your state optometric association for
referral to a local optometrist.

American Psychiatric Association
1400 K Street NW
Washington, DC 20005
202–682–6000
202–682–6114 (fax)
Web site: http://www.psych.org
Referral to your state psychiatric association for
referral to a local psychiatrist.

American Psychological Association
750 First Street NE
Washington, DC 20002-4242
202–336–5500 (main number)
202–336–5700 (public affairs)
202–436–5800 (professional practice)
Web site: http://www.apa.org
Referral to your state psychological association
for referral to a local psychologist.

National Association of Social Workers
750 First Street NE, Suite 700
Washington, DC 20002-4247
202–408–8600
800–638–8799
Referral to your state chapter of NASW for
referral to a local social worker.

Pedorthic Footwear Association
9861 Broken Land Parkway
Suite 255
Columbia, MD 21046-1151
410–381–7278
410–381–1167 (fax)
800–673–8447
Referral to a local certified pedorthist (a person
trained in fitting prescription footwear).

For Miscellaneous Health Information

American Academy of Ophthalmology
Customer Service Department
655 Beach Street
San Francisco, CA 94109-1336
415–561–8500
415–561–8533 (fax)
Web site: http://www.eyenet.org
For brochures on eye care and eye diseases,
send a self-addressed, stamped envelope.

American Heart Association
7272 Greenville Avenue
Dallas, TX 75231
800–242–8721
Web site: http://www.amhrt.org
For referral to local affiliate's *Heartline*, which
provides information on cardiovascular health
and disease prevention.

Impotence World Association
10400 Little Patuxent Parkway
Suite 485
Columbia, MD 21044
410–715–9609
800–669–1603
For information and guidance on impotence and
physician referral in your state, send a written
request and $2.00 for postage and handling.

Medic Alert Foundation
P.O. Box 1009
Turlock, CA 95381-1009
209–668–3331
209–669–2495 (fax)
800–432–5378
Web site: http://www.medicalert.org (may not
be up yet)
To order a medical I.D. bracelet.

National AIDS Hot Line
Centers for Disease Control and Prevention
800–342–2437 (24 hours)
800–344–7432 (Spanish)
800–243–7889 (TTY)
Information on HIV and AIDS, including
pamphlets and brochures, counseling, and
referral to local test sites, case managers, and
medical services.

National Chronic Pain Outreach Association
P.O. Box 274
Millboro, VA 24460
540–997–5004
540–997–1305 (fax)
e-mail: ncpoal@aol.com
To learn more about chronic pain and how to
deal with it.

National Kidney Foundation
30 E. 33rd Street
New York, NY 10016
212–889–2210
212–689–9261 (fax)
800–622–9010
Web site: http://www.mcw.edu/nkf
For donor cards and information about kidney
disease and transplants.

United Network for Organ Sharing
1100 Boulders Parkway, Suite 500
P.O. Box 13770
Richmond, VA 23225-8770
804–330–8602 (communications)
800–355–SHARE (for information on becoming
a donor)
800–24–DONOR
For information about organ transplants and a
list of organ transplant centers in the U.S.

For Travelers

U.S. Government Printing Office
Superintendent of Documents
P.O. Box 371954
Pittsburgh, PA 15250-7954
202–512–1800
202–512–2250 (fax)
Order the brochure *Health Information for
International Travelers* (stock #
017–023–001957) by phone with credit card or
send check or money order for $14.

**International Association for Medical
Assistance to Travelers**
417 Center Street
Lewiston, NY 14092
716–754–4883
519–836–3412 (fax)
For a list of doctors in foreign countries who
speak English and who received postgraduate
training in North America or Great Britain.

International Diabetes Federation
40 Washington Street
B–1050 Brussels, Belgium
For a list of International Diabetes Federation
groups that can offer assistance when you're
traveling.

For Exercisers

American College of Sports Medicine
P.O. Box 1440
Indianapolis, IN 46206-1440
317–637–9200
317–634–7817 (fax)
Web site: http://www.acsm.org/sportsmed
For information about health and fitness.

International Diabetic Athletes Association
1647 W. Bethany Home Road, #B
Phoenix, AZ 85015-2507
800–898–IDAA
e-mail: idaa@getnet.com
Web site: http://www.getnet.com/~idaa/
For people with diabetes and for health care
professionals interested in exercise and fitness at
all levels. Newsletter.

**President's Council on Physical Fitness
and Sports**
701 Pennsylvania Avenue NW
Suite 250
Washington, DC 20004
202–272–3421
202–504–2064 (fax)
For information about physical activity,
exercise, and fitness.

For People Over 50

American Association of Retired Persons (AARP)
601 E Street NW
Washington, DC 20049
202–434–2277
202–434–2558 (fax)
Web site: http://www.aarp.org
800–424–3410 (membership)
800–456–2277 (mail-order pharmacy)
Over-the-counter and prescription drugs delivered to your door in 7 to 10 days. Competitive prices that are the same for members and nonmembers. May pay by credit card or be billed.

National Council on the Aging
409 3rd Street SW
2nd Floor
Washington, DC 20024
202–479–1200
202–479–0735 (fax)
800–424–9046
Advocacy group concerned with developing and implementing high standards of care for the elderly. Referral to local agencies concerned with the elderly.

For Equal Employment Information

American Bar Association
Commission on Mental and Physical Disability Law
740 15th Street NW
Washington, DC 20005-1009
202–662–1570
202–662–1032 (fax)
202–662–1012 (TTY)
Web site: http://www.abanet.org/disability
Provides information and technical assistance on all aspects of disability law.

Disability Rights Education and Defense Fund, Inc.
2212 6th Street
Berkeley, CA 94710
510–644–2555 (voice/TDD)
510–841–8645 (fax)
800–466–4232 (voice/TDD)
e-mail: dredfca@aol.com
Provides technical assistance and information to employers and individuals with disabilities on disability rights legislation and policies. Assists with legal representation.

Equal Employment Opportunity Commission
1801 L Street NW
Washington, DC 20507
For technical assistance and filing a charge:
202–663–4900
202–663–4912 (fax)

800–669–4000 (connects to nearest local EEOC office)

800–669–3362 (for publications)

800–800–3302 (TDD)

National Information Center for Children and Youth With Disabilities

P.O. Box 1492

Washington, DC 20013-1492

202–884–8200 (voice and TDD)

202–884–8441 (fax)

800–695–0285 (voice and TTY)

Web site: http://www.aed.org/nichcy

Provides technical assistance and information on disabilities and disability-related issues.

For Health Insurance Information

AARP health insurance

800–523–5800

The AARP administers 10 health insurance plans. For some plans, individuals with diabetes or other chronic illnesses are eligible within 6 months after enrolling in Medicare Part B. For other plans, a 3-month waiting period is required for those with conditions preexistent in the 6 months preceding the effective date of the insurance, if not replacing previous coverage.

Medicare Hot Line

800–638–6833

U.S. Department of Health and Human Services

Health Care Financing Administration

6325 Security Boulevard

Baltimore, MD 21207

For information and various publications about Medicare.

Social Security Administration

800–772–1213

For information and various publications about Medicare.

Helpful Websites

www.diabetes.org (ADA website)

www.diabeteswebsite.com (site of popular authors and diabetes mentors June Biermann and Barbara Toohey)

www.niddk.nih.gov/health/diabetes/diabetes.htm (NIH/NIDDK government website)

www.childrenwithdiabetes.com (created by a father; offers many chat rooms and answers to more than 3,000 questions online)

www.diabetesmonitor.com (supplies information on upcoming medications and research, plus a mentor section)

www.mendosa.com/diabetes.htm (a diabetes dictionary)

dnet.ori.org/newuser (Oregon Research Institute's diabetes network) www.diabetes.com (lots of news from medical journals)

You can also subscribe to the following list servers (groups of people who share information about a topic):

listserv@lehigh.edu. To subscribe, send an e-mail to the list serve. In
the message box write the words "subscribe diabetic your name" (write your
name here).

majordomo@world.std.com. To subscribe, send an e-mail to the list serve. In
the message box write the words "subscribe diabetes".

ADA Regional Offices

New England Region

7 Washington Square
Albany, NY 12205
518/218-1755
Joyce Waite, Regional Executive
Vice President

Massachusetts Area Office
617/482-4580

Northern New England Area Office
603/627-9579

Rhode Island Area Office
401/738-6464

Pacific Northwest Region

2480 West 26th Avenue
Suite 120B
Denver, CO 80211
720/855-1102
Mike Van Abel, Regional Executive
Vice President

Alaska Area Office
907/272-1424

Hawaii Area Office
808/521-1142

Idaho Area Office
208/342-2774

Montana Area Office
406/761-0908

Oregon Area Office
503/736-2770

Washington Area Office
206/352-7950

South Central Region

4425 West Airport Freeway
Suite 130

Irving, TX 75062
972/255-6900
Quincy Neal, Regional Executive Vice
President

Arkansas Area Office
501/221-7444

Louisiana Area Office
504/831-0278

Northeast Texas/Northern Louisiana Area
Office
972/392-1181

Oklahoma Area Office
918/492-3839

South Texas Area Office
210/829-1765

West Texas Area Office
806/794-0691

South Coastal Region

1101 North Lake Destiny Road Suite 415
Maitland, Florida 32751
407/660-1926
Nancy Carlton, Regional Executive Vice
President

Atlanta Metro Area Office
404/320-7100

Central Florida Area Office
407/660-1926

Northeast Florida/Southeast Georgia Area
Office
904/703-7200

Northwest Florida/Southern Alabama Area
Office
850/478-5957

Outstate Georgia Area Office
912/353-8110

Southeast Florida Area Office
305/477-8999

Southwest Florida Area Office
813/885-5007

Upstate Alabama Area Office
205/870-5172

Southern Region

2 Hanover Square
434 Fayetteville Square Mall
Suite 1600
Raleigh, NC 27601
919/743-5400
Edward L. Owens, Regional Executive
Vice President

Central North Carolina Area Office
704/373-9111

Eastern North Carolina Area Office
919/743-5400

Greater Hampton Roads Area Office
757/455-6335

Kentucky Area Office
502/452-6072

South Carolina Area Office
803/799-4246

Tennessee Area Office
615/298-3066

Virginia Area Office
804/974-9905

Los Angeles Area Office
213/966-2890

Nevada Area Office
702/369-9995

Sacramento Area Office
916/369-0999

San Diego Area Office
619/234-9897

San Francisco Area Office
510/654-4499

Western Region

10445 Old Placerville Road
Sacramento, CA 95827-2508
916/369-0999
Michael Clinkenbeard, Regional Executive
Vice President

INDEX

The American Diabetes Association Complete Library of Self-Care and Nutrition

Self-Care

Type 2 Diabetes: Your Healthy Living Guide, Second Edition

A thorough guide to staying healthy with type 2 diabetes—everything from choosing a health care team and eating and exercising to self-monitoring, insulin, dealing with complications, and keeping mentally fit. You'll also find tips on employment and health insurance.
Softcover. #4804-01
Nonmember: $16.95/ADA Member: $14.95

The Ten Keys to Helping Your Child Grow Up With Diabetes

Here's help for parents who face the problems, feelings, and situations that can accompany managing diabetes. *Ten Keys* is a practical book for parents and caregivers of children with diabetes that addresses in detail the psychological, social, and emotional hurdles that often complicate the lives of youngsters with diabetes.
Softcover. #4908-01
Nonmember: $14.95/ADA Member: $13.95

Women & Diabetes

Designed for women, and filled with complete, thorough, and up-to-date discussions about a broad range of real-life topics such PMS, lactation, sex, pregnancy, child rearing, and menopause. Also includes dozens of checklists, charts, and exercises to help you create an individualized road map to living a healthy life with diabetes.
Softcover. #4907-01
Nonmember: $14.95/ADA Member: $13.95

Caring for the Diabetic Soul

You'll learn about coping with denial, controlling your stress and anger, building self-esteem, using a sense of humor, giving support, and much more. Written by professionals whose lives have been touched by diabetes—nurses, counselors, professors, doctors, and parents—each chapter reflects a personal experience that will touch you, too.
Softcover. #4815-01
Nonmember: $9.95/ADA Member: $8.95

101 Tips for Staying Healthy with Diabetes

Get the inside track on the latest tips, techniques, and strategies for preventing and treating diabetes complications. You'll learn how to treat and prevent skin infections, which cold and flu medicines to avoid, and how to eat the foods you like healthfully.
Softcover. #4810-01
Nonmember: $12.50/ADA Member: $10.50

How to Get Great Diabetes Care

This book explains the *ADA Standards of Care* and informs you of the importance of seeking medical attention that meets these standards. Includes discussions on the different types of diabetes, the goals of treatment, how to choose and effectively talk to your doctor, and more.
Softcover. #4811-01
Nonmember: $11.95/ADA Member: $9.95

Sweet Kids: How to Balance Diabetes Control & Good Nutrition with Family Peace

This new guide addresses behavioral and developmental issues of nutrition management in the families of children with diabetes. Each chapter begins with a story of a child with diabetes to help introduce you to each of the book's topics.
Softcover. #4905-01
Nonmember: $14.95/ADA Member: $11.95

Reflections on Diabetes

A collection of stories written by people who have learned from the experience of living with the disease. Selected from the Reflections column of *Diabetes Forecast* magazine.
Softcover. #5004-01
Nonmember: $9.95/ADA Member: $8.95

101 Tips for Improving Your Blood Sugar

101 Tips offers a practical, easy-to-follow road map to tight blood sugar control. One question appears on each page, with the answers or "tips" below each question. Tips on diet, exercise, travel, weight loss, insulin, illness, and more.
Softcover. #4805-01
Nonmember: $12.50/ADA Member: $10.50

Diabetes A to Z, Third Edition

In clear, simple terms, you'll learn all about blood sugar, complications, diet, exercise, heart disease, insulin, kidney disease, meal planning, pregnancy, sex, weight loss, and much more. Alphabetized for quick reference.
Softcover. #4801-01
Nonmember: $11.95/ADA Member: $9.95

Managing Diabetes on a Budget

For less than $10 you can begin saving hundreds and hundreds on your diabetes
self-care. An inexpensive, sure-fire collection of tips and hints to save you money on everything from medications and diet to exercise and health care.
Softcover. #5002-01
Nonmember: $7.95/ADA Member: $6.95

The Fitness Book: For People with Diabetes

You'll learn how to exercise to lose weight, exercise safely, increase your competitive edge, get your mind and body ready to exercise, much more.
Softcover. #4803-01
Nonmember: $18.95/ADA Member: $16.95

Raising a Child with Diabetes

Learn how to help your child adjust insulin to allow for foods kids like to eat, have a busy schedule and still feel healthy and strong, negotiate the twists and turns of being 'different,' and much more.
Softcover. #4901-01
Nonmember: $14.95/ADA Member: $12.95

The Dinosaur Tamer

Enjoy 25 fictional stories that will entertain, enlighten, and ease your child's frustrations about having diabetes. Each tale warmly evaporates the fear of insulin shots, blood tests, going to diabetes camp, and more. Ages 8–12.
Softcover. #4906-01
Nonmember: $9.95/ADA Member: $8.95

Grilled Cheese at Four O'Clock in the Morning

Your child's fears and frustrations of having diabetes will be eased when they read about Scott, a young boy who develops diabetes.
Softcover. #4904-01
Nonmember: $6.95/ ADA Member: $5.95

The Take-Charge Guide to Type I Diabetes

Discover how to prevent complications, increase your chances of having a healthy baby, learn all you can from testing your blood sugar, much more.
Softcover. #4806-01
Nonmember: $16.95/ADA Member: $13.50

Diabetes & Pregnancy: What to Expect

You'll learn about an unborn baby's development, tests to expect, labor and delivery, birth control, much more.
Softcover. #4903-01
Nonmember: $9.95/ADA Member: $8.95

Gestational Diabetes: What to Expect

Discover what gestational diabetes is and how to care for yourself during your pregnancy. You'll learn about an unborn baby's development, tests to expect, labor and delivery, birth control, much more.
Softcover. #4902-01
Nonmember: $9.95/ADA Member: $8.95

Necessary Toughness

You'll be inspired by this story of an athlete with the courage to face not only NFL linemen but also the threat of diabetes. You'll learn that you can live a healthy, happy life.
Softcover. #4807-01
Nonmember: $7.95/ADA Member: $6.95

Diabetes: A Positive Approach—Video

#4802-01
Nonmember: $19.95/ADA Member: $17.95

The American Diabetes Association 1999 Resource Guide

#5512-01
Nonmember: $4.95/ADA Member: $3.95

Cookbooks & Meal Planners

The Diabetes Carbohydrate and Fat Gram Guide

Calories are important, but knowing the fat and carbohydrate content of the foods you eat is the key to eating right. Registered dietitian Lee Ann Holzmeister shows you how to count carbohydrate and fat grams and exchanges, and why it's important. Dozens of charts list foods, serving sizes, and nutrient data for hundreds of products.
Softcover. #4708-01
Nonmember: $11.95/ADA Member: $9.95

Brand-Name Diabetic Meals in Minutes

Save time cooking with these popular taste-tested recipes from the kitchens of Campbell Soup, Kraft Foods, Weetabix, Dean Foods, Eskimo Pie, and Equal. Features more than 200 recipes from appetizers to desserts that will help make your meals tastier and your life easier. Nutrient information included. Softcover. #4620-01
Nonmember: $12.95/ADA Member: $10.95

How to Cook for People with Diabetes

Finally, a collection of reader favorites from the delicious, nutritious recipes featured every month in *Diabetes Forecast*. But you don't only get ideas for pizza, chicken, unique holiday foods, vegetarian recipes and more, you also get nutrient analysis and exchanges for each recipe.
Softcover. #4616-01
Nonmember: $11.95/ADA Member: $9.95

Magic Menus

Now you can plan all your meals from more than 50 breakfasts, 50 lunches, 75 dinners, and 30 snacks. Like magic, this book figures fats, calories, and exchanges for you automatically. The day's calories will still equal 1,500. Thousands of combinations are possible.
Softcover. #4707-01
Nonmember: $14.95/ADA Member: $12.95

World-Class Diabetic Cooking

Travel around the world at every meal with a collection of 200 exciting new low-fat, low-calorie recipes. Features recipes from Thailand, Italy, Greece, Spain, China, Japan, Africa, Mexico, Germany, and more. Appetizers, soups, salads, pastas, meats, breads, and desserts are highlighted.
Softcover. #4617-01
Nonmember: $12.95/ADA Member: $10.95

Southern-Style Diabetic Cooking

This cookbook takes traditional Southern dishes and turns them into great-tasting recipes you'll come back to again and again. Features more than 100 recipes including appetizers, main dishes, and desserts; complete nutrient analysis with each recipe, and suggestions for modifying recipes to meet individual nutritional needs.
Softcover. #4615-01
Nonmember: $11.95/ADA Member: $9.95

Flavorful Seasons Cookbook

Warm up your winter with recipes for Christmas, welcome spring with an Easter recipe, and cool off those hot summer days with more recipes for the Fourth of July. More than 400 unforgettable choices that combine great taste with all the good-for-you benefits of a well-balanced meal. Cornish Game Hens, Orange Sea Bass, Ginger Bread Pudding, many others.
Softcover. #4613-01
Nonmember: $16.95/ADA Member: $14.95

Diabetic Meals in 30 Minutes—Or Less!

Put an end to bland, time-consuming meals with more than 140 fast, flavorful recipes. Complete nutrition information accompanies every recipe. A number of "quick tips" will have you out of the kitchen and into the dining room even faster! Salsa Salad, Oven-Baked Parmesan Zucchini, Roasted Red Pepper Soup, Layered Vanilla Parfait, and more.
Softcover. #4614-01
Nonmember: $11.95/ADA Member: $9.95

Diabetes Meal Planning Made Easy

Learn quick and easy ways to eat more starches, fruits, vegetables, and milk; make changes in your eating habits to reach your goals; and understand how to use the Nutrition Facts on food labels. You'll also master the intricacies of each food group in the new Diabetes Food Pyramid.
Softcover. #4706-01
Nonmember: $14.95/ADA Member: $12.95

Month of Meals: Classic Cooking

When celebrations begin, go ahead—dig in! Includes a Special Occasion section that offers tips for brunches, holidays, and restaurants to give you a delicious dining options anytime, anywhere. Menu choices include Chicken Cacciatore, Oven Fried Fish, Sloppy Joes, Crab Cakes, and many others.
Spiral Bound. #4701 01
$14.95

Month of Meals: Ethnic Delights

Automatic menu planning goes ethnic! Tips and meal suggestions for Mexican, Italian, and Chinese restaurants are featured. Quick-to-fix and ethnic recipes are also included. Beef Burritos, Chop Suey, Veal Piccata, Stuffed Peppers, and others.
Spiral Bound. #4702-01
$14.95

Month of Meals: Meals in Minutes

Enjoy fast food without guilt! Make delicious choices at McDonald's, Wendy's, Taco Bell, and other fast food restaurants. Special sections offer valuable tips such as reading ingredient labels, preparing meals for picnics, and meal planning when you're ill.
Spiral Bound. #4703-01
$14.95

Month of Meals: Old-Time Favorites

Meat and potatoes menu planning! Enjoy with old-time family favorites like Meatloaf and Pot Roast, Crispy Fried Chicken, Beef Stroganoff, and many others. Hints for turning family-size meals into delicious left-overs will keep generous portions from going to waste. Meal plans for one or two people are also featured. Spiral-bound.
Spiral Bound. #4704-01
$14.95

Month of Meals: Vegetarian Pleasures

Meatless meals picked fresh from the garden. Choose from a garden of fresh vegetarian selections like Eggplant Italian, Stuffed Zucchini, Cucumbers with Dill Dressing, Vegetable Lasagna, and many others. Plus, you'll reap all the health benefits of a vegetarian diet.
Spiral Bound. #4705-01
$14.95

How to Order

1. **To order by phone:** just call us at **1-800-232-6733** and have your credit card ready. VISA, Master-Card, and American Express are accepted. Please mention code CK99701 when ordering.
2. **To order by mail:** on a separate sheet of paper, write down the books you're ordering and calculate the total using the shipping & handling chart below. (NOTE: Virginia residents add 4.5% sales tax; Georgia residents add 7.0% sales tax.) Then include your check, written to the American Diabetes Association, with your order and mail to:

American Diabetes Association
Order Fulfillment Department
P.O. Box 930850
Atlanta, GA 31193-0850

Shipping & Handling Chart
up to $25.00.........add $4.99
$25.01–$60.00......add $5.99
over $60.00 ....add 10%

Allow 2–3 weeks for shipment. Add $4.00 to shipping & handling for each extra shipping address. Add $15 for each overseas shipment. Prices subject to change without notice.

About the American Diabetes Association

The American Diabetes Association is the nation's leading voluntary health organization supporting diabetes research, information, and advocacy. Founded in 1940, the Association provides services to communities across the country. Its mission is to prevent and cure diabetes and to improve the lives of all people affected by diabetes.

For more than 50 years, the American Diabetes Association has been the leading publisher of comprehensive diabetes information for people with diabetes and the health care professionals who treat them. Its huge library of practical and authoritative books for people with diabetes covers every aspect of self-care—cooking and nutrition, fitness, weight control, medications, complications, emotional issues, and general self-care. The Association also publishes books and medical treatment guides for physicians and other health care professionals.

Membership in the Association is available to health care professionals and people with diabetes and includes subscriptions to one or more of the Association's periodicals. People with diabetes receive Diabetes Forecast, the nation's leading health and wellness magazine for people with diabetes. Health care professionals receive one or more of the Association's five scientific and medical journals.

For more information, please call toll-free:

Questions about diabetes:	1-800-DIABETES
Membership, people with diabetes:	1-800-806-7801
Membership, health professionals:	1-800-232-3472
To order ADA books or receive a free catalog:	1-800-232-6733
Visit us on the Web:	www.diabetes.org
Visit us at our Web bookstore:	merchant.diabetes.org